ASLIB READER SERIES

Previously published titles in the *Aslib Reader Series*

No. 1 NATIONAL LIBRARIES — M. B. Line and J. Line
No. 2 THE SCIENTIFIC JOURNAL — A. J. Meadows
No. 3 THE PROFESSIONAL DEVELOPMENT OF THE LIBRARIAN AND INFORMATION WORKER — P. Layzell Ward
No. 4 THE MARKETING OF LIBRARY AND INFORMATION SERVICES — B. Cronin

Dr Stephen Roberts is a lecturer in the Library Management Division of the School of Library and Information Studies, at Ealing College of Higher Education in London. After entering librarianship as a graduate assistant at Dundee University Library, and taking the MA course at the Postgraduate School of Librarianship and Information Science (now the Department of Information Studies) at Sheffield University, he worked as a research fellow at Bath University on the Design of Information Systems in the Social Sciences (DISISS) project, and then went to join the Library Management Research Unit at Cambridge University Library. As research fellow at the Centre for Library and Information Management (CLAIM) at Loughborough University he developed a research interest in library resource allocation and the costing of library and information services. He is the author of a number of reports and articles dealing with library economic investigations.

British Library Cataloguing in Publication Data

Costing and the economics of library and information services.—(Aslib reader series; v. 5)
   1. Libraries—Great Britain—Costs
   2. Information services—Great Britain—Costs
   I. Roberts, Stephen A.   II. Series
   025.1´1   Z683

ISBN 0-85142-176-8
ISBN 0-85142-177-6 Pbk

© Aslib 1984

3 Belgrave Square, London SW1X 8PL

Printed in Great Britain by Henry Ling Ltd., at the Dorset Press, Dorchester, Dorset

ASLIB READER SERIES
VOLUME 5

COSTING AND THE ECONOMICS OF LIBRARY AND INFORMATION SERVICES

EDITED BY
STEPHEN A. ROBERTS

Ministry of Education, Ontario
Information Centre, 13th Floor,
Mowat Block, Queen's Park,
Toronto, Ont. M7A 1L2

Aslib

SERIES EDITORS: PETER J. TAYLOR and RUTH FINER

This book consists of five main sections on specific themes, each section consisting of a group of readings preceded by the editor's commentary and notes on suggested further reading. There is an author index of all literature cited.

CONTENTS

INTRODUCTION 1

1. LIBRARY AND INFORMATION SERVICE COSTS: CONTEXT AND CONCEPTS ... 3

Introductory Notes 5

Cost accounting in libraries *R. M. Hayes and J. Becker* ... 7

The economic analysis and evaluation of information and documentation systems *W. Schwuchow* ... 26

2. INVESTIGATING AND MEASURING THE SYSTEM ... 33

Introductory notes ... 35

Systems analysis as a tool for research in scientific management of libraries: a state of the art review *M. Mahapatra* ... 37

A generalized methodology for library systems analysis *R. W. Burns Jr* ... 46

The analysis of library processes *Aslib Research Department* ... 55

Standard costing for information systems: background to a current study *S. E. Robertson, R. Reynolds and A. P. Wilkin* ... 71

Work analysis by random sampling *J. L. Divilbiss and P. C. Self* ... 77

3. BASIC APPROACHES TO SERVICE COSTING ... 83

Introductory notes ... 85

Management accounting and library activities *J. C. R. Hewgill* ... 87

The costing of library systems *D. W. G. Clements* ... 93

Analysing industrial information service costs: a simple checklist *A. Armstrong* ... 107

Administrative effectiveness: times and costs of library operations	G. C. K. Smith and J. L. Schofield	112
Cost accounting and analysis for university libraries	F. F. Leimkuhler and M. D. Cooper	134

4. PRACTICE AND PRACTICAL STUDIES 151

Introductory notes		153
Analyzing acquisitions and cataloging costs	J. M. Maier	155
Costing manual and computerised library circulation	J. Ross and J. Brooks	165
Determination of unit costs for library services systems	J. A. Nachlas and A. R. Pierce	176
Unit times in studies of academic library operations	D. H. Revill	184
Programmed budgeting and cost effectiveness	D. Mason	202
An application of managerial cost accounting to a science information center	M. L. Cochran, A. G. Smith Jr. and A. D. Bender	212
Teaching costing techniques to librarians and information scientists of the future	R. Sturt	216

5. TOWARDS MANAGERIAL ECONOMICS 223

Introductory notes		225
From economic to political analysis of library decision making	J. A. Raffel	228
Measuring the goodness of library services: a general framework for considering quantitative measures	R. H. Orr	240
Concepts of library goodness	M. K. Buckland	258
Cost-effectiveness	A. Gilchrist	263

User valuations and resource management for information services	*T. Whitehall*	273
University libraries as economic systems	*M. P. Marchant*	292
Application of the theory of the firm to library costing	*D. Rowe*	301
An economic model of library service	*A. Bookstein*	305
The psychopathology of uneconomics	*M. B. Line*	324
Towards the development of a library management information system	*R. S. Runyon*	337

CONCLUSION 347

AUTHOR INDEX 348

INTRODUCTION

In due course definitive treatises will be written on costing and management accounting for libraries, and on the theory of library economics. For the time being the selection of papers in this volume of readings may help to fill part of that gap in the literature, at the same time as making some of the more significant contributions more readily available and better known. In the last twenty years a growing body of literature on costing and library economics has appeared, to reinforce the already considerable and growing literature on library finance, operational research, library and information service evaluation, and performance measurement. Yet in spite of this volume of professional thought and writing there has been only a very slow emergence of consensus about the most appropriate body of theory, and the practical importance of supporting techniques of costing, accounting and performance measurement. However, the growing economic pressures upon libraries and the effects of technological change must bring the time closer when the essentials of new theories and practices will emerge as part of the operational corpus of library management.

It is the editor's conviction that an interest in, and understanding of, the costs of library and information service operations provide a good introduction to other and often deeper realms of economic analysis. At its best, economics is a practical discipline, using theory where necessary to understand the fundamental aspects of the economic process of choice, and to address the question of the best use of resources applied to given ends of production and service.

With these observations and considerations in mind the selected readings are designed to provide a progressive introduction from the cost analysis to the economic analysis of library operations. Economic analysis is hardly possible in empirical terms without cost data, and on the other hand cost data alone is of little value if its economic contexts are not appreciated and understood. Four out of the five sections of this reader are concerned broadly with cost studies and cost accounting. In the fifth section there is a deliberate shift to a more synthetic approach, offering what might come in future to be the outlines of a managerial economics for libraries. In these terms managerial economics would be envisaged as a blend of management accounting and applied economics directed towards the decision problems which library managers have to face in the area of resource allocation and service performance.

The first section deals with the context and concepts of library and information service costs by presenting two descriptions of cost accounting and economic analysis. The second section covers papers concerned with investigating and measuring the system being costed. Whether the 'system' is a relatively minor task or group of tasks, or a major segment of a library service, common principles of analysis apply. Many cost analyses have to begin with some systems analysis in order to determine exactly what has to be costed, by whom it is done, and what resources are allocated to and consumed by the process. The third section, entitled basic approaches to service costing, shows how the concepts introduced in the first section, coupled with the techniques discussed in the second, can be melded together to provide operational techniques for cost analysis. The emphasis in this section is on methods, and it is followed in section four by papers which discuss practical cost studies. It is not possible to reproduce papers exemplifying every type of cost study, and those selected are mainly concerned with the cost analysis of direct process operations. The concept of cost-effectiveness is introduced and exemplified in the context of budgeting. The extensive literature on library budgeting is not reviewed in this reader, but it must be remembered that the budget as a plan of projected expenditure should be built upon a basis of rational economic choice and decision making — that at least is the laudable theory to follow. The achievement of that rational choice would be part of the substance of managerial economics. The fifth section is a broad selection of papers dealing with some of the main issues in library economics. Cost-effectiveness and cost-benefit analysis loom large in these wider discussions of library economics. Thus, the thread of cost data is drawn through basic cost analysis of library operations in order to reach a better understanding of multivariate economic reality.

FURTHER READING

COOPER, A. *Financial aspects of library and information services: a bibliography.* Loughborough, Centre for Library and Information Management, 1980. (CLAIM Report no. 5).

DOUGHERTY, R. M. and LEONARD, L. E. *Management and costs of technical processes: a bibliographical review 1876–1969.* Metuchen, N.J., Scarecrow Press, 1970.

HINDLE, A. and RAPER, D. The economics of information. *Annual Review of Information Science and Technology,* 11, 1976, 27–54.

MICK, C. K. Cost analysis of information systems and services. *Annual Review of Information Science and Technology,* 14, 1979, 37–64.

WILSON, J. H. Costs, budgeting and economics of information processing. *Annual Review of Information Science and Technology,* 7, 1972, 39–67.

Cooper and Dougherty are two useful bibliographies for exploring topics on costing, finance and library economics. The review chapters in *ARIST* by Hindle and Raper, Mick, and Wilson provide a varied selection of references and leads to further papers, and the commentaries trace the evolution of professional discussion on the topic.

GENERAL NOTE ON FURTHER READINGS

The suggestions for further reading given at the end of each introductory section are chosen very selectively. It is doubtful whether even the most carefully chosen list would be representative or comprehensive of relevant papers, and users' needs for additional reading vary a good deal. Those papers cited will help the reader broaden the search for knowledge on the topic concerned. The bibliographies in many of the papers reproduced could also be used as a source for further reading. The papers chosen for further reading are from UK and US sources, but it should be noted that contributions to cost and economic studies of libraries and information services have been made particularly by German, Australian, Canadian and Scandinavian authors. The literature for further reading not cited here is quite scattered and not especially coherent; many useful contributions are made at conferences and are to be found in volumes of proceedings and/or book chapters.

1 LIBRARY AND INFORMATION SERVICE COSTS: CONTEXT AND CONCEPTS

1. LIBRARY AND INFORMATION SERVICE COSTS: CONTEXT AND CONCEPTS

The purpose of the two introductory papers is to provide basic familiarity with the main concepts of costing, cost accounting and their application in a number of broader areas of economic analysis. Even the experienced practitioner may still encounter problems created by the lack of standard definitions and concepts; at the very least some revision is always profitable. In reviewing the literature of costing for library and information management there is a dearth of papers which could be read as a broad general introduction to the topic. The papers by Hayes and Becker (1970) and Schwuchow (1977) together summarize some of the essential concepts, even though their original intention was perhaps not directly considered with that service in mind. Hayes and Becker's paper forms a chapter in their well known monograph on library automation, which has become a classic source from the early days of library computer applications in the late 1960s. Schwuchow's paper also takes the perspective of computer-based documentation services, although it has its origins in some very specific cost study research. The respective origins of these papers in the literature of libraries and computers is significant. The computerization of library and information processes has provided a driving force for a revitalized study of all the economic aspects of the processes of information transfer and management. The computer revolution in libraries and information led to the application of system study and systems analysis techniques, and these are often a useful and necessary prerequisite to cost studies. Computer applications have challenged the bases upon which all library and information tasks have been undertaken. The question of alternatives to manual operations and the variety of optional methods for implementing computer techniques have called for cost analysis, so that resource allocation decisions are economically based and buttressed by measurements of the cost consequences of different decisions.

Hayes and Becker begin by summarizing what they then felt to be the state of the art on cost studies — largely inadequate for management purposes. After offering definitions of what cost accounting is and is not, they proceed to a discussion of general principles. The essential point made is that cost accounting is a wide ranging and systematic activity; it is considerably more than just the establishment of the cost for a task. Four main stages in cost accounting are then discussed. The first stage is the collection and recording of cost data, involving the identification of processes and tasks, the identification of the sources of expense, a system of coding the sources of cost and expense, the packaging and repackaging of cost data by focus (for example, by document type, by department, by subject, by type of resource consumed and input), and the identification of labour times expended with the associated volume of material handled. The second stage concerns the allocation of overhead costs; basically the indirect costs as distinct from the direct variable costs of production. The third stage deals with the input of cost accounting data to some form of management information system, which includes the fourth stage of reporting. Two further topics are raised. Cost accounting and budgeting are related to each other, and must be explored by reference to the generation of unit cost data. These topics are logically related to a mode of operation which, within an overall framework of resource allocation, would relate costing and work measurement to cost accounting, budgeting and performance measurement by means of a management information and/or decision support system. Such matters provide the substance of the editor's monograph: Roberts, S. A. *Cost management for library and information services*. London, Butterworths, 1984 (In press).

The introduction to Schwuchow's paper begins with the simple cost accounting theme espoused by Hayes and Becker, but then goes on to the wider perspective of economic analysis and evaluation. The essential point of this paper, which uses the general model of an I&D system (information and documentation system), is to show the need for basic cost data as an essential element of more sophisticated measures of evaluation and performance. Cost-efficiency, cost-effectiveness, cost-value and cost-benefit are introduced as management tools. The latter part of Schwuchow's paper goes on to stress that cost analysis carried out in isolation is of limited value. However, the difficulty of integrating cost analysis with the other variables which enter into information service has to be realized. Schwuchow's research group nevertheless believes a start can be made on tackling these problems. Later papers in this reader develop these themes of the relationship between economic indices and measures and more embracing concepts of service, value, benefit and performance.

FURTHER READING

FLOWERDEW, A. D. J. and WHITEHEAD, C. M. E. *Cost-effectiveness and cost-benefit analysis in information science.* London, London School of Economics, 1974. (OSTI Report 5206).

SIZER, J. *Insight into management accounting.* 2nd edition. Harmondsworth, Penguin Books, 1979.

The report by Flowerdew and Whitehead is a useful discussion of principles not easily obtained in such convenient form elsewhere. The monograph by Sizer is typical in content and approach of many discussions of management accounting, and provides an idea of the scope of the topic, and the place of cost studies, in the management of the business enterprise.

COST ACCOUNTING IN LIBRARIES

R. M. Hayes and J. Becker

Very few libraries have a sufficiently detailed picture of costs for their present operations to support scientific management. This lack of a cost picture has been long recognized in the historical and continuing discussion of the need for adequate cost accounting in library operations.[1-4] In fact, the need relates not so much to the issue of data processing as to the issue of good library management. Basically, good cost data is a prerequisite for the development and support of adequate budgets, and for the evaluation of alternative services and procedures, whether mechanized or not.

For these reasons it is essential to consider the introduction into the library of an adequate, detailed, cost accounting system. Although we are viewing the matter in the context of mechanization, it is important to reiterate that it has meaning to the library independent of this context.

DEFINITIONS

Before discussing the issues in cost accounting, let us make some important distinctions so that cost accounting is viewed in the proper perspective.

[1] Adams, Charles, J., "Statistical Chaos: Technical Services in Public Libraries," *Library Journal*, 91 (9) (May 1, 1966), 2278-2280.
[2] Parker, Ralph H., "Aspects of the Financial Administration of Libraries," *Library Trends*, April 1963.
[3] Rider, Fremont, "Library Cost Accounting," *Library Quarterly*, 6 (1936), 331-381.
[4] Brutcher, Constance, et al., "Cost Accounting for the Library," *Library Resources and Technical Services*, 8 (Fall 1964), 413-431.

Reprinted from HAYES, R. M. and BECKER, J. *Handbook of data processing for libraries.* New York: Wiley/Becker-Hayes, 1970, pp. 85-103, by permission of John Wiley and Sons, Inc.

1. *The distinction between cost accounting and methods analysis.* Many of the articles written about the measurement of costs in library operation have focused on detailed work measurement as part of a general methods analysis approach.[5,6] It is, therefore, important to recognize that a cost accounting system is basically different from methods analysis, although there is an important role for each. Specifically, in methods analysis (and work measurement), the intent is to evaluate quite detailed differences between ways of executing specific operations. In contrast, cost accounting is a management tool for control of an entire organization.[7] As a result, the level of detail required for work measurement is considerably finer than that involved in a cost accounting system.

2. *Cost accounting versus ad hoc cost studies.* Again, most of the articles written concerning library costs have reported one-time studies. In contrast to them, the value of the cost accounting system lies precisely in the continuing picture that it provides. We must emphasize that a cost accounting system is a tool for management of the library. It is valuable not only in providing a continuing picture of costs but also in the highlighting of *changes* in costs, in the single library, over time.

3. *Cost accounting versus library statistics.* Libraries have a tradition of maintaining various statistics—the number of books acquired, the number of titles cataloged, the number of volumes circulated, and the number of reference questions handled. But there is a great difference between statistics and cost accounting. In a sense, statistics provide only one side of the picture; they fail to describe what it costs to acquire a book, to catalog a title, to circulate a volume, or to answer reference questions.

4. *Cost accounting versus bookkeeping.* It might be argued that any library must maintain cost data in order to control its budget.[8,9] The problem, however, is that only rarely are the general bookkeeping accounts adequate for the evaluation of costs. Again, budget control presents only part of the picture, since it separates costs from the statistics of performance. However, it is clear

---

[5] Niteck, A., et al, "Cost Accounting Forms (Guides to aid librarians to determine the unit cost of technical services of a library)," *Michigan Librarian,* 29 (December 1963), 19-21.

[6] Pierce, Watson O'D, *Work Measurement in Public Libraries.* New York: Social Science Research Council, 1949.

[7] Horngren, Charles T., *Cost Accounting: A Managerial Emphasis.* Englewood Cliffs, N.J.: Prentice-Hall, 1962.

[8] Price, Paxton P., "Budgeting and Budget Control in Public Libraries," *Library trends,* XI (April 1963), 402-412.

[9] Price, Paxton P., "Financial Administration" *in Local Public Library Administration,* edited by Roberta Bowler, Chicago: International City Managers' Association, 1964, pp. 114-147.

that most libraries, in fact, now acquire almost all of the data—in statistics and in budget control—required for a cost accounting system. The cost accounting system, by tying together the statistics with costs, provides the total picture. The necessity is to do this in detail sufficient for the purposes of management control, but not in such detail as to impose an unbearable burden.

In summary, a cost accounting system is continuing rather than intermittent; it is concerned with the total library and not with some detailed aspect of it; and it ties together costs with effectiveness rather than being concerned with simply one or the other. Cost accounting is a management tool of primary value to the librarian in his day-to-day control of his own library. It is only of incidental value in comparisons of one library to another. The importance to good management is illustrated by the listing (Figure 4.1) of typical management reports that would be the continuing product of a good cost accounting system.

It must be recognized, however, that a cost accounting system for library operation does pose some significant problems. It is relatively easy to accumulate statistics or to control budgets; it requires a recording system to tie the two together. As a result, a cost accounting system represents a cost in itself. Its costs must be weighed against values received.

Figure 4.1 Management and Cost Accounting Reports

Management Reports

1. Direct cost total by account and by unit of work, for each account.
2. Overhead cost, by category, and as a percentage of both direct salary and total direct cost.
3. Total cost—direct and indirect, by administrative unit.
4. Each of these by time, by time period.
5. Time delays and backlogs, by department and by type of material.

Cost Accounting Reports

1. Weekly Transaction Listing
2. Weekly Labor Report
3. Weekly Inventory Usage Report
4. Weekly Cost Distribution Report
5. Cost Center Cost by Account Report
6. Cost Center Product Allocation Report
7. Fringe Calculation Report
8. Work-In-Progress Count Report
9. Work-In-Progress Calculation Report
10. Work-In-Progress Ledger Report
11. Work-In-Progress Summary Report
12. Cost Center Analytical Report
13. Cost Center Rate Report

Furthermore, the library represents a kind of organization for which accounting practice has developed few guidelines. First, the "product" of the library is a set of services, based on continuing investment in acquiring and cataloging a collection of information (the books and journals). There are still no standards for capitalizing such investment or for determining how overhead should be calculated. Second, most libraries are not "profit-making" institutions. Yet, most accounting practice is oriented to the need to determine the *profitability* of individual products of an organization. It is only recently that the value of cost-accounting data has been considered as part of the decision processes in *allocation of resources*. It is the latter, however, which is usually of importance in the library.

A fact that, in the past, has complicated the problem in introducing a cost accounting system in libraries has been the general lack of availability of the mechanized equipment for processing the comparatively large volume of recorded data involved. For many libraries this may still represent a significant barrier, but as the larger libraries gradually introduce mechanical procedures for various clerical operations, and as the smaller libraries combine into library systems, these difficulties should become relatively minor. In fact, the principle should be adopted that whenever a program for mechanization is initiated, a parallel system for cost accounting should be considered as well.

Perhaps the most significant barrier to the introduction of a cost accounting system in the library is the extent to which it will find acceptance by the library staff itself. Professionals rightly are very reluctant to have their performance, in any way, "measured." Actually, intellectual work is, by its nature, difficult (if not impossible) to measure and, where measurement is attempted, all too frequently it causes a misunderstanding of what was actually accomplished. Library work, in particular, involves such an intermixture of intellectual with clerical processes that measurement of them is almost certain to create many difficulties. Thus, even if we recognize the value of a cost accounting system to library administration, we must be aware of its effect on the professional staff. Basically, the only answer to this problem lies in the extent to which the system for recording, processing, and reporting is simple and includes a means for recognizing the intellectual content of library work. But it is useful to provide the staff with advance explanation of the value of a cost accounting system to both the organization and the individual, with emphasis on the fact that cost data is used to aid in making valid judgments not to replace them.

GENERAL PRINCIPLES OF COST ACCOUNTING

A cost accounting system is a procedure for recording operations, times, and costs for various parts of an organization, together with a procedure for processing, reporting on, and acting upon the resulting data. It must include provision for representing all sources of costs, including the salaries of staff and administrative personnel, capital investment, and all categories of expense. It must include provision for the measurement of work performed in terms of both quantity and, for library operations, quality and complexity. It must include provision for the recording of the time required to handle given operations.

In the recording of this data, a distinction is usually made between "process costing," where the data is related to a specific process, and "job costing" where the data is related to a specific item being processed. Let us explain the basis of the distinction. In the acquisition of a single book, we see a succession of processes—ordering, receiving, cataloging, mechanical preparation, and shelving.[10] If we are concerned only with the issue of costs for these individual processes, it would be sufficient to have a cost accounting system that simply recorded data about each of them. But if we wish to relate costs to different types, forms or kinds of material, we need the more detailed job costing system that ties costs to the specific item being processed as well. The point is that job costing involves the same processes that process costing would account for, but the detail will be much greater. Figure 4.2 is an approximate classification for operations in the library into those for which process costing seems appropriate and those for which job costing may be desired. It further summarizes some of the distinguishing characteristics of the two.

No matter what form of recording and amount of detail is utilized, there are always certain costs that cannot reasonably be assigned directly to a process or to a job. Administration, for example, is required for all operations in the library, and its costs cannot rationally be ascribed specifically, say, to the cataloging of a particular book. The distinction, therefore, is made between these costs that can be related to a specific process or job (called direct costs) and the costs that cannot be (called indirect costs or overhead). The importance of this distinction arises when we ask the question, for example, "What does it cost to catalog a book?" Clearly the costs of administering the library, of payroll accounting, of rent, and of utilities must, in some sense, be considered as part of the costs of cataloging a book. The issue is: How should these indirect costs be allocated to particular processes or jobs? The variety of possibilities for such allocation is great, but the usual basis is to allocate the indirect costs proportionally to the direct ones. However, some specific issues must be resolved: (1) Should the storage space for the collection be regarded as an overhead expense, or should it be included in the allocation to cataloging or to reader services for which the collection seems more directly related? (2) In the allocation of administrative expenses, should the costs of the book be regarded

[10] Franklin, Robert D., "Book Acquisition Costs," *Library Journal*, 90 (April 1, 1965), 1512-1513.

Figure 4.2 Examples of types of operations.

Examples

Process-Type Operation	Job-Type Operation
Selection	Unique orders
Ordering	Blanket orders
	Standing orders
	Approval orders
Receiving	
Fund accounting	
Catalog production	Monograph cataloging
	Serial cataloging
	Document cataloging
	Microform cataloging
	Magnetic tape cataloging
Circulation control	
Ready reference	Bibliographical work
	Catalog reference
	Information specialty service

CHARACTERISTICS

Process Costing	Job Costing
1. Less effort	1. More detailed
2. Periodic recording rather than continual	2. Specific costs continually available
3. Unit averages more easily obtained	3. Clarifies differences among materials or service groups
4. Responsibility for costs more clearly defined	
5. Overhead allocation is simpler	

as part of the direct costs of acquisition or should the allocation of administrative costs be based solely on the salaries of the personnel involved? We raise these issues, here, solely to illustrate some of the detailed problems that must be resolved in the introduction of a cost accounting system. The particular decision made as to the basis for allocation will reflect the management needs of the library.

A final problem, in the creation of a cost accounting system, concerns the distinction between capital costs, which must in some way be amortized over the useful life of the capital investment, and expense costs which are charged as costs as they are incurred. Let us comment on the significant points. If capital costs are not amortized, they distort the cost picture, since they unduly increase costs at one point in time and decrease them later. To illustrate, if equipment is acquired to aid in the circulation function of the library and if this major capital expense is allocated to the cost of circulation at the time of purchase, the expenses in this department will be unnaturally high; later, if it serves its function properly, the costs of service will be significantly lower. The cost accounting system would completely fail to provide precisely that kind of management information for which it is intended, that is, describing what the effect of this capital investment was on operational costs. If, alternatively, the purchase of this piece of equipment is regarded as a capital investment, with costs amortized over the useful life of equipment and allocated against operating costs on that basis, a truer picture is obtained and the cost accounting system indeed serves its purpose. But the question now is: What constitutes capital investment? Most particularly, it seems that the book collection itself should be treated as a capital investment. The U.S. government curricula A-21 (concerning acceptable overhead accounting practice for universities on government grants and contracts) requires that books be treated as current operating expense (because there is a continuing budget for it). However, there is a huge initial investment represented in the university library's collection, the value of which should be recognized and which should be amortized. Of course, there are significant issues that must be resolved concerning the basis for an amortization schedule and standard depreciation rates, but the principle should be clearly established that the book collection represents the major capital investment in the library.

ISSUES IN OPERATION

The normal operation of a cost accounting system can be conveniently divided into four aspects: (1) operations involved in the actual recording of direct cost data; (2) operations involved in the allocation of overhead to that data and in its distribution to cost accounts; (3) operations involved in the analysis, preparation, printing, and distribution of management reports; and (4) operations involved in revision of the system, particularly toward the end of introducing more specific detail. In the following sections we will discuss each of these categories.

Direct-Cost Recording Operations

The major element of cost and cause of difficulty in acceptance of a cost accounting system lies in the recording of data for operation and jobs.

Figure 4.3 Chart of cost-accounts—direct expenses.

	A		B		C		D		E	
Account Code	1	2	3	4	5	6	7	8	9	10

The following chart should be regarded as tentative and illustrative. Any final list will require a very careful examination of the actual needs for management reporting in the individual library.

A. *Type of Process* — *Unit of Work*

- 100. Acquisition .... Title order
  - 110. Selection
  - 120. Ordering
  - 130. Fund accounting
  - 140. Receiving
- 200. Preparation .... Volume
  - 210. Labeling
  - 220. Jacketing
  - 230. Book cards and pockets
  - 240. Distribution
  - 250. Binding
- 300. Cataloging .... Title
  - 310. Descriptive cataloging
  - 320. Subject cataloging
  - 330. Classification
  - 340. Subject authority revision
  - 350. Shelf-listing
- 400. Production of catalogs .... Entry printed
  - 410. Key-punching
  - 420. Sorting and merging
  - 430. Creation of master
  - 440. Printing
- 500. Circulation .... Volume
- 600. Reference .... Request
  - 610. Formulation of request
  - 620. Initial searching
  - 630. Compilation of answer
  - 640. Transmission to request
- 700. Administration and general

B. *Level of Complexity*

- 0. Simple
- 5. Averages
- 9. Complex

COSTING AND ECONOMICS

C. Source of Cost

- 10. Salary
  - 11. Professional library
  - 12. Professional technical
  - 13. Clerical
- 20. Expenses
- 30. Capital investment (including book funds)

D. Type of Material

- 10. Books
  - 11. Fiction
  - 12. Nonfiction
  - 13. Juvenile
- 20. Serials
- 30. Phonograph records
- 40. Documents
- 50. Microform
- 60. Magnetic tape

E. Administrative Unit

- 10.
- 20. Departmental
- 30. or branch
- 40. Library organization

Therefore, it is vital that this recording be made as simple, as uncomplicated, and as easy to perform as possible.

The requisite data that must be recorded are the cost, time, and amount of work performed (in terms of some appropriate units for measurement of work). Usually, cost associated with a process is determined from the salary of the staff or equipment performing it; for most libraries, it is important to identify uniquely each person or piece of equipment, although for certain purposes (such as circulation charging) it is sufficient to identify the type of person. The data concerning time are relatively easy to define, the only real issue being the degree of precision with which it is recorded (usually, in library operations, we might reasonably record time to five minute intervals).

The real difficulty lies in the definition of the categories of processes and of suitable units for measurement of the work performed in each of them. In accounting terms, this is represented by a "chart of accounts." A representative chart for a typical library is shown in Figure 4.3. As this chart of accounts shows, the processes being measured can be identified at as many levels of detail as may be appropriate to management needs at the moment. Presumably, one would start a system at a relative gross level (even so gross as "ordering," "cataloging," "circulation," and "reference") and then refine the detail when necessary or desirable.

As should be evident from the chart of accounts (Figure 4.3), several considerations are relevent in the definition of process accounts. In addition to the process itself, the type of material being processed, the level of complexity, special features (such as language), the department, and required response times all become significant in the exact specifications of a process account.

Since qualitative judgment is so important in library work, the chart of accounts pays particular attention to the issue of complexity. Although we recognize that complexity is difficult (if not impossible) to define, it is essential to provide some mechanism for the recognition of it. The chart of accounts does so by providing a relative coarse measure, divided into three categories: simple, typical, and difficult. These could be determined by the type of material, the language, or other factors relating to the difficulty in the task. (Of course, they need not be applicable to all classes of operation.)

As mentioned previously, a distinction is usually made between "process-

Process-cost reporting form.

Process		Date	
Person	Time In	Time Out	Volume of Activity

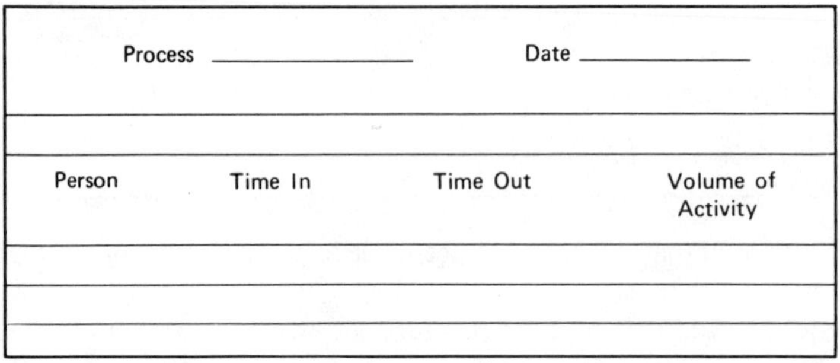

(a)

Process-cost punched card.

Card Code 3 Cols.	Blank 10 Columns	Account Code 10 Columns	Person Code 10 Columns	Time In 10 Columns	Time Out of Columns	Volume 3 Columns

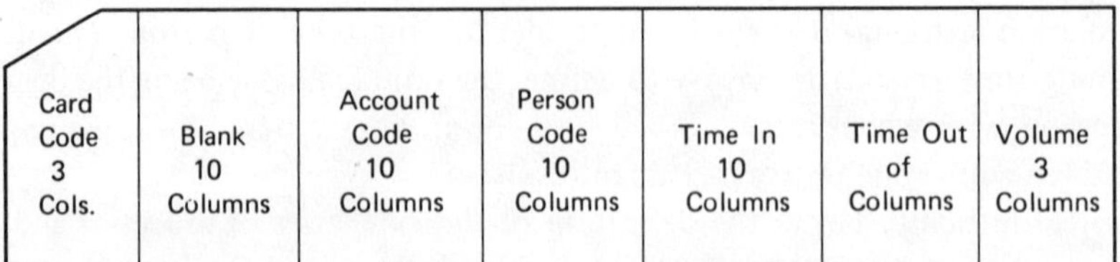

(b)

Figure 4.4 (a) Process-cost reporting form. (b) Process-cost punched card.

COSTING AND ECONOMICS 17

type" operations and "job-type" operations. Figure 4.4 shows a typical form for the recording of cost accounting data for a normal process-type operation. There would be a separate form for each such process, in which the recording on each line identifies the person (or machine) performing that operation, the starting time and ending time for each, and the volume of the activity handled at each of the three levels of complexity. Usually, such a form will be placed at a charge-out desk, and the clerk will then simply record his identity, starting and ending times, and tallies of the number of items charged out in the defined categories.

	Acquisition Number		Vendor		Date of Ordering	
	Author					
	Title					
	Process Code	Complexity		Person	Time In	Time Out
1	Ordering					
2	Receiving					
3	Cataloging					

(a)

Card Code	Acquisition Number	Account Code	Person Code	Time In	Time Out
3 Cols.	10 Columns	10 Columns	10 Columns	10 Columns	10 Columns

(b)

Figure 4.5 (a) Job-cost reporting form (illustrated by ordering and cataloging) (b) Job-cost punched card.

The recording of data for job-type operations involves a somewhat different form (Figure 4.5). As shown, each line in this form would allow the recording of one in the succession of processes through which the job moves, together with the identification of the persons (or machines) performing the successive jobs and the time taken for the level of complexity of the particular process for the particular job. Generally, this form will be, in some sense, physically attached to the job and will move with it from one process to the next. For example, if a request for information services is received which, from its nature, warrants the establishment of a job for it, a job accounting sheet would be created and would follow the job through the successive steps of (1) definition of request, (2) catalog searching, (3) acquisition of material, (4) analysis of relevant data, and (5) development of report.

Such a form thus serves a variety of purposes:

1. Issued by person responsible for initiation.
2. Authorizes the work and provides for a chronological record of the time consumed.
3. Describes the nature of the job and indicates what should be produced.
4. Outlines the steps to be taken.
5. Follows physical work through production.
6. Controls the accumulation of cost data.
7. Becomes the source record for cost accounting.
8. Can provide a permanent record.

In both process and job costing, the form of recording would be manual, on preprinted forms with self-explanatory codes to facilitate both the recording and subsequent key-punching. This raises a basic assumption: if a cost accounting system is to have any real chance of success, the later stages of processing and reporting should be performed with data processing equipment. This implies that the data in the manual recording forms must be transferred to machine language by key-punch operations. Figures 4.4 and 4.5 include typical punched-card formats. For each line entry in the manual recording form, a single punched card will be created.

Allocation of Overhead

Certain categories of data, as we have indicated, cannot be directly attributed to particular processes or jobs. For example, these include administrative expenses, rent and utilities, and certain generally used supplies. Figure 4.6 lists some of the usual kinds of overhead costs. Although the costs from these sources cannot be determined from the forms of recording defined above, they must be included in the later processing. Normally, this is handled by assigning several costs on an a priori basis to specific overhead categories. The salaries of administrative personnel, for example, would be automatically accumulated as an overhead expense without the necessity of a recording operation. Where a staff member may, during some portion of time, be performing direct work, that time will be recorded as part of a process or a job, and the remainder of this salary will be automatically allocated to overhead. Similarly, expense items such as rent, utilities, and supplies will be automatically charged to overhead as they

Figure 4.6 Overhead cost accounts

100.	Salary related		
	110.	Benefits	
		111.	Social Security
		112.	Insurance
		113.	Etc.
	120.	Vacations, leaves, holidays	
	130.	Nondirect time	
	140.	Overtime Premium	
200.	Supervision		
300.	Rent, utilities, maintenance		
400.	Supplies		
500.	Travel		
600.	Depreciation of collection		
700.	Depreciation of equipment		
800.	Legal and other services		

are incurred. For direct personnel, the time such as sick leave, vacations and holidays, and the like, which cannot be assigned directly to jobs or processes, will be determined by the difference between total salary and that charged directly to jobs or processes.

As a result, the total of all costs of operation—including both those recorded and those automatically allocated—must equal the actual costs of operation as accumulated in the General Account (Figure 4.7). The intent of allocating overhead is then to arrive at a figure for the total costs assignable to each process and/or job in the library. To arrive at these costs, the following sequence of steps are followed.

1. The costs directly associated with each line item recorded in a report form must be determined by multiplying the salary or machine costs by the amount of time spent.

2. These resulting costs are then accumulated to the level of detail appropriate to reporting needs.

3. The overhead costs must then be allocated, proportionate either to the direct salary costs, where this is appropriate, or to the total direct costs where other categories of expenses are significant.

The Effects of Rules for Overhead Allocation. The choice of a rule for the allocation of overhead has some unexpected effects of which the library must be aware—not only in the context of its own internal accounting but in the larger

Figure 4.7 Budget of accounts versus cost accounts.

General Accounts	Cost Accounts
Accounts payable	Direct material
Rent and utilities	Processes
Supplies	Jobs
Materials	Direct labor
Payroll	Processes
Prepaid expenses	Jobs
Insurance	Overhead allocations
Depreciation	Salary related
	Administration
	Indirect expenses
Total cost of service equals	Total cost of service

context of any organization of which it is a part. The usual rule is "allocate overhead in proportion to the amount of costs for direct *labor*." The word "labor" is italicized to emphasize the contrast with total costs. The effect of this rule is to provide positive encouragement to the replacement of labor by other kinds of direct cost and, especially, by mechanization. It also has the effect of penalizing the parts of an organization that do not attempt to use mechanization.

To highlight these effects, consider two departments as an organization: (1) the library, and (2) some other department—each with comparable manpower and costs.

	Department A	*Department L*	*Total*
Direct salaries	$30,000	$30,000	$60,000
Other costs	5,000	5,000	10,000
Overhead	30,000	30,000	60,000
Total	$65,000	$65,000	$130,000

Now, suppose that Department A decides to mechanize, replacing personnel with machinery. If the overhead is allocated proportional to direct salaries, the figures might change as follows.

	Department A	*Department L*	*Total*
Direct Salaries	$10,000	$30,000	$40,000
Other Costs	40,000	5,000	45,000
Overhead	15,000	45,000	60,000
Total	$65,000	$80,000	$145,000

COSTING AND ECONOMICS

It appears that the *library* is the cause of the increase in costs! Of course, to some extent, this is an extreme picture, since the overhead total will probably also be reduced, but not usually by a comparable proportion. The lesson is clear: accounting practice is almost designed to favor mechanization, and the library should be distinctly aware of its effects.

Input for Machine Processing

Purpose of the Machine Processable Input. An effective cost accounting system implies more than just recording data on cost forms. Although this might be the initial step in the process, the full system will include procedures for the processing of the data and the preparation of the resulting information generated in report form. In order to process the large volume of data that would be forthcoming from the library network operations, the use of electronic data processing equipment is inescapable. Thus, to provide input for this equipment, the data on the reporting forms must be transferred to machine readable form.

Development of the Input Format. Given the library's job control form, the next stage in the development of the cost accounting system is to provide a medium and format for the translation of data from that report form to machine readable input. In the choice of a medium, it would appear logical to treat each activity performed by the researcher and listed on the reporting form as a unit record, and thus to use punched cards to hold the data, with each punched card acting as a unit record.

Reporting Operations

A cost accounting system is of value only to the extent that reports useful to the library management can be produced from the resultant data. The principle of such management reporting is that it makes evident long-term trends in cost, it highlights exceptional situations, it clarifies effects of changes and unusual situations, it pinpoints problem areas, and generally it allows the library management to maintain control, not only over costs but over the quality of services produced. To these ends, reports of various kinds can be rapidly produced from basic recorded data.

1. "Reports by person," which allow for comparison of productivity, particularly in terms of the "level of complexity" of work done. Admittedly, this is a sensitive issue, but has great importance for good library management.

2. "Reports by process" so that the cost of various parts of library operation are clearly and explicitly known.

3. "Reports by job" or by type of job so that the costs of handling particular types of requests for references or for cataloging particular types of books can be clearly known.

4. "Reports by time period" so that explicit comparisons between time periods can be made and seasonal variations can be exhibited.

Cost or financial reports should be based on the following fundamental qualities and characteristics.

(a) Reports must fit the organization chart; that is, the report should be addressed to the individual who is responsible for the items covered by it and who, in turn, will be able to control those costs which fall under his jurisdiction.

(b) Reports must be prompt and timely. Reports issued long after the occurrence of events lose their control value. Prompt issuance of a report requires that cost records be organized so that information is available when needed. Delaying a report until all data is assembled can become a costly matter, since it prevents the executive from taking immediate remedial measures.

(c) Reports must be issued with regularity. Executives regard the receipt of reports at a definite hour of the day or week as the best means of arranging their plans and operations.

(d) Reports must give comparative figures, that is, a comparison of actual with budgeted figures or a comparison of predetermined standards with actual results and the isolation of variances. Other reports might compare this week's results with last week's or with the same week of the previous year. The reporting of differences or exceptions is important.

(e) Reports must be analytical. Merely the development of figures cannot suffice in the complexity of present-day management. If variances indicate good or bad performance, the reasons for the conditions should be stated.

(f) Reports should, if possible, be stated in physical units. To make cost reports more valuable and useful, an effort should be made to show physical units as well as dollar values.

COST ACCOUNTING AND PROGRAM BUDGETING

Increasingly, governmental and industrial organizations are turning to "program budgeting" as a means of financial planning.[11] The principles of

[11] Young, Helen A., "Performance and Program Budgeting: An Annotated Bibliography," *ALA Bulletin*, 61, pp. 63-67.

program budgeting are quite straightforward. The organization defines a set of "programs" representing the aims and objectives of its management. Usually, there will be some *a priori* estimate of what investment management is willing to make in achieving each of these programs. Each part of the organization must then justify its *administrative* budget by showing how it contributes to each program.

For example, in a university, the library serves students, faculty research, organized research projects, the administration, other libraries, and perhaps local industry. Each of these activities represents a program of service which the university regards as more or less important and to which the library contributes. If a university were to adopt program budgeting, the library would need to demonstrate the extent to which its administrative budget was allocable to each program—faculties, schools, institutes, research projects, and students, for instance. Comparable examples are evident in public libraries (service to children, to the disadvantaged, to industry, and to other libraries), school libraries, or special libraries.

As libraries of all kinds move toward greater service to a broader clientele, program budgeting will become a necessity for the library itself. When it does, an adequate cost accounting system is an absolute necessity. It is the only way to evaluate what each program will cost, in terms of the magnitude of service required. For example, suppose a university decided that service to local industry was a significant program (perhaps represented by a research center). If it is undertaken, the burden on the library represented by information requests from industry is likely to increase a hundredfold. Without cost data on which to project the effects on such an increased burden, the library is virtually helpless in justifying the increase in budget which will really be required.

ILLUSTRATIVE UNIT COSTS

As we have pointed out, it is extremely difficult to find useful cost data in the library literature. What data are available are based on different units of work, different methods of measuring production and costs, and different allocations of overhead. Therefore, to provide at least a starting point for anyone considering use of cost accounting in libraries, we provide, in Figure 4.8, a summary of illustrative unit costs. These have been derived from a careful review of the literature and have been compared with the actual costs in several libraries. We consider them to be realistic, but whether or not they are, at least they can be used to highlight the effects of different methods of measurement and different allocations of overhead. To do so, we have listed these illustrative unit costs in four categories: minimum, basic, standard, and burdened.

Figure 4.8 Illustrative unit costs.

Function	Unit of Work	Nominal Hourly Rate	Minimum	Basic	Standard	Burdened
General and Administrative						
Processing	/employee	$3	$1.50	$2.10	$3.00	$4.00
Acquisition						
Selection	/order	$5	1.20	1.70	2.40	3.30
Ordering	/order	$3	.70	1.00	1.40	1.90
Invoicing	/invoice	$3	.70	1.00	1.40	1.90
Cataloging						
Cataloging	/title	$5	1.80	2.50	3.50	5.00
Creation of master	/title	$3	.25	.35	.50	.70
Printing	/title/catalog	$3	.13	.18	.25	.36
Sorting and Filing	/title/catalog	$2	.13	.18	.26	.36
Reader Service						
Circulation	/volume	$2	.07	.10	.14	.19
Shelving	/volume	$2	.05	.07	.10	.14
Serials						
Receiving	/serial/month	$2	.10	.14	.20	.28
Recording	/serial/month	$2	.10	.14	.20	.28
Physical Handling						
Receiving	/volume	$2	.03	.04	.06	.08
Labeling, etc.	/volume	$2	.12	.18	.24	.32

Minimum Unit Costs

These represent the costs one would expect to find in a time and motion study (averaged over a number of units of work), based on the nominal hourly rate indicated for the salary or wages of personnel assigned to the function. They do not represent peak rates of work, but rather typical rates for actually handling a single unit. The figures given are representative of several reported in time and motion studies and are similar to those discussed in Chapters 14 through 18.

Basic Unit Costs

These represent the costs one would expect to find as the "direct costs" (per unit of work) reported by a cost accounting system. They are therefore the average cost per unit of work including nonproductive time (such as coffee breaks), inefficiencies, and variations in workload.

Standard Unit Costs

These represent the costs for the same rates of production as the basic unit costs but include recognition of all "salary-related benefits," such as vacations, holidays, sick leave, unallocated time, severance pay, overtime premium, insurance, and social security.

Burdened Unit Costs

These represent the actual costs of providing the services of the library, including supervision, operational expenses (space, utilities, maintenance), and amortization of capital investments.

Suggested Reading

There are very few discussions of cost accounting in the library literature which provide more than a superficial or incomplete picture. It is therefore suggested that one or another basic text in "managerial accounting" be read in order to establish a proper framework within which to view the comments in this chapter:

Horngren, Charles T., *Cost Accounting: A Managerial Emphasis.* Englewood Cliffs, N.J.: Prentice-Hall, 1962.

THE ECONOMIC ANALYSIS AND EVALUATION OF INFORMATION AND DOCUMENTATION SYSTEMS

Werner Schwuchow

Abstract—Significant results of a project carried out by the Studiengruppe für System-forschung e.V. (Heidelberg, W. Germany) on the "Economy of Information and Documentation Systems" are described. The aims of this project in the framework of the German national "Program of the Federal Government for the Promotion of Information and Documentation (I&D-Program) 1974–77" were to develop methods for measuring the efficiency of information and documentation systems and services and to test such methods in actual practice.

INTRODUCTION

The following report presents several internationally relevant findings of a research project carried out by the Studiengruppe für Systemforschung e.V. dealing with the topic The Efficiency of Information and Documentation Systems (WID I Project)". The project extended from mid-1974 to mid-1976 and was commissioned by the Federal Ministry of Research and Technology (Bundesministerium für Forschung und Technologie) in connection with the "Federal Program for the Promotion of Information and Documentation (I&D-Program) 1974–77"[1].

The main objectives of this project were:

(1) To develop and test *standard systems and methods for cost accounting* in information and documentation systems (I&D-systems)[2]. The term *I&D-systems* comprehends libraries, archives, documentation agencies, information analysis centers, information referral centers, etc. Methods for cost accounting were first developed specifically for those I&D-systems concerned primarily with the documentation of literature. A step-by-step expansion of the methodology to include other I&D-activities (such as library functions, the documentation of data, of projects, etc.) is anticipated.

(2) To establish *indices for the costs* of individual activities in I&D-systems: e.g. (i) acquisition costs/information source of unit of documentation† (for the various types of information sources: periodical articles, books, reports, patents, etc.) (ii) cost of bibliographic description per documentation unit (iii) cost of textual analysis (indexing, abstracting, etc.) per unit of documentation (iv) cost of keyboarding per unit of documentation (v) storage costs per unit of documentation (vi) output costs per search, SDI-profile or issue of an abstracting journal (vii) output costs + proportion of input costs + proportion of overhead expenses per search, SDI-profile or issue of an abstracting journal.

(3) To develop different practicable *approaches to and methods of determining the level of performance, the efficiency and the usefulness of I&D-systems.*

In our attempts to accomplish this third objective, we encountered familiar difficulties, as they are, for example, described in the more recent publications of Tressel and Brown[4], Hindle and Raper[5] and Murdok and Sherrod[6].

COST ACCOUNTING AND ANALYSIS

The ascertainment and analysis of *costs* form the basis for determining the efficiency of I&D-systems. Cost accounting should essentially accomplish the following tasks:

(1) Specification of the cost structure, i.e. the way in which the total annual budget is composed of the various types of costs (employment costs, equipment costs, cost of materials,

†A *documentation unit* is the amount of data which the text and bibliography of a book, a periodical article or other source of information contain (see [3], p. 51).

etc.) and how it is distributed over the particular operational functions (acquisition, indexing and abstracting, storage, search service, SDI service, administration, etc.).

(2) Supervision of the efficiency of individual operational functions and activities.

(3) Provision of material for the calculation of e.g. the prices of different kinds of I&D services (retrospective searches, SDI-services, abstracting services, bibliographies, data bases, etc.).

(4) Provision of decision-making aids for dealing with the question of whether to carry out certain operational functions and services within the system or whether to farm them out.

(5) Performance of comparative calculations among systems.

(6) Provision of material for forecasting costs in planning new or reorganizing existing I&D-systems (cost indices).

In the I&D-systems existing in Germany today, one rarely finds a policy of continuous, detailed cost accounting. In the few cases where certain cost calculations are made, they are not based on uniform systems and methods, nor are they detailed enough to come near accomplishing the tasks mentioned.

In performing tests on methods of standardized I&D-cost accounting compatible with those methods adopted by other members of the Common Market (see Refs.[7–10], we encountered the following difficulties: (i) I&D-systems are often part of a larger organization. This complicates the determination of the proportions in which management, administration, real estate, buildings, etc. contribute to the total overhead expenses. (ii) In smaller I&D-agencies, individual staff members assume several operational functions (e.g. indexing and abstracting, retrieval, user service, management). It is thus difficult to break down the overall expenses into the single components of the operational process. (iii) In addition to their main activities, I&D-systems exercise a number of secondary functions, e.g.; research, professionally qualified evaluations, publication of research reports and literature series, training of technical personnel. Under certain conditions, the costs of such activities should be set apart from the costs incurred by the "operation of the information service". (iv) Modern I&D-systems often cover a broad spectrum of services, they are "multiple product enterprises" and pose all the familiar problems associated with the distribution of partial overhead and input costs over a number of different services with no common denominator (the problem of finding a calculation scheme for such assessment).

Because of these problems in cost accounting and the fact that it is difficult to compare I&D-systems with one another (differing subject fields and user needs; differing technical equipment: from simple card catalogues to peek-a-boo systems, to computers; differing forms of cooperation, etc.), it is highly problematic to attempt to make comparative calculations and deduce cost indices for purposes of planning in the I&D area (see points 5 and 6 in the catalogue of objectives listed above). For such purposes, there is no sense in considering the overall costs of I&D-systems. Rather, one must take into account only those cost components which can be *directly* related (as in direct costing) to distinctly definable and comparable functions and activities (e.g. indexing, abstracting, keyboarding, searching).

Within the framework of our project, we have carried out two types of empirical investigations on the costs of I&D-systems:

(a) *General surveys* to obtain basic statements about the costs of different types of I&D-systems (I&D-cost theory), to derive cost indices for individual I&D-activities and (with great reservations) to draw comparisons between systems.

With the help of mailed questionnaires and subsequent interviews and panel discussions, we examined the costs and the factors influencing them in *26 I&D-systems* (13 operating conventionally; 13 partially computerized) in W. Germany for a longer period of time (approx. 6 months). The extensive statistical results for the year 1974 can be found in the project report[11]. There is scarcely any point in presenting an extract on this occasion, since the particular figures are hardly of interest beyond the borders of the Federal Republic of Germany (see[12]) and since, moreover, the figures are already partially outdated due to the rapid developments in the I&D-area.

(b) Detailed *case studies* in two of the 26 systems (one large, partially computerized and one large, conventional system) with the objective of carefully checking the results of investigation (a) in two specific cases and testing detailed procedures for cost accounting.

If the objective is to analyse costs and efficiency within individual systems (see points 2-4 of the list of tasks given above), case studies represent effective means; they are not, however, a satisfactory approach to the problems of comparisons among systems and general planning (points 5 and 6 of the task catalogue).

EVALUATION OF PERFORMANCE AND ANALYSIS OF EFFICIENCY

It is only meaningful to compare systems in the I&D-area if one considers not only the costs, but also the differing user needs, the types and number of information sources, the different organizational frameworks and conditions, technical equipment, the varying "amounts" of information processed, the varying amounts and characteristics of the services offered, etc. The cost analysis must be extended to an efficiency analysis (cost-performance or cost-effectiveness analysis).

The *performance* (effectiveness) of an I&D-system is evaluated on the basis of the degree to which the services offered by the system in question within a given period satisfy the needs of the users in both quantitative and qualitative terms (see Refs. [13-15]).

This performance can be evaluated according to a number of criteria, e.g. according to the *amount* of services dispensed per unit time, according to *revenue* (amount marketed times price) per unit time for individual types of services, according to *speed* or frequency at which specific services are produced or delivered, according to the *up-to-dateness* of the information transmitted, its *completeness* and *relevance* (recall, precision, etc.), according to the *ease* with which the system can be used and the *effort* involved, according to the *reliability* of the various services, the *flexibility* of the services offered (capacity for quick adjustments to shifts in demand), etc.

These *criteria of performance* are dependent upon the composition of the user population, the purpose and time of the performance evaluation, the services evaluated, etc. *Performance criterion* is our term for quantitative measures with which one can determine the level of performance achieved by an I&D-system, taking all the different aspects into consideration. These criteria must also be specified for each of the various kinds of I&D-services.

For search systems (retrospective searches) by way of an example, some of the relevant performance criteria are as follows: (i) Total number of searches carried out annually. (ii) Number of actual users of this service compared with the number of potential users (market penetration). (iii) The average time span between the agency's receipt of an enquiry and the user's receipt of the response (average response time). (iv) The average time span between the initial appearance of a publication and its inclusion in the system's store of information (the up-to-dateness of the information stored). (v) Recall ratio (see e.g. [15] p. 26 ff.). (vi) Precision ratio (see e.g. [15] p. 26 ff.). (vii) The average number of relevant references previously unknown to the users as compared with the total number of references supplied within a given time period (novelty ratio). (viii) The average number of previously unknown references which the users utilized in finding solutions to their problems as compared with the total number of references supplied within a given time period (pertinence). (ix) The number of unanswered enquiries as compared with the total number of enquiries received annually. (x) The average investment in terms of time and money by the user (user effort): effort required to gain access to the I&D-system (commuting expenses and time, telephone costs, usage fees, etc.), search time (if the search is made in person, as e.g. in an on-line system), time required for screening the transmitted search results, etc.

Performance criteria which can only be quantified with difficulty—if at all—(e.g. the appearance, legibility, etc. of the transmitted search results) can be taken into consideration by plotting judgments on an ordinal scale.

We have already on a previous occasion [16, 17] given a detailed presentation of a procedure for systematically recording judgments in connection with performance evaluations in I&D-systems (multi-dimensional evaluation). Applying this procedure in successive steps, it is possible to consolidate the partial judgments of individual users regarding specific aspects of an I&D-system to an overall judgment on its performance—although the process of establishing the specific aspects, their relative importance and their evaluation (with or without recourse to the values of performance criteria) will never cease to arouse debate and new considerations. Using ordinal value scales: (i) One aggregates the user's partial judgments on specific criteria of performance to determine his overall judgment on a service offered by an I&D-system. (ii) One aggregates the overall judgments of the individual users in order to obtain the collective overall judgment of all the users on this particular service. (iii) One aggregates the collective judgments on the various services in order to arrive at the collective overall judgment of a group of users on all the services offered by an I&D-system.

There is no other way to evaluate the *total* performance of I&D-systems, i.e. to evaluate the *totality* of services offered over a given time period, while simultaneously taking a large number of performance criteria into consideration—unless one were to decide in favor of introducing market and price mechanisms which would regulate supply and demand in the I&D-area (if indeed such an arrangement could even be completely effective in this field). Our project report[11] suggested a whole series of practical procedures, based on KING and BRYANT[15], for more or less comprehensive evaluations of I&D-systems' performances (macroevaluation, microevaluation).

The *efficiency* of an I&D-system is the relationship between its performance and the resources necessary to achieve this level of performance (manpower, equipment, materials, real estate and buildings, energy, etc.). These resources, evaluated in terms of monetary units over given periods of time, are equivalent to the costs of the system.

A detailed analysis of the effciency of an I&D-system (microevaluation) must take all factors into consideration which influence the costs and performance of said system. These factors, which we call *systems parameters* as does VICKERY[18], are many in number. We distinguish among three classes of such parameters (by this term we mean influences upon the organization, performance and costs of I&D-systems which can be regarded as constant within the framework and for the purposes of a given efficiency analysis):

"Environmental" parameters = influences largely determined by the "environment of the system in question (e.g. the number, kinds and languages of the information sources relevant to a certain specialized field; the information needs and behavior of the users; government planning; the financial resources at the disposal of I&D in general and of the system observed in particular; the international development of the I&D-area; the general economic situation).

Institutional parameters = influences which may be largely determined within the I&D-system itself (or by its immediate financial sponsor(s) or other responsible organization(s)) and which affect the general organizational structure of the system (e.g. organizational and legal form, manner of financing, geographic location, area of information to be covered, forms of cooperation with other agencies, size, organization of labor, composition of the personnel, type and capacity of mechanical equipment).

Functional parameters = influences which may be largely determined by the management of the observed system itself and which are related to the organizational structures of individual operational functions (e.g. kinds and number of information sources acquired, analysed and stored per unit time (coverage ratio, etc.); classification and indexing systems; depth of indexing, volume and characteristics of the indexing language; keyboarding and storage techniques; retrieval techniques; types and forms of the various services; techniques of data output).

While the boundaries between these three types of systems parameters are not always entirely clear, they are distinguished by the manners in which they can be influenced by I&D-systems' managers on a short, medium or long-term basis.

The structure of every single operational function is influenced by a number of such parameters. For example, the cost of the function "indexing and abstracting" alone is influenced by the following parameters:

(i) Kinds of information sources processed (percentage of periodical articles, books, reports, etc.). (ii) Subject field (e.g., in chemistry documentation, the cost of analysis tends to be higher than in other fields). (iii) Number of information sources processed per unit time (by the system as a whole, by the individuals working within the system, etc.). (iv) Qualifications and subjective conscientiousness of the "indexing and abstracting" personell. (v) Specific organization of labor (e.g. the integration of diverse activities into I&D-systems: cataloguing, indexing and abstracting, keyboarding, etc.). (vi) Documentary language (classification system, thesaurus, vocabulary commanded, etc.). (vii) Volume and characteristics of vocabulary used (keywords, subject headings, descriptors, preferred index terms etc.). (viii) Exhaustiveness of depth of indexing. (ix) Manner and scope of the supervision of indexing and abstracting. (x) Content and average dimensions of the units of documentation (bibliographic data, descriptors, abstracts, average number of words per abstract, average number of characters per documentation unit, etc.).

According to our studies, the influences exerted by systems parameters on the costs and performance of I&D-systems and/or their individual operational functions overlap to such an extent that the influences of particular parameters on separate functions (e.g. the influence of "the exhaustiveness of indexing" on "indexing costs") can only—if indeed at all—be very roughly ascertained within the framework of general surveys.

Should one wish to trace these influences and complex interrelations quantitatively, extremely detailed and costly case studies would have to be carried out in individual I&D-systems. Our project report[11] proposes a systems approach for such investigations.

For the time being, owing to the complexity of the subject matter, it seems advisable to restrict practical efficiency analyses in I&D-systems to individual operational functions or to the production of specific types of I&D-services. STANDERA[19], for example, suggests a simple technique for analysing the efficiency of search and SDI services while considering only a few performance criteria.

ANALYSIS AND EVALUATION OF THE BENEFITS OF I&D

As to the most difficult area of economic analysis in I&D[20], only a few approaches and definitions will be briefly introduced.

The *benefit* of I&D services is determined by the degree to which these services contribute toward the attainment of specific individual goals (e.g. increase in revenue and profit, improvement of personal performance and productivity, increase in individual creativity, reduction of time and money invested in the acquisition of information, cost reduction through elimination of unnecessary research) and the attainment of certain social goals (e.g. improvement of the living and working conditions within a society, elevation of the general level of education, general improvement of every man's access to information, increase in the capacity for research and development, improvement of competition in the economy, strengthening of the decision-making abilities of governments, public administrations, parliaments, judicial organs, etc.).

Accordingly, one distinguishes two kinds of benefits deriving from I&D-services.

As far as the *individual benefit* is concerned, there are several criteria which are relatively easy to measure; for example: (i) Time and expense saved by the individual users or their institutions (as a result of quicker and better information, avoidance of superfluous research and development, etc.). (ii) Increase revenues and profits in industrial enterprises (as a result of quicker and better information).

The *social benefit* derived from I&D-systems can, however, hardly be quantified with any degree of reliability. It manifests itself in, e.g. (iii) Improvement of the economic situation (higher profits, greater markets, fewer unemployed, higher incomes, etc.). (iv) Quicker and better solutions in public affairs (in the health system, in education, environmental policy, social policy, in the fight against crime, in traffic safety, etc.). (v) Improvement of the vocational opportunities of individual citizen through improvement of his access to information.

The quantification of this social benefit in the context of a comprehensive *cost-benefit analysis* is as problematic an undertaking in the I&D-area as in many other areas of public activity.

Therefore, a cost-benefit investigation in the I&D-area should not be carried out with the objective of establishing what portion of the public resources should be appropriated for this entire sector (as opposed to other public functions). Rather, such an investigation should proceed from a fixed public budget covering the whole I&D-area and restrict itself to determining how to distribute this budget most rationally (i.e. fulfilling the best possible benefit-cost conditions) among the individual I&D-activities and systems. With this end in mind, it is meaningful to correlate a benefit evaluation with a performance evaluation.

FUTURE PROSPECTS

The Studiengruppe für Systemforschung is currently involved in a WID II project, whose objective is to continue the work started in WID I, with particular emphasis on: (i) The introduction of running, standardized cost accounting systems in centralized I&D-systems of the Federal Republic of Germany (by developing "guidelines for cost accounting in I&D-systems," which will enable these systems and their staffs to carry out cost accounting independently). (ii) Cost analysis of information networks. (iii) Performance and benefit evaluation in centralized I&D-systems (case studies). (iv) Analysis of the problems of financing I&D-systems (including the problem of pricing the different types of I&D services). (v) Determination of the demand for running statistical surveys in the I&D-area in Germany and development of a system for carrying out such surveys.

REFERENCES

[1] The Federal Minister of Research and Technology (ed.), Programm der Bundesregierung zur Förderung der Information und Dokumentation (IuD-Programm) 1974–77, Bonn (1975).
[2] This method for cost accounting is based on several years of preliminary work in the Federal Republic of Germany: see R. FUNK, P. GENTH and W. SCHWUCHOW, Kostenschemata für Dokumentationseinrichtungen. In *Nachrichten für Dokumentation* 1976 27(1), 23–29; and in the nations within the Common Market: see P. H. VICKERS, Final Report on Project 2: Extension and Revision of the Cost/Accounting Scheme to Interactive Systems of the Network. ASLIB London (June 1976).
[3] Kommittee Terminologie und Sprachfragen (KTS) of the Deutsche Gesellschaft für Dokumentation e.V. (ed.), *Terminologie der Information und Dokumentation*, Vol. 4 of the DGD literature series, Verlag Dokumentation, Munich.
[4] G. W. TRESSEL and P. L. BROWN, A critical review of research related to the economics of the scientific and technical information industry. Prepared for National Science Foundation, Rept. No. PB245665, Batelle Columbus Labs., Columbus (Ohio), 1975.
[5] A. HINDLE and D. RAPER, The Economics of Information. *Ann. Rev. Inform. Sci. Tech.* 1976 11, 27–54.
[6] I. MURDOCK and I. Sherrod, Library and information center management. *Ann. Rev. Inform. Sci. Tech.* 1976 11, 381–402.
[7] P. H. VICKERS, A cost survey of mechanized information systems. *J. Docum.* 1973, 29(3), 258–280.
[8] G. DUBOID and E. PEETERS, Couts Du Traitment Automatique fr l'Information Documentaire, Brussels (1974).
[9] E. ALLAIRE, Enquete sur les Couts de Systemes de Documentation Automatique en France. Centre National de la Recherche Scientifique, Paris (1975).
[10] Commission of the European Communities, Directorate General Scientific and Technical Information and Information Management. Cost of Scientific and Technical Information and Documentation Systems, 194 pp., EUR 5531 dlelf, Luxembourg (1976).
[11] K. EUSTACHI, W. HACK and W. SCHWUCHOW, Wirtschaftlichkeit von Informations- und Dokumentationseinrichtungen, Part A: *Project Report*, Part B: appendices to project report. Studiengruppe für Systemforschung e.V., Heidelberg (1976). Will appear in 1977 in the report series of the Federal Ministry of Research and Technology (Bundesministerium für Forschung und Technologie). Obtainable from: Bundesministerium für Forschung und Technologie, Referat für Presse und Öffentlichkeitsarbeit, Postfach 120 370, 5300 Bonn 12.
[12] K. EUSTACHI, W. HACK and W. SCHWUCHOW, Die Wirtschaftlichkeit von IuD-Einrichtungen. *Nachrichten für Dokumentation* 1977, 28(2), 68–73.
[13] F. W. LANCASTER and W. D. CLIMENSON, Evaluating the economic efficiency of a document retrieval system. *J. Docum.* 1968, 24(1), 16–40.
[14] F. W. LANCASTER, The cost-effectiveness analysis of information retrieval and disseminations systems. *J. Am. Soc. Inform. Sci.* 1971, 22(1), 12–27.
[15] D. W. KING and E. C. BRYANT, *The Evaluation of Information Services and Products*. Information Resources Press, Washington, D.C. (1971).
[16] W. KUNZ, H. RITTEL and W. SCHWUCHOW, Zur Berwertung Von Informationssystemen. *EURIM. A European Conference on Research into the Management of Information Services and Libraries* (Paris, 20–22 Nov., 1974), pp. 5–14. ASLIB, London (1974).
[17] W. KUNZ, H. RITTEL and W. SCHWUCHOW, *Methods of Analysis and Evaluation of Information Needs*. Verlag Dokumentation (pub.), ISBN 3-7940-3450-3, Müchen (1977).
[18] B. C. VICKERY, *On Retrieval System Theory*; 2nd Edn, p. 155 ff., London (1965).
[19] O. R. STANDERA, Costs and effectiveness in the evaluation of an information system: *J. Am. Soc. Inform. Sci.* 1974, 25(3), 203–207.
[20] D. I. URQUHART, Economic analysis of information services. *J. Docum.* 1976, 32(2), 123–125.

2 INVESTIGATING AND MEASURING THE SYSTEM

2. INVESTIGATING AND MEASURING THE SYSTEM

The implementation of successful cost accounting in libraries depends on at least two initial processes: the first is an understanding of the total system which is being costed, and of the structure of the component parts of that system; the second is the definition of the part of the process and system to be costed, especially regarding its operational context and the location and definition of boundaries. So, for example, what is the organizational position of areas such as technical processing and inter-library loan service within the overall structure of the organization; and what tasks, operations and flows of resources and effort go to make up the component parts of technical processing and inter-library loans?

The first paper by Mahapatra (1980) takes a global view of systems analysis applied to library and information services. Of particular importance is the sequential process of system study outlined, which can guide the conduct of a management investigation. The position of cost study is specifically mentioned in the design and development phase. The main techniques of system study are discussed, with cost analysis related to the overall task of analysis and appreciation, and with the cost factor as a part of evaluation and measurement. Systems study is used to assess the feasibility of different methods and developments, and cost data may then be used to assess which option should be chosen for implementation.

Burns (1971) discusses a generalized methodology for systems analysis, and deals with some more specific aspects raised by Mahapatra. Burns observes that historic costs used in system design may be considerably modified once the system procedures are implemented. There is no simple solution to cope with this problem, but it suggests that operational systems should be able to draw on a back-up of management costing, to provide a necessary source of feedback. The paper by the staff of the Aslib Research Department (1970) provides a further narrowing of the field of view towards the detailed application of systems analysis. It is concerned with the analysis of library processes as a contribution to the improvement of procedures and performance. As library processes are reviewed the analyst must be aware of the cost implications of differences in procedure. The standardization of process descriptions and means of describing and recording are also discussed in this paper. The basic principles are related to work study (method study and work measurement) processes, and are directly relevant to detailed types of cost study where the first stage is the analysis of times taken to perform tasks.

Directly pertinent to the previous paper is a contribution by Robertson, Reynolds and Wilkin (1970), which addresses the question of standard costing for information systems. Standard costing focusses on the concepts of standard tasks and task components; provided these can be ascertained, then approximate and/or real costs for actual library processes could be modelled. Such a procedure might save managers' time and effort when they need to cost elements of systems, particularly in development work and the consideration of optional process methods. The novel ideas mentioned in this paper have perhaps not worked into common practice, although the idea of standard costs and times (average costs and average times) is both potent and attractive. Standard costing is a technique for synthesizing costs. Most cost analysis proceeds from the opposite direction: the analysis of actual tasks to derive cost components.

This selection of readings ends with a paper on work analysis by random sampling, by Divilbiss and Self (1978). Sampling of observations is often the only economic way to cope with the field collection of time data for detailed cost study, and various trials have shown that these methods are reliable. This paper should be considered in conjunction with the papers by Smith and Schofield (1971) in section 3, and Revill (1977) and Nachlas and Pierce (1979) in section 4.

FURTHER READING

CHAPMAN, E. A., ST. PIERRE, P. L. and LUBANS, J. *Library systems analysis guidelines.* New York, Wiley-Interscience, 1970.
GILDER, L. and SCHOFIELD, J. L. *Work measurement techniques and library management: methods and data collection.* Cambridge, University of Cambridge — Library Management Research Unit, 1976. (LMRU Report No. 2).
LUBANS, J. and CHAPMAN, E. A. *Reader in library systems analysis.* Englewood, Microcard Edition Books, 1975.
MARSTERSON, W. A. J. Work study in a polytechnic library. *Aslib Proceedings,* 28 (9), 1976, 288–304.

The two publications by Chapman and Lubans are useful background sources which will develop further ideas on the scope and application of systems analysis. Gilder and Schofield review techniques of library work measurement and discuss practical examples and problems. Marsterson is a good exemplification of the practice of the principles.

Systems Analysis as a Tool for Research in Scientific Management of Libraries: A State of the Art Review

by M. MAHAPATRA

1. Systems approach

The problem of research in library and information science can be small scale or large scale; can be specific or general, can be short term or long term; can be very practical or very theoretical (50). Kajberg (27) evaluates research methods in librarianship, with American viewpoint where as Slamecka (43) observes some of the pragmatic approaches to theoretical research in information science. Vickery (50) illustrates the various 'analytical techniques for investigating libraries'. Priscilla Rose's (40) approach is through the following three manners: i) Behavioral approach, ii) Systems approach and iii) Other less important varieties of approaches. Bellomy (2) solves library problems through systems approach, whereas Elton and Vickery (17) suggest the scope of operational research in the library and information field.

Of all the above approaches, this state of the art review discusses only the *systems approach* for research in library and information field. An attempt has been made to discover the fundamental concepts behind *systems analysis* and its possible application to library administration and operation. Much emphasis has been paid to the *technique* aspect of the subject. The review deals with the following phases of the subject:

   i)   systems and systems characteristics,
   ii) systems analysis, its definition, scope and application,
   iii) phases of systems study,
   iv) techniques of systems study, and
   v)   future prospects.

2. Systems and systems characteristics

Moore (38) quoting Webster defines a system as "a set or arrangement of things so related or connected as to form a unity or organic whole, a set of facts, principles, rules, etc; classified or arranged in an orderly form so as to show a logical plan linking the various parts". He further says, "a system is a set of operations organized to satisfy adequate user requirement".

Systems have definite characteristics. Chamis (8) enumerates a set of characteristics which differentiates one system from any other system. They are as follows:

i) Systems are dynamic in various degrees.
ii) Each system has its own objectives.
iii) There are alternative ways of reaching a given objective in a given system.
iv) Each system has its own environment.
v) The criteria used to judge the value differ for each system.
vi) Each system has its own limiting factors.
vii) The optimum design differs for each system.

Some systems may not have all these characteristics while other systems may have additional characteristics not mentioned here.

Herner (25) deals with the range of systems, out of which two main types can be distinguished, i.e. i) Information systems which include effective organization and utilization of available resources; the development of remote access; time shared, digital computer systems; extensive memory systems; information storage and retrieval systems; data processing systems, etc. (8), and ii) Library systems which include in library operation the total picture from the library's objectives, its reasons for being, the demand made upon it and its user needs and requirements; it also includes the equipment and the personnel (38).

Whatever may be the case, whether it is an information system or library system, it can be investigated or traced into its modes of hierarchy, for every system has its own subsystems, procedures, etc. in a hierarchical fashion. Stafford Beer calls them 'cones of resolution' and suggests that any investigation of an organization will result in a hierarchy of modes – working down from the most generalized picture of the situation to more elaborate and detailed levels (49).

3. Systems analysis

3.1. Definition and scope

A concise generally accepted definition of systems analysis does not exist. Different workers have defined it in different manner. The range of definitions can be noted from the articles of Fasana (19), Chapman (9), Moore (38) and Burns (6) to name a few. However, for the present context, we can define systems analysis according to Chapman as the logical analysis of the present systems, the evaluation of the efficiency, economy, accuracy, productivity and timeliness of existing methods and procedures measured against the established goals of the library, and the design of new methods and procedures or modifications of existing methods and procedures to imporove the flow of information through the system. Like its definition, its scope also varies to a great extent (8,19,38).

3.2. Application

Whether systems analysis is a method (or a technique) for research in effective library management or a descipline in itself raises doubt. However, authors like Salverson (41), Vickery (50), Lamkin (30, 31), Chamis (8), Fasana (19), and a few others (27, 30, 34, 46) give their opinion regarding systems analysis as a tool for research in scientific management of libraries.

Fasana says that systems analysis is not a solution in itself. At best it is a methodology, technique or tool that has promise. He further explains that it is a methodology especially designed to facilitate the continuing adjustment of a system to its environment. Chamis concludes that systems engineering approach is a very powerful technique for analysing an existing information system to investigate whether it is organized in the most efficient way as well as making the maximum use of its available resources. Lamkin writes this as a tool that will serve the librarians richly by facilitating their ability to improve operational performance and to communicate with top management. Mackenzie (34) suggests systems analysis as a decision-making tool for the library manager whereas Salverson treats this as another method of evaluation in library and information services. Mason (36) discusses the systems analysis, operations research, market research, personnel management, etc. and their interrelationships.

4. Phases of systems study

Burns (6) recognized five basic phases of systems study. They are, i) Systems study, ii) Analyzing the system, iii) Design of system, iv) Implementation and evaluation of the new system, and v) Continuation. But according to Fasana (19) approximately six phases or steps in a systems study can be distinguished and though the phases are overlapping in operation, in theory should be done in the following sequence.

I   Preliminary phase
   i) begins with a decision by top management
   ii) selection and authorization of person or persons to undertake the effort

II Description phase
   i) to gather data by describing and measuring all aspects of current operations

III Analysis phase
   i) analysis of the raw data that has been gathered
   ii) to assemble and display it in a useful form
   iii) to begin to identify and compare alternative ways of accomplishing the same results.

IV Design and development phase
   i) to prepare a detailed systems proposal, including work schedule development and operating costs, equipment requirements, etc. of one or more alternative systems
   ii) to develop test and document all aspects of working systems for implementation. Hays (23) has developed a methodology for systems design and suggested its usefulness in effective library management.

V   Implementation phase
   The key to successful implementation of the new system is
   i) creation of a hospitable environment
   ii) training the proper staff
   iii) demonstration of the new systems for building confidence in the new procedure
   iv) and others such as file conversion, if necessary systematic phase out of old procedures, site preparation, follow up on training, adopting of documentation, etc.

VI Evaluation and feedback

5. Techniques of Systems study

5.1. Survey methods

Surveys fall under the category 'direct method of measuring use by scientists and technicians' (13). There may be descriptive surveys which are limited to enumeration and description and there may be analytical surveys which are subject oriented and relate data to identify factors and patterns. The combination between the above two types, descriptive – analytical, is also used (20,40). The general method choosen to gather the pertinent information is what is commonly called 'the user needs survey' (32). The first step in developing a survey is to decide who should be involved in the survey and what areas should be covered. Three major methods have been used for this purpose – the questionnaire methods, the diary method and the interview method (1).

Davis (13) puts the questionnaire method into three types – free answer questions, categorical answer questions and ranking system answer questions. Bare (1) suggests important characteristics for formulating a questionnaire, where as Herner (25) adopted certain characteristics of the questionnaire while developing a rather complex system for an information centre dealing with a broad range of social sciences. The diary method is dealt by Bare (1) for conducting user requirement studies in special libraries.

Interview is another direct method of survey. There are two types of interviews – unstructured and structured (13). In other words, Landau (32) names them as 'subjective survey techniques' and 'participant – completed questionnaire'.

Other methods like observation, critical incident study (13), sampling which includes random sampling (4, 16), and purposive selection sampling (32), work sampling and random-time-techniques are also used to sample library users (24).

5.2. Charting and graphical methods

Librarians in special libraries and information centres are employing several management devices or techniques to assist them in the operative and administrative research of libraries (11,12). Some of the techniques as Gull (21) enumerates are relatively old as, operation charts; operating manuals (also known as staff manuals, individual manuals, sectional manuals, etc.); position descriptions; personnel or job adminstrative procedures; and standardized forms; and others are relatively new and unusual in libraries, such as, functional block diagrams; logical flow charts or decision flow charts, decision tables and flow process charts. For definition and types of flow charting articles of Bolles(3), Gull (21) and Heinritz (24) are highly recommended; specially Gull has dealt in detail the technique for preparation of block diagrams and logical flow charts.

The application of flow charting to systems analysis is rather essential (47). For example, Bolles has charted all the clerical routines in the Esso Research and Engineering Company's Central Library (USA) (3). Another interesting hypothetical analysis was done by Jestes for locating a reference book in a large university library. The analysis was made of the sequence of steps and the time and cost of the patron in locating the book. The steps and decisions the patron takes were graphically displayed in a flow chart (26).

5.3. Analysis

The other technique which is required for systems study is analysis (14). It can be the analysis of staff, procedure, cost, time and others if any. The analysis is done by various methods. Chamis describes the analysis of information system responsibilities and procedures, i.e. the nature of specific responsibilities and how do they relate to one another and to the whole information system, and how each responsibility consists of a number of procedures or activities which must be carried out. Chamis also deals with information staff time analysis (8). Heinritz describes about the cost analysis and cost determination, and cites how the library profession has made a small start toward the use of industrial cost techniques such as break-even analysis (24). Bare describes the methods of analysis of various other data (1).

5.4. Evaluation and measurement

Different workers have approached differently to the evaluation and measurement of library operations, services in relation to systems study.

Salverson (41) and Carnovsky (7) suggest for the subjective evaluation of the library operations. In evaluating the library one must consider the efficiency of its internal operations and its effectiveness in implementing the goal of service to users (37, 41). These two criteria are necessarily interrelated. The most basic formula as suggested by Salverson for determining efficiency of an operation is:

$$E = \frac{O}{I} \qquad \text{Efficiency} = \frac{\text{Output}}{\text{Input}}$$

Lipetz translated this into terms useful for communication systems

$$E = \frac{\text{Useful results (services)}}{\text{Costs involved}}$$

The cost factor includes expenditures in terms of materials, supplies, personnel and equipment. The cost can be determined by various methods (35, 44, 48). Chamis (8) provides an analytical method for determining the overall value of an information system while treating the various criteria for its evaluation. Heinritz (24), Kozumplik (29) and Logsdon (33) deal with work measurements, time and motion studies for various library tasks. Such measurement is necessary to establish fair performance standards and to calculate systems costs. Kozumplik applies the standard work measurement techniques to acquisitions, cataloguing and circulation functions of the library (29). As suggested by Chapman (9) the time schedule is not only important to the orderly and expeditious prosecution of the study, but also to the administrative knowledge and acceptance of how long current library operation will be showed or otherwise adversely effected by the study's demands on the operating time. Pizer and Cain's work briefly reports in a battery of tests and methods that are now available to librarians as tools for assessing the performance of their library objectively (39). These tools like 'document delivery test', 'a test of inter-library loan service', 'time sampling techniques', etc., serve to clarify the picture of library services, enable the administrator to compare his services with those of another library in directly comparable terms and provide a means of establishing baselines against which he can measure progress towards improved services.

6. Future prospects

Systems analysis has already proved useful in libraries, first by fostering a critical, systems approach to operations and problems; and secondly by providing librarians with new techniques useful in analyzing, evaluating and understanding library operations (19). To cite an example for its effective application, Buckland *et al* have applied the technique in the University of Lancaster Library (5). Kennington (28) and Stanton (46) have suggested some important tips for its application in the field of special librarianship.

If systems analysis is periodically and continuously done, then Moore (38) suggests some of the important benefits to be gained by the library which undergoes such a study, where-as Fasana (19) points out some of its limitations. The future of systems analysis in libraries is promising, but will not be realised without effort on the part of the librarians. Since systems analysis is an emerging discipline developed primarily for use in non-service environment, the technique currently available will have to be evaluated and adopted before they can be applied indiscriminately to libraries. This will take time and considerable effort.

REFERENCES

1. Bare, Carole E.: "Conducting user requirement studies in special libraries", *Special Libraries*, 57 (1966): 103–106.

2. Bellomy, Fred L.: "Systems approach solves library problems," *ALA Bulletin*, 62 (1968): 1121–1125.
3. Bolles, Shirley W.: "Use of flow charts in the analysis of library operations", *Special Libraries*, 58 (1967): 95–99.
4. Bookstein, A.: "How to sample badly", *Library Quarterly*, 44 (1974): 124–131.
5. Buckland, M. K., Hindle, A., Mackenzie, A. G. and Woodburn, I.: "Systems analysis of a University library: University of Lancaster Library, *University of Lancaster Library Occasional papers no 4*, (1970).
6. Burns, R. W.: "Generalized methodology for library systems analysis", *College and Research Libraries*, 32 (1971): 295–303.
7. Carnovsky, L.: "Evaluation of library services", *Unesco Bulletin for Libraries*, 13 (1959): 221–225.
8. Chamis, Alice: "Design of information systems, the use of system analysis", *Special Libraries*, 60 (1969): 21–31.
9. Chapman, Edward A.: "Planning for systems study and systems development", *Library Trends*, 21 (1973): 479–492.
10. Cleverdon, C. W.: "User evaluation of information retrieval systems", *Journal of Documentation*, 30 (1974): 170–180.
11. Collins, K. A.: "Data management systems. Part I. A model approach to automatic small library files", *Special Libraries*, 66 (1975): 121–125.
12. Collins, K. A. and West, W. W.: "Data management systems. Part II. Journal routing – An example of library applications", *Special Libraries*, 66 (1975): 205–211.
13. Davis, Diana L.: "New approaches to studying Library use", *Drexel Library Quarterly*, 7 (1971): 4–12.
14. Deprospo, E. R.: "Use of community analysis in the measurement process", *Library Trends*, 24 (1976): 557–567.
15. Dronberger, G. B. and Kowitz, G. T.: "Abstract readability as a factor in information systems", *Journal of the American Society for Information Science*, 26 (1975): 108–111.
16. Drott, M. C.: "Random sampling; a tool for library research", *College and Research Libraries*, 30 (1969): 119–125.
17. Elton, M. and Vickery, B.: "The scope for operational research in the library and information field", *Aslib Proceedings*, 25 (1973): 305–319.
18. Farradane, J.: "Evaluation of information retrieval systems", *Journal of Documentation*, 30 (1974): 195–205.
19. Fasana, Paul J.: "Systems analysis", *Library Trends*, 21 (1973): 465–478.
20. Fatcheric, J. P.: "Survey of users of a medium-sized technical library", *Special Libraries*, 66 (1975): 245–251.
21. Gull, C. D.: "Logical flow charts and other new techniques for the administration of libraries and information centers", *Library Resources & Technical Services*, 12 (1968): 47–66.
22. Hamberg, M., Ramist, L. E. and Bommer, M. R. W.: "Library objectives and performance measures and their use in decision – making", *Library Quarterly*, 42 (1972): 107–128.
23. Hays, Robert M.: "Development of a methodology for systems design and its role in library education", *Library Quarterly*, 35 (1964): 339–351.
24. Heinritz, Fred J.: "Analysis and evaluation current library procedures", *Library Trends*, 21 (1973): 522–532.
25. Herner, Saul: "Systems design, evaluation, and costing", *Special Libraries*, 58 (1967): 576–581.

26. Jestes, Edward C.: "Example of system analysis: locating a book in a reference room", *Special Libraries*, 59 (1968) 722–728.
27. Kajberg, Leif: "Research methods for librarianship in retrospect: some observations on American achievements", *Libri*, 23 (1973): 52–57.
28. Kennington, Don.: "Managing effectively: some tips for special librarians", *Aslib Proceedings*, 23 (1971): 287–291.
29. Kozumplik, William A.: "Time and motion study of library operations", *Special Libraries*, 58 (1967): 585–588.
30. Lamkin, Burton E.: "Decision – making tools for improved library operations", *Special Libraries*, 56 (1965): 642–646.
31. Lamkin, Burton E.: "Systems analysis in top management communication", *Special Libraries*, 58 (1967): 90–94.
32. Landau, Herbert B.: "Methodology for a technical information use study", *Special Libraries*, 60 (1969): 340–346.
33. Logsdon, Richard H.: "Time and motion studies in libraries", *Library Trends*, 2 (1954): 401–409.
34. Mackenzie, A. G.: "Systems analysis as a decision-making tool for the library manager", *Library Trends*, 21 (1973): 493–504.
35. Magson, M. S.: "Techniques for the measurement of cost-benefit in the information centres", *Aslib Proceedings*, 25 (1973): 164–185.
36. Mason, D.: "Management techniques applied to the operation of information services", *Aslib Proceedings*, 25 (1973): 445–458.
37. Meier, R. L.: "Efficiency criteria for the operation of large libraries", *Library Quarterly*, 31 (1961): 215–234.
38. Moore, Edythe: "Systems analysis: an overview", *Special Libraries*, 58 (1967): 87–90.
39. Pizer, Irwin H. and Cain, Alexander: "Objective tests of library performance", *Special Libraries*, 59 (1968): 704–711.
40. Rose, Priscilla: "Innovation and evaluation of libraries and library services", *Drexel Library Quarterly*, 7 (1971): 28–41.
41. Salverson, Carol A.: "Relevance of statistics to library evaluation", *College and Research Libraries*, 30 (1969): 352–361.
42. Shaw, W. M.: "Library – user interface: a simulation of the circulation subsystem", *Information Processing and Management*, 12 (1976): 77–91.
43. Slamecka, V.: "Pragmatic observations on theretical research in information science", *Journal of the American Society for Information Science*, 26 (1975): 313–317.
44. Smith, G. C. K. and Schofield, J. L.: "Administrative effectiveness: times and costs of library operation *Journal of Librarianship*, 3 (1971): 245–266.
45. Snowball, George L.: "Survey of social science and humanities monograph circulation by random sampling of the stock", *Canadian Library Journal*, 28 (1971): 352–360.
46. Stanton, R. O.: "Applying the management-by-objectives technique in an industrial library", *Journal of the American Society for Information Science*, 26 (1975): 313–317.
47. Swenson, Sally: "Flow chart on library searching technique", *Special Libraries*, 56 (1965): 239–242.
48. Taylor, L.: "Cost research on a library service", *Aslib Proceedings*, 13 (1961): 238–248.
49. Thomas, P. A.: "Tasks and the analysis of library systems", *Aslib Proceedings*, 22 (1970): 336–343.
50. Vickery, B. C.: "Methodology in research", *Aslib Proceedings*, 22 (1970): 597–606.

ROBERT W. BURNS, JR.

A Generalized Methodology for Library Systems Analysis

THIS ARTICLE IS DIRECTED toward the novice in systems work. Its purpose is to generalize at a very elementary level a methodology or approach which can be used in conducting a systems study. Systems work is discussed here as a point of view; a logical, coherent, from the top down, preface to decision-making and resource allocation which utilizes a very powerful body of sophisticated techniques. The approach and techniques reviewed in this paper, however, will be those on the most elementary level. No attempt will be made to discuss the techniques of queueing, inventory management, linear programming, simulation, marginal analysis, game theory, statistical inference, or any of the other highly sophisticated techniques available to the operations research/systems analysis (OR/SA) analyst. When the systems approach is clearly understood and properly used, it becomes a potent weapon in the arsenal of the administrator. Rather than a review of the tools themselves, a delineation of this systems methodology and point of view will be considered in this article. The methodology discussed here embraces a number of standard techniques used by the systems engineer, time and motion analyst, operations researcher, and occasionally, even the librarian. Examples of these techniques are scattered through the professional literature of librarianship/information science, management, industrial engineering, and operations research/systems analysis. Some of the more important references describing OR/SA in the library have been included in the bibliography which accompanies this article. Unfortunately, many of the most basic concepts of these twin fields remain poorly understood and as a result are seldom applied by the library profession. Two glossaries of terms have been added to the bibliography for the benefit of the user who wishes additional help in understanding the terminology of OR/SA.

In the past six to eight years, only a few publications of merit have appeared in the literature showing how and under what conditions a systems study can be conducted in a library environment. Some of these were prepared by librarians, but many of the best have been written in a highly technical jargon by individuals whose credentials are in fields other than library science. Indeed, one of the most significant developments has been the number of articles written about the library/information science field by individuals whose backgrounds are in other disciplines but who, nevertheless, have successfully used the library as a laboratory, and in doing so have given the library profession some of its most substantial contributions.

Reprinted by permission of the American Library Association and the author from *College & Research Libraries* 32(4): 295–303 (July 1971).

A true systems study should be able to document for the administrative officer the goals of the administrative unit being studied and the resources available to the unit, as well as suggest alternative methods for achieving these goals within a given set of constraints. All of this must be accomplished in such a fashion that the administrator is permitted to select the proper alternatives by manipulating resources to reach his preselected goals. Fundamentally, this is a process of balancing goals with resources based on the facts gathered by the analyst. Facts needed by the administrator include such items as unit costs, unit times, costs of materials and equipment, opportunity costs, configuration and availability of equipment, movement of staff and material, and staffing patterns. It is the job of the analyst/designer to ferret out these facts and present them to the administrator with a full display of available options.

A systems study must examine both the economic efficiency of the unit being studied as well as its operational efficiency, always being careful to study each *in vivo*. Economic efficiency can be judged in either of two ways: the ability of the system to produce or process the same number of units for less cost; or the ability to produce more units for the same cost. The savings achieved by library automation seem largely to accrue from the second advantage. Operational efficiency is a much more subtle concept and, indeed, involves many of the intangible values with which all librarians doing systems work are constantly confronted. One measure of operational efficiency derives from user satisfaction and can be determined by the questionnaire/interview method.

The achievement of maximum efficiency within a system is an extremely subtle process requiring the fine tuning and sensitive ear which one expects of a skilled violinist. It is in no sense of the word the obvious undertaking that some managers believe it to be. An efficient system is one which has reached a correct balance between the resources and the system's achievement of its goals, or performance. However, there is a distinction between efficiency and the measures of efficiency. It is quite common for the novice in systems work to confuse the ways of measuring efficiency within a subsystem such as decreased costs, increased production, etc., with the efficiency goals of the total system. True efficiency can only be discussed validly in the context of a total system's operation.

What Is a System?

In discussing systems work, the first problem is to develop an unambiguous definition for the word system. Although it is used often and widely, the implications of this concept are seldom fully understood. As Nadler points out, there are almost as many definitions as there are people writing about the field.[1] The Random House dictionary stresses the concept of a system as "an assemblage or combination of things or parts forming a complex or unitary whole. . . ." The U.S. General Accounting Office, in its systems glossary, expands this to point out that "systems analysis may be viewed as the search for and evaluation of alternatives which are relevant to defined objectives, based on judgment and, wherever possible, on quantitative methods, with the objective of presenting such evaluations to decision makers for their consideration. . . ."[2] Bellomy refers to a system as "an assemblage of interdependent things and ideas necessary to achieve a set of related objectives . . . characterized by inputs which are processed to produce the outputs required to achieve specified objectives. . . ."[3] After examining these definitions, several ideas begin to emerge which are common to any systems effort, no matter what it may be called. The ideas of interrelated parts bound into a coherent whole possessing a common goal or objective are central to the systems concept. It is on these basic attributes that we shall build our methodology for a systems study.

In this article attention will be focused on the four steps or phases of a systems study which we shall call the systems survey, the systems analysis phase, the systems design phase, and the implementation/evaluation phase. This somewhat arbitrary division should not be taken to infer that these are discrete operations with a systems design proceeding only when the systems analysis effort has been completed. This would be a highly idealized solution since in actual practice the pressures to get on with the job will usually force the telescoping of these efforts. When this is done with care and in a recursive fashion, the chances of success are usually good. Each of these phases should be viewed as complementary to the others and, although they are similar and related, each must be performed in a sequential and discrete fashion, preferably in tandem. Some overlap is permitted, but the analysis phase always begins before the design phase, and the design phase always begins before the implementation phase.

General Characteristics of a Systems Effort

Before discussing each phase in detail, several generalizations should be made about the entire systems effort. These will help the reader develop an understanding of the type of problem to which we are addressing ourselves; they are as follows:

(1) Attention to detail lies at the very heart of the systems effort and thorough precise work demands an intense preoccupation with every detail, no matter how small. Indeed, the entire systems effort hangs on the ability of the analyst/designer to unearth and articulate *all* the minutiae of a procedure. It would be difficult to overemphasize the importance of this aspect of systems work, for the most minute detail can jeopardize the success of an entire operation. This becomes even more critical when the systems effort involves machine planning, for machines, unlike people, will not tolerate ambiguity. This will suggest to the perceptive reader that it is wise, indeed essential, to plan several alternatives for each proposal, since the smallest miscalculation could force the scrapping of an entire proposal and change the direction of all work done up to that point.

(2) Every system is a subsystem of some larger system and each system is itself composed of a number of component subsystems. Therefore, all systems exist in both a micro and macro hierarchy depending on the perspective of the analyst. Knowing this, the analyst must constantly guard against suboptimization, i.e., the design of a component subsystem such that it operates in an optimum fashion to the detriment of the system as a whole.

(3) Systems work is a much more subtle process than simply fact gathering. It involves a thorough understanding not only of who, what, when, where, why, and how, but of the relationships which exist between the system under review and all of the other systems with which it interfaces, as well as the component subsystems which make up the system being studied.

(4) There is no single definitive measure for the effectiveness of a system— only circumstantial optimums, each of which must be weighed against all other possible options available to the manager.

(5) Systems are generally designed for the normal operation (quantitatively, the mean or median), and only rarely will the goals of the system permit design for the exceptional conditions.

(6) All systems work is by nature re-

cursive with each successive repetition performed either at the same or at a different level.

(7) Continuous feedback and monitoring are essential components of the systems effort.[4] One of the major difficulties in optimizing present manual library systems has been the lack of adequate provision for valid feedback.

(8) By definition, all systems must exist within an environment. The environmental factors are those which affect or relate to the system under discussion but which are not a part of that system. The analyst cannot fully describe the system without also delineating its environment.

(9) There is a danger in any systems work that it will attempt to quantify that which cannot be quantified—the intangible factors. Overquantification can become a very serious problem and often leads to a credibility gap in the entire systems effort.

(10) Documentation is as much an essential part of the systems effort as analysis, and to ignore or discount this aspect of systems work is to invite disaster.

(11) There is never any final phase to a systems effort, only iteration.

Library systems work provides us with excellent illustrations for each of the above axioms. For example, the failure to write down and describe all the steps in a systems effort *as they take place*, has forced many SA projects to start again whenever a change of personnel takes place. Or, how many librarians have unknowingly insisted upon a system which will handle all exception routines and then wondered why the system took so long to develop or refused even to work at all? Library systems are difficult to analyze, not because of their size, but because they are often unstructured, lack adequate provision for feedback and monitoring, and are always so interrelated and interdependent that the best descriptions of them are of dynamic systems which have "evolved" over a long period of time through a trial and error process. Developing models for this type of a system, especially mathematical models, is a particularly difficult undertaking and can lead to very misleading conclusions unless the model builder understands the proclivity of mathematical modeling for oversimplification.

In fact, most of the dilemmas which plague all systems work also exist in the library systems effort. As with any systems work of magnitude, the analyst finds himself on the horns of a dilemma at the very beginning of his study. Machol has pointed out that the problems of designing a large system are often of such magnitude as to make the problem indigestible and even unsolvable if attacked all at once.[5] Yet the analyst cannot arbitrarily divide the problem to study it piecemeal without running the risk of losing the continuity of the whole. Where then does a realistic approach exist between these two extremes? A partial answer lies in the perspective of the analyst, in his ability to maintain a continuing balance between the unity of the whole and the detail of the part.

Steps in the Systems Study

The systems effort begins with a problem defined by the analyst as a system existing in an environment of other systems and bound by certain constraints. The first step is to isolate the system under review so that it can be described in an unambiguous fashion. This is the systems survey stage and marks the beginning of a series of successive partitionings which take place until the system has been divided into the smallest logical component still capable of being identified with the system being studied. This process of system dissection is analogous to the molecular theory of chemistry which defines a molecule as the smallest particle of matter still exhibiting all the characteristics of the larger mass (system) from which it came. After dividing the system into its molecular components, the analyst then proceeds to delineate the alternatives he has created by rearranging these component parts in whatever fashion the resources and goals of the system will allow, always being careful to work within the constraints which the system's environment dictates. The analyst then proceeds to evaluate these alternative solutions in the light of the stated goals or objectives and selects from them a preferred course of action which he recommends to the decision-maker. Thus, evaluation/implementation becomes the last sequential step of the systems effort and is followed by whatever iterations are deemed necessary by the decision-maker to reach the goals of his agency.

Systems Work from the Administrator's Viewpoint

At this point it might be appropriate to shift perspective and discuss systems work from the administrator's point of view; that is, in terms of the agency's goals, choices, resources, and inputs/outputs. Each administrator has at his disposal four categories of resources: staff, space, funds, and time. (To this some would add a fifth resource—information.) The mix a manager adopts to meet the goals of his administrative unit has depended in large measure upon his own judgment which up to now has been, at least in part, intuitive. In the course of getting the job done or reaching a goal these resources will of necessity be consumed to a greater or lesser degree. It is the responsibility of the manager to balance continuously the availability and consumption of these resources with his goals in order to assure that the goals are reached in the most efficient fashion possible.

Furthermore, a large portion of systems work consists of no more than asking questions about all those assumptions and operating norms which up to now have been accepted as obvious, axiomatic, or based on historical prerogative, and in so doing to pare away the obfuscation which tends to grow up around a deep-seated procedure.

But how does all this apply in a library environment where the goal is that nebulous entity "service"? In order to answer this question realistically, one must first decide what constitutes the library's service goal. The author has chosen to adopt the definition of the library's goal that Mackenzie has used: "to assist in the identification, provision and use of the document or piece of information which would best help the user in his study, teaching or research, at the optimal combination of cost and elapsed time...."[6] Efficiency, when used in this context, becomes either answering more of the "needs" of a reader while holding costs and elapsed time constant, or meeting the same needs while cutting down costs and elapsed time. However, neither explanation of efficiency is entirely satisfactory when used in this fashion because the process described here is one using only quantification as the valid criterion for evaluating its success. This is not to imply that there are no areas in library systems analysis which can be evaluated in a quantitative sense—there most definitely are. It is merely to emphasize for the systems person that he cannot quantify all aspects of a library system. Indeed, insofar as any systems study attempts to use quantitative methods where they are not appropriate, the study will fail and, unfortunately, the reason will not always be clear to all concerned. What the analyst cannot do is quantify the intangible benefits from a course of action, and it is here that the administrator will need to depend most heavily upon his own experience and intuition for guidance. What follows is a generalized methodology for the systems approach to problem-solving.

First Phase: The Systems Survey

In the first phase of the systems study, the analyst conducts what is called the systems survey, during which he relates the system under review to other systems in which it is embedded—to its environment if you will—by determining what is germane to the problem being studied. Once these boundaries have been established, the analyst begins to lay out the problem in very general terms, specifying the goals and functions of the system under review. This involves familiarization and departmental orientation of the analyst, preparation of such tools as a list of the files maintained, their contents, and the organization of each; a list of the forms being used with examples of each; and a description of their movement, and associated activities; a review of all procedural manuals and job descriptions; and finally a documented statement of the system's goals.[7] When used in this context, a goal can be thought of as either a direction or an objective or a combination of both. It can be a point to be reached or a line of march to be followed in moving toward this point. But each goal must also be defined in terms of the expected performance of the system. In fact, any discussion of goals which does not include a statement of the performance expected from the system is so innocuous as to be irrelevant and makes the entire discussion meaningless. Statements of performance coupled with goals have the added advantage of helping to prevent a dichotomy from developing between the real and stated goals.

Second Phase: Analyzing the System

The analyst is now ready to begin the second phase of his study, preparation of a block diagram or system schematic, which outlines in a very general way the tasks performed by the system and the relationships which exist between the subsystems.[8] This is the first level of definition and is, of necessity, very gross. For a library circulation system these boxes might be charging, discharging, searching, shelving, etc. Each box is then further subdivided into its appropriate tasks down to the procedural level, showing the movement of people and materials through all subsystems. This is accomplished by using flow process charts first and then by using flow decision charts.

Construction of the block diagram and the flow charts are the first concrete expressions of an analysis effort which up to now has been primarily a data gathering and intellectual exercise. Flow process charts enable the user to visualize at once the movement of a person and, for example, the distances traveled in checking out a book. The chart will also point out for the user how many times a book is "inspected" as it moves through a given routine. The flow decision chart, on the other hand, uses a different set of symbols and shows at what points decisions are made and how these decisions affect the flow of materials/people. In his charting, the analyst works at a very specific level where he is concerned with discrete entities capable of quantification in terms of how long, how many, how much, and how often. Indeed, his next task is to begin the quantification of these steps by carefully tabulating the number of times a given symbol was used on the flow process chart and the time necessary to move through these steps. Parallel with this effort, the analyst should be identifying activities and compiling these into a document known as a standardized activities list. It is also customary to document the levels of personnel performing these tasks.

Thus far, the analyst has dissected the system—in this case, a library loan desk—through the activities (charging, discharging, etc.) and procedures (how a card is returned to a book in the discharging activity) levels with all the components enunciated at each level. As he does this he also begins the timing of these component subsystems at the procedural or task level. At the same time, the analyst should begin the process of deriving costs by determining what are the real wages (direct + indirect/productive time on job) paid to staff in order that he may translate unit times into unit costs. When this exercise has been finished, the analyst can measure quantitatively the available alternatives, at least in terms of costs, and offer these to the decision-maker for review.

There still remains the difficult problem of evaluating intangibles—those factors which cannot be quantified, such as convenience, availability, prestige, etc.—and if the cost studies have been close, intangibles become crucial to the decision-making process. Intangibles will add support to a program only when definable costs can actually be used to demonstrate a more efficient operation. In other words, the intangible factors can only be used to buttress an argument and never as the sole reason for modification of a system, experience and intuition aside. The point is that more subtle techniques of quantification must be used before funds can be invested in any change which intuitively appears to yield better results.

Third Phase: Design of the System

The next phase, systems design, usually follows when the analysis efforts have been completed and carefully digested. In theory, these steps should be discrete. In actual practice, however, they seldom are, for the design efforts will often overlay the analysis studies. Usually design consists of a modification of the existing system—a rearrangement of the components in the old system—but with possible additions or deletions modifying any or all inputs of the resources discussed earlier, and always within the context of the systems goals.

Fourth Phase: Implementation and Evaluation of the New System

The final phase begins with the implementation of the prototype system and its test/evaluation. This is often the most expensive single phase and its success depends on all earlier phases being in a state of completion. Up to this point the entire process has been a recursive one of dividing, measuring, charting relationships, defining, then repeating the whole process of quantifying the characteristics of the component systems, charting relationships again, and repeating the cycle. Because of economic constraints, however, the implementation and prototype phase cannot always be repeated easily. Therefore, it behooves the analyst to work with meticulous care once this phase of the systems effort has been entered. Another point which should be brought to the reader's attention here is that first-time processing costs, procedures, etc., are normally atypical and cannot be judged to remain constant throughout the life of a system. These are not the nonrecurring costs normally associated with the activation of a system, but those unit costs and unit times which would normally be expected to remain constant throughout the life of the system. The first complete operating cycle is never typical, no matter how carefully the planning and design work was done. There is always the problem of the unforeseen, and no analyst, no matter how good, is ever able to plan for all contingencies.

Conclusion

Hopefully, the reader now has a better understanding of the intricacies and nuances inherent in systems work. It is obvious that such work is a prerequisite to library automation, but it does not necessarily follow that automation will automatically succeed the systems efforts. Indeed, the study can easily indicate that library automation is not appropriate given the existing resources of time, money, staff, or space. In essence then, systems work is a method—part science, part art—whereby one determines the correct balance between constraints and the resources necessary to realize predetermined goals, and leads to the establishment of realistic priorities based upon a thorough understanding of the total system being studied and its relationship to all other systems having a common interface.

References

1. Gerald Nadler, *Work Design* (Homewood, Ill.: Richard D. Irwin, 1963), p.87ff.
2. U.S. General Accounting Office, *Planning—Programming—Budgeting and Systems Analysis Glossary* (Washington: U.S. G.A.O., 1968) p.40.
3. Fred L. Bellomy, "Management Planning for Library Systems Development," *Journal of Library Automation* 2:187-217 (Dec. 1969).
4. "Feedback," *The Systemation Letter* 166: 4p. (1965).
5. Robert E. Machol, ed., *System Engineering Handbook* (New York: McGraw-Hill, 1965), p.1-5.
6. A. Graham Mackenzie, "Systems Analysis of a University Library," *Program* 2:7-14 (April 1968).
7. Ibid.
8. Robert Hayes, "Library Systems Analysis," in *Data Processing in Public and University Libraries*, ed. by John Harvey (Washington: Spartan Books, 1966), p.5-20; and C. D. Gull, "Logical Flow Charts and Other New Techniques for the Administration of Libraries and Information Centers," *Library Resources & Technical Services* 12:47-66 (Winter 1968).

Bibliography

I. Basic and Introductory Material of Special Value to Librarians

1. Herner, Saul. "Systems Design, Evaluation, and Costing," *Special Libraries* 58:576-81 (Oct. 1967).
2. Bellomy, Fred L. "Management Planning for Library Systems Development," *Journal of Library Automation* 2:187-217 (Dec. 1969).
3. Dougherty, Richard M., and Heinritz, Fred J. *Scientific Management of Library Operations*. New York: The Scarecrow Press, 1966. 258p.
4. Hayes, Robert. "Library Systems Analysis," in John Harvey, ed., *Data Processing in Public and University Libraries*, p.5-20. Washington: Spartan Books, 1966.
5. Becker, Joseph. "System Analysis—Prelude to Library Data Processing," *ALA Bulletin* 59:293-96 (April 1965).
6. Leimkuhler, Ferdinand F. *Mathematical Models for Library Systems Analysis*. School of Industrial Engineering, Purdue University, Sept. 1967. PB 176 113.
7. MacKenzie, A. Graham. "Systems Analysis of a University Library," *Program* 2:7-14 (April 1968).
8. Burkhalter, Barton R. *Case Studies in Systems Analysis in a University Library*. Metuchen: The Scarecrow Press, 1968. 186p.
9. MacKenzie. ibid.
10. Kilgour, Frederick G. "Systems Concepts and Libraries," *CRL* 28:167-70 (May 1967).

II. Advanced Texts

11. Morse, Philip M. *Library Effectiveness: A Systems Approach*. Cambridge: The M.I.T. Press, 1968. 207p.
12. Raffel, J. A., and Shishko, Robert. *Systematic Analysis of University Libraries: An Application of Cost-Benefit Analysis to the M.I.T. Libraries*. Cambridge: The M.I.T. Press, 1969. 107p.
13. Machol, Robert E., ed. *System Engineering Handbook*. New York: McGraw-Hill, 1965. p.1-5.
14. Nadler, Gerald. *Work Design*. Homewood, Ill.: Richard D. Irwin, 1963. p.87ff.

III. Specialized Articles Covering Techniques

15. Poage, Scott T. "Work Sampling in Library Administration," *Library Quarterly* 30:213-18 (July 1969).
16. Fazar, Willard. "Program Planning and

Budgeting Theory," *Special Libraries* 60: 423–33 (Sept. 1969).
17. Kozumplik, William A. "Time and Motion Study of Library Operations," *Special Libraries* 58:585–88 (Oct. 1967).
18. Gull, C. D. "Logical Flow Charts and Other New Techniques for the Administration of Libraries and Information Centers," *Library Resources & Technical Services* 12:47–66 (Winter 1968).
19. Aslib Research Department. "The Analysis of Library Processes," *Journal of Documentation* 26:30–45 (March 1970).

IV. General Material

20. U.S. General Accounting Office. *Planning—Programming—Budgeting and Systems Analysis Glossary.* Washington: U.S. G.A.O., 1968). p.40.
21. Spencer, Donald D. *The Computer Programmer's Dictionary and Handbook.* Waltham, Mass.: Blaisdell, 1968. p.41.
22. Rivett, Patrick. *An Introduction to Operations Research.* New York: Basic Books, 1968. 206p.
23. Churchman, C. West. *The Systems Approach.* New York: The Delacorte Press, 1968. 243p.
24. "Feedback," *The Systemation Letter* 166: 4p. (1965).
25. "Analysis . . . The Second Essential Step," *Systemation: A Semi-Monthly Letter on System Trends and Techniques* 12:4p. (1 Oct. 1958).
26. Heyel, Carl, ed. *The Encyclopedia of Management.* New York: Reinhold Publishing Co., 1963. p.613. Taken from Pocock, John W. "Operations Research; Challenge to Management," Special Report no. 13. New York: American Management Association, 1956.

THE ANALYSIS OF LIBRARY PROCESSES

ASLIB RESEARCH DEPARTMENT

A LIBRARY, like any other man-made system, exists to provide services that are believed to meet certain needs. It will be effective to the extent that user needs have been correctly gauged, and that the services provided do in fact meet them.

As well as being effective, a library strives also to be efficient—to provide its services as economically as possible. Many factors enter into library economics—such as the cost of stock, accommodation, equipment, and so on—but one major factor is staff time. In many large libraries, perhaps 80 per cent of staff time is devoted to 'technical services' (acquisition, processing, circulation, etc.). To save some of this time by improving procedures can certainly contribute to efficiency.

Before a procedure can be improved it must be analysed. Analysis of library processes can be piecemeal, but is likely to produce better results if it is undertaken systematically, using tested techniques. Library systems analysis is increasingly relying on techniques developed in industry, but it does not always prove easy to adapt them to the library situation.[1] There is a good case, therefore, for examining carefully any techniques especially developed for library use. This paper is concerned with a development of this kind.

In 1965, the Lehigh University Center for the Information Sciences published a manual for the analysis of library systems, prepared by Taylor and Hieber.[2] The essence of the proposed analysis of library processes is to regard each process to be describable as an *activity* carried out using a *form*. 'Forms' include not only the records generally recognized as such in libraries, but also catalogue cards, user requests, and the documents themselves. Sending a recall notice, typing an author card, or labelling a book, are therefore all regarded as activities involving forms.

The systems analysis proceeds as follows: 1. identify each type of 'form' used in the library, 2. describe each form in terms of a standard code, 3. identify each activity associated with each form, 4. describe each activity in terms of a standard code, 5. record associated codes on punched cards, 6. analyse the data by appropriate manipulation and printout of the cards.

Taylor and Hieber noted: 'Systems studies have traditionally relied on such techniques as flow charts, written procedure manuals, time and motion studies, and time standards. Most of these methods ... are of limited practicality'. They offered their technique as a more flexible alternative.

In 1967, Aslib Research Department decided to try out the technique in

Reprinted from *Journal of Documentation,* 26(1), 1970, by permission.

the analysis of university library processes. The purpose of the trial was three-fold: *a*) to provide, if possible, systems analyses useful to the particular libraries investigated, *b*) to draw lessons, if possible, from a comparison of analyses made of two or more libraries, and *c*) to determine the value of the Lehigh method, or some modification of it, in the systems analysis of library processes. With kind co-operation and help from the staffs of two university libraries (acknowledged at the end of this report), data was collected during the period April 1967 to September 1968.

This paper is concerned to report on purpose *c*)—to assess the value of the Lehigh technique. As noted above, their manual provides a standard code for forms and another for activities. The form code had to be slightly amended to conform to British conditions. The activity code was amended drastically, partly to adapt it to British conditions, but mainly to simplify it.

THE FORM CODE

The following information was recorded about each form:
1. Purpose (columns 1–3 of the punched card), e.g. 213 = purchase of library materials, 531 = interlibrary loan request.
2. Number (columns 4–6)—a consecutive number for each form identified.
3. Copy number (column 7)—for multipart forms.
4. Name (columns 8–23)—an abbreviation in alphabetic characters, e.g. ISSUE SLIP.
5. Physical size (columns 24–25), e.g. 01 = 3 × 5 inches.
6. Physical characteristics (columns 26–28), e.g. 230 = card, 110 = paper sheet. The third digit indicates colour, e.g. 3 = white.
7. Secondary purpose (column 29), e.g. 2 = acquisition.
8. Point of origin, personnel (column 30), e.g. 1 librarian, 2 deputy, 6 library assistant.
9. Point of origin, departmental (columns 31–32), e.g. 21 = acquisitions, 22 = cataloguing, 31 = issue desk.
10. Point of origin, external (columns 33–34), e.g. 12 = student, 24 = academic department, 41 = a named bookseller.
11. Point of disposal (columns 35–38, as 31–34).
12. Frequency of use (column 39), e.g. 0 = constantly, 4 = monthly, 5 = quarterly.
13. Average monthly volume of use (column 40), e.g. code 4 = 101 to 250 per month, code 7 = 1501 to 2500.

THE ACTIVITY CODE

The following information was recorded about each activity. This differs substantially from the original Lehigh code.

COSTING AND ECONOMICS

1. Point of activity, personnel (column 41), coded as column 30.
2. Point of activity, departmental (columns 42-43), coded as columns 31-32.
3. Regularity (column 44), e.g. I=irregular infrequent, J=continual frequent, D=once per day, M=once a month.
4. Description of activity (columns 45-47). The full code schedule is given overleaf:

100	Direct transfer of information to/from
110	Initialization of information
120	Adding information
130	Transcribed initialization
140	Transcribed addition
150	Transfer from form

In the units position is coded the transfer method

1	Handwriting
2	Typing
3	Punching
4	Telex
5	Automatic printout, e.g. computer
6	Via carbon or NCR paper
7	Stamping
8	Duplicating

200	Manipulation of information
210	Statistics compilation
220	Verification
230	Answering question
500	File handling
510	Filing
520	File searching
530	File amendment
540	File sorting
550	Attachment to other forms

In the units position was coded the key to any matching, taken from columns 48-53.

700	Removal of record from system
710	Mailing
720	Handing to outsider
730	Destroying
900	Peripheral activities
910	Duplicating, reproducing in same format
920	Displaying, exhibiting
930	Reproducing in different format
999	Unanalysable activity outside system

5. Information transferred (columns 48–53). The full code schedule is:

A	Author name
B	Borrower name and/or address, including borrowing library
C	Class, location, or item number
D	Date published or expected
E	Order number
F	Financial report or synthesis
G	Numerical report or synthesis
H	Invoice number
I	Date issued or sent
J	Date returned
K	Price
L	Frequency of publication
M	Current holding details
N	Accession number
O	Date ordered or requested
P	Publisher name and/or address
Q	Date received or due for return
R	(not yet used)
S	Supplier name and/or address, including lending library
T	Title
U	Department name
V	Volume number
W	Subject heading, abstract, statement of interest
X	Material, colour, type of document
Y	Decision report
Z	Miscellaneous

Six of these items can be placed in columns 48–53. If there were more than six, an asterisk was coded into column 54, and extra information was punched into a trailer card. An asterisk in this column was also used to refer to any other footnote recorded on a trailer card, e.g. the ILL PHOTOCOP OUT RECORD form has a footnote, INFO TRANSFERRED TO MAIN RECORD BOOK.

6. Machine used (column 55), e.g. T=typewriter, D=duplicator, K=keypunch.
7. Machine control (column 56), e.g. L=library control, C=company or organization control.
8. Decision maker (columns 57–59, as 41–43). If a decision was made at this point, its maker was recorded.
9. Reason for variation (columns 60–61), e.g. 02=buy on standing order, 03=suggestion rejected, 30=fuller entry required.
10. Order number where variation is recorded (columns 62–63, as 79–80).
11. Batch size (column 68, as 40).
12. Code of associated form (columns 72–78, as 1–7).
13. Order number of activity card (columns 79–80). The main sequence

COSTING AND ECONOMICS 59

of activities is numbered 01 to 09. Variations may be numbered 20 to 29, 30 to 39, etc.

DATA RECORDS

Examples of form and activity coding sheets are shown in Figures 1 and 2. The information was then transferred to 80-column punched cards. Each punched card recorded a single activity applied to a single form. The deck of punched cards was sorted into an appropriate sequence and a printout obtained. Consider the sequence in Figure 3, each line being the printout from a single card. All lines refer to activities on a single form, number 211003, a 'book order form'.

Code 211 (columns 1–3) refers to the purpose of the form, a request for acquisition. The next three figures, 003, record that this was the third form examined during the study, and the seventh figure 1 that this was part 1 of a multipart form. Then comes the abbreviated name of the form. The next two digits refer to its size (01 = 3 × 5 inches), and the following three to its physical characteristics (123 = white NCR paper). The next digit, 2, is a broad 'secondary function' code, here meaning 'acquisition'. We then come to code 4, implying 'section head', as personal point of origin, in department 21 = acquisitions. The following two zeros are in the unused columns 33–34. The next two digits indicate the departmental point of disposal, 29 = general office, followed by two zeroes for unused columns 37–38. The third zero in the sequence, however, is in column 39, and means 'in constant use', and the next digit 6 = average monthly usage 601 to 1500.

All the lines (a) to (j) are the same up to this point, since this completes the description of the form. The ensuing digits in each line code various activities. In line (a), the first 9 = external, i.e. the first activity arises outside the library, and the following 99 = all academic departments. To make this quite clear, there is an asterisk to a footnote that appears in line (k). Next comes J = the activity is continual and frequent, followed by 131 = initialization transcribed by handwriting: the activity starts the form off on its career. We next find the letters ATPD: the transcribed information usually includes author, title, publisher, date of publication. At the end of the line is 01, indicating that this is the first card relating to form 2110031.

Line (a) is in fact a coding of the information in Figures 1 and 2. It can be summarized as follows: Part 1 of the book order form is transcribed, by people at all levels in all academic departments, and is received by the acquisitions department. The requests arise continually and frequently (between 601 and 1500 per month). The transcribed information is as stated above. Subsequent lines and footnotes trace ensuing activities involving this form. Beginning with line (r), activities associated with Part 2 of the form are recorded.

The coding technique does not in itself enhance the descriptions already available in Figures 1 and 2—in fact, the code must be laboriously interpreted in the manner just described. Its value will lie only in the further possibilities that punched card manipulation may provide.

USE IN CHARTING PROCESSES

Taylor and Hieber argue that 'a detailed flow chart of all library processes will cover an area of several hundred square feet and will be intelligible, if at all, only to its creator'. Still, they agree that 'because many forms must be traced through a multitude of activities, it is frequently necessary to make flow charts... The deck of punched cards is in essence a flow chart... and is considerably more flexible than a corresponding flow chart'.

In Figure 4 data in Figure 3 is represented as a flow chart. The bracketed letters indicate the line or lines of the printout relating to each box of the chart. It is probably fair to say that the logic of the procedure cannot be adequately grasped unless the printout is—at least mentally—translated into flow chart form. Only then do certain unclarities appear.

For example, what happens at line (e) if the form does not come back from the supplier? Why in fact does it accompany the book during cataloguing? Is it, or could it be used to receive a draft catalogue entry? If the data recorded in (a) is inadequate, is it amplified before (d)? Does the verification in (h) include a check of the Reject file? Is this ever weeded? Is the rewriting of data at (i) necessary—could not Part 1 of the form be used for this, and Part 2 be put into the Reject file? What in fact happens to Part 2 of Reject forms? Is there a procedure for chasing unfilled orders (for example, by searching the On Order file?) Only the clear display of a flow chart gives such thoughts a real chance to emerge.

This particular example therefore suggests, first, that the Lehigh technique does enable one to record compactly data about the processing of forms, and that this information can be expanded into flow-chart form, but second, that such expansion is necessary if full benefit is to be derived from the analysis. What one gains is that the full record is indeed compact—not 'covering an area of several hundred square feet' (in fact, the processes of each library examined occupied about 400 punched cards, the printout less than 6 square feet). From this record, particular small sections can be extracted for expansion and study. What one loses is that the record contains nothing but detail, and it is not easy to see how a broader picture of the library's activity might be extracted from it.

USE IN ISOLATING PARTICULAR ASPECTS OF WORK

Taylor and Hieber stress the possibility of analysis by manipulating the punched card deck in various ways, for example:
—the extent to which human decisions figure in the procedures (by listing cards with an entry in our columns 57–59),

—the amount of file handling, that could conceivably be mechanized (entries in our columns 45–47),
—the duplication of information on several forms (entries in our columns 48–53),
—the tasks performed by different grades of staff (entries in our column 41), or different departments (our columns 42–43),
—the extent to which variations occur (by listing cards with an entry in our columns 60–63).

The possibility of manipulation arises only incidentally from the fact that punched cards are used (we have also used visual scanning of printout). The important point is that the characteristics of forms and activities have been reduced to standard codes, so that a characteristic appearing at a number of points in the whole process can readily be recognized.

We can, for example, sort out all cards coded 51=filing, in columns 45–46, print out their contents, and examine the grade of staff doing the filing (column 41). Results might be as follows (the bracketed figure is the number of filing activities of the type indicated):

Filing by	Done by	Frequency
Author	Librarian	Irregular infrequent (1)
	Section head	Irregular infrequent (1)
	,,	Continual frequent (2)
	Other professional	Continual frequent (1)
	Library assistant	Continual frequent (1)
	,,	Irregular infrequent (2)
Title	Section head	Irregular infrequent (4)
	,,	Continual frequent (3)
	,,	Once per term (1)
	,,	Once per year (1)
	Other professional	Continual frequent (1)
	Library assistant	Continual frequent (1)
Class, location,	Section head	Continual frequent (1)
order, or item no.	,,	Once per week (1)
	Other professional	Continual frequent (2)
	Library assistant	Continual frequent (5)
	Clerical assistant	Continual frequent (1)
Date	Librarian	Once per month (1)
	Section head	Continual frequent (1)
	Other professional	Continual frequent (1)
	,,	Once per month (1)
	,,	Once per day (1)
	Technician	Continual frequent (1)
	,,	Once per quarter (1)
Name	Library assistant	Continual frequent (3)
	,,	Irregular infrequent (4)
	Clerical assistant	Continual frequent (1)

Thus of the 25 'continual frequent' filing activities, 17 were carried out by section heads, 5 by other professionals, 10 by library assistants, 2 by clerical assistants, and 1 by a technician. From column 40 of the printout (average form usage) we can estimate that over 13,000 units were filed each month. Of the 10 heaviest filing burdens, 3 were apparently borne by section heads, 1 by another professional, and the rest by library assistants. An analysis such as this does raise queries as to the most suitable allocation of filing work.

As a second example, we can sort out cards coded 13 and 14 (=transcribed information) in columns 45-46, and look at information transcribed from one form to another (excluding cases where the source form is a document such as a book, and excluding transfer by carbon paper, etc.) We obtain a list of instances of clerical copying. As set out below, a sample list shows the abbreviated names of the receiving and source forms, the information transferred (coded as in columns 48-53) and the frequency.

	Receiving form	Source form	Information	Frequency
(a)	ISSUE STATS	DLY ISSUE STATS	G	Once per day
(b)	PCPYG STATS	PCOPY REQ	FU	Continual frequent
(c)	PCPYG QRLY REC	PCPYG STATS	FU	Once per quarter
(d)	PCPYG QRLY ACC	PCPYG QRLY REC	FU	,,
(e)	PER INDEX REQ	PER CARDEX	PTV	Irregular infrequent
(f)	PER BACKRUN REQ	PER USE REC	TV	,,
(g)	PER NONREC NOTE	PER CARDEX	PT	,,
(h)	CAT CARD	STOCK CARD	ACDPTV	Continual frequent
(i)	PUNCHED CARD	SOURCE FORM	CW	,,
(j)	PER PUNCHED CARD	PER PC AMEND	CKLT	,,
(k)	BURO PER UN CAT	,,	LMT	Irregular infrequent
(m)	ADDNS BULL	CAT CARD	ACTV	Once per month
(n)	ODUE REMINDER (1)	LOAN SLIP	ABC	Continual frequent
(p)	,, (2)	,,	ABCT	,,
(q)	,, (3)	,,	ABCT	Irregular infrequent
(r)	PL LOAN REQ	REQ ILL	ATV	,,
(s)	ASLIB ENQ	,,	ADPTV	,,
(t)	BURO REQ	,,	ADKPTV	Continual frequent
(u)	NLL REQ	,,	ADPTV	,,
(v)	ILL EXT REQ	LOAN SLIP	AQTV	Irregular infrequent
(w)	PAT SPEC ORDER	REQ ILL	CT	,,
(x)	SML PCPY REQ	PCOPY REQ	ADTV	Continual frequent

Since this is only an illustration, we need not consider the exact nature of each case, but the kind of data obtained can be seen from line (n): there was continual and frequent copying of information from loan slips to overdue reminders. Such an analysis raises queries as to whether such copying could be carried out photographically, or by the use of a multipart form.

The examples suggest that the Lehigh technique can be useful in the detailed analysis of activities within a library, to aid proper division of labour, simplification of work, and general improvement of routines.

USE IN COMPARING LIBRARIES

The purpose in comparing library processing is not to establish whether one library is 'better' than another. Contrasting two ways of carrying out a particular process may indeed suggest improvements, but in any overall comparison each library is likely to derive ideas from the other. Library comparison is basically concerned with establishing common standards. What are the processes common to all libraries? How uniform are the methods used? To what extent could common methods be developed? Whether standardization is desirable, even where possible, is of course an open question. The answer depends upon whether the advantages of standardization (for example, cutting development costs by adoption of an established technique, simplifying the use of standard input, aiding co-operation) outweigh its disadvantages (loss of a system closely moulded to local needs).

Leaving this question unanswered, we may consider some comparisons between the two libraries examined. Providing similar services to similar communities, they used almost the same number of forms: library A, 85 (102 if each part of a multipart form is counted separately), library B, 82 (96). The number of activities per form was distributed as follows (each part of a multipart form treated separately):

Activity/form	1	2	3	4	5	6	>6	total
Library A	16	41	22	11	6	4	2	102
Library B	6	44	18	10	5	5	8	96

Library B worked its forms a little harder than A—fewer single-activity forms, more with over 6 activities. The total numbers of form activities recorded were A 288, B 331 (including variations from the regular procedure). They were distributed as follows:

Code	Activity	A	B	B/A
110	Initialization of information	25	32	1·3
120	Adding information	10	18	1·8
130	Transcribed initialization	54	62	1·1
140	Transcribed addition	12	4	0·3
150	Transfer from form	37	24	0·7
200	Manipulation of information	14	23	1·6
510	Filing	46	70	1·5
520/540	File searching amendment, or sorting	4	20	5·0
550	Attachment to other forms	12	12	1·0
710	Mailing	45	40	0·9
720	Handing to outsider	4	2	0·5
730	Destroying	9	5	0·6
	Other	16	19	1·2
		288	331	1·2

The patterns were not widely different, although library B did relatively more of some activities (such as filing) than A, and relatively less of others (such as mailing). From column 40 of the printout (average form usage) the volume of each activity could be estimated.

Let us look in more detail at filing. This has already been analysed for library A. Similar analysis for library B is as follows:

Filing by	Done by	Frequency
Author	Other professional	Once per fortnight (10)
	Library assistant	Continual frequent (5)
	"	Irregular infrequent (1)
	"	Every 6 months (1)
Title	Section head	Continual frequent (4)
	Library assistant	Continual frequent (4)
	"	Irregular infrequent (4)
Class, location, order, or item no	Other professional	Once per fortnight (10)
	"	Irregular infrequent (1)
	Library assistant	Continual frequent (3)
	"	Irregular infrequent (1)
Date	Librarian	Once per fortnight (1)
	Other professional	Once per month (1)
	"	Once per term (2)
	Clerical assistant	Continual frequent (1)
	Secretary	Once a year (1)
Name	Section head	Continual frequent (1)
	Other professional	Irregular infrequent (3)
	Library assistant	Continual frequent (2)
	"	Irregular infrequent (12)

Of the 20 'continual frequent' filing activities, 5 were apparently carried out by section heads, 14 by library assistants, and 1 by a clerical assistant—it appears that less professional time was used for filing than in library A.

We can now follow the history of a particular form 211012 Book Order Suggestion Card, comparable in function to form 211003 already examined in library A. Data on 211012 is flow charted in Figure 5. Comparison with Figure 4 is facilitated by tagging Figure 5 with bracketed letters when individual blocks in each chart perform approximately the same function. A basic pattern (a-c/h-s-v) was preserved, but the flows differed, mainly because the multipart form 211003 had the secondary function of serving as an order.

This single example could be amplified, but it serves to illustrate a general point that has been demonstrated by Thomas and East in an extended study of bibliographic records.[3] While the clerical processes in libraries of all types *can* be reduced to a common pattern, 'no two libraries will necessarily use any one form in the same combination of procedures... There does not presently appear to be an innate reason for using a form in a particular way, nor for tying it to a particular additional set of procedures'. If this is true then detailed comparison of procedures associated with particular forms is not likely to be illuminating. Thomas and East also collected data on all uses made of each form and each file in a series of libraries, but they found it necessary to go behind the specific form activities examined, and to structure library procedures in the following more generalized pattern:

Acquisition	*Use*
select	locate
order	list
receive	lend
	reserve
Processing	recall
access	interlend
classify	photocopy
catalogue	
label	*Maintenance*
shelve	bind
	replace
	discard

Each procedure can in turn be analysed into (up to) six activities: initiate, authorize, activate, record, report, cancel. For details, the reader is referred to their report.

The comparison of detailed data on form activities, whether collected by the Lehigh technique or another, does not in any simple way lead to the derivation of a common standard. The data could be used—as Thomas and East used their data—as raw material for subsequent analysis, but there is no indication that the Lehigh technique offers any advantage for this purpose.

CONCLUSIONS

In the overall assessment of a library, its effectiveness must be studied as well as its efficiency. This was recognized by Taylor and Hieber, whose manual includes a section on the analysis of library use (not explored in our study). As far as efficiency is concerned, their technique examines only one aspect (though an important one), staff activity involving 'forms'—in the wide sense in which they defined them.

Within this framework, one general weakness is the lack of any explicit consideration of files. As may be seen in Figure 4, data is recorded about placing forms in files, or searching for forms in files, but characteristics of a file as a whole are either implicit or unrecorded. Consequently, problems arising from file organization cannot readily be identified.

The punched card record is a compact way of summarizing a mass of detailed data. By sorting, printout, and visual scan of the printouts, a good deal can be learnt about the procedures in a library, but the record is basically a quarry from which data must be extracted. To get benefit from it, extracted data must be expanded into flow chart or tabular form, which can then be analysed. We feel that we have not yet fully explored all that can be extracted in this way.[4]

Data recorded for two or more libraries can be compared, and for libraries of different types this might well reveal interesting differences in the pattern of activities. Since the linking of forms and activities is rather arbitrary, simple comparison of the forms used in various libraries is unlikely to lead to the development of a common standard.

This brings us to the basic weakness of the Lehigh technique as a method of systems analysis. The structure of any complex system is hierarchical. An information system as a whole transfers information from A to B—say, from publishers to library users. Each subsystem within it—acquisition, processing, use—carries out certain stages of this transfer. Each procedure within a subsystem—select, order, receive, etc.—carries out a substage. Each form activity is a step within a substage. Adequately to analyse a system requires a definition and description of processes at each level in it. The Lehigh record consists wholly of descriptions at the lowest level, form activities. A higher level—say, acquisition—can only be described by listing out all its component form activities—the acquisition process cannot be described at its own level.

The Lehigh procedure thus cannot truly be called a method of systems analysis. It is a technique of collecting, recording, and manipulating data that can contribute usefully to analysis, but it cannot perform all that the system analyst needs to do. Like other analytical techniques, it is a useful tool in the hands of the analyst, but not a machine that will do his job.

ACKNOWLEDGEMENTS

The work reported in this paper could not have been carried out without permission and help from two university librarians—Mr E. H. C. Driver of the University of Aston, and Dr A. J. Evans of the Loughborough University of Technology—together with the co-operation of their staffs. At Aston, we were particularly indebted to J. Seals of the library staff, and C. A. Cayless of the Department of Mathematics. At Loughborough, great help was given by R. Wall and Mrs J. Beaumont.

The work of data collection, the modification of the codes, and some preliminary analysis, was carried out for Aslib by R. Priest. Further analysis was made by Miss R. Reynolds. Comments on the work were contributed by Miss P. Thomas, H. East, and J. Martyn. The final paper was drafted by B. C. Vickery.

The whole project was carried out with the financial support of the UK Office for Scientific and Technical Information. We are grateful for their encouragement and for their permission to publish this report.

REFERENCES

1. DOUGHERTY, R. M. *and* HEINRITZ, F. J. *Scientific management of library operations.* New York & London, Scarecrow Press, 1966
2. TAYLOR, R. S. *and* HIEBER, C. E. *Manual for the analysis of library systems.* Library Systems Analysis report no. 3. Bethlehem, Pa., Center for the Information Sciences, Lehigh University, 1965.
3. THOMAS, P. A. *and* EAST, H. *The use of bibliographic records in libraries.* London, Aslib, 1969.
4. The Lehigh system is an adaptation to the library situation of a method first developed for office work (see ref. 2). Recently, J. M. Carroll has described other ways of manipulating the record (A methodology for information systems analysis, *Journal of Industrial Engineering*, vol. 18, p. 650–7, November 1967). Essentially, his method is to eliminate much of the detailed data, and to record about each form only (*a*) the successive 'stations' where it is handled (a station could be a section or a person) (*b*) whether the handling at each station is 'use' or 'file' (*c*) other forms generated in the handling of the recorded form. This data is punched on cards and manipulated to show (*a*) the overall flow of forms between stations, and (*b*) the overall load at each station. We have not explored this method with our data.

1	6	7	8		23	24 25	26 28	29	30	34	35	38	39 40
211003		1	BOOK ORDR FM PT 1			01	123	2	42100		2900		06

FORM NO. (1)	COPY NO.(7)	NAME OF FORM (8)	PHYSICAL SIZE (24)
211003	1	Book order form Part 1	3 x 5

PHYSICAL CHARACTER (26)	PRIMARY FUNCTION	SECONDARY FUNCTION (29)
NCR paper and copy, white	Request for purchase	Request for item on approval

POINT OF ORIGIN (30)	POINT OF DISPOSAL (35)	VOLUME PER MONTH (39)
Acquisitions Section head	General Office	1000

SPECIAL PUNCHING INSTRUCTIONS (IF ANY)	APPLICATION CODE

FIG. I

41	43	44	45	47	48		54	55	56	57	59	60		67	68	69	71	72		78	79 80
999		J	131		ATVP*																01

FORM NUMBER	COPY	PERFORMER (41)	REG (44)	ACTIVITY (45)	INFORMATION USED (48)
211003	1	999	Continual frequent	Transcr. initial – handwriting	Author Title Date Publisher

MACHINE INVOLVED (55)	MACHINE CONTROL (56)	DECISION MAKER (IF ANY) (57)	IF VARIATIONS REASON AND ORDER NO. OF NEXT STEP (60)

BATCH SIZE (68)	TIME TAKEN OVER ACTIVITY (69)	NUMBER AND NOTES IF ANY OTHER FORM INVOLVED (72)	ORDER NO. (79)
			01

FOOTNOTES. IF * IN COL 54 PUNCH FREE FORMAT CARD AS BELOW

* 2110031 01 999 REFERS TO ALL DEPTS AND ALL LEVELS

FIG. 2

COSTING AND ECONOMICS

```
(a) 2110031BOOK ORDR FM PT10112324210029000699J131ATPD    *                      01
(b) 2110031BOOK ORDR FM PT10112324210029000699J156ATPD         0120         211003202
(c) 2110031BOOK ORDR FM PT101123242100290006421J52A       *                      03
(d) 2110031BOOK ORDR FM PT101123242100290006421J710                              04
(e) 2110031BOOK ORDR FM PT101123242100290006421J550       *                 500090005
(f) 2110031BOOK ORDR FM PT101123242100290006421J730                              06
(g) 2110031BOOK ORDR FM PT10112324210029000691J111UB                             20
(h) 2110031BOOK ORDR FM PT101123242100290006421J220            4210330           21
(i) 2110031BOOK ORDR FM PT101123242100290006421I151BUATPD *                 000000030
(j) 2110031BOOK ORDR FM PT101123242100290006421I51A       *                      31
(k) * 2110031 01 999 REFERS TO ALL DEPTS AND ALL LEVELS
(m) * 2110031 05 FORM KEPT IN BOOK UNTIL CATALOGUED THEN DESTROYED
(n) * 2110031 03 00 AND BOOK RECEIVED FILE CHECKED
(p) * 2110031 30 0000000 REFERS TO HANDWRITTEN NOTE TO REQUESTER
(q) * 2110031 31 FILED IN REJECT FILE
(r) 2110032BOOK ORDR FM PT201235 42100290006999J136ATPD                     211003101
(s) 2110032BOOK ORDR FM PT201235 42100290006421J51A       *                      02
(t) 2110032BOOK ORDR FM PT201235 42100290006421J52A       *                      03
(u) 2110032BOOK ORDR FM PT201235 42100290006421J51A       *                      04
(v) 2110032BOOK ORDR FM PT201235 42100290006421M730       *                      05
(w) * 2110032 02 FILED IN BOOKS ON ORDER FILE
(x) * 2110032 04 FILED IN BOOKS RECEIVED FILE
(y) * 2110032 05 FORM 6 MONTHS IN BOOKS RECEIVED FILE
(z) * 2110032 05 MONTHLY WEEDING OF FILE
```

FIG. 3

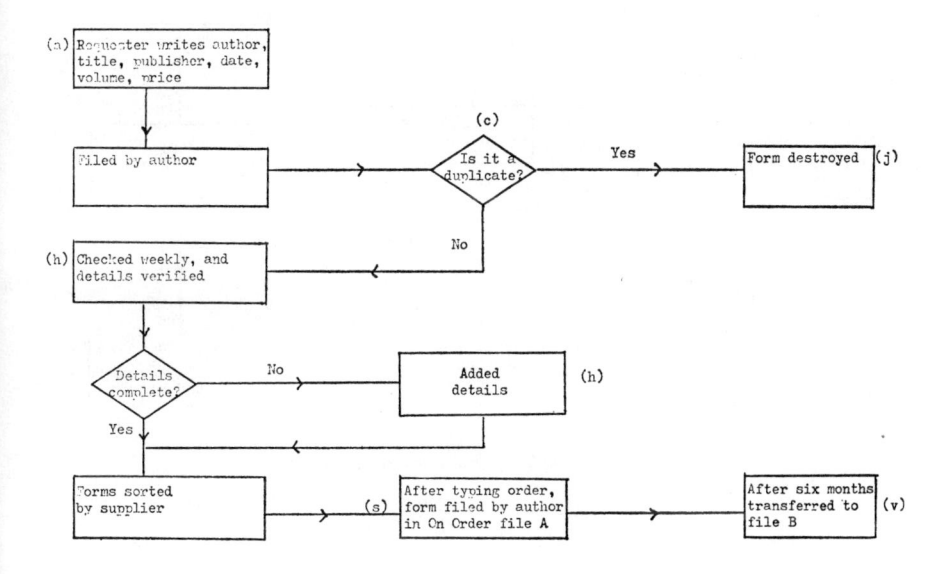

FIG. 4 Form 211003, Book order

Part 1

(a) Requester writes author, title, publisher, date

(c) (n) Checked by author in On Order and Books Received files

(d) Form mailed to supplier

(e) Returned form is attached to received book

(f) (m) After cataloguing, form is destroyed

(g) Staff or student adds name, dept.

(h) Section Head verifies request — Accepted / Rejected

(i) (p) Handwritten note sent to requester

(j) (o) Form filed by author in Reject file

Part 2

(b) (k) Data transferred by NCR paper

(s) (w) Filed by author in On Order file

(t) Searched by author when book received

(n) (x) Filed by author in Books Received file

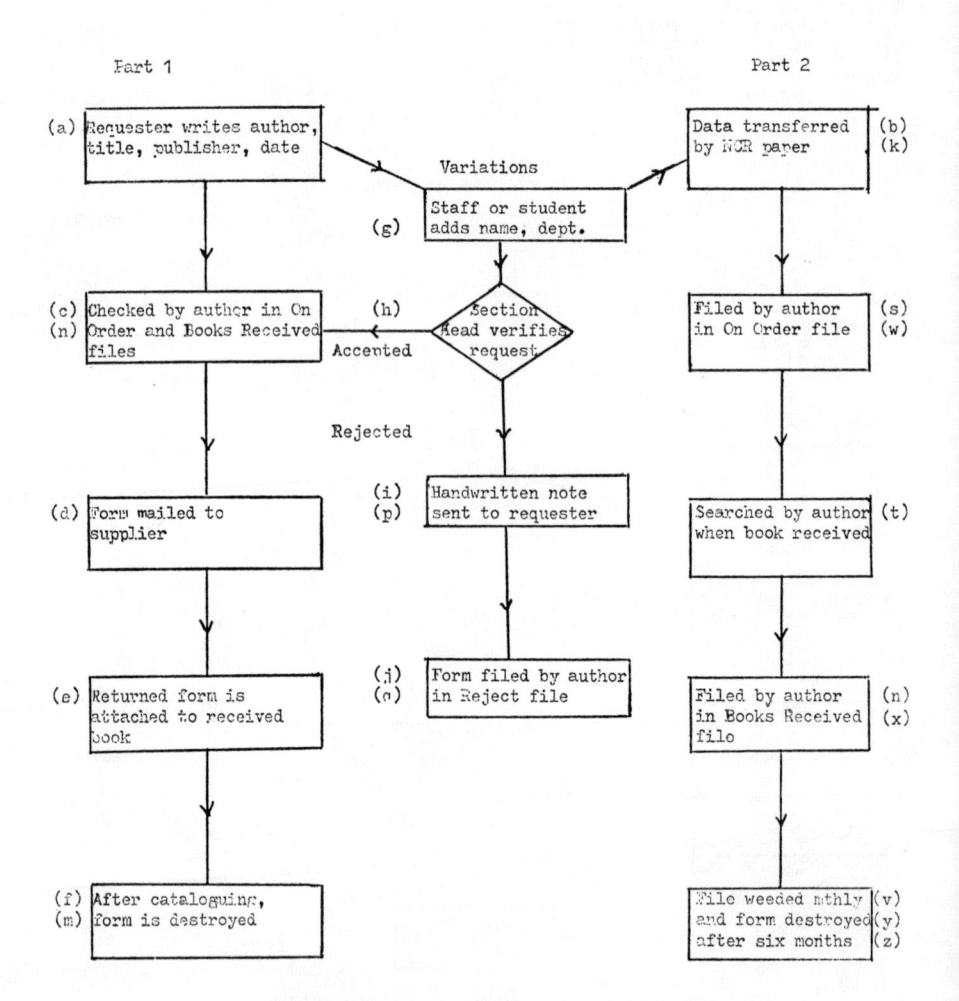

(v) (y) (z) File weeded monthly and form destroyed after six months

FIG. 5 Form 211012, Book order suggestion

STANDARD COSTING FOR INFORMATION SYSTEMS: BACKGROUND TO A CURRENT STUDY

S. E. ROBERTSON, R. REYNOLDS, *and* A. P. WILKIN

Aslib Research Department

Introduction

FOR SOME time past, interest has been developing within the Aslib Research Department in the problems of establishing standard costs for information systems.* A literature search recently conducted by the Department (R. Reynolds[1]) has revealed a scarcity of usable information on this subject: such data as is available is difficult to evaluate comparatively because of the differing definitions of the operations costed and of the terms used to describe them. It would seem, therefore, that a first step towards developing a costing method of widespread application would be the establishment of standard conventions for the analysis of information systems.

One might postulate two possible ways of arriving at comparative costs for these systems, namely:

(a) *General survey method*: The overall costs of a large number of information systems are broken down into a small number of categories, and analysed for correlation (see, for example, C. J. Wessel et al[2]).
(b) *In-depth study*: A small number of systems are studied in detail in an attempt to establish the true sources of the costs and factors affecting them.

In a current project, we are attempting to apply method (b) to the production of current-awareness bulletins. An outline of some of the preliminary work in this project follows.

Classification of costs

Helmkamp[8] suggests that an information system be regarded as a manufacturing concern, 'in which the product, information, is developed in various forms during a well-defined production process'. Sizer[3] gives the following basic classification of costs for cost accounting:

Prime expense	*Production overheads*
Direct material	Indirect material
Direct labour	Indirect labour
Direct expenses	Indirect expenses

Sizer distinguishes between direct and indirect costs in the following way: 'One *allocates* direct expenditure which can be directly associated with a cost centre or cost unit, but one *apportions* indirect expenditure'.

From Gilchrist's[4] classification of library systems, we can extract the following costs:

* Throughout this paper the phrase *information systems* is used in a general sense to include libraries.

Reprinted from *Aslib Proceedings*, 22(9), 1970, by permission.

Labour
  Operational subsystem (cost affected by variables such as layout, form design, document form, equipment form)
  Administrative subsystem

Material
  Capital equipment costs
  Rental of equipment
  Equipment running costs
  Consumables
  Documents

Overheads

To this list must be added the cost of use of outside services (e.g. for printing) which is not included in Gilchrist's classification.

These items fit easily into Sizer's classification, with the exception of documents, which unlike 'materials' in the generally accepted sense, are not consumed by the various processes they undergo. Therefore, we arrive at the following table of costs:

Prime expenses
  Documents: including information input from other services
  Direct material: Consumables such as blank forms
  Direct labour: Operational subsystem
  Direct expenses: Cost of use of outside services (e.g. for printing)
                    Direct equipment costs

Production overheads
  Indirect material: Consumables such as general stationery
  Indirect labour: Administrative subsystem
  Indirect expenses: Equipment (capital/fixed rental)

Our attention will be concentrated mainly on the problem of direct labour costs in terms of man-hours, but some of the other categories, in particular administrative costs, need further consideration.

Definitions

Following Thomas and East[5] and Gilchrist[6] we regard the library system hierarchically as:

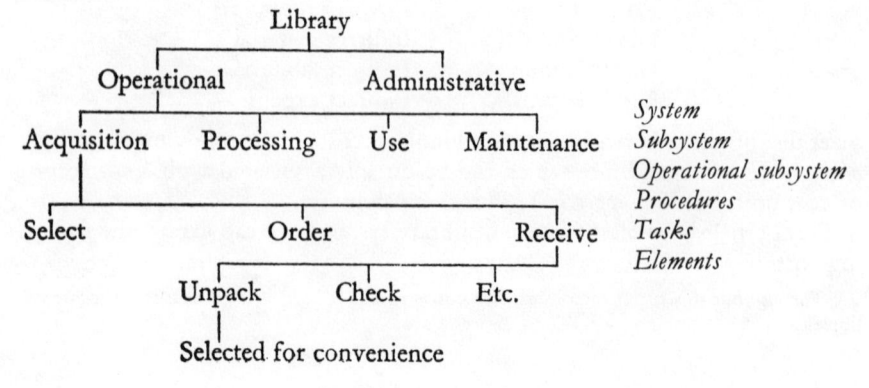

```
                        Library
            ┌──────────────┴──────────────┐
        Operational                 Administrative              System
    ┌────────┬────────┬────────┐                                Subsystem
Acquisition Processing  Use  Maintenance                        Operational subsystem
    │                                                           Procedures
┌───┼───────────────────────┐                                   Tasks
Select         Order        Receive                             Elements
        ┌────────┼────────┐
      Unpack   Check     Etc.
        │
    Selected for convenience
```

COSTING AND ECONOMICS

The terminology used in the above table is based on Institute of Office Management (IOM) definitions, and has mainly been applied to physical and clerical operations. However, a characteristic feature of libraries is the interweaving of intellectual and clerical operations and this creates problems in the application of this terminology to information systems, particularly at the task level and below.

For comparative costing, we consider it necessary to define within the hierarchy a standard level of widespread application, so that the operations on this level can be assigned standard times. Previous study has shown that the level chosen should as far as possible satisfy the following conditions:

1. Only one person should be involved in the operation.
2. The variables affecting the time taken for an operation in varying environments should be easily identifiable.
3. The beginning and end point of the operation should be easily observable.
4. The end product of the operation should be identifiable.

Points 1 and 2 require that the operation should be below the procedural level (see for example the eighteen library procedures of Thomas and East[5]). Points 3 and 4 define a minimal level, above the element level for operations with some intellectual content. The operations satisfying these conditions which we have called TASKS are equivalent to the clerical tasks as defined by IOM.

In practice, the beginning and end points are in some sense superficial, and may depend on the practice of the individual performing the task. Therefore, the aim has been to provide:

(a) A list of tasks capable of building up notional systems, but not necessarily sufficient for describing a real system.
(b) A framework for describing tasks which may emerge during the examination of real systems.

One problem in the definition of tasks is deciding how specifically they should be defined. For example 'Enter' is a very general task covering all operations in which information is recorded, ranging from simple, as in 'Copy', to complex, as in 'Abstract'. One might decide to use the specific word in each case, but this still would not be sufficient to identify the various factors involved, and therefore explain exactly the time taken to perform the task in a given instance. Thus, the time taken to 'Copy' will depend on the amount of information recorded, the sources consulted for this information, and the intellectual effort involved. The problem, therefore, is the identification of these variables. Given a method for taking these variables into consideration, the specificity of the task-names is not of primary importance, and so for convenience we have chosen a small list of general words.

Since it appears very difficult to identify *a priori* precisely those variables which significantly affect the task time, we have attempted to provide a framework which permits the inclusion of all possible variables.

The full framework (see Table 1, p. 455) is as follows: the task is split into *components,* and under each component is specified all the associated information, e.g. relevant forms and files, and bibliographic elements involved. These

TABLE I

Task components
Consult (including read, scan, search)
Compare
Think (including assign, select, decide, calculate)
Write (including handwrite, type, stamp)
Prepare
Put away
Take out
Separate
Affix
Sort
Operate
Discuss
Move

Classification of tasks

CLASS	COMPONENTS	SPECIFICATION
Enter	consult	Which sources are consulted
	think	'Select' etc., which elements of information involved
	prepare	What preparations are necessary for writing
	write	Method used, details recorded, where recorded
File	consult	Which sources and which file
	put away	Which item
Extract	consult	Which sources and which file
	take out	Which item
Place	put away	Which object, where
Remove	take out	Which object, from where
Verify	consult	Which sources
	compare	Which elements on which item
	(action)	Which action
Sort	sort	How many, of which object, in what order
Attach	prepare	Which items, how
	affix	How
Separate	separate	Which items, how attached
Duplicate	prepare	Which items, on which machine
	operate	How many copies
Discuss	discuss	Which elements of information (if possible) which people
Move	move	What to where

components are not necessarily sequentially separate (unlike 'elements' as defined by IOM), but may on occasion overlap or be performed concurrently.

Thomas[9] gives a list of tasks identified in a number of library studies. Although these tasks are not identical to ours, the level on which they are defined is the same, and they can all be defined in terms of our variables.

Modelling of systems

The aim of the present project, then, is to assign standard times to the various tasks, indicating how these times are affected by the variables we have identified.

But given a list of tasks with their associated times (and costs), how could these be usefully used in a system design situation to estimate the cost of a proposed system?

Clearly, the more detailed the data we provide, the more complex the synthesis of these costs will be. A similar scheme of standard times for typing (Burke and Watts[7]) consists of 13 pages of data and 96 pages of instructions on

COSTING AND ECONOMICS

their use. It seems that, for the application of our scheme, the following will be necessary:

(a) The basic data concerning the cost of the appropriate unit tasks.
(b) Environmental data concerning the particular system under consideration.
(c) A model of the proposed system indicating how these data are to be combined.

Because of the probable complexity of the model, it would appear necessary to provide a general-purpose, adaptable model of a particular class of system, as a basis for any more detailed modelling exercise. This general model we call the 'notional system'.

As mentioned above, the present project is concerned with the production of current awareness bulletins. More specifically, we are initially covering non-mechanized systems from the input of documents (excluding selection) to the distribution of the bulletin. An outline of the notional system for this class of system is given in Table 2. We do not expect real systems to follow this pattern exactly; the point is to identify all the different operations that

TABLE 2: *Outline of notional system for production of current awareness bulletin*

```
(Selection)    (Documents)
                    |
..................................................................
                    |
                (Worksheet)
Processing    Catalogue——>——|
                    |
              Classify———>——|
                    |
              Abstract———>——|
                    |
              Index (1)——>——|
                    |
              |——<——Check
                    |
                  Index (2)
..................................................................
                    |
                (Batch)
                    |
Production      Sort
                    |
                Number              (Typescript)
                    |
                Type main entry——>——|
                    |
(Typescript)        |——<——Check
    |               |
    |——<——Type index entry(ies)
    |               |
  Check——>——|       |
    |               |
  Sort              |
    |               |
..................................................................
    |               |
Printing   etc.                    etc.
```

'Index (1)' = 'index from original document'
'Index (2)' = 'index from abstract'

might be involved and to show how they are related, i.e., what is the input and output of each operation.

The model will also help to identify the system variables (b) which need to be measured in order to make the cost estimate. This is likely to be a major operation, and in some cases (for a proposed system in a new subject field) it may not be feasible to obtain all the desired data. For example, presumably abstracting time depends on the language and the form (periodical article/monograph etc.) of the document; therefore in order to estimate average abstracting time, one needs to know the relative frequency of different languages and different forms.

Because of the complexity of the modelling and data-gathering processes, it will be desirable to have some more approximate, more easily applied formulae for estimating costs. Thus we will attempt, with the aid of our notional system, to isolate the most important variables affecting the cost of larger units of operation, and give approximate formulae for these costs. For example, it may be possible to make an approximate estimate of the cost of producing an abstracts bulletin, with the aid of a few major variables such as number of items abstracted per year.

General comments

Some difficulties can be foreseen in the development and application of such a scheme of standard tasks with standard times. As previously mentioned, the accurate identification of all important variables is a major problem, which we have only begun to tackle. Those variables which we have specified above are generally closely associated with the relevant tasks, but there may be others equally important which are functions of the general environment, e.g. the size and nature of the organization might exert pressures on the staff which would be reflected in the performance of particular tasks. Similarly, the background, personality and experience of the individual worker might significantly affect the time taken. These, and other similar factors, may well warrant further study. The problem of deriving comparative costs is of great complexity, and requires careful definition of the many factors involved. Hopefully, this paper represents a first step towards such definition.

REFERENCES

1 REYNOLDS, R. *A selective bibliography on measurement in library and information services.* (To be published by Aslib).
2 WESSEL, C. J. *et al. Criteria for evaluating the effectiveness of library operations and services. Phase II: Data gathering and evaluation.* Washington, John I. Thompson & Co., 1968, p. 53.
3 SIZER, J. *An insight into management accounting.* Penguin, 1969, p. 51.
4 GILCHRIST, A. Work study in libraries. *Journal of Librarianship,* 2, 2, April 1970, p. 126-38.
5 THOMAS, P. A. *and* EAST, H. Comments on the terminology of the analysis of library systems and the function of forms therein. *Aslib Proceedings,* 20, 8, August 1968, p. 340-4.
6 GILCHRIST, A. Further comments on the terminology of the analysis of library systems. *Aslib Proceedings,* 20, 10, October 1968, p. 408-12.
7 BURKE, W. W. *and* WATTS, J. M. *Work measurement in typewriting.* London, Pitman, 1968.
8 HELMKAMP, J. G. Managerial cost accounting for a technical information centre. *American Documentation,* 20, 2, April 1969, p. 111-18.
9 THOMAS, P. A. Tasks and the analysis of library systems. *Aslib Proceedings,* 22, 7, July 1970, p. 336-43.

Work Analysis by Random Sampling

J. L. Divilbiss and Phyllis C. Self

ABSTRACT

Random sampling of work activities using an electronic random alarm mechanism provided a simple and effective way to determine how time was divided between various activities. At each random alarm the subject simply recorded the time and the activity. Analysis of the data led to reassignment of staff functions and also resulted in additional support for certain critical activities.

INTELLIGENT management of a library means that the most elusive and inelastic of resources, time, must be carefully allocated to various activities. Books on management generally state that this allocation (or reallocation) should follow a determination of how time is actually being spent [1]. While this is true of any library, it is especially true of a library which is expanding its collection or its services, because these changes often bring duplication of work and conflicts in priorities. The Library of the Health Sciences at the University of Illinois at Urbana-Champaign (LHS-UC) is an example of a rapidly changing library. In the last five years, the library staff has increased from one clerk to a total staff of eleven, the collection has increased from nothing to 5,000 volumes and 4,000 audiovisual items, and service has been extended to approximately 8,000 health care professionals in a sixteen-county region. Thus, the Library of the Health Sciences was the kind of library where determination of work activities was urgently needed if the library were to provide good service and extend the range of services.

The precipitating cause for this study was the desire to determine why audiovisual materials were not being cataloged. One of the authors (Self) had primary responsibility for audiovisual materials and had set as a goal that one-quarter of her time would be spent in cataloging them. Since it was not possible to set aside large blocks of uninterrupted time for cataloging, it was not clear just how much time was actually spent in that activity. It *was* clear that it would be necessary to examine all of her work activities to see where the time was spent.

CHOICE OF METHOD

How, then, does one determine how much time is actually spent in various activities? The diary method is simple and widely used by professionals such as lawyers who need the information for client billing. However, the librarian whose workday is fragmented into scores of activities will find the recording of diary entries an intolerable burden. In addition, the diary method tends to yield inaccurate results for many reasons, including a lack of objectivity on the part of the subject [2]. After all, who among us would record (accurately) that we spent fifteen minutes wool-gathering?

Another method of work analysis relies on an observer to record activities. This removes the burden of data taking for the person whose work is being studied and often improves the objectivity of the measurement. The familiar time-and-motion expert with stopwatch and clipboard does very well in observing assembly line activities but is much less successful in the library. For one thing, librarians are often flustered by having an observer hovering nearby. There is the additional problem that the observer may not be able to tell from observation alone just what activity is being performed. The observer must then ask the librarian something like "Who were you talking to on the telephone?" or "Are you working on a reference question or doing selection?" The librarian may find this kind of questioning as distracting and burdensome as recording diary entries. Finally, there is the problem that the ob-

Reprinted from *Bulletin of the Medical Library Association,* 66(1), 1978, by permission.

server method is too expensive for the average library since it ties up an employee in a nonproductive activity.

With the diary and observer methods ruled out, we decided to conduct our study using an electronic random alarm mechanism and self-observation [2]. In this method, the subject carries a small device which emits short tone bursts ("beeps") at random times through the day. At each beep the subject records what he was doing at that instant. This is, of course, a random sampling scheme but one which does *not* require the use of a prepared table of random times and close observation of the clock. Between beeps the subject can simply ignore both the clock and the beeper.

In any sampling technique the accuracy of the result depends on the number of samples taken [3]. For our study we felt that it would be adequate to determine to within about 3% how time was spent. This level of accuracy requires about 500 samples. (Determining activities to within 1% would require nearly 5,000 samples; this would involve much greater effort in data collection and would almost never be justified because distribution of work activities is not constant from month to month and year to year.)

Having established the number of samples needed, we then decided over what period of time to conduct the study. Selection of a suitable time-span depends primarily on the nature of the work. For example, reference work in a large public library might involve relatively little week-to-week variation; in this situation a one-week study might be adequate. Generally, however, librarians have monthly reports to prepare, meetings to attend, and similar scattered activities. A study lasting only one week would give a distorted measure of the time spent in these occasional activities. It was our feeling that activities in the Library of the Health Sciences varied substantially from one week to the next but were relatively uniform from one month to the next. Thus, we decided on a nominal one-month period for our study.

It would appear that the sampling rate (the average number of samples per hour) could be determined from the total number of samples and the total number of working hours in the study interval:

22 working days = 176 hours

$$\frac{500 \text{ samples}}{176 \text{ hours}} = 2.8 \text{ samples/hour}$$

Actually, it is not quite this simple. We have found in studies with students and faculty members that a sampling rate of three times per hour is acceptable; sampling rates of four or five times per hour create resentment. (Because the device is random, the time between beeps is often much less than the average interval. Even though subjects may spend only ten seconds each on thirty-five samples during a workday, they feel that too frequent sampling is distracting.) This psychological limitation on sampling rate means that a person who works halftime would need to sample for two months rather than to sample at a rate of 5.6 samples per hour for one month.

EQUIPMENT

Random alarm mechanisms are available commercially [4], but to our knowledge none are available with the properties required by this study. As a result, one of the authors (Divilbiss) designed a "beeper" which could be carried throughout the workday. The beeper is 2½ by 5 by ¾ inches, weighs a little less than six ounces, and operates for about two months on a single battery. The thinness and narrowness of the device allow it to fit comfortably in a man's shirt or jacket pocket. For a woman whose clothes do not include pockets, other carrying arrangements can be made. These include suspending the beeper from a belt in the manner of a calculator or carrying the beeper in a tray of catalog cards.

A simple on-off switch has been provided as the only external control. The sampling rate is seldom changed during a study, and thus there seems little reason to make the rate easily adjustable by the subject. On the other hand, a case *could* be made for external adjustment of the loudness of the beep. A beep that is loud enough to be heard while one is standing next to a Teletype machine may be embarrassingly loud in a quiet reading room. A simple subterfuge effectively solves the problem. In quiet areas the beeper can be muffled by putting it in an inner pocket, a purse, or a desk drawer. The subject is mentally tuned to the beeper pitch and will hear it when it is so faint that others in the same area do not hear it.

Subjects sometimes feel that the beeps are not truly random since they often occur at intervals much shorter than the average. Analysis of thousands of samples has shown that the beeps are in fact distributed randomly. Detailed discussion of the electronics is inappropriate in this journal, but the operation can be described by analogy. Every ten seconds drop seven coins on a table. If they come up seven heads, take a sample; otherwise do nothing. This procedure will result in an average of 2.81 samples per hour.

Data Collection

The study was based on a nine-hour day, which included the lunch hour. This was done because lunch was not taken at a predictable time. Categories chosen for this study were drawn from the subject's job description and from a prestudy of activities. Clearly, there will always be occasions when the activity being sampled does not correspond to any of the predefined categories. In this circumstance, it is essential to write a brief description of the activity rather than merely writing "miscellaneous," because subsequent analysis of the data may permit sorting of these miscellaneous activities into meaningful categories. The actual data collection involved recording the time and checking a category or writing a brief description of the activity.

The following tasks were chosen as predefined categories: MEDLINE, cataloging, reference, supervision of staff, administrative meetings, and professional meetings. MEDLINE included searching time, in-service training, demonstration, and arranging for MEDLINE appointments. Cataloging was defined as any procedure involved in preparing an audiovisual item from the time it was purchased to the time it was placed on the audiovisual shelf for circulation. Reference was that time spent in answering ready reference questions or noncomputer subject searches. Staff supervision included the training of new employees and the management of prescribed standard procedures. Administrative meetings were meetings between the librarian and the assistant librarian as distinguished from professional meetings, which included other librarians or other professionals in the health care field. Actual working definitions of activities were far more detailed than the brief descriptions listed here; considerable detail is needed if ambiguity is to be avoided.

Attitudes of Others

Most professional librarians realize that they need to know where time is being spent in order to improve their library service. They would like an easy and accurate study method in order to perform more professional activities and leave the clerical work to the clerks or nonacademic staff. While the study reported here describes only the work activities of the assistant librarian of the Library of the Health Sciences, we have worked with several other subjects doing similar time studies. We have found that the technique works very well when the subject is strongly motivated and feels that the results will be genuinely useful.

Subjects who are merely curious about how their time is spent generally lack the discipline to carry the beeper and record data conscientiously. A study of this kind could be imposed by a subject's supervisor, but the results would be questionable unless the subject actively cooperated.

Problems

If results of a sampling study are to be meaningful it is essential that samples not be missed through failure to have the beeper close at hand. For a librarian working at a desk this would not be a problem. In our case, the subject worked not only in her own library but in the six other departmental libraries that contain medical materials. We have attempted to make the beeper easily portable, but it nonetheless requires a conscientious effort on the part of the subject to carry it through the work day.

A second problem is that sampling can be distracting for the subject and others nearby. For example, the beeper might require the subject to pause during a MEDLINE search to record data. Recording the time and the letter "M" takes only a few seconds but it is still an interruption that hinders the search. As a related problem, staff members who were *not* subjects often mentally categorized their activities on hearing the beep; some were annoyed that the beeper called attention to idle time and time spent in personal activities.

Some users in the library noticed the beeps, but showed no concern when the sound did not persist. A possible explanation is that patrons in a medical library are accustomed to hearing physicians summoned by paging devices. When the subject sat at the reference desk for extended periods of time, users were not annoyed by the interruptions, and many were interested in the results of the study. A number of library users have now been subjects, using this method.

Under some circumstances, it can be socially awkward or impractical to use the beeper. During a lecture, it might distract the lecturer or students and interfere with the teaching function. For those circumstances, the subject merely recorded time when the beeper was turned off, the activity, and the time when it was turned on again. Data recorded this way are referred to as "diary" entries.

Analysis

Analysis of the collected data was relatively straightforward. We started by counting the number of samples for each of the predefined work categories. This left a number of samples which did not easily fit our categories; those samples were examined more closely and then assigned to existing or new categories. One new category that resulted from this process was "administrative," a term covering such activities as opening mail, using the Xerox copier, and straightening up a desk. While these activities may appear to be "clerical" they are actually tasks which cannot be delegated effectively.

Initially, time was recorded for each sample as a check on the randomness of the beeper. During the analysis of the data, we found that having this time information permitted us to reconstruct events and assign samples to categories with greater confidence. The slight extra effort of recording the time seems to have been well justified in terms of resolving ambiguities in the data. There were, of course, samples that defied attempts to reconstruct and categorize; fortunately, these amounted to less than 1% of the total.

As was mentioned in an earlier section, "diary" entries were made in circumstances where the use of the beeper would have been socially awkward. These diary entries were converted to "synthetic beeps" by multiplying the elapsed time by the average sampling rate. Thus, two hours spent in a particular activity with the beeper turned off would be counted as 5.6 beeps in order to combine "diary" data with actual samples. A serious attempt was made to minimize these diary entries, because they are less reliable than actual samples; only 15 out of a total of 525 samples were synthesized from diary entries.

The percentage of time spent in the various activities is shown in Table 1. In each case, the range represents the limits at the 95% confidence level. For example, we are 95% confident that the time spent in MEDLINE searching was between 23.0 and 30.8% of the total.

TABLE 1

Activity	% Time
MEDLINE searching	26.9 ± 3.9
Supervision of staff	13.5 ± 3.0
Administrative meetings	11.6 ± 2.8
Idle	10.7 ± 2.7
Reference	9.1 ± 2.5
Professional meetings	6.9 ± 2.2
Administrative	6.5 ± 2.2
Lunch	5.7 ± 2.0
Newsletter	5.0 ± 1.9
Cataloging	4.2 ± 1.8

INTERPRETATION

We had decided at the beginning of this project that a one-month period would be a suitable interval to examine. This appears to have been a reasonable choice because most major activities were fairly well distributed over the month. One notable exception was the writing of a newsletter, which took up a significant amount of time during one week. A sampling interval of much less than a month would have given an erroneous impression of the time actually spent in preparing the newsletter.

The most significant result of the study was that the subject spent an average of twelve hours per week in MEDLINE work. This work was shared with two other employees who spent comparable amounts of time at the MEDLINE terminal and in related activities. Since the MEDLINE computer was available only fifteen hours per week, this means that most of the time categorized as "MEDLINE" was spent making appointments, arranging for demonstrations, and conducting MEDLINE interviews.

The most surprising result of this study was that only 4.2% of the work time was spent in cataloging audiovisual materials, even though this had been regarded as a high-priority activity. Cataloging is an activity easily interrupted by more urgent business, such as answering reference questions and responding to staff problems.

Another area of concern was the amount of time spent on staff supervision. At the time of this study, the entire staff reported directly to the librarian, yet 13.5% of the assistant librarian's time was spent answering questions and directing staff members because the librarian was unavailable. Following this study, the assistant librarian was made responsible for supervising five of the ten staff members.

CONSEQUENCES

The data from this study helped us to reallocate work assignments, especially in the areas of MEDLINE and staff supervision. As a result, the librarian is now spending the greater portion of her time in administrative work, and the assistant librarian is spending her time in the areas of staff supervision and reference. More use is being made of student workers to run errands on the University of Illinois campus, and the nonacademic staff are now trained to give information about MEDLINE and to arrange for MEDLINE appointments. The result is that the professional staff spends more time in professional activities such as reference, cataloging, and acquisitions.

The results of this study also strengthened our request for MEDLINE support staff and for the creation of an Audiovisual Department by showing the percentage of time being spent on supervising staff and MEDLINE and how little time was being given to the areas of reference and audiovisual cataloging. The Library of the Health Sciences at Urbana-Champaign has the beginnings of an excellent audiovisual collection but has given little attention to this area because of the ever-increasing demand for MEDLINE services by health care professionals. After looking at our proposal and the supporting data, the School of Basic Medical Sciences provided additional staff to help in MEDLINE searching. The school was also concerned about the audiovisual collection, and supplied support staff to create an Audiovisual Department.

For the first time in months, we at LHS-UC feel that workloads are now at a manageable level, that services are being performed at a higher level of quality, and that the professional and nonacademic staff are being more efficiently utilized. The professional staff is no longer making MEDLINE appointments or mailing out MEDLINE searches, but using the time to plan for improved efficiency on the major tasks involved in operating a rapidly growing library.

RESTUDY

Work sampling should be a continuing activity. The data summarized here are believed to be accurate for the time when they were taken, but, of course, LHS is a constantly changing institution. Additional staff has been hired, new policies have been implemented, and new services have been offered. Two changes in the immediate future are likely to have great impact on LHS. Acquiring an additional retrieval service, Bibliographic Retrieval Services, Inc., will involve the senior staff in planning, scheduling, and training for its use. The other major change is that the University Library is installing an automated circulation system which will make the entire university collection accessible at each of the departmental libraries. Technological and policy changes of great magnitude will certainly necessitate a restudy of LHS in the near future.

REFERENCES

1. MACKENZIE, R. ALEC. The Time Trap. New York, AMACOM, 1972.
2. SPENCER, CAROL C. Random time sampling with self-observation for library cost studies: unit costs of interlibrary loans and photocopies at a regional medical library. J. Am. Soc. Inf. Sci. 32: 153-160, May-June 1971.
3. GOODELL, JOHN S. Libraries and Work Sampling. Littleton, Colorado, Libraries Unlimited, 1975.
4. Random Alarm Mechanism. Available from: Informer, Inc., 2218 Cotner Avenue, Los Angeles, California 90064.

3 BASIC APPROACHES TO SERVICE COSTING

3. BASIC APPROACHES TO SERVICE COSTING

The five papers reproduced in this section require very little introduction, since they deal with the central ground of costing as it can be applied to library and information services. The papers develop the initial message conveyed by Hayes and Becker in the opening contribution to this reader; on the other hand they do not perhaps go so far into the regions of complexity and contention raised by Schwuchow's paper.

Hewgill (1977) gives another general introduction to management accounting and library activities; it can be read in conjunction with and as a reinforcement to the Hayes and Becker paper. Because it was presented at a conference the message is both direct and simple, and highly effective. The first two figures summarize well the conceptual message of much basic cost analysis. Firstly, that costs can be presented in different ways; the same cost data can be rejigged in a variety of forms to meet different cost and management information needs. Secondly, the relationship between categories of expense incurred, and the fundamental cost classification of *direct* and *indirect* is made clear. Hewgill then goes on to identify many of the cost concerns of the operational manager as a series of questions, and as a series of principles for the effective use of accounting data. Clements (1975) develops the argument in Hewgill's paper, in the light of some pioneering experience of cost study in the British Library. The concepts of *routine costing* and *special exercise costing* are introduced, together with a very helpful discussion of methodological details. The appendix in his paper of measures of input, output and service functions is a particularly useful categorization, which should help to focus thinking in this area of library management.

The checklist in Armstrong's (1972) paper is a salutary reminder that cost study often means a preoccupation with detail; the message is that sources of cost are everywhere, and that even relatively minor aspects of processes are nonetheless tagged with a potential and/or actual cost. Smith and Schofield's paper (1971) has now become a frequently cited study, and is a standard exemplification of how the principles of work measurement can be applied to calculating the times and costs of library operations. Cost investigations of major library processes were carried out in a number of libraries, and the findings reported. The specimen data collection forms and the discussion of field methods are very useful. This paper is closely related to a number of others reproduced in the following section of practical studies (Maier, 1969; Nachlas and Pierce, 1979; Revill, 1977).

Leimkuhler and Cooper (1971) exemplify the further development of cost analysis and accounting, especially in the context of programme budgeting (in this regard contrast it with the paper by Mason (1973) in section 4). Again the authors initially note the weakness of library cost study methodology (a topic still not fully tackled, even at the present). A cost-flow model is developed for a university library, which is tested with historical data from the General Library at the University of California, Berkeley. The basic idea of the *cost centre* is introduced. The cost-performance of different organizational units is analysed, and unit costs, and overheads are discussed. The authors conclude positively about the value of such studies.

FURTHER READING

HUMPHREYS, K. W. Costing in university libraries. *LIBER Bulletin,* 5/6, 1974, 8–32.

MITCHELL, B. J. *Cost analysis of library functions: a total system approach.* Greenwich (Conn), JAI Press, 1978.

The two papers chosen for further reading are both concerned with the costs of operations in academic libraries. Both discussions contribute useful material on basic concepts and their application in practical contexts. The principles discussed are broadly applicable to any type of library organization.

Management accounting and library activities

J. C. R. Hewgill M.B.E. E.C.M.A.

Paper presented at a one-day conference, 'Value for money: costing and some aspects of cost effectiveness in the library/information unit', held at Gregory House, the Thomas Coram Foundation, Brunswick Square, London on 8th March 1977

ACCOUNTANCY IS NO mystic, druidic activity but a means devised by practical people to express the use of resources (and any returns from commercial activities) in a common measure—money.

Cost accounting is the simple process of breaking down resources to the activity being carried on and then collating the monetary cost to show the cost of the activity.

An oversimplified statement might be:

Cost of library	£1000
Number of loans made	1000
Cost of each loan	£1

However, this pays no attention to time. How long a period? Does it refer to time past—historic accounting? Does it mean a forecast—future accounting for management control?

This leads to **Management accounting** which is concerned with decision making and therefore with future events. For a precise definition of these and many other terms, the appropriate reference is *Terminology of Management and Financial Accounting* by the ICMA.

The statements about both these accounting processes also ignore the fact that organizations differ and carry on many different activities. Since managers can normally only make direct decisions on their own area of responsibility and desire to know the effect of those decisions, it is necessary to break down costs to specific functions as well as activities.

Since there is always more than one way to present any set of numbers, so there are three ways to present costs (Figure 1).

The same pile of gold can be represented to different people for various purposes. It is however well known to any accountant that Murphy's Law applies equally to accounts—'The analysis needed is always the one which is not available'.

At this point it is advisable to pause and remember that accounting is not an end in itself. There are usually two main reasons for keeping accounts:

1. Has the cash or resources been used for the purpose for which it was intended? *i.e.* no waste, fraud, defalcation or misdirection—stewardship.

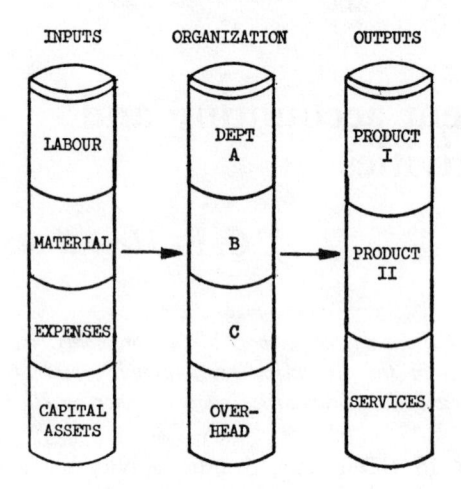

FIG 1. *Three ways to present costs*

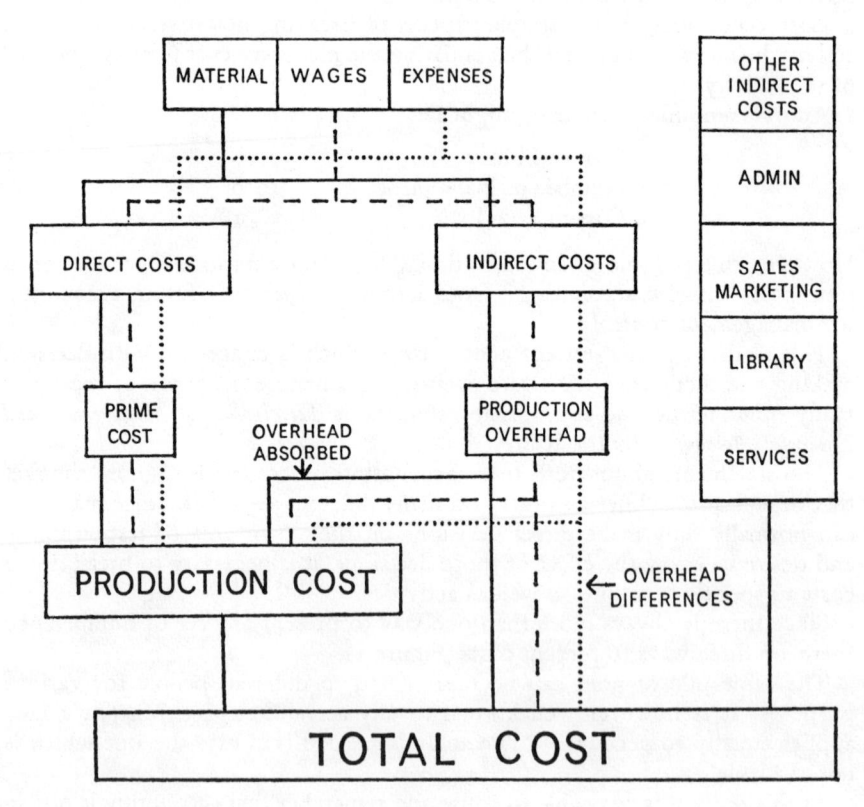

FIG 2.

COSTING AND ECONOMICS

2. Are the resources (cash is a resource too!) being used effectively? *i.e.* how can they be used more effectively?

The two sets of data derive from the same source. The purpose is different. Because accounts need to balance exactly there is a tendency to think of them both to the nearest penny. This is necessary for the first, but not for the second, where we are dealing with the future—any forecast is (by definition) uncertain and imprecise—accuracy to more than two or three significant figures is seldom worth the effort.

Any plan or budget therefore needs to be treated with circumspection. In fact this imprecision is the basis for managing the organization. By using actual results arising and recorded, compared with the forecast budget, with reasons for differences analysed (if it is worth the effort), managers can decide whether the differences are controllable and take appropriate action to contain overspending (or improve underspending).

Resources used may be directly related to the activities carried out, i.e. the number of parcels posted dictates postage cost (provided no action is taken to control weight), whereas in libraries labour cost tends to be fixed. This leads to the need to identify differential cash cost—(variable cost) from other costs (fixed costs). It depends upon the level of the manager, what is fixed and what is variable. Also cost in cash terms may be fixed, but the resources (usually labour) can be varied to different tasks, thus changing the departmental or activity cost without changing the total expenditure. Libraries tend to be in a situation where their outputs are not sold (or even saleable). They therefore have to be considered in the light of another type of analysis (Figure 2).

Indirect costs have their own characteristics, of which the four main ones are:

1. Not related to direct production/output quantity.
2. Not controlled easily.
3. Frequently not managed by the same managers as production.
4. Products/services are not sold.

This introduces another fudge factor into any cost calculation equation; overhead cost is (by definition) not easily directly related to the output activities, *e.g.* the head librarian is not easily costed out to loans, purchases, indexing or literature searches carried out by staff. It therefore becomes necessary to bring in some form of cost-sharing between departments of activities (Figure 1), this arbitrary sharing (apportionment or allocation) means that ouput costs will always be imprecise, which means that management should not be too concerned with small changes caused by this process.

Having derived an organizational breakdown in order to devise the second analysis in Figure 1, it might look like this.

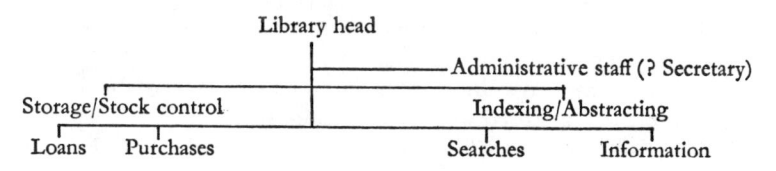

FIG. 3: *Organization of a library*

From this organization it is probably fairly straightforward to find the second and third analyses in Figure 1. However the organization will be more likely to look like this

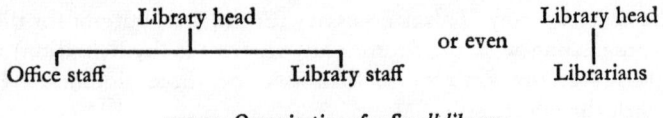

```
            Library head                                Library head
        ┌────────┴────────┐         or even                 │
   Office staff      Library staff                      Librarians
```

FIG. 4: *Organisation of a Small library*

The activities of any of these may be direct or indirect and it is necessary to derive some sort of set of records of activity to find out what proportion of time (and material) is used for each. Once this has been done, the framework for cost analysis and control exists and steps can be taken to establish cost behaviour related to activity and management decisions.

$$\textit{Cash} \longrightarrow \text{Differential costs based on} \longrightarrow \textit{Cost behaviour}$$

$$\textit{from} \text{ knowledge of} \begin{cases} \text{variable} \\ \text{(marginal)} \\ \text{semi-variable} \\ \text{fixed} \end{cases}$$

Cost/output or cost/activity ratios are easy to find, *e.g.* £/loan, broken down to direct (postage, packing and labour)+indirect (control, accommodation, electricity, etc). The management problem is to find out whether this is the 'right' cost. Various methods are available such as:

1. Internal comparison within an organization, (however lower cost may mean poor service!)
2. External comparison between organizations, (*e.g.* via Centre for Inter Firm Comparison)
3. How much will managers stand being charged to their overheads?
4. How much would the service cost commercially?

However, these ignore the quality and 'rightness' of the service—the customer's view point. This is probably much more difficult to measure. Possible methods are:

5. How satisfied is the customer?
6. Cost/Benefit analysis—*i.e.* does the measured benefit justify the cost? This implies finding a measure (not easy).
7. Cost-effectiveness analysis—how effective is the service, *e.g.* 100 per cent effectiveness may or may not be a good thing?
8. Reaction speed—how long does it take to produce the service, *e.g.* within one day or three weeks (on average!)?
9. Penalty cost—how much does the organization lose if the service is reduced or discontinued?

Continuous monitoring of these compared with a unit or activity cost will also provide a measure of control of indirect costs. Other possibilities are:

(a) Restriction of inputs.
(b) Measurement of outputs.
(c) Arbitrary regulation of activity.
(d) Management by objectives (MbO).
(e) Incentives.

However, managers also like to know the effects of their decisions and these may take various forms. These effects should not just happen, they should be planned and objectives set, which brings us back to the forecasting aspect. Whilst it is quite acceptable to continue the service as before at the same cost as last year, it is seldom that circumstances or organizations allow this, so targets should be set realistically, assumptions stated and understood and accepted by all concerned.

How to measure changes in cost/performance

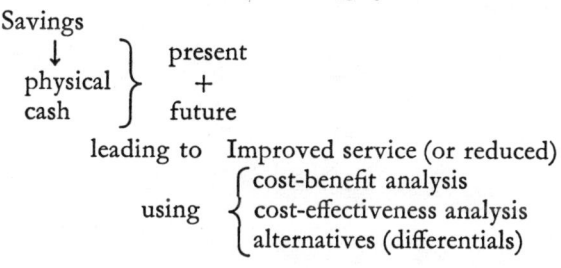

$$\left.\begin{array}{l}\text{Savings}\\ \downarrow\\ \text{physical}\\ \text{cash}\end{array}\right\}\left.\begin{array}{l}\text{present}\\ +\\ \text{future}\end{array}\right\}$$

leading to Improved service (or reduced)

using $\left\{\begin{array}{l}\text{cost-benefit analysis}\\ \text{cost-effectiveness analysis}\\ \text{alternatives (differentials)}\end{array}\right.$

• Reduced to basic principles, the effective use of accounting data must be founded on good and sensible management practice on the following lines:

1. The use of forethought to assess future workloads.
2. To set performance targets for work done, *e.g.* speed or reaction.
3. To decide on staffing levels and processes to be used, *e.g.* second class post.

These lead to

4. Preparation of a forecast budget in both physical and monetary terms.
5. This is analysed as simply as possible to show who *controls* the expenditure and distribution of resources.
6. Records are kept to show actual results to be compared with the forecast.
7. These are *formally* reviewed at regular intervals to ensure that decisions are taken, when needed, to get closer to the forecast *or* to recognize and cater for inescapable changes of circumstances.
8. Staff are educated to carry out this process, sensibly with understanding, so as to avoid the process being one of inquest and blame and to make it one of positive forward thinking and better management.

BIBLIOGRAPHY

BAGGOTT, J. *Cost and Management Accounting Made Simple.* Allen, 1973.
BALDWIN, D. R. Managerial Competence and Librarians. *Pennsylvania Library Association Bulletin,* Vol. 26, January 1971, p. 17-25.
BUCKMAN, T. R. PPBS in University, National, and Large Public Libraries in the USA. *Libri,* Vol. 22, No. 3, p. 256-70.
DOUGHERTY, R. M. *and* HEINRITZ, F. J. *Scientific Management of Library Operations.* New York, Scarecrow, 1966.
ICMA. *Engineer's Guide to Costing.* ICMA/IProdE, 1969.
ICMA. *Terminology of Management and Financial Accounting.* ICMA, 1974.
JOHNSON, E. R. Applying MbO to the University Library. *College and Research Libraries,* Vol. 34, No. 6, p. 436-9.
KELLER, J. E. Program Budgeting and Cost Benefit Analysis in Libraries. *College and Research Libraries,* Vol. 30, March 1969, p. 156-60.
MASON, D. Programmed Budgeting and Cost Effectiveness. *ASLIB Proceedings,* 25 (3), March 1973, p. 100-10.
MORSE, P. M. *Library Effectiveness: A System Approach.* Cambridge, Mass., MIT Press, 1968.
NOYCE, J. L. *PPBS and MbO in Libraries.* An Annotated List of References, 3rd ed. Brighton: Smoothie, 1974.
YOUNG, H. Performance and Program Budgeting: An Annotated Bibliography. *ALA Bulletin,* Vol. 61, No. 1, January 1967, p. 63-7.

The costing of library systems

D. W. G. Clements

Introduction
LIBRARIES, LIKE OTHER organizations, are bodies trying to achieve certain objectives within set financial constraints and it is desirable that they operate as effectively as possible trying to achieve their objectives. Many libraries and information services have been developed on the understanding that they are 'a good thing' and this offers considerable scope for confusion about operating objectives and justification of the library's existence. It is therefore essential that the overall objectives of the library and information service are defined as far as possible and that progress towards these objectives is measured and monitored. The definition of objectives need not be difficult and indeed consideration of a 'Management by Objectives' approach could be of use in helping to define meaningful objectives. The hard core of any system that aims at measuring and monitoring progress towards stated objectives is costing. It is therefore essential that libraries are familiar with problems of costing and with the handling of financial information because it is of use in controlling day-to-day operations, in improving overall effectiveness, in ensuring an adequate and effective case is made out for the library or information budget and in planning for the future.

Background
Costing can be considered from two aspects, (i) routine costing to provide regular financial and management information and, (ii) special exercise costing to deal with particular questions such as whether to mechanize a given procedure or how much does it cost to process a new acquisition.

To enable library systems to be costed in a uniform and comparative manner, it is necessary to define a number of standards which must be used in all costing exercises in any organization. These standards include the following:

(i) a list of expense and revenue heads under which data must be recorded;
(ii) agreed methods of apportionment of costs on an arbitrary basis where exact analysis cannot be made economically, *e.g.* accommodation costs;
(iii) a standard list of library operations so that similar tasks can be compared;
(iv) an agreed list of units of measurement of output or service so that statistics are meaningful and comparable.

A standard list of expenditure and revenue heads under which data must be recorded is not difficult to produce and every organization will have its own accounting system which should provide the basis for such a list.

Reprinted from *Aslib Proceedings*, 27(3), 1975, by permission.

Certain costs obviously vary directly with a process and can easily be allocated to the correct part of the organization and/or the correct product or service. Other costs are more general and need to be arbitrarily assigned. For example, the costs of rent, rates, electricity, telephones etc. are generally known only for the organization and have to be arbitrarily assigned to various parts of the organization. Thus the rent and rates may be apportioned to departments on the basis of floor space, lighting by light points, heating by cubic capacity of a room, telephones by the number of phones, etc. Even after allocating direct costs and apportioning indirect costs to individual departments, there will still be considerable amounts of expenditure which may need to be spread over operating departments of an organization including the library or within the library departments. These charges include the cost of the administrative departments such as the finance section and personnel section. Such expenses are often loosely called overheads and can be apportioned on one of several arbitrary bases such as a percentage on direct labour costs, a percentage on total direct costs, etc. Geoffrey Ford in a report he has prepared for OSTI on the costing of library procedures[1] has suggested a basis for the apportionment of indirect costs.

When one comes down to comparative costing of library procedures it is useful to have a standard list of library operations so that similar tasks can be compared. The need for such a standard list has long been recognized. An early example was produced by the Library Association in 1963[2] and gave a descriptive list of the professional and non-professional duties in libraries. Aslib did further work in this field[3] and developed a procedural model to illustrate the use of various forms in performing the basic activities of a library. This provided an attempt to standardize the nomenclature of activities within a broad framework. Other work in this area by Aslib has built on and extended this earlier work.[4,5] Similarly, work carried out on Colorado Academic Libraries by Leonard and others[6] contained a list of standardized technical processing activities which is of interest. None of these, however, attained anything approaching a broad coverage of all library operations nor provided a means of describing them in any standard form. During late 1972 the British Library was experimenting in the use of diary survey techniques and developed a faceted list of tasks that was intended to enable an operation to be defined in a standard way facilitating comparison both within and between libraries. This list was reproduced in Geoffrey Ford's costing report mentioned above. It serves as a tentative basis for discussion on which a standard could be based though in the general administrative area further work needs to be done.

Finally, in any costing exercise it is necessary to relate costs to units of output or service provided. Some standard units of measurement of work completed or outputs produced are therefore needed if statistics are to be meaningful and comparable. This is an area in which further work needs to be done by libraries and a provisional list of units of measurement is given in the Appendix. It has not been developed very far but is intended to serve as a starting point from which a standard might evolve. It clearly needs to be tested in practice in libraries and its units measured up against the yardstick of practical experience and application. It illustrates, however, the need for a basic list of units of measurement so that comparison of data within one library or between libraries can be made.

Routine costing
Routine costing information comes from a cost accounting system that provides regular data for use by management. Many cost accounting systems exist and the system currently in use in the British Library will be used for illustration. Cost accounting involves the collection of costs for every job, process, service or unit, in order that suitably arranged data may be presented as a guide in the control of an organization. In the British Library a computer-based accounting system has been established and has followed the practice of amalgamating the cost accounts and financial accounts into a single co-ordinated system.

The first stage in the analysis of costs is to allocate expenditure, and revenue, to sections of an organization (cost centres) and produce sectional cost accounts that should be available for sectional management to plan and control their operations, especially if there are budgets with which to compare to actual expenditure. The extent to which an organization is divided into sections will be a matter of judgment but it is best to start with only a few major sections and to provide capacity for a more detailed breakdown in the light of experience. In the British Library, for example, ten major sections or cost divisions have been established (see below) and each of these major cost divisions can be subdivided into thirty sections on average though most of these have not as yet been utilized.

Cost Division
　Board
　Bibliographic Services
　Lending Services
　Central Administration and Research and Development Department
　BL General
　Reference Division General
　Department of Printed Books
　Department of Manuscripts
　Department of Oriental Manuscripts and Printed Books
　Science Reference Library

The second stage consists of analysing the sectional costs by activities and associating them with units of output or service. In library terms care needs to be taken when considering what outputs or services are provided. In the Bibliographic Services Division of the British Library, it is easy to identify the outputs as these are catalogues, bibliographies and other publications that are produced for internal use or for sale. In either case the costs need to be known and related to income where they are sold. In other parts of the British Library such as the Reference Services, outputs are generally units of service provided, often free, to users and one is trying to establish, in broad terms at least, the expenditure on the various types of service provided. Definition of outputs or services for these library activities is more difficult and the following is illustrative of one approach:

Provision of enquiry-based reference and information services
Provision of exhibition services
Provision of photo services (a) photocopying
                            (b) microfilming
                            (c) photography
Conservation of library holdings
Additions to stock

In practice invoices are received by divisional staff to check to ensure the goods or services have been supplied and authorize the invoices for payment. The staff then code the invoices prior to batching and forwarding to the finance section for entry into the computer and payment. For coding purposes pre-printed 'allocation slips' are attached to the invoices. Details of the VAT rate, VAT value and goods value have to be entered on the slip. The goods value of the invoice then has to be coded to show the type of expenditure and has to be allocated to the appropriate cost centre and analysed by the appropriate output or service with which it is associated. This coding operation is carried out by the divisional clerical staff and has caused no major difficulties once the system was familiar to them. The system also provides for a detailed analysis of book purchases while revenue is analysed on a similar basis to expenditure prior to entry into the computer.

The mini computer—a Molecular 18—is programmed so that as invoice details and cost codings are entered, they are checked and, if arithmetically correct, the computer prints out payable orders and schedules, automatically maintains the cost accounts and provides a separate VAT account. The only form of output is *via* a serial printer and all printed outputs can be obtained on demand as well as at regular monthly intervals. For audit purposes a daily audit trail is produced detailing all information fed into the mini computer.

Such a system, whether computer based or not, can produce cost accounts at several levels of detail, can maintain the standard financial accounts, and can be flexible enough to provide for further refinement in the analysis of costs. In order to make the best use of any cost accounting system it is necessary to have the full backing of top management and to discuss the proposed system fully with all levels of management concerned so as to ensure that the analyses provided suit their needs. It is also useful if the system provides for a regular comparison with a budget so that actual performance can be compared with that expected in monthly reviews of progress of expenditure. At one level, monthly cumulative figures can be compared with the annual budget to review progress and experience has to be used to judge whether the position seems satisfactory for that part of the financial year. Once figures have been obtained for several years, however, it is often possible to estimate monthly budgeted figures that take account of seasonal variations so that the comparison of actual and expected expenditure is more realistic. The British Library system has made provision for monthly and yearly budgeted figures to be incorporated for all individual cost centres and outputs. Initially only annual budgets will be used for comparison within the major cost divisions but given further experience and at least one year's complete figures, it will be possible to calculate monthly budgets that take account of seasonal fluctuations, though this need not be done for all cost centres nor for all expenditure heads.

Comparison of actual and expected performance in cost terms can clearly be of value and for management purposes some measure of units of output or service produced would help to relate costs to productivity and to 'unit costs', though this latter term cannot be used too strictly. The use of a system of budgetary control not only provides useful information on a routine basis but is also invaluable when preparing estimates for next year's operations and in establishing a good case for increases in the existing budget. Besides the usual starting point of the current budget plus allowances for price rises, the existence of data showing trends in work input and productivity rates help to quantify needs when planning for the next year or so and such supporting evidence can be invaluable when preparing a case for the library' budget. It is of course not only necessary to consider the growth of the budget due to existing operations, price rises and work throughputs but also to consider any major changes envisaged such as new services, changes in cataloguing policies, expansion of acquisitions, proposals to alter procedures using new equipment. All such changes must be quantified and supported by evidence, much of which will be derived from special costing exercises.

Special exercise costing

Special costing exercises are concerned with particular activities or groups of activities and will generally be concerned with costs of current operations and with estimated costs of alternative methods. In this, labour costs represent the major factor in total costs, generally accounting for about 50 per cent of the total recurrent costs as in the British Library and in the public library system in the UK. This section will therefore start by considering this aspect of costing.

All library activities are susceptible to measurement and costing, given time to collect the relevant data. For a technique to be practicable, it must be simple to operate, economical to run and able to produce reliable results that can be repeated at different times and/or different places. In considering the measurement of labour costs, some form of measurement is required to establish a time for an experienced worker to carry out a specified job at a defined level of performance. Traditional work study techniques have been developed in industry especially for measuring production processes, but can be applied to some library operations. The direct observation stopwatch-technique is not ideal for many clerical and most administrative tasks and cannot easily be applied to large numbers of staff in short periods of time. Another direct observation method is the use of activity sampling. This provides a percentage of time during which an activity occurs and enables more members of the staff to be studied. With clerical and administrative types of activities, it is, however, difficult to easily identify which tasks are being performed at a specific time since so much is based on thought processes. This technique is not easily applicable for many library activities though is suitable in certain circumstances.

An approach that can be used is based on diary recording by individuals and has been used in the past by various organizations. The Library Management Research Unit at Cambridge became particularly interested in this approach as a possible basis for a simple do-it-yourself technique that could be applied in any type of library easily and cheaply and produce reliable results. The principle of the Library Management Research Unit method is a simple standard recording technique based on diary recording by individuals of secondary tasks.[7] Any individual's job can generally be divided into main and other or secondary tasks and the aim is to identify the one main task on which most time is spent (this need not be the most important task) and then for the individual to record the amount of time he spends on his other tasks only. Tea and coffee breaks are not separately recorded in the diary. It is also necessary to have some measure of throughput, *i.e.* the number of units completed (*e.g.* items catalogued, enquiries answered, cards filed) though it is unimportant whether these units are recorded individually or for groups. It is then possible after a few weeks' recording to allocate the time spent by members of staff on each task and therefore to estimate the labour costs and compare this with some appropriate unit of work completed. This simple technique was tested and developed in part of the British Library to try to provide a standard tool that could be applied to give a broad analysis of staff costs in all parts of the organization.

Both for systems investigation within any one library and for comparison of costs between libraries it is necessary to have at least a brief description of the procedures used in each task (presented generally in the form of flow charts) and these descriptions or flow charts should follow standards such as those laid down in the National Computing Centre 'System Documentation Manual'. Besides a detailed description of individual tasks, it is necessary to have a standard list of tasks that can be used to classify the tasks recorded by the staff on their forms so that similar library operations can be compared. The detailed procedures used to perform each operation may differ from place to place or over time and would be identified under the flow charting when required, but the overriding need is the ability to compare primary operations such as 'preparation of catalogue entries'. Such a standard list has been mentioned previously in this paper. A further requirement to facilitate comparison of library operations is an agreed list of units of output or work completed and again the need is to concentrate on the most important and useful statistics for comparative purposes. Again the Appendix gives a provisional list of units of measurement that could be used for comparative purposes.

The following outline methodology was tested in the British Library and can be adopted in any study:

(i) Staff will be asked to complete a separate form for each day of the survey.
(ii) The form will record their name, grade, etc., on the top section.
(iii) The form will record their normal hours of work *e.g.* 9.00 am to 5.30 pm (from which is deducted 1 hour for lunch) plus any time worked outside normal hours.
(iv) All tasks should be recorded on separate lines on the form including sickness, leave, time off, etc. while any tasks carried out in paid overtime should be separately recorded at the bottom of the form. The

amount of time spent on each activity should be recorded and these times should add up to the total daily hours less time for lunch.

(v) Many people have a clearly defined main task which can account for about half or more of the day. In such cases they should enter the description of all tasks on the form but only record the time for the secondary tasks. The survey officer will later calculate the appropriate time for the main task when coding the forms.

(vi) Tea and coffee breaks do not need to be separately recorded but can be included in the time logged against the appropriate tasks.

(vii) Units of work completed will be required and can either be recorded on a group basis or individually depending on the existing statistics and the type of activity. Only for those tasks which have meaningful outputs will the units of work be recorded.

(viii) Activities carried out in paid overtime should be separately recorded so they can be charged for at overtime rates

(ix) The forms after completion should be passed to the survey officer for checking and coding according to coding tables and for calculating times for main tasks where only secondary tasks have had their times recorded. It was found generally useful to take each person's forms for one week at a time and to summarize the results on a clean form for punching and subsequent analysis. This helped to ensure that the times recorded checked with the hours of work and that the coding of tasks was meaningful and consistent.

Before any studies are initiated it is essential to hold preliminary discussions with the head of the institution or department concerned to explain the methodology, to indicate the results that can be obtained and to establish the areas to be surveyed and their priorities. Having agreed a broad plan of approach, any staff associations or unions should be informed of the proposed studies and then a general meeting should be held with all staff concerned to briefly explain what will be involved. Specific studies will be preceded by a three or four week preparation period during which the survey officer will obtain a general picture of the work of the units concerned and collect details of statistics currently collected on a group or individual basis, officially and unofficially. He will then meet each member of staff to explain the nature and purpose of the studies, to show how to complete the form, to identify the principal tasks carried out and how to record them, to identify where statistics of work completed need to be collected individually and to answer any queries. The data should be gathered for four weeks initially and could then be repeated for fortnightly periods at random times during the year if required. It is advisable to go round during the first day or two of data collection to answer any queries and to see if the forms are being completed correctly. It is always worth while carrying out a pilot study in a small part of an institution to gain experience in running the study and to see if any snags arise. This pilot need not be carried out for more than a week. It is also easier to start by considering processing departments, where jobs are more clear cut, rather than administrative departments. Finally, it was found that one person could explain the study to about sixty to seventy people in a week (*i.e.* instal the survey) and could successfully manage the study and analyse the results.

Once the basic data have been collected and analysed, certain summary tabulations can be prepared. One tabulation should present an analysis of the amount of time (and the appropriate cost) spent on the main library operations performed by the staff of the section together with a record of the number of units of work completed while a second tabulation should analyse the time spent on these operations by grades of staff.

The next stage consists of the preparation of a short report for management. This aims at concentrating attention on the main results and would be accompanied by copies of the summary tabulations.

A survey of an organization can, if required, be carried out in steps and each step analysed on the basis described above. At the end all the results can be brought together if required to prepare summary tabulations across the whole organization presenting detailed analyses and the comparison of data from section to section. This latter can prove of use especially where some tasks are carried out by staff from several sections of the organization. Public service work is a typical example of those jobs that are spread out over the organization, but it is surprising how many other tasks overlap over two or more sections.

The results of the studies present a detailed picture of the operations performed by staff and time spent on these, and thus the labour costs. It is useful to repeat such surveys for a two-week period once or twice a year to see if the pattern has changed or to see if there are seasonal variations. This is especially useful if changes in methods of working are to be installed to obtain measurements of performance before and after such changes. The broad picture of time spent on tasks and of rates of throughput are useful for day-to-day control in providing a better understanding of the operating conditions and in estimating for the effects of increased workloads, of backlogs, of staff absences, etc.

The results of the studies may also be useful in analysing the tasks being carried out by various grades and their possible reallocation. At a higher level an analysis of costs on a functional basis provides a truer representation of actual costs of operations and services, and this is invaluable in any system development work aimed at improving the effectiveness of current operations, in budgeting and forward planning and in the control and review of policy by management. The rapid rise in unit labour costs shows only too clearly the problem of labour-intensive operations in any service organization and the need to plan for the long term and to economize in the use of labour.

So far this section has concentrated on the measurement of labour costs which of course should be done not only in the processing and service parts of the library but in the administration sections as well. Besides labour costs, many other costs need to be considered and the existence of a standard list of expenditure heads serves as an *aide memoire* to ensure items are not missed out. The first stage is identify those direct costs that can easily be allocated to the correct part of the organization and this includes direct material costs such as catalogue cards, order forms and so on especially in mechanized systems, and other direct costs such as computer time, equipment costs, binding costs, consultancy charges, etc. Problems of spreading equipment costs over the life of the equipment need to be considered but fairly simple rules will do for most purposes. Indirect costs, as have already been discussed, cover on the one hand general items that need to be arbitrarily assigned, such as accommodation costs, while on the other hand include the cost of the administration departments which themselves need to be checked for their efficiency. These latter costs will need to be spread over operating departments if one is trying to estimate a selling price or the true cost of a service to the user. Government bodies can of course make use of the 'Ready Reckoner for Staff Costs' issued by the Civil Service Department to provide a quick estimate of overall costs based on staff costs plus allowances for overheads and accommodation. Though not accurate such ready reckoners can be useful for broader studies of forward estimates when no other detailed data exist.

Estimating the cost of proposed or alternative systems is fairly straightforward in principle and to a large extent the existence of costs of current operations provides a starting point. Before any alternative system can be costed the level of detail required must be decided, as often broad estimates will be sufficient to identify likely alternatives worthy of further consideration. Detailed costings will require a similar detailed level of knowledge about proposed alternative procedures with estimates of time required to complete the necessary tasks, equipment types, costs and speeds, material costs and so on. Again a standard list of expenditure heads serves to ensure that all aspects of costs have been covered though it may be possible to consider only marginal costs, *i.e.* those immediately affected, and to ignore general overheads especially if there are no changes in accommodation requirements. Changeover costs should not be ignored, especially if a change of system results in large stocks of redundant materials or in redundant equipment which is still in reasonable condition.

The use of automated systems in libraries is one of the most common proposals considered. Although automation costs are frequently divided into developments costs and operating costs it is not easy to separate them in practice and it is essential to cost the automated system over the whole life of the system so that the initial investment in a proposed new system is spread over several years. Experience has shown that staff costs over the life of a typical computer installation amount to roughly two-thirds, and equipment to about a quarter of the total expenditure, which clearly focuses attention on the main elements. The Civil Service Department has considerable experience in this field and it is not proposed to go into these questions in detail. In library terms conversion costs can be a major factor when large data files may need to be converted into machine-readable form. It was estimated by the National Libraries ADP Feasibility Study that the cost of converting the BM catalogue into machine-readable form would be about £600,000–800,000 exclusive of the cost of setting up an automated system for the British Library's processing operation. Considering that something like six million records are involved, however, it may well be that conversion costs would be much higher, by a factor of about four or five.

It should not, however, be forgotten that the costs of proposed systems need to be related not only to the existing systems—and any labour-intensive system is going to rise rapidly in cost due to salary increases—but also to other benefits that will result, and in the end it may well be that the new system is authorized not so much on grounds of cost savings, though this is desirable, but on the benefits to be expected for the new system which outweighs all other considerations.

Conclusion

This paper has briefly covered some problems of the costing of library systems and has concentrated on the one hand on routine cost-accounting systems for regular management information, and on the other hand on special exercise costing and on the analysis of labour costs since these form such a major part in library expenditure. Once costs are collected for management purposes they will prove to be invaluable and they will provide a basis on which many other longer-term studies can be started and will often allow consideration of the more sophisticated techniques of research to be applied in an organization. For the majority of cases the existence of costs will be found to provide a benefit for management on a day-to-day basis in controlling their organization and in planning for the future.

REFERENCES

1 FORD, G. *Library automation: guidelines to costing.* Lancaster University, March 1973. (Report prepared for OSTI.)
2 *Professional and non-professional duties in libraries.* A descriptive list compiled by a sub-committee of the Membership Committee of the Library Association. The Library Association, 1963.
3 THOMAS, P. A. *A procedural model for the use of bibliograghaphic records in Libraries.* Aslib (Occasional Publication no. 4), 1970.
4 THOMAS, P. A. *Task analysis of library operations.* Aslib (Occasional Publication no. 8), 1971.
5 THOMAS, P. A., *and* WARD, V. A. *An analysis of managerial activities in libraries.* Aslib (Occasional Publication no. 14), 1974.
6 LEONARD, C. E. *and others. Centralised book processing: a feasibility study based on Colorado academic libraries.* Scarecrow Press, 1969.
7 SMITH, G. C. K. *and* SCHOFIELD, J. L. Administrative Effectiveness: times and costs of library operations. *Journal of Librarianship,* 3 (4), 1971, p. 245–66.

APPENDIX

Units of Measurement

DATA COLLECTED REGULARLY | DATA COLLECTED AS REQUIRED

A. New inputs to the library
1. *Items ordered*
1.1. Number of Titles Ordered
   (If possible count under the following headings)
   (i) by purchase
   (ii) by exchange
   (iii) by donation
   (iv) by legal deposit

(1) Proportion selected but not ordered
(2) Amount of second-hand material ordered
(3) Proportion of orders needing to be chased or hastened
(4) Performance of various sources of supply

COSTING AND ECONOMICS

DATA COLLECTED REGULARLY

2. *Items received*
2.1. Current Serial Titles (excluding monograph series)
Count the number of current serial titles received, counting each title once only (*i.e.* exclude duplicate copies)—this means counting bibliographic titles and not parts
2.2. Number of Patents received
 (i) UK Patents
 (ii) Non-UK Patents
2.3. Printed Materials (monographs, etc. excluding current serial titles, patents, printed maps, musical scores)
(If possible count under the following headings) (Count by volumes or units)
 (i) by purchase
 (ii) by exchange
 (iii) by donation
 (iv) by legal deposit
2.4. Printed Maps
(Count by number of sheets)
2.5. Music
(Count by number of separate scores)
2.6. Manuscript Material
(Includes full-size copies if not commercially published but excludes microform copies)
(Count by number of units to be catalogued)
2.7. Microforms
 (i) Microfilms by number of rolls
 (A standard roll is 30 metres long, approx. 100 ft.; 60 metre lengths count as 2 rolls, etc.)
 (ii) Other Microforms
 (Count by the number of physical units, e.g. sheets of microfiche, number of microcards)

B. Processing outputs of the library
1. *Stamping*
(Stamping of newly acquired material with appropriate library ownership and/or date-stamp)
2. *Item streaming*
(Sorting newly acquired material and routing according to processing steps required, *e.g.* type and level of cataloguing, need for classification, need for binding, etc.)
3. *Cataloguing and subject work*
3.1. Number of separate titles catalogued; and number of catalogue entries prepared.
(If possible count under the following headings)

DATA COLLECTED AS REQUIRED

(1) Number of new titles taken
(2) Number of titles ceasing publication
(3) Number of separate parts to be registered/recorded
(4) Number of modifications required to existing records, *e.g.* change of title, change of price, etc.

Applicable to all types of items received
(1) Number and type of items ordered but not received
(2) If appropriate, other types of material received should also be broken down by (i) purchase, (ii) exchange, (iii) donation and (iv) legal deposit

(1) Number of items stamped
(2) Delay between receipt of item by library and shelving (and date-stamping if appropriate)
(1) Proportion of items received undergoing each of the processing steps available
(2) Delays between receipt of items, completion of each processing step and final shelving

(1) Level of cataloguing used and amount and type of material going to each level
(2) Number of entries revised
(3) Number of existing entries in the catalogue altered/amended
(4) Amount of modification and revision

DATA COLLECTED REGULARLY	DATA COLLECTED AS REQUIRED
(i) monographs (ii) new serial titles (iii) individual serial articles (iv) other material 3.2. Number of separate titles subject analysed and/or indexed; number of separate titles classified; and number of subject entries prepared	needed to the authority files (5) Amount of time required for authority checking during preparation of catalogue entries (1) Type and level of subject work and amount and type of material going to each (2) Number of entries revised (3) Number of existing entries altered/amended
4. *Production of catalogue and other bibliographic tools* 4.1. Number of records typed and/or keyboarded 4.2. Number of entries proof-read prior to final production 4.3. Number of catalogue cards produced 4.4. Number of catalogue entries printed or produced (excluding catalogue cards). Please indicate whether produced in printed form, microfilm, COM, etc. 4.5. Number of other bibliographic tools produced (please specify)	(1) Delays between receipt of final entries and production of finished products (2) Proportion of entries produced by each of the processes used (3) Amount of machine time lost
5. *Binding, labelling, boxing, etc.* 5.1. Binding Control (Scheduling, etc. of items to be sent to the binders) (Count by number of physical units bound)	(1) Amount and type of material to be bound and rebound (2) Delays in binding (3) Proportion of items received from binders requiring further binding work
5.2. Shelf location system	(1) Type of shelf location system used, number of units dealt with
5.3. Labelling	(1) Type of labelling system used, number of physical units labelled
5.4. Boxing (Preparation of boxes for serial parts, loose material, etc.)	(1) Number of boxes prepared (2) Number of physical units boxed
5.5. Covering (Covering of books, etc. with protective jackets, etc.)	(1) Methods used and quantities dealt with
5.6. Filing and Shelving	(1) Number of physical units of new acquisitions shelved (2) Number of units of stock withdrawn for discarding (3) Number of units of stock replaced due to wear, outdated editions, etc. (4) Amount of tidying of material on open access shelves. Number of items on open shelves in wrong position (5) Number of catalogue cards filed (6) Number of existing catalogue entries replaced due to wear, damage, etc. (7) Number of existing catalogue entries withdrawn

COSTING AND ECONOMICS 105

DATA COLLECTED REGULARLY

C. Service functions of the library
1. *Reception/screening of readers*
2. *Book application and reservation*
   (Concerned with readers' applications for books stored in closed access)
   2.1. Number of applications received
   2.2. Number of volumes or units reserved
   2.3. Number of requests not satisfied

3. *Book supply*
   (Location and retrieval of material stored in closed access)
   3.1. Number of volumes or units requested
   3.2. Number of volumes or units supplied
   3.3. Number of requests not supplied
   3.4. Number of requests taking longer than 'x' minutes to supply
4. *Loan services*
   4.1. Loans to readers for use outside the library
      (i) Number of volumes lent
      (ii) Number of items reserved

   4.2. Lending to other libraries
      (i) Number of requests received
      (ii) Number of requests satisfied
      (iii) Delays in supply

   4.3. Circulation of literature to members of own organisation
   4.4. Borrowing from other libraries
      (i) Number of items requested
      (ii) Number of items received
   4.5. Location services
      (Supply of locations of items not held in stock)
      (i) Number of requests received
      (ii) Number of requests satisfied
      (iii) Delays in supply
5. *Information services*
   5.1. Number of enquiries received and number satisfied broken down by
      (i) readers' enquiries
      (ii) telephone enquiries
      (iii) postal enquiries
      (iv) telex enquiries

DATA COLLECTED AS REQUIRED

(1) Number of applications for readers' tickets dealt with
(1) Analysis of distribution of numbers of applications made during each day and of seasonal fluctuations
(2) Analysis of number of volumes reserved per reader and periods of reservation
(3) Analysis of requests not satisfied and reasons
(4) Analysis of reader failure in locating material in the catalogue
(1) Analysis of length of delays in delivery and their causes
(2) Analysis of type, age of publication and subject of items requested
(3) Analysis of reasons for requests not being satisfied
(4) Analysis of number and size of volumes requested per reader

(1) Analysis of loan requests by type, age of publication and subject
(2) Number of volumes overdue
(3) Number of reservations satisfied and length of delays
(4) Distribution of issues during the day showing peaks of use
(1) Originl items lent to libraries in UK and overseas
(2) Number of photo- or other copies issued to libraries in UK and overseas
(3) Analysis of type, age of publication and subject of requests received and sources of requests and analysis of unsatisfied requests
(1) Number of titles circulated and number of people on lists for each title
(1) Analysis of items requested
(2) Analysis of sources of supply
(3) Analysis of speed of supply
(1) Source of requests and source of supply
(2) Analysis of type, age of publication and subject of requests received, satisfied and unsatisfied

(1) Analysis of number and type of requests received and satisfied
(2) Analysis of requests unsatisfied
(3) Amount of time required to answer requests and material used to supply answer

DATA COLLECTED REGULARLY

5.2. Compilation of bibliographies, reading lists, etc.

5.3. Other services (e.g. translations, exhibitions, educational services, etc.)

6. *Reprographic services*
6.1. Photocopying (see also 4.2. above under loan services)
   (i) Number of requests received and satisfied and whether requests received by post or from readers in the library
   (ii) Number of sheets produced
6.2. Microfilming
   (i) Number of requests received and satisfied
   (ii) Number of frames produced

6.3. Other copying and photographic services
   (i) Number of requests received and satisfied
   (ii) Number of units produced (*e.g.* frames, prints, etc.)

DATA COLLECTED AS REQUIRED

(1) Number of bibliographies, reading lists, etc. compiled. Frequency of duplicate requests. Amount of time required to prepare these items.

(1) Analysis of requests for each type of service against demand, costs and charges

(1) Analysis of type, age of publication and subject of requests received, satisfied and unsatisfied
(2) Analysis of size of orders
(3) Analysis of speed of supply
(4) Analysis of costs and charges

(1) Analysis of type, age of publication and subject of requests received, satisfied and unsatisfied
(2) Analysis of size of orders
(3) Analysis of speed of supply
(4) Analysis of costs and charges

(1) Analysis of type, age of publication and subject of requests received, satisfied and unsatisfied
(2) Analysis of size of orders
(3) Analysis of speed of supply
(4) Analysis of costs and charges

Analysing industrial information service costs: a simple check list

Alan Armstrong

MANY of us younger and less experienced information officers flounder hopelessly (some in a delightful feminine helplessness) when asked to present an analysis of the cost of the information service we run.

The panic stems from three things: first, not knowing when asked; secondly, only having a short time to find the answers; thirdly, not knowing how to start.

An alternative to this panic is to precede any involuntary inquisition by a self-imposed costing exercise which can be done at leisure, regularly reviewed and revised at leisure, and pigeon-holed until required for presentation to the boss.

The costing exercise can be superficial to include salaries, stationery, books and journals or it can be done thoroughly. When it is called for and you have to present it, there can be a keen smell of corporate surgery in the air and it may be as well to have made a meticulously thorough analysis. Corporate surgeons lay every possible cost at your door. If you know what the costs are, you can defend them.

Whether cost analysis is done leisurely, or in haste, a simple checklist helps. For this text the author assumes you have leisure.

Cost analysis cannot be done alone. We have to consult and use the skills and goodwill of accountants and personnel officers. They will be helpful as long as we explain what we are doing. Never try to cost your operation by yourself. It must be done within the ground rules set by the company accountants. For example, find out whether the company charges each department for its postal costs. If so, add them; if not, note in your analysis that postal costs are not set against your operation. On almost every costing issue, you must talk to others.

Salaries
First of all add up the annual salaries of all your staff. If your organization pays overtime, ask the personnel or payroll section to give you the annual overtime payments for the last twelve months. Beware of exceptional workloads which may have made overtime payments unusually heavy.

Salary burden
These are the additional costs incurred by the company when employing library staff, or any staff.

Reprinted from *Aslib Proceedings*, 24(11), 1972, by permission.

How you actually get to your departmental figures is a matter which only you and your other office colleagues will ever understand. Salary burden has different ingredients in different companies, so any of the following items might be included. All are costs and none can be ignored.

National health insurance
How much does the organization pay per year in NHI stamps for the staff?

Pension
What amount does the company pay towards pensions and life insurance. If the personnel department are reluctant to give precise figures, ask for the information as a percentage of each person's salary. It could be as much as 6 per cent of annual salary.

Training board levy
Again this may be easier to obtain as a salary percentage, e.g. $2\frac{1}{2}$ per cent of annual salary.

Holidays and sickness
The company pays you for your national and annual holidays. It also pays you during sickness. The burden lies not in the salary payment (already accounted for in preceding paragraph on salaries) but in the cost to the company of up to thirty or more days per person per year as holiday, and sick days which must be written off by the employer as wholly non-productive. This could be 8–9 per cent of each person's salary. In a factory this could more easily be measured as loss of output.

Paid absence
If your Aunt Maud died, and you took time off, the same principle applies as in the preceding paragraph.

Recruitment costs
Did you recruit staff during the year? What were the costs of recruiting—include advertisements, etc?

Temporary staff
What was the cost of temporary staff for your department?

Canteen subsidy, or luncheon vouchers
One usually gets either one or the other. Both cost the employer money. What is your share of the cost?

Group insurance
In addition to life insurance and pension fund, there could be widows benefits, salary continuance, group travel accident, etc.

Some or all of these items could be charged to you in your organization. There will be more, peculiar to your own situation.

Ask Personnel to help you to determine the costs of each. If Personnel are vague and non-committal, ask for annual salary burden items to be costed as a percentage of each employee's annual salary. It could be about 25–26 per cent of annual salary.

Occupancy costs

Rent
How many square feet does the information service cover? Multiply the number of square feet by the rent that the organization pays per square foot. Outside London it could be £2 per square foot, inside London it could be £7 or more per square foot. If your company owns its building, maybe nobody pays anything. I doubt it—check with financial people, bearing in mind that usable space rate is higher than just plain square footage. Rents in the City of London have risen very sharply during the past few years and have now reached figures of between £10 and £12 per square foot. On average each person employed occupies a little over 100 square feet of working space, so that in the City the cost is more than £1,000 a year per head of staff. The equivalent cost in the country, for example in Knutsford, Cheshire, is no more than £150 a year.

Rates
Divide the total rates charge of your building by that percentage portion you and the library occupy and find how much in rates the library pays.

Heating
Ask for an estimated departmental heating charge. You may find this information a little difficult to find, but if you say why you want to know, you should get a sensible answer. If in doubt, estimate it using your knowledge of domestic charges.

Lighting
Use the same procedure as for heating; estimate from your annual home bills if you have to—but ask for help first.

Cleaning
The office is cleaned each evening—ask the administrators for your departmental charge. If necessary, take the total company annual bill and divide it by the number of employees to find the cost per employee.

Dilapidations
Many companies and organizations subdivide annual dilapidations (painting repairs and maintenance of fabric) to departments. Most do not. Find out whether your employer does.

Departmental costs

Stationery
Ask the administrators the cost of what you ordered over the previous twelve months. They delight in knowing this or working it out for you.

Postage
Like the telephone, it could be apportioning of letter charges by department plus recorded parcel charges. Again it will be more than you expect.

Other staff
This is one really difficult to assess. The company messengers, commissionaires, telephonists and other non-productive staff, such as the legal and financial departments, are there to assist and support your function and service. As such, their costs may be apportioned to those who use them, you included. It's tempting to disclaim this item, but when you are in full operation, can you deny using telephonists, telex operators, messengers, company postmen, and so on? Be prepared to find that you are being charged for the use of this support staff. (This is why you should always encourage the minimum number of personnel officers possible.)

These can be described as overheads transferred into your budget, for which you are accountable. One example is printing. Do you pay for photocopies? Does the charge apportion operator's salary and occupancy costs or is this charged separately, perhaps annually, on a department usage system?

Telex
If you have telex, are you charged in any way for costs of sending your telexes? If so how much? Who pays the equipment rental?

Furniture
Is your furniture rented or purchased? What are the rental charges—for instance, on electric typewriters or calculating machines? If purchased—what has been purchased in the last twelve months and what previously, if you depreciate your costing over some years? Check with the financial people on how they apportion furniture costs to you.

Telephone
This cost will usually be a mixture of recorded long distance calls plus a random division by department of local and self-dialled STD calls. The cost will be higher than you think.

Books, journals
Some charges must be absorbed by the information department for books, directories and journals. Follow precedent in determining those purchases which are yours and those which are paid for by other budgets.

Travel
What have been the staff travelling costs for the period?

Consultants
Did you use consultants, e.g. Aslib, during the year—what was the cost?

Hotel and other expenses
What expenses have been incurred in hotels, restaurants?

COSTING AND ECONOMICS

Corporate subscriptions
If your company is a member of Aslib, add this corporate charge here. You can try to offset this cost to user departments on the grounds that it is useful to them, but this invites reciprocation; for example, you may be invited to help pay the fee to the Personnel Officers Association—as if it helped you in some way. It would be better to absorb the Aslib subscription charge as your own, if possible. Add other corporate subscriptions here too, e.g. British Standards Institution, but only if it really is your departmental subscription.

Professional fees
Some organizations pay employees' professional institute fees: Is your company paying yours? If so, how much per annum for your staff?

Training expenses
Internal or external training courses for staff can be costly. How much did your department spend during the year?

Conferences
We all like to go to one or two a year and only churlish organizations say no. How many have you been to at £50 per day? This usually can be tied in with hotel, restaurant and travelling expenses.

Others
There are many—space does not allow a longer list. Each of us can add items peculiar to our organizations. If you feel like it, add £3 per member of your staff for the annual Christmas party—it has to be paid for!

In summary, there are obviously more charges and costs to be considered than salary alone. Some items in the checklist may plainly not apply in your organization. However, it is sensible to eliminate them. Adding up the costs can be more than a little frightening. Real operating costs can be as much as 200-300 per cent higher than total annual salaries. If this is so, then the earlier and more carefully the unit is costed by the librarian, the sooner can self-analysis of cost-benefit comparisons get underway.

For this is always the supplementary question after submitting the total cost: 'What measurable or tangible benefits to the organization are derived from this annual expenditure?'

If the annual expenditure is £20,000, we all need to have a good list of benefits ready when asked: especially if the company surgeon is already leading you to the operating theatre.

Administrative Effectiveness: Times and Costs of Library Operations

G C K Smith and J L Schofield

The kinds of information needed by managing librarians to make correct decisions are considered, with emphasis on the value of current data on the exceptional situation. Management information in a library is of greatest use in comparison, either internally, or with data from other libraries. A simple, standard method of recording and costing is urged, so that librarians may readily identify procedures requiring improvement.

Development of the present costing method is traced from its original state as a simple management information system based on exception reporting (i.e. reporting the exceptions which occur in any particular survey), through a pilot study in a large university library, to its full installation in two further university libraries. The method of analysing the raw data is described, and examples of the tables are given, together with brief background information on the libraries concerned.

After a note on the limitations of the present costing method and of unit costs in general, unit times and costs are given for numerous operations in both the libraries surveyed, covering both reader and technical services. There is agreement between results of several American studies and those of the present investigation. For further comparison, the information on times and salaries has been used in conjunction with a standard civil service costing procedure.

Finally, it is shown how far the system has achieved its original aims, and recommendations are made for the development of a ready-made costing method for librarians using suggested statistical units of work.

Reprinted from *Journal of Librarianship*, 3(4), 1971, by permission.

INTRODUCTION

One of the main items proposed to the Library Management Research Unit, Cambridge (LMRU) for investigation was the organization of library operations. Starting from the assumption that in the past librarians all too often acted upon the basis of guesses or out-of-date information, we were required to discover, for example, what steps could be taken to ensure that library routines are subjected to methodical flow chart studies, and to examine the cost breakdown of the various activities in a university library. Our first consideration was the nature of information which a librarian in middle and senior management grades needs to help him make satisfactory short- and long-term decisions on running and developing a whole library or one of its subsystems. While senior librarians are not slow to admit that they often act upon inadequate or faulty information, they are more reticent about stating specific information requirements. We had therefore to use our own imagination in deciding what was required, before we could plan a method of extracting and channelling it in the most suitable form to the people who need it most.

We made an early distinction, largely for our own convenience, between management information on users of the library and management information on operations and staff of the library. Projects were devised separately in each field, but we have never lost sight of the principle that all library operations are ultimately directed towards the user's satisfaction. Certain other important considerations have also affected the choice of our method of investigation. For example, the need to control flows of information has encouraged us to adopt some of the practices of *management by exception*.* We also accept the desirability of developing a system which librarians can use themselves, without having to budget for a systems analyst or a consultant, to examine their libraries' efficiency and effectiveness. These considerations have led us to recommend recording not the regular tasks but the less regular or unusual activities when records are needed, and to encourage self-recording whenever possible by all grades of staff.

Unit costs of various library processes had been suggested to us as among the most valuable types of management information. To discover these, it was clear that records of productivity, in terms of units of work accomplished, would first be required. Output figures themselves would be valuable information upon

---

* "Management by exception": an arrangement under which only exceptional cases are referred to management, other cases being dealt with accordingly to precise instructions or general principles in accordance with the objectives of the undertaking. GB Treasury. *Glossary of management techniques.* HMSO, 1967, 12.

which to base decisions on methods and staffing arrangements. Work being taken on and work waiting, if quantifiable, were also considered important, particularly for planning to meet peaks and to reduce backlogs. In addition to productivity records, the librarian must also have information on the hours worked and lost by his staff, and the exact procedure which they are following, as a basis for planning to cope with crises and changes. As a valuable check on the service provided by his staff, information on the quality of their work is of further assistance to the librarian. Where continuous checks are not part of the system, or where they could be reduced, he can employ sampling for quality control of procedures like catalogue filing and book labelling. Scientific managers will not increase productivity without careful checks on standards of accuracy.

Bearing in mind the need for sifting the upward flow of information, by summarizing and by reporting in detail only when an exceptional situation—peak, trough or bottleneck—appears, we must look at what the librarian can do with the information he receives. For one thing, he will be able to *make comparisons*: although only two weeks' output of cataloguing may be considered, he will be able to compare the first week with the second, and over a longer period a "standard" or "norm" will begin to emerge for this subsystem. Also, given auxiliary information on hours worked, including details of work which took staff away from their regular duties, he will be able to *identify problems, see the results of changes* in method and *make outline plans* for future contingencies. From these times, he can *calculate labour costs* (the most important and difficult area of costing—it can account for 75% of total unit cost) and see the effects of re-grading tasks.

If the librarian is not content with setting his own standards, he can use his management information on norms of time, output and cost to compare his system with other libraries, provided that they count the same way, and that he knows the differences in their working methods. Alternatively he can compare his own system's norms with the theoretical (i.e. synthetic) standards, built up from detailed timing of elements, tasks and procedures in a wide range of libraries. Improvements may then be effected by adopting more efficient methods practised elsewhere or by combining standard elements to perform the same function or at least achieve the same result.

Any one of these three types of comparison can lead to improvement in both quality of decisions and efficiency of methods; but naturally we hope for the best results from *inter-library comparisons*.* A nationally, perhaps even internationally, agreed set of statistical units for recording work created and completed (input and output) must be developed, and a generally acceptable list of task elements must be compiled, so that we can identify differences in procedure and, if necessary,

* Cp. "Interfirm comparisons": the exchange of comparative information between firms with the object of helping their management to increase their firms' efficiency. *Op. cit.*, 7.

derive a set of standard or "national norm" unit times. Deciding on units of output and identifying task elements are surely the jobs of special studies by co-operative bodies of librarians (SCONUL, UC & R Section, etc.) or by research teams (Aslib, LMRU, etc.), or perhaps by both in co-operation; but they must develop guidelines by which librarians themselves can study their operations. There should be a straightforward management information, and therefore costing, system which can be either installed permanently or used as a regular test for obtaining information for decisions. The system must be simple, so that staff do not lose more than a small amount of time in recording; it is therefore better for them to record exceptions to their normal tasks—their secondary tasks, rather than their primary ones.

From records of work units and time the librarian can begin to identify areas for improvement in methods; from cost records the adequacy of staffing arrangements can also be reviewed. If one library's acquisition procedure not only takes longer but costs more than another's, and if the elements are basically the same—that is, if they are both doing the same things and one is not, say, pre-cataloguing as well—then it is clear that some rethinking of both methods and staffing may be needed by the former.

If the procedures cost roughly the same, but one takes longer, then methods should be examined first; if the time is the same, but the cost greater in one, job grading ought to be critically reviewed. There are, of course, a number of other factors which must be taken into account. When a problem area is identified, more detailed study may be necessary, of times, office layout and so on, with the librarian asking at every stage why, when, where, by whom, what and how things are done and records kept.

FIRST IDEAS

Our first thoughts were directed to producing a very basic, unsophisticated system of rationalizing information on the output of various library processes and on the times taken to achieve them, and of directing such information to the proper quarters. The hours worked by each identifiable department or section were to be aggregated, not broken down according to the grade of staff members, while units of work (or output) were to be only roughly defined. Ready-made "statistics" counted for the annual report were to be accepted as units of work whenever possible. Results and applications were expected to be quite limited; but it was hoped that the very recording of output would help to increase productivity. We were also hoping that with the system's help a librarian would be able to assess:

(i) the labour cost per unit of output, with cost based on a departmental average hourly rate;
(ii) the work rate of a department, section or individual;

(iii) the time required to clear outstanding work;
(iv) the spare capacity in a department;
(v) the extent of inter-departmental lending of staff;
(vi) the amount of absence from a department.

The germ of the projected system was a simple reporting form, to be completed in duplicate by heads of department or by individuals performing single tasks. One copy was to be sent to the Librarian at regular intervals, from which he could build up a file for each department or procedure. The form contained details of hours worked under these headings: gross hours available—own staff, other staff; hours not available, including sickness, holiday; net available hours. It also recorded units of work received and completed during the hours accounted for. To assist in compiling this summary form, each member of staff was to have a second, even simpler form upon which to record all details of "secondary" tasks—the tasks which did not contribute directly to the department's output figure—and of absences. Of course, one man's secondary task could be another's primary, and vice versa. This second, individual form is really the cornerstone of our more developed recording system.

PILOT STUDY

In order to test our unsophisticated method, we arranged a month's pilot study at a large university library (over 750 000 vols.) during part of one term and part of a vacation. It was planned to discover the suitability of forms, the best method of installation and the reactions of the staff involved. Appropriateness of the various units of work and the ease with which these were recorded were also to be reviewed. We hoped to achieve such results as an improved set of forms, more precise and acceptable definitions of units of work and a satisfactory way of introducing the system to a library. The interval for reporting was in this case set at one week, and every kind of department was involved in the trial: processing, reader service, multi-activity (e.g. periodicals) and technical (e.g. photography).

Naturally enough, there was some variation among departments in the amount of information which they could record without undue additional effort by the staff, and in the amount of co-operation extended to us. In several cases a department willingly recorded much more information than it would normally gather for its annual statistics. This was especially true when the departmental head was concerned to present a thoroughly representative picture of all work done by his staff. Nearly all of the departments unfortunately found it impossible to give regular reports on their backlogs, in view of the time which they said a count would involve. Once a year was felt to be a manageable frequency. One reader service department also pointed out to us that considerable time was needed to calculate hours worked, owing to the degree of staff borrowing upon which it was compelled to rely, and the complexities of its lunch and evening duties.

The general impression gained from our pilot study was that in this library, at least, purely processing departments lent a lot of their time to purely reader service departments, which depended on borrowed staff for between 4% and 13% of their gross available time. Loss of time due to all causes was most notable among processing departments and least serious in technical ones. Actual information obtained was confined to departmental totals of time worked, borrowed and lost, which together with output figures showed the effect of changes in available time on productivity. It was clear that a longer survey period would be required before firm conclusions could be made, while a great deal of work remained to be done in evolving definitions of tasks and units of work. It was agreed that an important result of the system would eventually be the comparison of unit costs between different libraries. Some refinement of the costing arrangements was therefore given a high priority.

We decided that our system could, with a little development, provide a means of obtaining net unit labour costs. Departments would naturally have to be broken down by grades of staff and by procedures (or related jobs); more precise details of time, output and salary would need to be obtained. We should have to record and count backlogs at the beginning, then perhaps once a year. Self-recording at an individual level seemed to involve least work and least resistance. The two-tiered diary aspect of the system was therefore retained, but we decided to adopt a modified form, adjusted better to the needs of an individual library, a more thorough set of instructions for staff, and an interval for recording suited to existing compensatory leave arrangements. One Saturday off in two, for example, would imply a recording period of multiples of a fortnight.

MAIN SURVEYS

Our first main installation took place in another large (over 700 000 vols.) university library (Library Q) from late May to mid-August 1970. This library is in a transitional stage of organization, with a subject-based reader service staff distributed throughout the building and performing some formerly centralized technical service functions. About 102 full-time equivalent (f.t.e.) staff were involved. The time of year was interesting, since it covered a portion of term, a lot of vacation and the whole of the Annual Inspection. The three-month period was long enough for rates of work to be established quite accurately and the causes of variation determined. We decided on a two-week period of recording, and forms were regularly collected from departments and sent to the Unit for analysis. Tasks which heads of departments wished to have highlighted were recorded, particularly those which took staff away from their regular places of work; time spent on Inspection duties was also carefully noted. Detailed records were sought only for time worked or lost between 09.00 and 17.00 hours; but where units of work completed were partly achieved during evenings, this was taken into account when calculating unit costs. All departmental heads and most other staff were interviewed before the survey began.

Analysis of the information gathered by our forms was carried out in three stages. First of all we prepared a table from the individuals' forms for each department, to give a personal and departmental picture of the time and tasks (Fig. 1). Then, from these tables, with the aid of average salary figures supplied by the librarian, we constructed a second table, showing costs within departments for each of the specified tasks or other time categories, such as leave or time lent to other departments (Fig. 2). Finally, the costing tables were broken down by related tasks and procedures (e.g. inter-library loans) throughout the library, and then built up again into a table of costs for each period and for the whole twelve weeks (Fig. 3). Most of the analysis was complete within six weeks of the end of the survey, and the library concerned has examined the results and already found them useful. The information has proved itself valuable as a check on slow or costly procedures, and a means of clearly identifying points of possible re-grading, and of preventing the unofficial introduction of unnecessary operations. Unfortunately, in only certain cases did we link units of output directly with time recorded, a limitation which has left us with only a small number of true labour costs. These are given in a section below in tabular form, Library Q wherever possible being set against comparable information obtained from a second university library (Library R). However, there was no shortage of useful information on the cost per hour of nearly every operation in the library.

The most important lesson learned from the installation at Library Q was the need for even more precise definitions of the primary tasks of individuals or departments which we did *not* want recorded. We were also determined in future to ally units of work completed more closely to the time taken to complete them. In the field of analysis we found that it would take very little longer to analyse four-weekly records than fortnightly. The frequency of recording should really depend upon the Librarian's need for current information; but if his own departmental heads or administrative assistants are to do the analysis, then the frequency must be modified by the time available for analysing. We think that four weeks is the optimum period, short enough for close control and long enough to reduce analysis time to an acceptable level.

Our second full-scale test took place in a smaller university library (c. 600 000 vols.), Library R, with a staff of about 45 in the main building, which houses principal collections in Arts and Social Sciences and incorporates centralized processing for a number of branches. This library has a more traditional organizational structure, with mainly functional divisions. Again a total of twelve weeks was covered, but this time in three periods only. We conducted a thorough preliminary series of interviews with departmental heads and all their staff, before exact instructions were devised for what was to be recorded (secondary tasks) or omitted (primary tasks). Individual forms were made up into pads for convenience and distributed with final advice to the staff. The survey started early in September and finished at the end of November 1970; evenings were included in as much detail as the period 9–5.30. No problems occurred during the course of this test which the library staff could not sort out for themselves, and more precise unit labour costs have been achieved without any additional effort at the analysis stage. The time involved in analysing and costing data from Library R was $31\frac{1}{2}$ hours net for each four-week period, or 42 minutes at 65p per member of staff analysed. An examination of time only would have cost only $28\frac{1}{2}$p per staff member per four weeks.

RESULTS IN DETAIL

A selection of the final results of our investigations in Libraries Q and R has been made for the purposes of this article. We have presented nearly all the real unit labour costs which were obtained, and particular emphasis is placed on points of comparison between the two libraries. Examples of procedures have been drawn from most stages of the acquisition, processing and use subsystems. There are, however, one or two qualifications which apply to all the results, while some of the problems met during analysis need to be described first.

The answer to university librarians' problems does not lie in unit costs alone, but unit costs can provide useful indicators of problems. A study of organization and methods, without a single operation timed or costed, can achieve simplification and savings. Unit costs from one library at one time are not helpful. Unless comparisons can be made with different periods or other libraries, there will be no indication of where to begin making improvements. Even then comparisons cannot be made without an exhaustive study of the variables involved: a library may have changed its methods between two costing exercises, or two libraries may differ so widely in design that unit costs of several operations are consequently at variance. However, when the variables have been noted and their influence identified, there will remain points of comparison where unit costs may reveal true opportunities for economy and improved method.

The costs which we have calculated are all net labour costs; that is, they represent the cost only of time actually devoted to producing the unit of output; cost of leave, sickness, special and secondary tasks is excluded. Secondly, the cost of time has been based on average salary figures, i.e. the average salaries of staff in each grade calculated from the actual salaries of staff employed at the time. They are not median salaries. Lastly, the salaries are, unless otherwise stated, net figures, excluding the cost of pensions and National Insurance. To arrive at a fairly accurate gross unit labour cost, 10% should be added to the amounts given below; while, if times and costs are required which exclude allowances for tea and coffee breaks, fatigue, personal needs and waiting for work, between 12½% and 16% should be added to our figures. All times and costs are given to the nearest minute or new penny. Full-time equivalent staff (f.t.e.) is given in terms of regular hours.

Acquisitions (Books)

TABLE IA

Library Q. All incoming suggestions for purchase checked by subject specialist library staff. F.t.e. staff in Acquisitions Department = 9·4 average, including Accounts section. Time on selection excluded.

Weeks		Units: Items* accessioned	Unit time m	Unit cost £
1–4	Term	1393	41	0·46
5–8	Vacation (incl. Inspection)	2273	29	0·33
9–12	Vacation	1040	67	0·72
Total		4706	38	0·45

* Items = "books".

TABLE IB

Library R. All suggestions processed by Acquisitions Department. Accounts work included, but not selection; there is no accessions record kept. F.t.e. staff = 5·8 average.

Weeks		Units: Items* passed to Cataloguing	Unit time m	Unit cost £
1–4	Vacation	1551	29	0·31
5–8	Term	1398	34	0·35
9–12	Term	1311	36	0·38
Total		4260	33	0·35

* Items = "volumes".

Cataloguing (Books)

TABLE 2A

Library Q. Cataloguing for departmental libraries only: cataloguing and classification operation only, excluding typing and filing of slips. BNB copy from weekly lists (*not* cards) is used. F.t.e. staff = 4·6.

Weeks		Units: Items catalogued	Unit time m	Unit cost £
1–4	Term	323	78	0·71
5–8	Vacation (incl. Inspection)	397	56	0·56
9–12	Vacation	342	76	0·75
Total		1062	69	0·68

TABLE 2B1

Library R. Original cataloguing for main and departmental libraries. Net = cataloguing and classification only; gross = all processes, including supervision, typing and filing cards, labelling books. F.t.e. cataloguers = 5, auxiliary staff = 5·4.

Weeks		Units: Items catalogued	Unit time Net m	Unit time Gross m	Unit cost Net £	Unit cost Gross £
1–4	Vacation	1387	20	53	0·25	0·60
5–8	Term	1178	29	75	0·39	0·88
9–12	Term	1336	24	66	0·33	0·78
Total		3901	24	64	0·32	0·75

TABLE 2B2

Library R. Revision of catalogue. Includes relocation, recataloguing, reclassification as a result of the adoption of AACR, revision of classification schedules, transfers of material, etc. Definitions of "net" and "gross" as above. F.t.e. cataloguers = 3·4, auxiliary staff = 5·4.

		Units: Items revised	Unit time		Unit cost	
Weeks			Net m	Gross m	Net £	Gross
1–4	Vacation	993	15	58	0.13	0.57
5–8	Term	1717	12	41	0·11	0·42
9–12	Term	873	20	79	0·17	0·81
Total		3583	15	55	0·13	0·56

Binding preparation

Operations in these departments at both libraries are similar.

TABLE 3A

Library Q. All material is sent to commercial binders. F.t.e. staff = 3·9.

Weeks		Units: Items received from binders	Unit time m	Unit cost £
1–4	Term	1707	6	0·06
5–8	Vacation (incl. Inspection)	c. 1143*	8	0·09
9–12	Vacation	c. 1140*	9	0·10
Total		c. 3990*	7	0·08

* Figures based on estimates.

COSTING AND ECONOMICS

TABLE 3B

Library R. About 42% of material is sent to the Library's own bindery, but everything passes through this department. F.t.e. staff = 1·0.

Weeks		Units: Items received from binders	Unit time m	Unit cost £
1–4	Vacation	1663	5	0·03
5–8	Term	567	14	0·10
9–12	Term	467	12	0·09
Total		2697	8	0·06

Lending and Enquiries

Our figures for both libraries include time spent answering readers' enquiries, maintaining circulation records and recalling overdue books.

TABLE 4A

Library Q. There are a separate Reference Department and subject enquiry desks throughout the library, but enquiry times at these are not included here. Issue desk f.t.e. staff = 9·7.

Weeks		Units: Items borrowed	Unit time m	Unit cost £
1–4	Term	7042	9	0·08
5–8	Vacation (incl. Inspection)	2922	10	0·09
9–12	Vacation	4044	9	0·08
Total		14 008	10	0·08

TABLE 4B

Library R. There is no separate Reference Department, but enquiries about periodicals, government publications and law books are directed to the appropriate departments. F.t.e. staff = 3·7.

Weeks		Units: Items borrowed	Unit time m	Unit cost £
1–4	Vacation	2893	8	0·07
5–8	Term	8854	5	0·05
9–12	Term	10 704	3	0·03
Total		22 451	4*	0·04

* Further investigation has shown that the observed actual time for all issue and return processes is nearly 40 seconds per unit.

Inter-library loans

Costs and times cover all aspects of inter-library loans processes in Tables 5A and 5B. "Items received on inter-library loan" were selected as the primary units, since it was considered that the main function of i.l.l. activities in a library was to obtain books for readers of that library. However, times and costs include effort on providing books for other libraries and passing on unfilled requests.

TABLE 5A

Library Q. F.t.e. staff = 3·0.

Weeks		Units: Items received on i.l.l.	Unit time m	Unit cost £
1–4	Term	244	87	0·75
5–8	Vacation (incl. Inspection)	115	140	1·25
9–12	Vacation	190	92	0·74
Total		549	100	0·85

COSTING AND ECONOMICS 125

TABLE 5B1

Library R. F.t.e. staff = 2·0.

Weeks		Units: Items received on i.l.l.	Unit time m	Unit cost £
1–4	Vacation	144	78	0·78
5–8	Term	143	82	0·81
9–12	Term	197	58	0·64
Total		484	71	0·73

TABLE 5B2

In the following table, costs at Library R have been further broken down into inter-library borrowing and lending processes. The arrangement is similar to tables of inter-library loans costs in Williams' study of four American university libraries.[1]

Process	Number of f.t.e.s	Labour £	Items requested	Items filled	Cost per item requested	Cost per item filled
Borrowing	0·72*	249·21	593	484	0·42	0·51
Lending	0·61*	104·37	1031	487	0·10	0·21

* Not f.t.e. of gross hours (i.e. regular working hours), but f.t.e. of actual time spent on inter-library loans, as in Williams.

OTHER COSTING METHODS

Since it appears to be a difficult task to decide upon any period of the year which can be called "typical" for a university library, we think that labour costing of operations should be based upon fairly simple records kept over a fairly long period, not complex ones over a short time. During the course of our investigations, various exercises in both the USA and Britain have come to our attention. The most comprehensive of these was conducted in Colorado, as part of a feasibility study for a centralized book processing system for a group of academic libraries.[2] Detailed descriptions of methods and results were given for acquisitions, cataloguing and processing activities. There is a certain similarity between Colorado's "Daily Time–Function Record" and the LMRU individual secondary task record form. The diary study in these libraries, however, lasted only for two periods of five consecutive work days, compared with our twelve weeks. We found the chapter on current library operations and some of the appendices of results very useful for purposes of comparison, and we feel that the CALBPC list of

"Standardized technical processing activities" should be carefully considered as a possible basis for a national British standard list such as Aslib is interested in developing.[3] Two figures of particular interest from Colorado for comparison with LMRU results are the "mean normalized" and "standardized" times for original cataloguing and classifying, 19·9 minutes and 29·1 minutes. (Cf. our own 24 minutes net at Library R.)

A second study of acquisition and processing operations was carried out by Wynar and others at the University of Denver.[4] Only a summary article on this has been examined, but it appears that some form of "time and motion" study involving a diary technique was employed, with a manual of detailed instructions given to the library staff. At Denver in 1960 the acquisitions processes, excluding selection, came to a norm of c. 36 minutes, while original cataloguing took c. 25 minutes (cf. Library R, with 33 and 24 minutes). This report is one of the most useful we have found for comparative purposes. Cataloguing costs only were reported on by Peterman at the Waldo Library, Western Michigan University.[5] Here the labour cost per book "was determined from man hours utilized and was prorated from annual salary expenditure". All operations from accessioning to filing catalogue cards were examined, and a time of 66 minutes per book was arrived at, costing $3.20 in 1962 (cf. at Library R, 64 minutes at 75p in 1970). A very thorough costing operation on inter-library lending and acquisition of periodicals was conducted by Williams and others with information from four anonymous American university research libraries.[1] Aspects of this investigation which we found useful were the checklist of library functions and the related form to record allocation of employee time under these headings. Labour costs for four libraries were calculated from f.t.e. figures based upon the employees' time forms, which were completed by obtaining estimates of percentages of time (spent on serials acquisition, inter-library loans of serials) from every employee. The only direct comparison with our results can be seen for Library R in Table 5B2 above.

Other research which we have consulted during our study included the more instructional work of Burkhalter[6] and Dougherty and Heinritz.[7] The most relevant sections of these were Burkhalter's memo on effective labour costs, and three chapters on time study cost and performance standards in Dougherty and Heinritz. This latter textbook suggests observation with a stop-watch as the best method of time study, while the case studies in the former use very precise times, presumably obtained by an observer.

In the tables below (6A and 6B) we have tried to provide some comparison between our own costing technique and another method, generally accepted in Britain, especially in government departments. An operation has been chosen which does not differ greatly at each library, and from the twelve weeks of diary forms we have calculated the percentage of regular hours spent by staff on

COSTING AND ECONOMICS

acquisitions work. On the left of each table a gross unit cost has been derived from the mid-points of standardized salary scales and an annual output figure; on the right we have substituted the average salaries of actual grades in the library, as submitted to us by the Librarian.

It is thus possible to see the effect of real average salaries on the accepted costing method, compared with results obtained from standard, mean salaries. We can also set both of these gross unit costs against net costs calculated by our own technique; but we must first add about 10% to the net costs to cover employers' pension contributions.

Annual staff costs of existing acquisition systems

TABLE 6A

Library Q

Standard grades, mean salaries   *Actual grades, average salaries*

F.t.e.			£	£	
1	Sub-Librarian level (96%)*	salary	2665	2975	1 Sub-Librarian
		FSSU	265	297	
		Nat. Ins.	40	40	
2	Senior Library Assistant level (96%, 91·5%)*	salary	2500	2437	2 Senior Assistants
		pension	250	244	
		Nat. Ins.	78	78	
4¼	Library Assistant level (93%, 92·5%, 89%, 96%)*	salary	2919	3576	2 Assistants (p.t.)
		pension	—	—	3 Junior Assistants
		Nat. Ins.	164	164	
2	Clerical level (100%, 94·5%)*	salary	1397	1556	2 Clerical
		pension	140	156	
		Nat. Ins.	81	81	

Total labour cost, including queries   £10 499   £11 604

Assuming an intake of 20 500 items per year, based on items accessioned over 12 weeks, unit cost is   £0·51   £0·56

* Percentage of regular hours spent on acquisitions work.

TABLE 6B1

Library R
1. With Assistant Librarian

Standard grades, mean salaries   Actual grades, average salaries

F.t.e   £   £

F.t.e			£	£	
1	Sub-Librarian level (89·2%)*	salary	2462	2575	1 Sub-Librarian
		FSSU	246	257	
		Nat. Ins.	37	37	
1	Assistant Librarian level (96·8%)*	salary	1948	1875	1 Assistant Librarian
		FSSU	195	187	
		Nat. Ins.	40	40	
2	Library Assistant level (92·3%, 95·9%)*	salary	1393	1084	1 Library Assistant 1 Junior Library Assistant
		pension	—	—	
		Nat. Ins.	78	78	
1	Senior Clerical level (94·5%)*	salary	1087	1052	1 Clerical B
		pension	109	105	
		Nat. Ins.	39	39	
1	Clerical level (98·4%)*	salary	707	879	1 Clerical C
		pension	71	88	
		Nat. Ins.	40	40	

Total labour cost, including queries   £8452   £8336

Assuming an intake of 18 500 items
per year, based on items passed to
Cataloguing over 12 weeks, unit
cost is   £0·46   £0·45

2. With Senior Library Assistant

Standard grades, mean salaries   Actual grades, average salaries
                                              £   £

Total labour cost, including queries,
for all grades except Assistant
Librarian   6269   6234

1	Senior Library Assistant level (96·8%)*	salary	1291	1368	1 Senior Library Assistant
		pension	129	137	
		Nat. Ins.	40	40	

Total labour cost with SLA   £7729   £7779

Unit cost is therefore   £0·42   £0·42

* Percentage of regular hours spent on acquisitions work.

CONCLUSIONS AND FURTHER RESEARCH

We have in the course of our research amplified and refined our original objectives of the method of assessing "administrative effectiveness". Labour costs per unit of output have been assessed, with costs based on actual salaries, not merely a departmental average rate. The work rate of a department, section or individual can be simply summarized on forms such as those shown in Figures 1 and 2, using information taken from staff diary forms. Time required to clear outstanding work is readily estimated by multiplying waiting units by unit times discovered for recorded or primary tasks. A department's spare capacity may be assessed by recording all its operations and finding the time remaining, or by comparing unit times of primary tasks under ordinary conditions with unit times obtained in a controlled experiment. The extent of inter-departmental staff exchanges and absence from a department are clearly shown on the forms in Figures 2 and 3, which are compiled from individual diaries and departmental records.

After a pilot study and two full-scale tests, we have come near to the point when a practical "package" can be offered to any university librarian who wants to examine his operations and costs without calling in a team of consultants. However, before a package is quite ready, we should like to have national agreement on certain parts of its contents. For example, we have found that when a full-scale costing and standard time operation is required for one process or for a whole system, some form of flow process chart should be compiled to cover all procedures under review. Also, as we have suggested already, a generally agreed list of task definitions is an essential foundation, if any useful inter-library comparisons are to be made. The LMRU is currently co-operating with Aslib's Research Department, who have, through their consultancy work in various types of libraries, built up a valuable reserve of experience in the field of task definitions.[3, 8] Further approval would be required on the most suitable "statistics" or units of output, and on some standard method of computing salaries. The blessing of SCONUL, or some equivalent body, would be a final and very significant complement to the package.

The proposed package would most probably consist of the following: a set of instructions on flow charting, with specifications of forms; a checklist of library tasks; a list of units of output, input and service given; a set of form specifications for the diary recording method; full instructions on installation and running; and specifications of tables for analysis and notes on the method. Results would, of course, be completely within the knowledge and control of the library concerned, but private comparisons with other libraries would be possible, and SCONUL would be able to collect results if general approval was obtained.

"Statistics" are currently being given much consideration in the university library world. Our opinion is that there are three types of statistical units which could usefully be recorded, not only for the purposes of costing, but also for broader inter-library comparisons: (1) that which causes a library process to be put into operation; (2) that which represents the end product of a process (e.g.

a book ready for use); and (3) that which indicates the amount of service given (e.g. inter-library loan request filled).

We suggest that any library carrying out an investigation into all its subsystems would be well advised to conduct installation, maintenance and analysis at a departmental level, to spread the total work required. Obviously analysis will take the most time, but we have found that for every member of staff only about 42 minutes are required for analysis.

REFERENCES

[1] Williams, G., *and others*. *Library cost models: owning versus borrowing serial publications*. National Science Foundation, 1968.

[2] Leonard, L. E., *and others*. *Centralized book processing: a feasibility study based on Colorado academic libraries*. Scarecrow P., 1969. 45–88, 257–333.

[3] Gilchrist, A. Work study in libraries. *J. Librarianship*, 2 (2) April 1970, 126–138.

[4] Wynar, B. S., *and others*. Cost analysis in a technical services division. *Lib. Res. Tech. Serv.*, 7 (4) Fall 1963, 312–326.

[5] Peterman, E. A study of the cataloguing costs in the Waldo Library, Western Michigan University. Brief details in *Lib. Res. Tech. Serv.*, 14 (1) Winter 1970, 63.

[6] Burkhalter, B. R., *editor*. *Case studies in systems analysis in a university library*. Scarecrow P., 1968. 9–10.

[7] Dougherty, R. M., *and* Heinritz, F. J. *Scientific management of library operations*. Scarecrow P., 1966. 99–114, 150–181.

[8] Thomas, P. A. *A procedural model for the use of bibliographic records in libraries*. Aslib, 1970.

Figure 1

DEPARTMENT		NAME				
SECTION		GRADE				
PERIOD		£ PER HR.				
			h. m.	h. m.	h. m.	
BASIC	Full Time Part Time Temporary					
		TOTAL				
GAINED	Work by					
		TOTAL				
GROSS AVAILABLE TIME						
LOST	Compensatory Time Off Leave Sick Leave Other Absence					
		TOTAL				
LENT	Work for					
		TOTAL				
ALL TIME LOST AND LENT						
NET AVAILABLE TIME						
RECORDED (SECONDARY) TASKS						
		TOTAL				
TIME REMAINING (FOR PRIMARY TASKS)						
			Units	Units	Units	
INPUT OUTPUT						

FIGURE 2

			h. m.	£	h. m.
BASIC	Full Time Part Time Temporary				
		TOTAL			
GAINED	Work by				
		TOTAL			
GROSS AVAILABLE TIME					
LOST	Compensatory Time Off Leave Sick Leave Other Absence				
		TOTAL			
LENT	Work for				
		TOTAL			
ALL TIME LOST AND LENT					
NET AVAILABLE TIME					
RECORDED (SECONDARY) TASKS					
		TOTAL			
TIME REMAINING (FOR PRIMARY TASKS)					
				Units	U
INPUT OUTPUT					

Figure 3

TIME CATEGORY OR ACTIVITY			h.	m.	£	Units	h
BASIC	Full Time					—	
	Part Time					—	
	Temporary					—	
	TOTAL					—	
GAINED	Paid Overtime					—	
	Unpaid Overtime					—	
	TOTAL					—	
LOST	Leave					—	
	Sick Leave					—	
	Other Absence					—	
	TOTAL					—	
NET AVAILABLE TIME						—	
TIME REDISTRIBUTED WITHIN LIBRARY						—	
READER SERVICES	Circulation						
	Reference						
	Short Loan Coll.						
	Inter-Library Loans	Borrowing					
		Lending					
		TOTAL					
	TOTAL						
TECHNICAL SERVICES	Acquisitions (Books)						
	Accounts						
	Cataloguing and Classification						
	Catalogue Entry Preparation						
	Labelling etc.						
	Binding Preparation						
	TOTAL						
MIXED SERVICES	Periodicals						
	Government Publications						
	TOTAL						
RESHELVING AND MOVING BOOKS							
TIME REMAINING							

FERDINAND F. LEIMKUHLER and MICHAEL D. COOPER

Cost Accounting and Analysis for University Libraries

The approach to library planning studied in this paper is the use of accounting models to measure library costs and implement program budgets. A cost-flow model for a university library is developed and tested with historical data from the General Library at the University of California, Berkeley. Various comparisons of an exploratory nature are made of the unit costs and total costs for different parts of the Berkeley system.

THE COST-FLOW ACCOUNTING MODEL

THERE DOES NOT APPEAR to be any uniform method by which libraries account for their internal costs. Considerable attention is given to the development of budgets along organizational lines and to the control of expenditures for labor and materials. But these data are not used to measure the cost of performing some function or rendering some service in the manner of industrial cost accounting. For example, in order to estimate the cost of holding a journal and to compare it with the cost of using a regional lending service, Williams[4] had to develop his own basic data in four libraries by means of interviews and other sampling techniques. In their recent study of the M.I.T. Libraries, Raffel and Shishko[3] had to augment the existing data base considerably in order to estimate the cost of various library functions and programs. In addition, the papers of Penner[2] and Landau[1] provide a good review of previous cost studies.

A basic notion in the development of a cost control system is the idea of a "cost center" for which there is a clear definition of function and responsibility. The cost centers serve as focal points in the system for the collection and evaluation of cost data. There appear to be two major kinds of cost centers in libraries: processing centers and service centers. The processing centers serve an intermediate role in the flow of resources to the service centers, and all of their costs are passed on to the service units. The service centers can include branch libraries or specialized facilities within a central library. These units offer a schedule of services to certain users at certain "prices" which together comprise the output of the library. A library program may be identified with a single service unit or may cut across several or all units. Shishko divided the mission of the M.I.T. Libraries between research and instruction without subdi-

Reprinted by permission of the American Library Association and the authors from *College & Research Libraries* 32(6): 449–464 (Nov. 1971).

viding it by subject area. In a branch library system most branches would contribute to both research and instructional programs and their individual output would have to be divided under the two main headings, if this is desired. In accounting for costs and developing costs of service estimates it is important that these figures be related to a true decision-making function in the organization; that is, they should have a quality called "accountability." It is meaningless to develop numbers about which nothing can be done.

A simplified cost accounting plan for modelling the flow of cost through a library organization is shown in Figure 1. This plan incorporates the notion of standard cost as a measure of performance. The standard costs are based on the number of items processed, acquired, or held by the library unit. Other measures of performance could be used to gauge the flow of costs. These standards should be evaluated each year and modified accordingly so as to provide the best estimate of what is expected for the next year. "Variance" accounts can be used to collect the difference between what is expected and actually occurs; that is, between standard cost and "full" cost. This is a common and useful way to maintain control over costs and to generate management-by-exception reports. In Figure 1 only one variance account is shown for each category, but in practice one may develop separate variance measures for the amount and the unit cost of a flow. For example, if labor is costed at different wage rates for different kinds of labor hours used, it would be possible to maintain separate variance accounts for the wage rate and the labor hours to explain total labor variance. Standard costing assumes that the cost is directly proportional to the basis for unit cost; however, routine corrections can be made to account for any predictable bias from the variance figures.

A Cost Model of the Berkeley Libraries

The cost accounting plan in Figure 1 was applied to the Libraries of the University of California at Berkeley in order to show how costs are generated and flow through the system to the various branch and special libraries. The resulting simplified cost model of the Berkeley Libraries is shown in Figure 2. No variance accounts are included in this model, since it is based on the cost history of a single year. However, variance accounts and standard costing could be introduced. The model conforms closely to the organizational structure of the Berkeley Libraries except in the case of the Serials and Documents Department, where a division had to be made between their function as a central processing unit and their function as a special service unit for readers. A similar division was made at the branch libraries to separate the cost of selecting and accessioning new items from the cost of maintaining and providing service from the shelved collection.

The main kinds of costs in the model are the direct costs for materials and labor and the indirect costs for space and overhead. The costs of space and university overhead do not enter into the ordinary budget estimates of operating costs, but they are important parts of the total cost of operating libraries and cannot be ignored. All space for the libraries was costed at the same unit price except for the depository space, and the university overhead was applied at a uniform rate. This permitted the development of a total labor, space, and overhead figure for each organizational unit of the library.

The main distinction in the flow of materials is between monographs and serials, and between purchased items and gift and exchange items, although the latter distinction is dropped after acquisition processing. For serials, a dis-

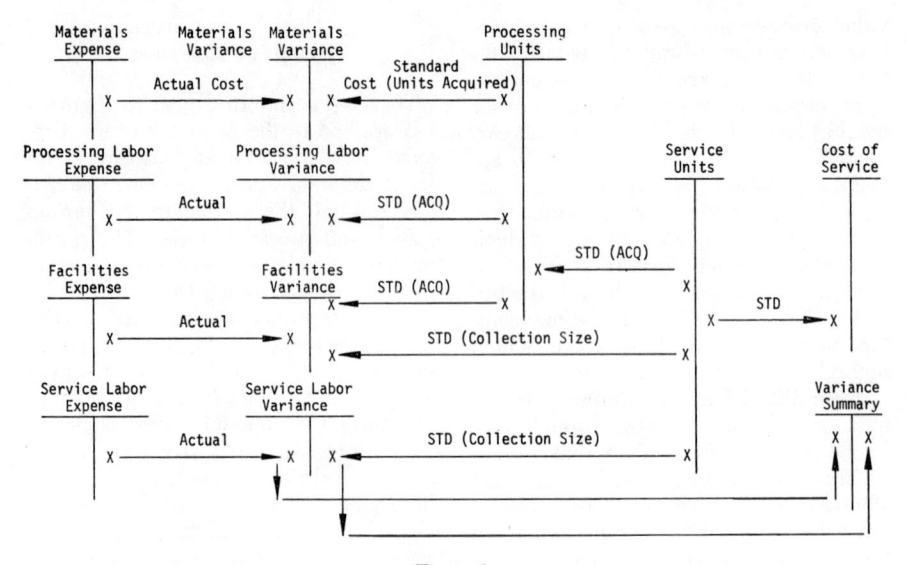

Figure 1
FLOW OF LIBRARY COSTS IN A SIMPLIFIED STANDARD COST ACCOUNTING PLAN

tinction is maintained between new items and continuing items because of the difference in cataloging treatment. The total number of items and their distribution through the system are based on data from the annual reports of the Berkeley Libraries for the year July 1, 1967, to June 30, 1968 (1967/1968), although in some instances it was necessary to develop estimates from the Libraries' files of orders.

DIRECT COSTS: MATERIALS

Materials costs for the Berkeley library are limited to two classes of items: monographs and serials. Any type of library material for which a standing order can be placed is considered a serial.

Through the budgeting process each branch library is allocated money for purchase of monographs. For each branch a branch fund is maintained from which all disbursements are made. In all, more than 150 funds are used for materials purchasing for the General Library.

Each order for a monograph may call for the receipt of one or more volumes. A random sampling procedure was undertaken to determine the number of volumes per order. Eighteen hundred orders from thirteen funds were examined. From this data, the number of volumes per order was determined to be 1.20. Certain funds such as those used to buy back sets and serials and duplicate copies of high usage monographs had significantly different ratios—2.20 for both. For these funds, the latter factor was used.

Table 1 summarizes the number of monographs acquired during the fiscal year 1967/1968. The average price per monograph for the Berkeley General Library was $7.44, for a total of 81,350 items acquired. The number of items acquired by the branches was 21 percent of the total, while expenditures were 20 percent of the total ($605,588).

COSTING AND ECONOMICS

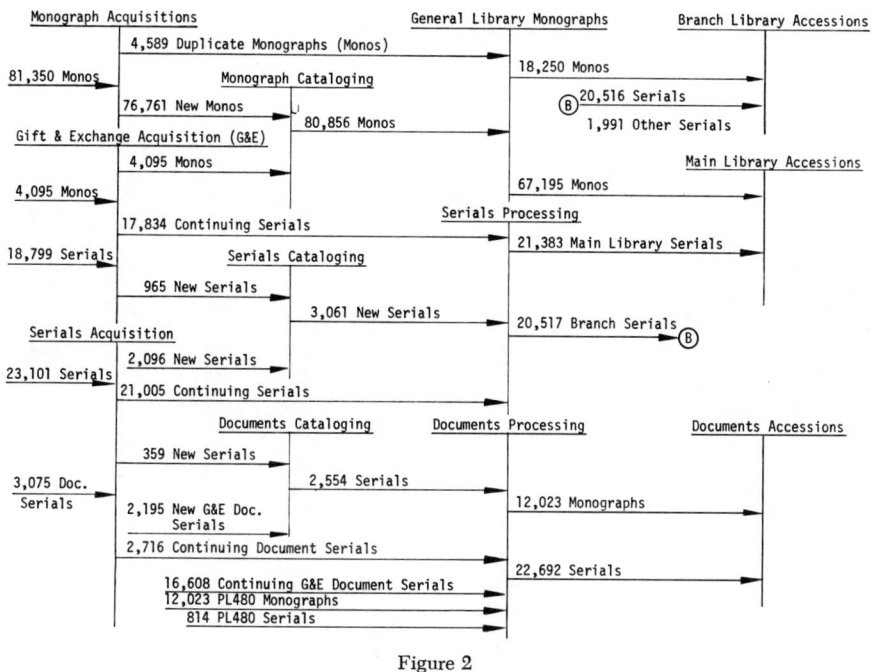

Figure 2
ITEMS PROCESSED

A second category of materials that enter into the library system is serials. To determine the average price per paid serial for the libraries, a sample of the order file of 25,450 cards was taken. Of the 1,378 orders (5.4 percent) examined, 975 (3.8 percent) were found to be related to items received and paid for in the 1967/1968 fiscal year. The results of the sample are also shown in Table 1. The average price of a serial received by a branch library was $27.23 while all other General Library units averaged $13.13 per serial. The overall average price per serial was $20.01.

Williams [1968] reports that for the four university libraries he sampled, the subscription prices per title year were $12.62, $22.62, $21.55, and $17.06.

In addition to paid serials representing 54 percent of the total received, more than 19,000 serials are received through gift and exchange operations. Table 2 shows the distribution of all serial items across branches.

DIRECT COSTS: LABOR

Aside from materials cost, the second component of direct costs is labor. The Berkeley library divides the labor force into three classes: professional, nonprofessional, and general assistance. Almost all student employees are hired in the general assistance category. Mean salary rates per year for each category are shown in Table 3. The nonprofessional category includes the "library assistant" job titles as well as secretary, bookmender, editor, etc.

Organization charts for the library, in conjunction with published salary

TABLE 1
Monograph and Serials Purchase Costs 1967/1968

Branch Library	Number of New Monographs Purchased (vol.)	Purchase Expenditure ($) for Monographs	Unit Price for Monographs	Number of Items in Serials Sample	Cost of Serials Items Sampled ($)/Year	Sample Cost/Serial Title/Year
Agriculture (AG)	790	5,879	7.44	48	2,682	55.88[1]
Art/Anthropology (A/A)	812	5,217	6.42	13	96	7.38
Astronomy/Math/Stat (AMS)	390	3,550	9.10	15	309	20.60
Biochemistry (BIOCHEM)	72	930	12.92	9	231	25.67
Biology (BIOL)	658	6,358	9.66	76	2,848	37.47[2]
Chemistry (CHEM)	181	2,373	13.11	22	535	24.32
Earth Sciences (ES)	489	4,065	8.31	9	85	9.44
East Asiatic (EAL)	4,665	21,620	4.63	28	455	16.25
Education/Psychology (E/P)	1,841	9,878	5.37	40	351	8.78
Engineering (ENG)	713	8,670	12.16	55	2,118	38.51
Entomology (ENT)	NA	NA	NA	NA	NA	NA
Environmental Design (ED)	1,564	11,925	7.62	28	1,376	49.14
Forestry (FOR)	272	2,706	9.95	14	188	13.43
Graduate Soc. Sci. (GSSL)	1,468	9,607	6.54	32	360	11.25
Library School (LSL)	465	1,857	3.99	22	374	23.38
Music (MUS)	1,258	11,922	9.48	14	171	12.21
Optometry (OPT)	195	1,716	8.80	2	12	6.00
Physics (PHY)	313	3,284	10.49	13	259	19.92
Public Health	976	7,522	7.71	26	441	16.96
Social Welfare/Crim (SW)	425	2,347	5.52	10	71	7.10
Branch Libraries Total	17,547	121,426	6.95	476	12,962	27.23
Main Library Total	63,803	484,162	7.59	499	6,550	13.13
TOTAL	81,350	605,588	7.44	975	19,512	20.01

[1] Includes one $2,000 item.
[2] Includes one $1,250 item.

schedules, were used to calculate the direct labor cost per branch and main library unit (see Tables 4 and 5). To the extent that the organization charts do not reflect the true staffing situation, and to the extent that the mean salary figures do not represent the true salaries, the data in Tables 4 and 5 are biased.

Total direct labor expenditure amounts to $3.6 million, and of this, 22 percent is branch labor. Of the 120 Full Time Equivalent (FTE) employees in the branches, 31 percent are professional, 39 percent are nonprofessional, and 30 percent are general assistance. The 443 FTE for the Main Library is made up of 22 percent professionals, 49 percent nonprofessionals, and 29 percent general assistance.

INDIRECT COSTS: OVERHEAD AND SPACE

The cost of library building space is estimated to be about $5.00 per square foot per year. This figure is intended to represent current replacement value of the building space including equipment and fixtures and the cost of utilities and maintenance. The simplified method used to make this estimate is shown below. The numbers used were obtained from the studies by Raffel and Shishko[3] and Williams,[4] and from consultation with the Berkeley and University Architects Offices, the Berkeley Grounds and Building Office, and the University Real Estate Office. These numbers, however,

COSTING AND ECONOMICS

TABLE 2
SIZE OF THE GENERAL LIBRARY
JUNE 30, 1968

Branch Library	Volumes	Current Serials	Total Items[2]	Ratio of Volumes to Serials
Agriculture	63,799	2,437	66,236	26.18
Art/Anthropology	27,024	1,158	28,182	23.34
Astronomy/Math/Stat	24,574	827	25,401	29.71
Biochemistry	5,427	140	5,567	38.76
Biology	144,090	3,221	147,311	44.73
Chemistry	18,342	335	18,677	54.75
Earth Sciences	42,199	977	43,176	43.19
East Asiatic	241,811	1,237	243,048	19.55
Education/Psychology	65,455	1,385	66,840	47.26
Engineering	63,162	1,638	64,800	38.56
Entomology	8,579	246	8,825	34.87
Environmental Design	50,728	1,293	52,021	39.23
Forestry	20,281	1,334	21,615	15.20
Graduate Social Sciences	39,014	2,616	41,630	14.91
Library School	25,520	2,014	27,534	12.67
Music	70,360	197	70,557	357.16
Optometry	2,872	82	2,954	35.02
Physics	15,276	190	15,466	80.40
Public Health	41,111	906	42,017	45.38
Social Welfare/Crim	12,857	275	13,132	46.75
Branch Total	982,481	22,508	1,004,989	43.65
Main Building	2,200,562	44,075[1]	2,244,637	49.93
Total General Library	3,183,043	66,583	3,249,626	47.81

[1] Includes 22,692 documents.
[2] A serial title is considered as an item.

TABLE 3
SALARY SCHEDULE

Title	1967/1968 Mean Salary ($) Per Year
Professional	
Librarian I	$ 7,075
Librarian II	8,450
Librarian III	9,975
Librarian IV	11,575
Librarian V	13,725
Nonprofessional	
Library Assistant I	5,250
Library Assistant II	6,078
Library Assistant III	7,044
General Assistance	
Clerk	4,650

are not to be considered as official or certified figures in any sense, but only as representative cost figures for the purpose of analysis.

The annual cost for the Richmond Inter-Campus Library Facility ICLF(N) is estimated to be about $2.50 per square foot per year to cover the cost of purchase, remodeling, equipment, utilities, and maintenance. Tables 4 and 5 summarize the space costs for the General Library.

In addition to direct labor costs, the library incurs expenses for fringe benefits and salary administrative overhead for its employees. Discussions with the University Office of the Vice President for Planning and Analysis indicated that administrative overhead is approximately 10 percent of direct labor cost. Salary administrative overhead ranges between 9 and 13 percent of direct labor, depending on job title. This study assumed that administrative overhead was 10 percent. Thus, fringe benefits plus administration total 20 percent.

Within the library itself, the costs of the librarian's office, the business office, the personnel office, and the space used by these departments were considered as part of the library overhead charge. In addition, supplies and general ex-

TABLE 4
LABOR AND SPACE COSTS—MAIN LIBRARY 1967/1968

Main Library Unit	Total FTE	Total Direct Salary Expenditures ($)	Total Assignable Square Feet (ASF)	Total Annual Space Cost at $5.00/ Square Foot
Acquisitions Department	66.75	481,763	13,793	68,965
Bancroft Library	35.075	249,355	31,599	157,995
Business Office	17.375	105,742	4,358	21,790
Catalog Department	76.75	500,420	6,375	31,875
Catalogs (Public)	—	—	9,899	49,495
Documents Department	26.045	162,584	31,064	155,320
General Reference Service	17.25	128,369	3,066	15,330
Inter-Campus Library Facility North (ICLF) Depository	3.50	16,875	55,840	139,600[2]
Librarians Office	6.75	83,891[1]	1,566	7,830
Library Pers. Office	3.375	23,470	447	2,235
Library Photo. Service	23.50	141,285	4,665	23,325
Loan Department	88.125	464,667	100,901	504,505
Morrison Library	3.745	20,708	5,487	27,435
Reading Rooms	—	—	16,748	83,740
Serials Department	69.125	381,007	31,440	157,200
Storage Selection	1.25	5,813	—	—
Undergrad. Library Selection Project	4.50	32,906	4,791	23,955
Total Main Library	443.115	2,798,855	322,039	1,470,595

[1] Estimated.
[2] Total annual cost of $2.50 per square foot.

TABLE 5
LABOR AND SPACE COSTS—BRANCH LIBRARIES 1967/1968

Branch Library	Total FTE	Total Direct Salary Expenditure ($)	Total ASF	Total Annual Space Cost at $5.00/ Square Foot
Agriculture	4.805	33,009	7,746	38,730
Art/Anthropology	4.045	24,387	5,307	26,535
Astronomy/Math/Stat	3.94	23,783	4,009	20,045
Biochemistry	.512	4,014	1,503	7,515
Biology	14.225	81,617	21,480	107,400
Chemistry	3.08	19,276	11,025	55,125
Earth Sciences	3.08	20,104	5,782	28,910
East Asiatic	18.875	153,834	13,698	68,490
Education/Psyc.	13.50	84,532	13,308	66,540
Engineering	5.875	35,498	6,125	30,625
Entomology	1.52	9,947	1,796	8,980
Environmental Des.	8.08	54,376	14,522	72,610
Forestry	4.97	37,436	5,319	26,595
Grad. Soc. Sci.	11.69	77,415	23,713	118,565
Library School	2.75	17,679	3,321	16,605
Music	6.375	44,096	8,858	44,290
Optometry	1.03	6,897	1,014	5,070
Physics	3.58	23,958	4,833	24,165
Public Health	5.64	36,149	7,873	39,365
Social Welfare	3.20	17,439	4,205	21,025
Total Branch Library	120.772	805,446	165,437	827,185
Total Main Library	443.115	2,798,855	322,039	1,470,595
TOTAL	563.887	3,604,301	487,476	2,297,780

Cost of on-campus or nearby real estate	$12.00 per gross sq. ft.
Total building construction project cost	38.00 per gross sq. ft.
Total building and site cost	$50.00 per gross sq. ft.
Assignable space factor with 80 percent utilization	1.25
Effective cost of assignable space	$62.50 per sq. ft.
Cost of fixtures, furniture, shelving, etc.	4.00 per sq. ft.
Total initial cost of space and furnishings	$66.50 per sq. ft.
Capital recovery factor	0.06
Equivalent annual cost of space and furnishings	$ 3.99 per sq. ft. per yr.
Annual cost of utilities and maintenance	1.00 per sq. ft. per yr.
Total annual cost for library building space	$ 4.99 per sq. ft. per yr.

penses as well as equipment and fixtures were included in the overhead charge and allocated to library units on a salary basis. The overhead charges for these departments and items amounted to 21 percent. The total overhead charge for library units was 41 percent (20 percent + 21 percent).

PROCESSING COST CENTERS: ACQUISITION AND CATALOGING COSTS

As materials are introduced into the processing centers of the library, they undergo transformations which ultimately result in items ready for circulation. Figure 2 shows the flow of items through the processing centers, and Table 6 indicates unit costs. The monographs and/or serials enter at each processing center. To these "raw materials" is added a labor, space, and overhead charge. Thus, as a unit passes out of the processing center, a value is added corresponding to the cost of processing the item.

For purposes of the model, monographs are considered to be acquired from two sources—purchases and gifts. Purchased monographs enter the system at a cost of $7.44 per item. Gift monographs enter at zero cost per item. To the direct material cost for purchased monographs is added a labor and space charge of $3.04 per item. The $3.04 is the cost for the Administrative and Processing Divisions of the Acquisitions Department, plus overhead.

New monographs enter the cataloging department from the Gifts Division and the normal acquisition ordering procedure. Once in the cataloging department, a labor, space, and overhead charge of $5.40 per monograph is added. Binding, selection, and other miscellaneous charges are also added.

A monograph acquired by a branch has a final cost of $25.00, while a monograph acquired by the main library costs $19.85.

Similar flows can be observed for serials and documents. A paid serial has an

TABLE 6
UNIT COSTS

	Monographs	Serials
Purchase Price	$ 7.44	$20.00
Selection		
Main Library	2.84	2.84
Branch Library	4.00	4.00
Acquisition Labor and Space	3.04	2.65
Cataloging Labor and Space	5.40	49.61
Serials Check-In Labor and Space		3.04
Miscellaneous		
Binding	1.54	5.03
Postage, Insurance, Taxes	.15	.15
Total*		
Main Library	19.85	33.87
Branch Library	25.01	39.03

* Columns do not add to total since not all units are processed by all departments.

initial subscription cost of $20.00. After cataloging for a new serial and processing (check in/entering) for all serials, the branch cost is raised to $39.03 and the main library cost becomes $33.87.

Miscellaneous charges include binding expenditures as well as postage, insurance, and taxes on acquisitions. Binding charges are made up of the cost to operate the bindery, the Bindery Preparation Division, and the Binding Pickup Department. Including space and overhead charges, this amounts to $337,197 for 55,880 items bound (excluding mending). When the total expenditure is divided between monographs and serials in the ratio 20,899 to 34,981 (1 to 1.67) and the resulting cost divided by the total monograph and serial items processed, a cost of $1.54 per monograph and $5.03 per serial results. These amounts represent proportional charges for future binding that a processed item incurs.

In addition to binding and postage charges, a received serial has added to it a charge reflecting its check-in cost. This amounts to $3.24 per serial title per year.

Service Cost Centers: Main Library and Branch Libraries Costs

Once the labor and space costs have been established for the processing functions, it is then possible to determine the service costs and the total library costs. Tables 7 and 8 summarize the total library cost for the system. Out of a total of $8.3 million, $3.7 million (46 percent) is spent in the process of acquisition of materials. Of this, only $1.2 million (14 percent) is for the purchase of raw materials, i.e., monographs and serials.

Total acquisition cost of $3.7 million has three components: materials cost, labor cost, and space cost. Materials are either monographs or serials, and enter the system at a unit price of $7.44 and $20.00, respectively. Gift items enter at zero cost. Acquisition labor cost includes the cost of all units involved in processing the items; i.e., acquisitions processing, cataloging, serials processing, documents processing, and branch processing. The space cost is that associated with each of the processing units.

Branch labor acquisition cost was determined by means of interviews with each branch librarian. The librarian was asked to indicate what percentage of time each employee spent in the acquisitions process. This time was intended to reflect the cost of selection of materials, typing of orders, and other associated tasks. The cost of branch processing of items (cataloging, filing, etc.) was estimated from a survey of three branch libraries.

Service labor and service space costs reflect the cost of providing service to the patron. This is in distinction to the total processing cost which reflects the cost of obtaining and processing raw materials.

Comparison of the Costs of Circulation, Holding, and Acquisition

Several measures have been selected for use in evaluating the performance of the library and aiding in planning and analysis. If the total cost for the branch service operations is divided by the total number of items held, a measure of the holding and acquisition cost per item is obtained. Figure 3 plots this relationship for the branch libraries. The plot exhibits a declining cost per item held as the number of items held by the library increases. Evidently some economies of scale are present. The smallest branch library, Optometry, has the second highest cost among all branches ($7.05). (Libraries cited are circled in subsequent figures to aid the reader in interpreting the data.) The Graduate Social Science Library has the

TABLE 7
Total Library Cost—Branch Libraries
1967/1968

Branch	Service Labor Cost	Service Space Cost	Total[*] Processing Cost	Total Library Cost
Agriculture	21,372	37,749	115,916	175,037
Art/Anthropology	18,886	25,931	66,572	111,389
Astronomy/Math/Stat	23,938	19,674	42,553	86,165
Biochemistry	3,997	7,450	7,364	18,811
Biology	84,942	106,226	143,041	334,209
Chemistry	23,129	54,967	17,850	95,946
Earth Sciences	16,859	28,462	51,007	96,328
East Asiatic	171,330	66,714	165,330	403,374
Education/Psychology	93,595	65,543	102,532	261,670
Engineering	31,657	29,908	82,706	144,271
Entomology	12,131	8,906	9,601	30,638
Environmental Design	53,969	71,728	91,641	217,338
Forestry	40,311	26,109	59,216	125,636
Graduate Social Sciences	77,108	117,313	140,752	335,173
Library School	5,646	15,854	90,856	112,356
Music	50,456	43,833	70,476	164,765
Optometry	7,515	4,984	8,325	20,824
Physics	29,777	24,009	15,666	69,452
Public Health	36,078	38,785	61,061	135,924
Social Welfare	19,022	20,808	21,934	61,764
Branch Total	821,718	814,953	1,364,399	3,001,070
Main Total	1,618,531	1,282,612	2,425,481	5,328,624
TOTAL	2,440,249	2,097,565	3,789,880	8,327,694

[*] Includes materials, labor, space, and overhead costs connected with nonservice activities.

TABLE 8
Total Library Cost—Main Library
1967/1968

Unit	Service Labor Cost	Service Space Cost	Total Materials Acquisition Cost	Total Library Cost
Central Collection				
Loan Department	$ 435,940	$ 430,115		
Public Catalog		49,495		
Reading Rooms		83,740		
Reference Department	181,000	14,050		
Reserve Book Room	196,224	49,240		
Humanities Grad. Service	23,045	25,150		
Bancroft Library	301,310	125,360		
Rare Books Room	33,249	30,495		
Mark Twain Collection	17,030	2,140		
Morrison Library	29,198	27,435		
Serials Department	49,425	43,482		
Newspapers Room	48,799	95,870		
Undergrad. Library Project			$ 76,783	
Documents Department	61,469	128,790	353,586	
Maps Room	10,640	16,325		
Library Photo Service	199,212	23,325		
ICLF(N) Depository	23,794	139,600		
Storage Selection	8,196			
Subtotal	1,618,531	1,284,612	430,369	
Main Library Materials Acquisition			1,995,112	
Total	$1,618,531	$1,284,612	$2,425,481	$5,328,624

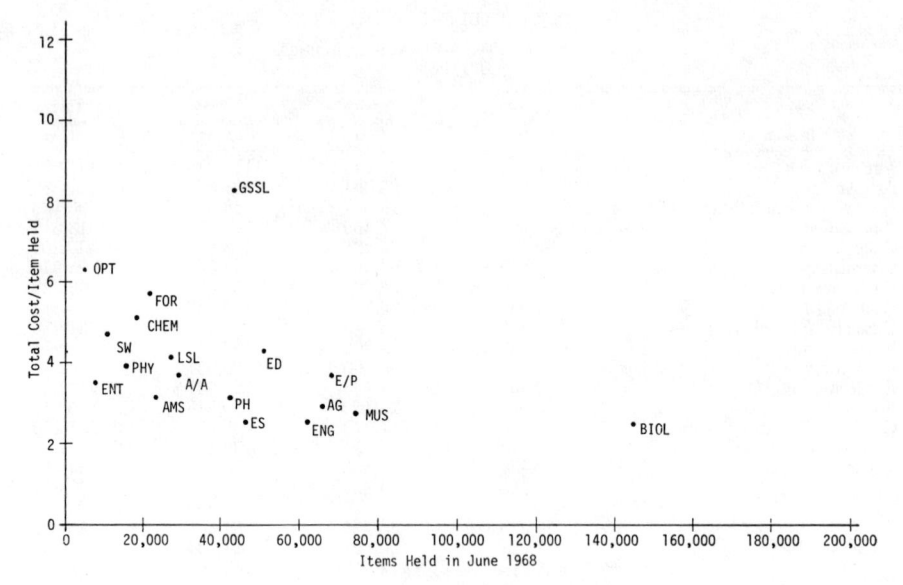

Figure 3
TOTAL COST PER ITEM HELD

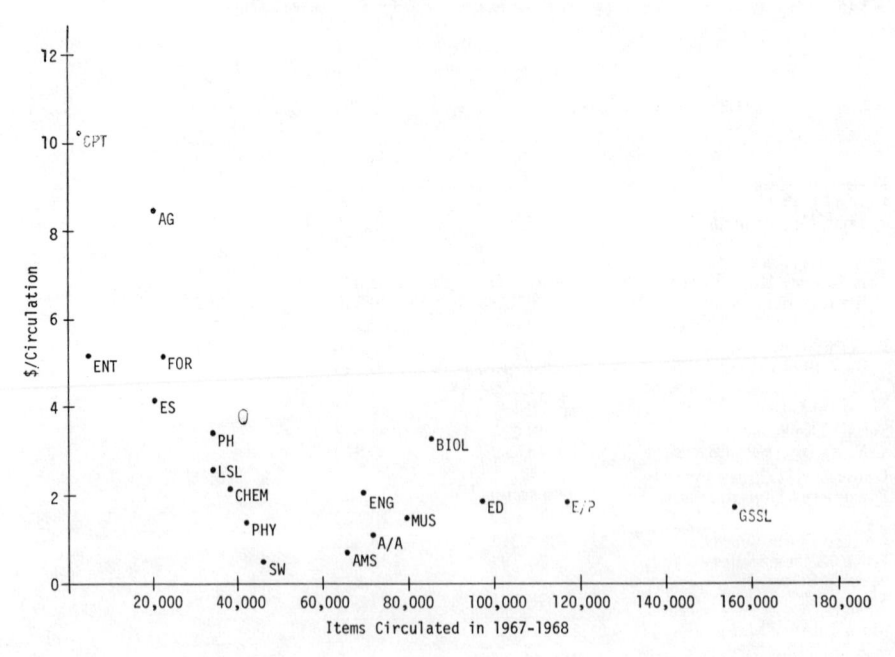

Figure 4
TOTAL COST PER UNIT OF CIRCULATION

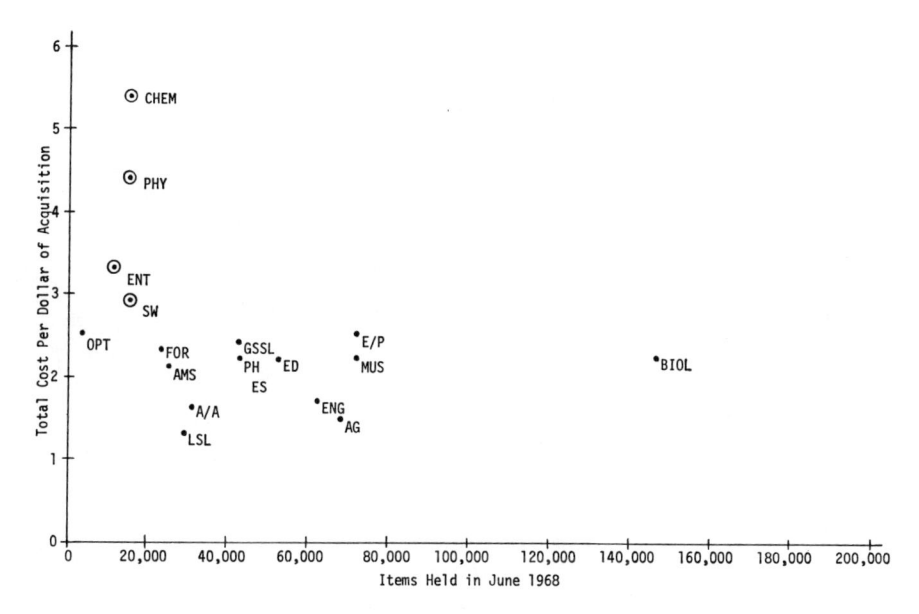

FIGURE 5

TOTAL COST PER DOLLAR OF ACQUISITION

highest cost per item held, but this can be accounted for by the large amount of unused stack capacity of the library. The largest branch library (not shown on graph), East Asiatic, has the lowest cost per item held ($1.66).

Branch libraries average $2.99 while the main library averages $2.37 per item held. The overall average holding cost per item is $2.56.

The total cost per unit of circulation is plotted for branch libraries in Figure 4. Each data point represents the total cost of the branch service center divided by the total circulation for that branch. The average cost per unit of circulation is $3.53 for the General Library. Main library cost is $4.16 per item, while branch cost is $2.77.

The minimum cost per unit of circulation is reached for branches having 50,000 to 70,000 circulations per year. The highest cost per unit of circulation is recorded for the branch library having the smallest circulation. The branch library with the highest circulation, the Graduate Social Sciences Library, has a cost of $2.07 per unit of circulation as compared with the $2.77 average branch cost.

Total cost per dollar of acquisition is calculated as the total library cost by branch divided by the total acquisition cost for that branch. A lower cost per dollar of acquisition reflects the fact that more money is being put into materials than labor or space. Figure 5 shows that the Library School Library devotes a major share of its resources to acquisition. The Chemistry library, on the other hand, spends a small amount of money on acquisitions relative to labor and space. In general, small branches (Social Welfare, Entomology, Physics, and Chemistry) exhibit a much higher than average cost per dollar of

Figure 6
VOLUMES—FTE BY BRANCH LIBRARY

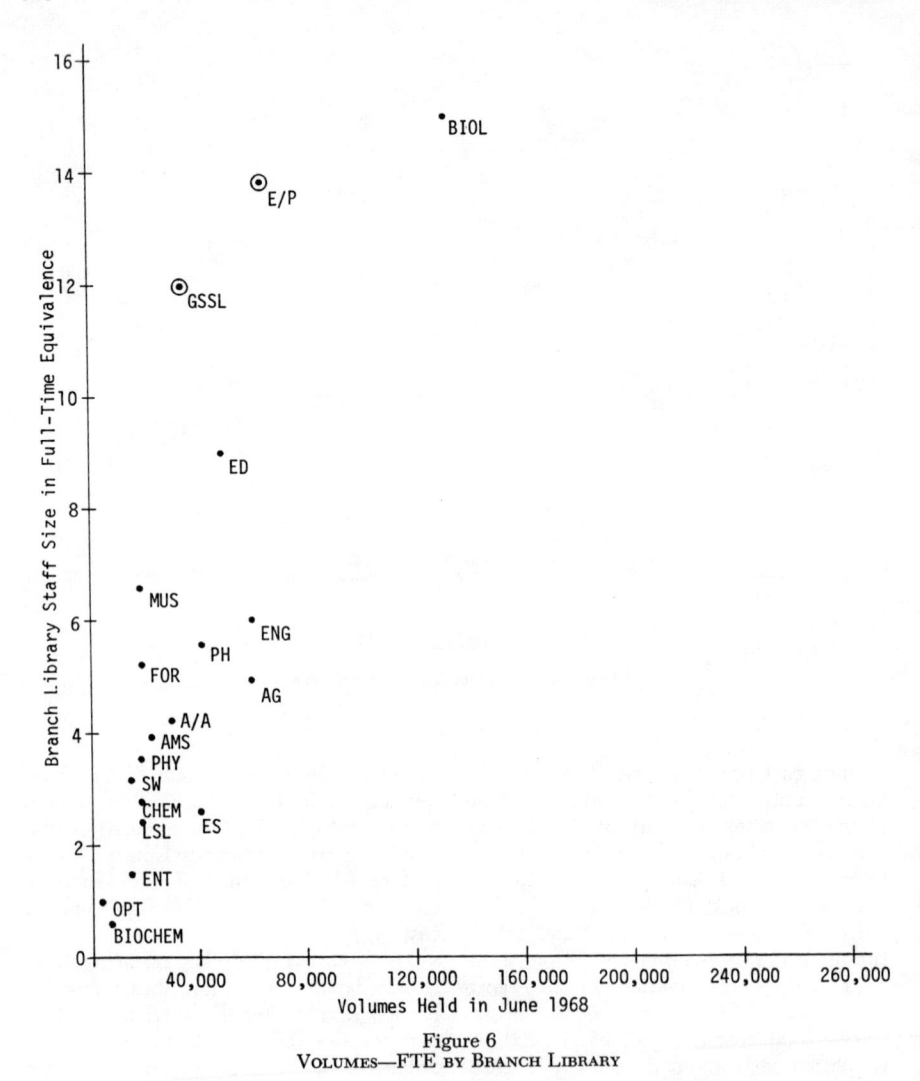

acquisition. The cost for the remaining branch libraries seems to stabilize in the $1.20 to $2.70 range.

COMPARISONS OF LABOR AND SPACE COSTS

Nearly $3.6 million out of $8.3 million was spent for direct labor in the General Library in 1967/1968. Since this constitutes a relatively large expenditure, it is important to try to develop tools for detecting significant changes in staffing needs.

The relation between FTE and the number of volumes held is presented in Figure 6. As the number of volumes

COSTING AND ECONOMICS 147

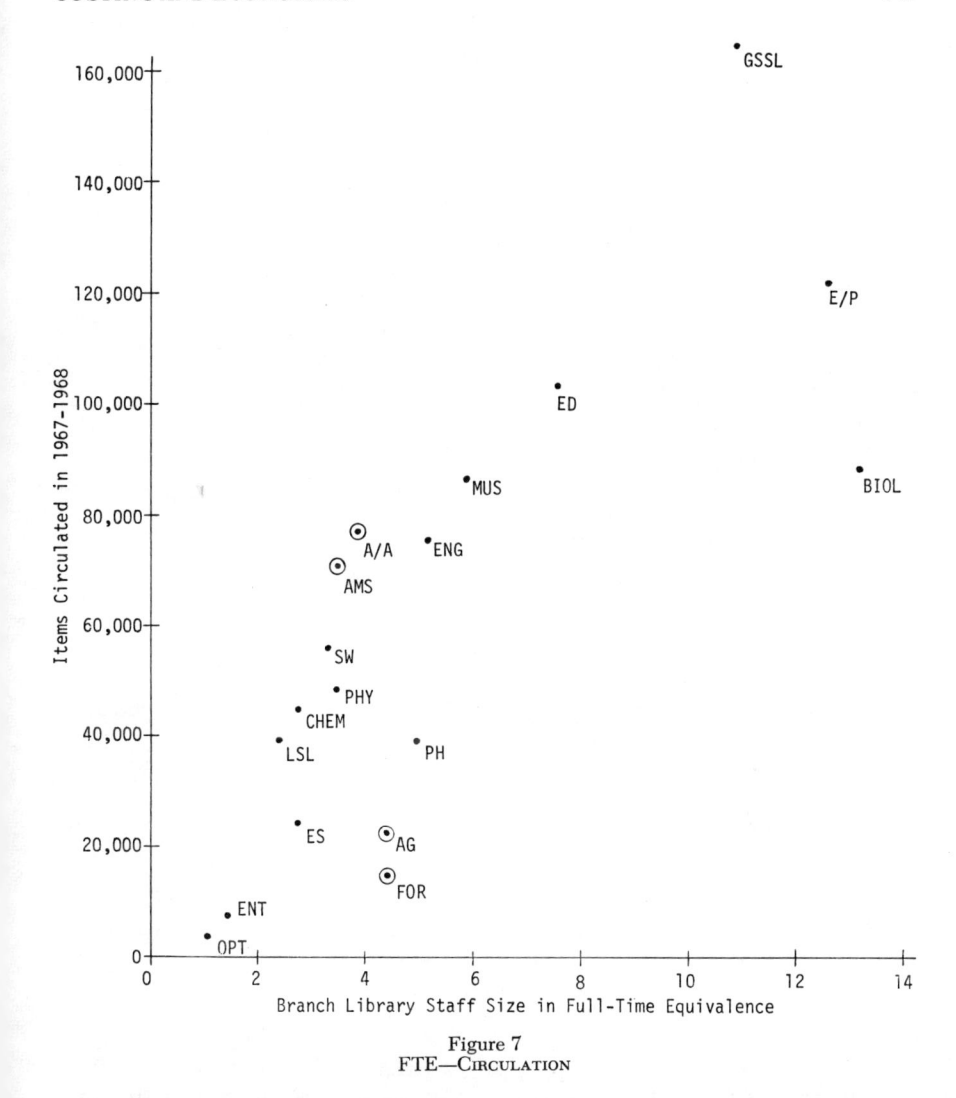

Figure 7
FTE—CIRCULATION

held increases, FTE staff increases. This relationship may be due to the manner in which staff is allocated to the branches.

When FTE and circulation by branch are compared (Figure 7), the same increasing pattern emerges. If a curve were fitted to the data of Figure 6, it would seem that the Graduate Social Sciences library and the Education/Psychology library fall in line with the staffing-circulation relationships of the other branches.

Interviews with the Art/Anthropology and Astronomy/Mathematics/Statistics librarians have indicated a shortage in FTE for the amount of circulation of their respective branches. This seems to be confirmed by Figure 7. In addition, the graph indicates that Agricul-

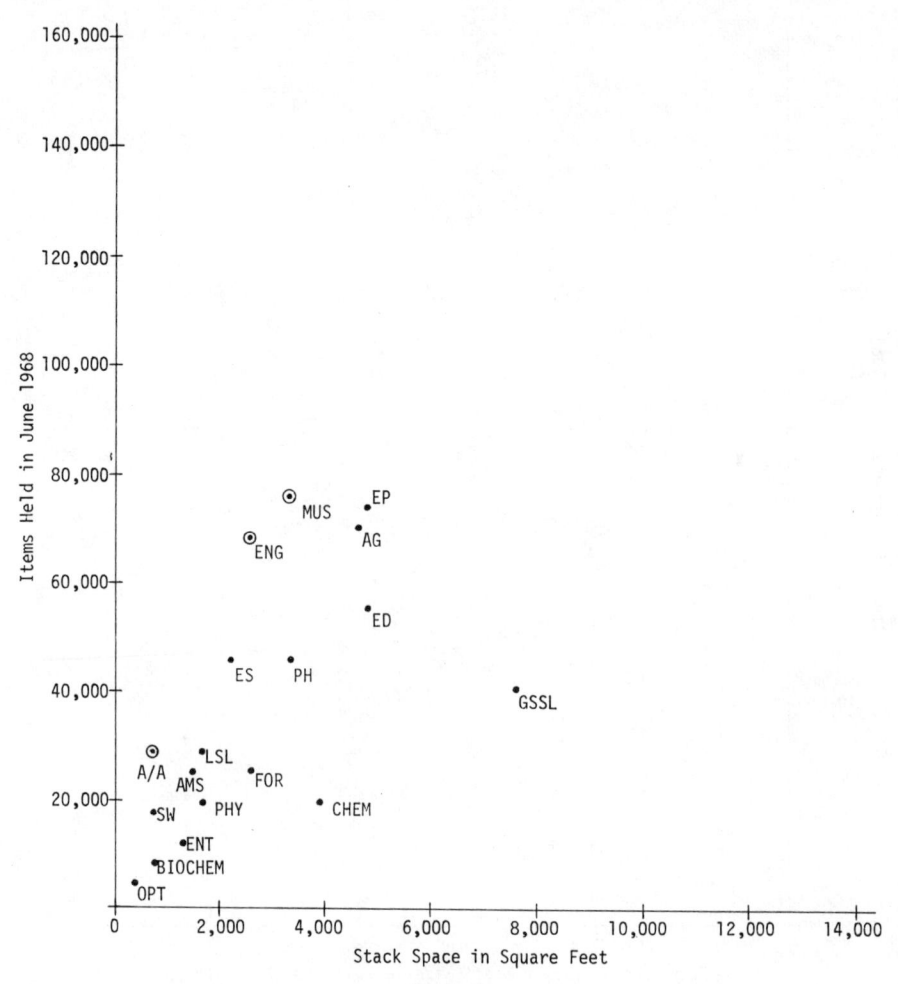

Figure 8
STACK CAPACITY

ture, Biology, and Forestry are overstaffed for the amount of circulation.

The storage of materials constitutes a second area in which planning and control must be exercised. Since facilities cannot be constructed in short periods of time, management must be in a position to predict when a branch will no longer be able to store all the items it would like.

The stack capacity (in square feet) for each of the branches is plotted against the total items held by that branch in Figure 8. From the graph it is apparent that the Chemistry and Graduate Social Sciences library have room for expansion while Art/Anthropology, Engineering, and Music seem to be relatively crowded.

SUMMARY

A cost-flow accounting model has been presented and data from the University of California Berkeley General Library has been used to illustrate the model's applicability. Unit and total cost comparisons have been made and evaluative tools have been proposed for use in library management. From the analysis, a number of conclusions can be drawn.

With respect to circulation, holding, and acquisition costs, it appears that a lower cost per item held is found in branch libraries having a large number of items. In addition, branch libraries with a circulation in the range of 50,000 to 70,000 are found to have the minimum cost per unit of circulation. The analysis also indicates that small branch libraries spend more of their resources on acquisition of material than they devote to labor.

Analyses of labor and space costs also yield useful planning information. From these costs it is possible to detect staffing needs and staffing patterns. This is done by determining the relationship between FTE and circulation and FTE and items held for the branch libraries. In addition, by determining the relation between volumes held and stock capacity across all branches, the librarian is in a position to see where construction resources can be used most effectively, or where collection weeding might take place.

ACKNOWLEDGMENTS

The authors acknowledge the generous assistance of Dr. James E. Skipper, university librarian, for making available all necessary data for the cost analysis. Mrs. Helen M. Worden, associate university librarian, was especially helpful in clarifying many of the problems incurred in the analysis of the Berkeley library. Miss Coralia Serafim conducted the survey of branch librarians. Dr. Robert M. Hayes and Dr. Patrick Wilson made valuable suggestions to preliminary drafts of this document.

BIBLIOGRAPHY AND REFERENCES

1. Landau, Herbert B. "The Cost Analysis of Document Surrogation: A Literature Review," *American Documentation* 20:302-10 (Oct. 1969).
2. Penner, Rudolph J. "The Practice of Charging Users for Information Services: A State of the Art Report," *Journal of the American Society for Information Science* 21:67-74 (Jan.-Feb. 1970).
3. Raffel, Jeffrey, and Shisko, Robert. *Systematic Analysis of University Libraries.* M.I.T. Press, 1969.
4. Williams, Gordon. *Library Cost Models: Owning Versus Borrowing Serial Publications.* Center for Research Libraries: Chicago, 1968. PB 182 304.

4 PRACTICE AND PRACTICAL STUDIES

4. PRACTICE AND PRACTICAL STUDIES

The Colorado Academic Libraries Book Processing Center project is recognized as one of the seminal studies of its kind to examine technical processes in libraries and to apply work measurement to the analysis of unit times in order to produce unit costs. The paper by Maier (1969) provides a useful summary of the methods and results of the project, which have been reported in full elsewhere (Leonard et al., 1969). Maier discusses the essential elements of a practical cost study technique, and emphasizes the importance of output measures in contributing to a balanced picture of library costs. Output measures are often difficult to obtain, and it is regrettable that often they are assessed only after the event. The corollary is that the collection of library statistics and management data are ongoing aspects of the manager's work. Ross and Brooks (1972) report a practical and comparative study of the costing of manual and computerized library circulation systems at the University of Essex. It was the problems and questions arising from the application of computer technology in libraries that focussed attention on the need to obtain cost data in the late 1960s. The study, which is fairly typical of its kind, is interesting in that it attempts to cost user time as a stage on the road to making a useful cost-benefit calculation; a similar exercise is discussed in the paper by Mason, also included in this section.

The paper by Nachlas and Pierce (1979) adds further detail to the examples of practical cost studies. The concepts of macro and micro-costing are discussed; the former concerned with the broad spread of costs and cost trends in a system; the latter with obtaining cost data useful for specific decision-making by management, especially by the use of unit cost data. The paper is mostly concerned with unit costing. There is a useful discussion of the use of work sampling to obtain work time data, and an illustration of practical systems study of a library operation in order to establish sampling points for data collection. Nachlas and Pierce place their work in the context of industrial engineering and work study, and urge the adaptation of such approaches by library managers. Revill (1977) reviews the concepts of unit times and unit costs, and stresses the fundamental importance of the former as a source of management data. However, there may well be problems in establishing a consensus over standard values for different operations, and local differences in task performance and methods clearly have to be recognized. Standardization of task descriptions and job content has to be achieved if unit times are to be used for inter-system comparison. Revill's paper is particularly valuable for its survey of recorded unit times, and it is an account rich in useful detail gained from practical experience. Examples are given as to how unit time data can be used to draw up staff budgets.

Mason's paper (1973) develops the theme of practical cost study and the practical use of cost data, this time for budgeting. The account of PPBS is of intrinsic interest, but the treatment of cost data handling within the budgeting exercise is especially apposite as an encouraging illustration of why cost techniques and data should form one of the foci of management's repertoire of techniques. Mason's main concern is with the problem of the effectiveness of resource allocation. Programme budgeting and cost-effectiveness analysis are regarded as the next best approach to the more difficult question of estimating value of service outputs. Mason argues convincingly that costing is an essential part of budgeting activity and the development of sound budget structures. The simple practical illustrations in his paper should be helpful to those who wish to explore practical applications elsewhere. The short paper by Cochran et al. (1970) verifies from practical experience the importance of cost analysis and cost accounting. In essence the authors address the question of value raised by Mason. The authors make a convincing case for trying to assess both direct and indirect (overhead) costs, and variable and fixed costs. Cost factors must be visible and brought to the attention of management and users. Costing makes a major contribution to value analysis in the opinion of the authors.

The final paper by Sturt (1972) looks at the question of cost awareness amongst library managers from the point of view of library educator and practitioner. The diagnosis was relatively pessimistic when the author wrote this paper, but it is hoped that there are now some grounds for optimism; the number of papers produced currently on library and information service costing is at least a steady if not a growing stream. Like Revill, Sturt argues that managers should develop a battery of hard costs for their service activities, and concludes that for effective teaching a body of case studies and authentic costing is required.

FURTHER READING

ASSOCIATION OF RESEARCH LIBRARIES. OFFICE OF MANAGEMENT STUDIES. *Determining indirect cost rates in research libraries.* Washington, ARL, 1977. (SPEC Kit No. 34).

ASSOCIATION OF RESEARCH LIBRARIES. OFFICE OF MANAGEMENT STUDIES. *Cost studies and financial planning.* Washington, ARL, 1979. (SPEC Kit No. 52).

BIRMINGHAM LIBRARIES CO-OPERATIVE MECHANIZATION PROJECT. *Costing catalogue systems in three libraries.* Birmingham, BLCMP, 1972.

BRYANT, P. and NEEDHAM, A. *Costing different forms of library catalogues.* Bath, University Library, 1975. (BUCCS Final Report: paper no. 7).

DRAKE, M. A. Attribution of library costs. *College and Research Libraries,* 38 (6), 1977, 514–519.

DRUSCHEL, J. Cost analysis of an automated and manual cataloguing and book processing system. *Journal of Library Automation,* 14 (1), 1981, 147–160.

HAYES, R. M. Managerial accounting in library and information science education. *Library Quarterly,* 53 (3), 1983, 313–327.

LANCASTER, F. W. Cost-effectiveness analysis of information retrieval and dissemination systems. *Journal of the American Society for Information Science,* 22(1), 1971, 12–27.

LEONARD, L. E. and others. *Centralized book processing: a feasibility study based on Colorado Academic Libraries.* Metuchen (N.J.), Scarecrow, 1969.

MAGSON, M. S. Techniques for the measurement of cost-benefit in information centres. *Aslib Proceedings,* 25(5), 1973, 164–185.

TUCKER, C. J. A comparison of the production costs of different physical forms of catalogue output. *Program,* 8 (2), 1974, 59–74.

TUTTLE, H. W. Standards for technical service cost studies. In *Advances in Librarianship,* 1, 1970, 95–111.

Leonard has become a classic example of a library cost study and contains useful methodological discussion. The SPEC kits produced by the ARL contain material gathered from various libraries in the form of internal papers and documents discussing cost topics and methods. Four of the papers (BLCMP, Bryant and Needham, Druschel, and Tucker) report cost studies of technical processes and systems of interest to all library and information units. Tuttle considers the question of standards for cost studies. Drake deals with the problems of allocating costs to different institutional programmes and user groups. Lancaster and Magson develop the themes of cost-effectiveness and cost-benefit, and serve as an introduction to their application in managerial economic studies.

Analyzing Acquisitions and Cataloging Costs

JOAN M. MAIER

Because the need for more precise techniques in analyzing the costs of technical services in libraries has been discussed for a number of years, this paper is frankly methodological. The procedures described were developed as part of a feasibility study to establish a book processing center for the state-supported academic libraries in Colorado.

Lawrence Leonard has already outlined the techniques by which job performance data were collected at nine libraries. Mean times in minutes for specified technical processing activities were calculated from time observations. It is upon these data and related statistics that the cost analysis was based.

The problem in essence is to convert the time required to perform each task into dollars and cents, then to cumulate these individual task costs to obtain a unit cost for book processing for a given library.

The end product of the Colorado Academic Libraries Book Processing Center (CALBPC) method is the Summary Cost Sheet (Table 1) illustrating the five elements of the cost analysis: labor, supplies, overhead, transportation, and commercial binding fees. It should be clarified here that "transportation" refers not to shipping charges but to the distance a book is moved through the acquisitions and cataloging system as delineated on a flow process chart.

Output Statistics

The difficulty in completing the cost analysis itself arose not so much out of the tedium of collecting the original time observation data but in collecting budgetary, personnel, and output statistics. Examples of output are the number of catalog cards produced annually, the number of authority cards typed, the number of books pamphlet-bound at a library, etc.

TABLE I
SUMMARY COST SHEET

Cost of Processing per Volume (in dollars) by Member Library

Library	L	S	O	T	M	C
#1	$3.412	$.158	$.821	$.036	$ .108	$4.54
#2	3.010	.292	.692	.031	...	4.02
#3	2.807	.169	.450	.053	.047	3.53
#4	4.965	.400	.416	.028	.063	5.87
#5	6.691	.149	.846	.024	...	7.71
#6	1.809	.408	.434	.020	...	2.67
#7	2.775	.300	.389	.026	.058	3.55
#8	3.568	.180	.278	.057	.074	4.16
#9	1.490	.572	.567	.010	1.850(U)	4.49
Average	3.392	.292	.544	.032	.367	4.50
CALBPC	$2.346	$.292	$.310	$.057	$ .092	$3.10

Volume predicted for CALBPC is 119,505, based upon the sum of the volumes added to each member library in FY 1967 (i.e., 160,993) prorated by the averaged percentage of new titles added (i.e., 74.23%).

KEY:
L = Labor Cost
S = Supply Cost per Book
O = Overhead (Equipment and Institutional)
T = Transportation Factor
M = Commercial Binding Cost for Paperback Books Prorated
U = Cost per Volume of Utilizing a Commercial Firm for Processing
C = Cost of Processing per Volume per Member Library

COSTING AND ECONOMICS

The format and degree of specificity for collecting statistics varied so widely from library to library that for some tasks performed, the only means for measuring output was to take a sample. For instance, to answer the question, "How many claims were made on outstanding orders during the fiscal year?" th eanaiyst had to gather a sample of claim slips from the order file; or, if a small file, count the total number of claims in the file and extrapolate from this the number of claims executed in one year. The importance of output statistics becomes apparent upon examination of the Frequency Chart (Table 2). These statistics are also crucial for computing the wage-per-minute column that is part of the labor cost analysis (Table 3) and the other four major elements on the Summary Cost Sheet.

Statistics on output, otherwise thought unobtainable "after-the-fact," can often be estimated by judicious sampling. Once the number of items in the file or collection to be sampled has been determined, the question of how large a sample to take can be settled by using the formula:

$$\sigma p = \sqrt{\frac{\theta(1-\theta)}{N} \times \frac{N_p - N}{N_p - 1}}$$

where
- σp = the confidence level desired (normally .05 to denote the probability that the sample is a 95% accurate representation of the entire file)
- θ = .50 (the probability requiring the maximum sample size)
- Np = total items (slips, cards, books, etc.) from which the sample will be drawn
- N = sample size needed (the unknown)

For example, to sample an orders-completed file of 30,000 titles to estimate how many paperbound books the library processed during a given calendar period, the sample size would be computed from the equation:

$$.05 = \sqrt{\frac{(.50)(.50)}{N} \times \frac{30{,}000 - N}{30{,}000 - 1}}$$

Once the sample is drawn from the file, the percentage of paperbound books can be established for the sample itself, and the estimated number of paperbound books in the total file derived from taking that percentage of the 30,000 titles.

Some fundamental output statistics are:[1]

Volumes added to the collection during a given period.
New titles added.
Added copies processed.

---

[1] A complete list of output statistics useful in cost analyses are included in the complete report.

Table 2
Frequency Chart: Acquisitions

Activity Description	Frequency Percentage Formula
1. Open, sort and distribute incoming mail.	1
2. Review book order requests; review selection media.	$\dfrac{\text{titles purchased}}{\text{volumes processed}}$
3. Select titles to be ordered.	Same as #2
*4. Type library order request card.	Same as #2
5. Search and verify bibliographic information.	Same as #2
6. Assign vendor and fund.	Same as #2
7. Prepare multiple order record.	Same as #2
*8. Type purchase requisition, etc.	$\dfrac{\text{purchase requisitions prepared}}{\text{volumes processed}}$
9. Revise typing. Sign and mail requests.	Same as #8
10. Burst forms.	Same as #2
11. File forms in appropriate files.	Same as #2
12. Encumbrance or prepayment routine.	Same as #2
13. Unpack books; check against packing list or invoice. Check outstanding order file.	Same as #2 → 1 (if gifts are handled this way)
14. Check in serials on Kardex.	$\dfrac{\text{added volumes}}{\text{volumes processed}}$
*15. Collate books.	0 → 1
16. Book return procedure (incorrect shipment, defective copy, approval books).	$\dfrac{\text{volumes returned}}{\text{volumes processed}}$
17. Book accessioning routine.	0 or 1
*18. Write sourcing information.	0 or 1
19. Prepare gift record form.	$\dfrac{\text{gift volumes received}}{\text{volumes processed}}$
20. Book distribution routine.	1
*21. Prepare receiving report.	Same as #2

* The use of these functions varied widely.
Assumption: Volumes processed entered the system during a given fiscal year.

COSTING AND ECONOMICS

TABLE 3
LABOR (L)
Unit Cost Calculation for Technical Processing Activities[1]
Acquisitions

LIBRARY #2

Activity Description	a Observed Mean Time	b Frequency	c Adjusted Time	d Personal Rating Factor	f Standard Time	g Category of Worker	h Wage/Minute	i Cost of Activity
1. Open, sort and distribute incoming mail.	.279	1.000	.279	1.15	.4739	2	.0272	.129
2. Review book order requests; review selection media.	(.856)	1.000	.856	1.10	1.3908	3	.0874	.122
3. Select titles to be ordered.	AF	...	...	...	...	...	...	...
4. Type library order request card.	.641	1.038	.665	1.10	1.0805	1	.0233	.025
5. Search and verify bibliographic information.	2.359	1.000	2.359	1.10	3.8329	1	.0233	.089
6. Assign vendor and fund.	(.475)	1.000	.475	1.10	.7718	3	.0874	.068
7. Prepare multiple order record.	.687	1.000	.687	1.10	1.1162	2	.0272	.030
8. Type purchase requisition, etc.	3.676	.013	.048	1.10	.0780	2	.0272	.002

[1] Seventy-six activities are listed in the full report.

KEY: AF = Another function incorporated this activity at this library.
( ) = Simulated data.

Added volumes processed.
Library of Congress cards filed in the card catalog.
Total actual work days that a technical services department was in operation during a given period.
Total hours worked by each category of personnel.

Ideally, a cost analysis would begin with the collection of the necessary statistics as a part of the data gathering process. Unfortunately, the CALBPC team recognized the need for some statistics only after the time observation phase had been concluded. Hindsight being the wonderful thing it is, the investigators used "historical" and sampling statistics to complete the cost study—which was doing it the hard way. It can be recommended that others engaged in similar studies collect all needed output statistics early in the study.

Methodology

The following discussion explains step-by-step how the cost per volume processed can be calculated. The method is built upon the theoretical model of one book progressing through the system such that every task performed in the system is performed on that book *proportionally* (see Frequency Chart and explanation). The unit cost obtained, therefore, applies to the generalized model of a book being processed at that library, not to any specific category of books such as those originally cataloged, those needing plastic jackets, etc.

Unit Labor Cost Calculation. Let us assume that the observed mean times (a) have been entered in the Labor Chart (see Table 3). The symbols in parentheses refer to the symbols in Table 3. Let us also assume one fiscal year is being studied. Is it correct to use these unit times as they are, to represent accurately the amount of work being accomplished? Does every book that passes through the system receive the benefit of each function for which there is time on the chart? Probably not. For instance, added copies are not searched (Function #5) nor are they cataloged with LC card sets or originally. Gift books, on the other hand, might receive an extra bit of processing (Function #19 in the full report). Therefore, to assume all books receive exactly the same treatment is an erroneous and costly assumption to make.

How then is it possible to assign weights to each time (b), i.e., to express accurately the importance of each function to a given library in quantitative terms? Using a percentage concept, the investigator could construct a Frequency Computation Table (Table 2), which indicates what statistics must be ratioed to provide a weighting percentage. Thus, in answer to the question, "How important is Function #19 (Prepare Gift Record Form) to the processing system?" The answer is to use statistics of one fiscal year for gift books processed as well as total books processed, and compare the two. The result might be something like .10 or 10 percent, i.e., one out of every ten books processed is a gift. Consequently, .10 would be entered in the frequency column by Function #19. If a function occurs to every book once such as in the case of

#6, Assign vendor and fund, it receives a frequency weight of 1.0 (100%). By the same logic, if the same function occurs more than once to the same book, a frequency above one would be recorded. For instance, the same book might have six catalog cards prepared for it, this number established by taking the number of cards filed in the Public Catalog and Shelf List over the whole year divided by the number of books processed. A frequency count of 6 (600 percent) would be entered for sorting, filing, and revising of catalog cards.

As previously discussed, statistics necessary for assigning frequency percentages are sometimes not available or else not part of the normal reporting routines. If not, it is usually possible to derive them by sampling existing files, examining billing records, and by asking the staff to maintain statistics on certain items such as cancellations and authority cards for limited but well-defined periods, as for a three month period or every third month.

Once the frequencies have been assigned, it is possible to compute the adjusted times (c). But again, the accuracy of the adjusted times must be questioned. During the time observations, the person being timed was assigned a personal rating factor according to whether he seemed to be working above or below his normal pace, although this was recognized to be a purely subjective judgment (d). (See Leonard's paper for a fuller discussion.)

It is also important to consider such factors as administrative overhead, general supervision, and unproductive time such as coffee breaks, which cannot be assigned to any specific task but which apply to all functions. The additional time to allow for these general activities is provided for by using a standardizing factor (1.4771).

Therefore, the adjusted mean times must be multiplied by both the personal rating factor and the standardizing factor to obtain a "standardized time" (f) for each function performed in the library under investigation.

The flow process chart described by Leonard provides the information on what category of employee is assigned to a given function. Each library has its own categories, but three should serve for purposes of illustration. These are: (1) part-time or student clerks; (2) full-time clerks; and (3) full-time professional librarians (g).

The wages-per-minute per category in Table 3 is based on the total personnel budget or expenditure for a year by category of employee divided by the total number of work-minutes in each category for one year (h). To obtain the total work minutes by category, the steps followed are:

1. Total the actual number of work days for each individual. (*Note:* eliminate weekends, legal holidays, sick leave, professional leave, vacation days.) This total will vary according to the fringe benefits accruing to each category.
2. Convert the total work days to work minutes by multiplying by 8 (hours per day) and by 60 (minutes per hour).

3. Divide the amount of money spent per annum in a given category by the number of work minutes accrued in that same category. The quotient is the wage per minute by category. The wage rate for "productive" time is automatically higher than that spent for total "official" work-time.

The wage rates are entered on the Labor Chart (Table 3) matching the categories previously entered for each function. The standard time multiplied by the wages-per-minute yields the cost per function for each book. The sum of these function costs provides the total labor cost for processing a book at that library.

Other Costs. The remainder of the analysis is not nearly so complex as the labor cost computation. For example, the *supplies* cost is simply the supplies expenditure for technical processes divided by the total number of volumes processed in one year. See the Summary Cost Sheet, Table 1.

Overhead is treated here in two forms: institutional and equipment. Administrative overhead has already been taken care of as part of the standardizing factor in the labor computation. Institutional overhead includes the cost of items normally not charged to a library's budget. These include light, heat, telephone, water, insurance, interest on a building mortgage, janitorial labor and supplies, building and grounds maintenance, and depreciation on buildings. Most non-profit institutions carry an overall figure—x-dollars per square foot of usable internal floor space in the building. Such figures ranged from $2.50 to $5.00 per square foot per annum for the libraries studied. The comptroller may possess a figure because institutions which are recipients of federal grants are normally expected to establish an overhead rate and use that rate on all grant applications. It is sometimes expressed as a percentage of salaries. One participating institution in the CALBPC Study uses 53.3 percent of salaries as the method for computing overhead costs on grant proposals.

If a square footage figure is used, then the number of square feet assigned to technical services multiplied by the cost per square foot yields the annual institutional overhead cost. This figure divided by the total volumes processed in a year produces the unit overhead cost.

The other form of overhead pertains to equipment. It comprises depreciation on purchased equipment, rental fees, and contractual services. Depreciation schedules need to be set up for equipment owned by the library, based upon the purchase price or accepted appraised value and the expected life span so that the amount of depreciation per item can be summed for a total depreciation figure. Depreciation schedules are frequently not maintained in libraries. However, they are an excellent means for keeping an equipment inventory up-to-date and projecting replacement needs. Amounts spent on rental fees such as Xeroxing, sending cards away to be photocopied, or buying computer time should be a part of the accounting records.

The three elements of equipment overhead are summed and the results divided by the total volumes processed. The unit equipment overhead added to the institutional overhead yields the total unit overhead cost.

Transportation is a factor which depends upon the physical arrangement of the work facility. As part of the flow process chart preparation, the number of feet required to complete a transportation step is measured and entered on the chart. Then, these distances are summed to indicate the total number of feet that a book must theoretically travel while it is being processed. The problem is to convert distance to time and then to cost. Under timed observations the walking rate of the average library employee was found to be 241.2 feet per minute. Dividing the total feet on the flow process chart by 241.2 feet per minute produces the time taken to transport materials. Converting from time to dollars is an easy multiplication step using the wage-per-minute amount in the full-time clerk category.

Since books are normally moved in batches from one processing point to another, the transportation cost just computed must be divided by some batching factor. To determine a realistic batching factor for the CALBPC study, books on book trucks and purchase request cards in "to search" boxes were counted. The average batch factor was 85. A similar procedure could be conducted at any other library or libraries to obtain an average batching factor. The total "unit" transportation cost divided by the appropriate batching factor gives the actual unit (per book) cost.

The total dollars spent on commercial *binding* divided by the total books processed yields a unit binding cost. Once all five elements have been calculated, it is possible to sum them to obtain a total unit cost per book processed.

The Inductive vs. the Deductive Method

Through this discussion the thought has probably occurred to the reader: why not simply take the total budget for technical processes and divide it by the total books processed to get a unit processing cost? This method might come somewhere near telling *what* the cost is, but it will not tell *why* it is. For instance, why is library A's cost twice library B's when both have very similar budgets? A flow process charting of each operation may reveal that library A is using many more steps than library B, and time observation may indicate that the first library's mean times are much greater for similar steps. However, without basic data from which the costs can be analyzed inductively, there is no way of pinpointing the causes of inefficiency and therefore no way of concretely justifying existing costs.

Should the cost analysis reveal several inefficiencies in technical processing these same procedures described will point the way toward the remedies. For example, when a supervisor is confronted with actual dollar amounts attached to the labor of maintaining certain files, he is likely to reconsider the justification for these expenditures. Can the labor cost for any given function be reduced by means of a forms revision, a reallocation of the category of personnel, the adoption of new equipment and techniques, a rearrangement of furniture, elimination of certain records, etc.?

One final thought . . . The investigative procedures described deeply involved the library staff of nine libraries. It is of supreme importance that staff members be thoroughly briefed in the *reasons* for undertaking an investigation and that they be kept informed on the progress of a study. Change can be very disrupting unless a staff is psychologically prepared to accept it and is committed to the philosophy of finding a better way to do what they are now doing. Good will and cooperation from a staff is fundamental to the success of a self-study. Even after a study is finished, the staff will still be concerned. The most brilliantly conceived reorganization based upon scientifically collected data cannot succeed without the interest and support of the personnel on the operating level. This seems elementary, yet in the excitement of an investigation, it is easy to lose sight of the long range objective—organizing people to serve people. And it is people who can make even a bad system look good if they really like it.

Costing Manual and Computerised Library Circulation Systems

JOHN ROSS and JANE BROOKS

Abstract

The cost per loan for the manual circulation system at the University of Essex Library is calculated for 1970/71 and predicted for 1973/74 and 1976/77. An allowance is made for the time spent by library users when borrowing books. Likely costs for an on-line circulation system are also calculated. A table is given for manual, off-line and on-line circulation systems costs for several university libraries.

Introduction

The authors have based their calculations largely on work of Kimber at The Queen's University of Belfast (1) and McDowell, Phillips and Woods at the University of Southampton (2). Initially, the above reports were examined and altered to allow for the value of user time saved by automation and for a higher rate of salary increase.

When this was first done (December 1970) using Southampton's 1968/69 figures, the authors predicted 1970/71 figures of 11.7 new pence per loan for the manual circulation system (now 12.6 new pence) and 11.9 new pence for the automated version, (now 11.6 new pence). This example of overestimating the cost of a computer based circulation system is believed to be something of a record. The new figures, however, are again amendments of Southampton's own calculations.

Similar principles have been applied to costing the 1970/71 manual circulation system at the University of Essex, predicting costs up to 1976/77 and estimating the effects of automation. The benefit of any doubt has usually been given to the manual system alternative. All percentage increases are compound.

Evaluating library users' time

Following a suggestion made by Jeffreys (3) in a letter to *Program* a value is attached to the time spent by academic staff borrowing

Reprinted from *Program*, 6(3), 1972, by permission.

books. Ford, Hudson and Apling (4) included postgraduate and undergraduate time as well when they costed circulation for the South-West Universities.

The base value for academic staff time is taken as 137 new pence per hour in 1968/69. This is in line with the *National Prices and Incomes Board Report*, No. 98, (Cmnd. 3866) p. 26 quoted by Jeffreys, which gave the average academic salary as £2,200 per annum, on the basis of 46 thirty-five hour weeks per year. A fairly arbitrary figure of 7 per cent is used as the average annual increase since then.

The proportion of loans to academic staff seems a moot point. Jeffreys quoted 1/3 for Newcastle; Ford, Hudson and Apling used 1/6 for Bath, Bristol, Cardiff and Exeter and a recent sample at Southampton indicated 1/7. The proportion for Essex is not known but thought to be around 20 per cent. The value of academic staff time is therefore multiplied by 20 per cent and applied to every loan made.

At Essex several timing exercises produced an average of forty-eight seconds for filling in a loan voucher and twelve seconds for it to be checked and the book to be date-stamped etc. Queuing time was ignored. It was assumed that a computer based circulation system would eliminate filling in loan vouchers but not affect the time taken to date-stamp the book. This is almost certainly loading the results against the automated circulation system. E.g. for a loan taking one minute in 1968/69, user cost per loan is

$$\frac{137 \times 20}{60 \times 100} = 0.46 \text{ new pence.}$$

If student time were costed on the basis of the maximum undergraduate grant being the annual salary (£430 per annum) then student time is 20 per cent of the value of the average academic staff time i.e. 0.46 new pence per minute. Weighted for 80 per cent of the loans at one minute per loan this would give

$$\frac{0.46 \times 80}{100} = 0.37 \text{ new pence}$$

This figure would be increased by allowing for postgraduate grant scales. The authors do not propose to include student time in these calculations. Those readers who disagree with this could double all the user time values as a rough approximation.

University of Essex manual circulation system

A job time analysis sheet was completed by ten Junior Library Assistants for two weeks. These documents are not known for their accuracy but an average of twenty should improve the reliability and

COSTING AND ECONOMICS

a choice of fourteen categories, including 'Idle', 'Coffee Breaks' and 'Other', should not have required too much inventiveness. The analysis produced a further category: 'Unaccounted'.

Three categories were regarded as non-productive, namely 'Idle', 'Coffee Breaks' and 'Unaccounted', and the remaining categories were adjusted to give percentages of productive time (87 per cent of the total). Non-circulation work was taken to be 'Queries', 'Photocopying', 'Turnstile', and 'Other'. The remaining categories were adjusted again to give percentages of circulation work (75 per cent of the productive time).

Table 1 Analysis of circulation staff time

Category	Percentage of total	Percentage of productive work	Percentage of circulation work
Shelving	11.9	13.6	18.3
Charge	12.6	14.4	19.4
Discharge	14.3	16.4	22.1
Short loan collection	15.5	17.8	23.9
Overborrowing	1.6	1.8	2.4
Recalls	5.9	6.8	8.3
Reservations	3.6	4.1	5.6
Queries	1.9	2.2	—
Photocopying	6.0	6.9	—
Turnstile	2.4	2.8	—
Other	11.5	13.2	—
Coffee break	1.7	—	—
Idle	8.7	—	—
Unaccounted	2.4	—	—
	100.0	100.0	100.0

The Circulation department salary bill for 1970/71 was taken to be the salaries and national insurance for one Senior Library Assistant (plus superannuation in this case) and ten Junior Library Assistants working full-time at the circulation desk plus 3,400 hours worked part-time by other library staff (seven Senior Library Assistants, three Library Assistants and six Junior Library Assistants).

Full-time staff   £9,163 (gross)
Part-time staff   £2,564
———
£11,727

Circulation work bill $\frac{£11,727 \times 75}{100} = £8,800$

This is the actual cost for 1970/71 and does not assume that all staff are on the midpoint of their respective salary scales. The policy in the Library at Essex is to fill the Junior Library Assistants posts with school leavers who intend after a year or so to go on to some form of higher education or other training. Most of the junior staff, therefore, are paid less than the midpoint of their salary scale. This is a trend which is likely to continue.

Staff cost per loan

In 1970/71 there were 55,000 'normal' loans and 45,000 from the Short Loan Collection.

The labour involved on the Short Loan Collection was only 24 per cent of circulation work whereas the other loans required 76 per cent. This is slightly unfair to the 'normal' loans since this umbrella covers anything not specifically a Short Loan task but reservations, shelving, recall etc. are considerably streamlined for the Short Loan Collection.

1970/71 Staff cost per loan (new pence)

Normal loans $\frac{880,000 \times 76}{100 \times 55,000}$ = 12.16p

Short loans $\frac{880,000 \times 24}{100 \times 45,000}$ = 4.69p

Overall $\frac{880,000}{100,000}$ = 8.80p

Rate of inflation

The rate of salary increase will be taken from the average of the five years 1 January, 1967 to 31 December, 1971. During this time there were $3\frac{1}{2}$ per cent rises on four occasions (August, 1967, 1968 and 1969 and in February, 1970) plus a $12\frac{1}{2}$ per cent rise in July, 1970 and a further 10 per cent in July, 1971. This gives a total of 36.5 per cent in five years or 7.3 per annum. This represents the

COSTING AND ECONOMICS

average increase of the basic pay scales and does not include annual increments. The salary scales of non-academic library staff at Essex are allied to those of Local Government.

Assuming that the same trend will hold for the next six years and making no allowance for the decrease in efficiency as the desk becomes more crowded and the file size larger, this would give rise to another 23 per cent by 1973/74 and 52 per cent by 1976/77 in the staff cost per loan.

Staff cost per loan (new pence)

	1970/71	1973/74	1976/77
Manual	8.80	10.87	13.43

Value of library users' time

The manual circulation system has been timed at one minute per loan ignoring queuing time (i.e. time to fill in a loan voucher plus time for the book to be date-stamped etc.). The time of academic staff is taken to be worth an average of 137 new pence per hour in 1968/69. An arbitrary rate of increase of 7 per cent per annum is assumed and 20 per cent is used as the proportion of loans to staff. Only loans to academic staff are considered in our costing of library users' time.

User cost per loan (new pence)

	1970/71	1973/74	1976/77
Manual	0.54	0.66	0.81

Stationery costs

All three parts of the triplicate NCR loan voucher in use at Essex are printed throughout and are therefore more expensive than some other kinds, at £6.30 per thousand. Loan vouchers for the Short Loan Collection are single and are produced in the University Printing Centre for £0.08 per thousand.

Averaging 55 per cent at 0.63 new pence and 45 per cent at 0.08 new pence gives a figure of 0.38 new pence per loan for stationery. It will be assumed that this figure is constant over the years, rising costs being offset by longer printing runs. Other stationery costs will be ignored since they are small (about 0.1 new pence per loan) and should be unaltered by automation.

Stationery costs per loan (new pence)

	1970/71	1973/74	1976/77
Manual	0.38	0.38	0.38

Total cost of the manual circulation system at the University of Essex

These figures in new pence apply to the manual system as used in 1970/71 and include all loans whether from the Short Loan Collection or 'normal'.

	1970/71	1973/74	1976/77
Staff	8.80	10.86	13.40
User	0.54	0.66	0.81
Stationery	0.38	0.38	0.38
	9.72	11.90	14.59

Estimated cost of an on-line circulation system at the University of Essex

Any computer based circulation system requires a number to identify each separately loanable item. If badge readers rather than teletypes are to be used there must also be a machine readable version of the number, i.e. a punched card or coded label. The proposed system at Essex will be on-line and will therefore require a further stage, the creation of a computer record stored on a magnetic disk.

The cost of converting the book stock in the University of Essex Library is taken to be the cost of assigning cards to all books (by December, 1972 the book stock is expected to be about 200,000 volumes) and all new accessions (about 15,000 volumes per annum) at the same unit cost as given by Mrs. L. Seymour for the University of Surrey (5).

The creation of machine records for each book is not included. The basic operation is very simple but amendments to include author, title and various statistical data will take longer. As yet the work involved is unknown but the computer program for the creation of the book files should be available by the middle of 1972 and finer calculations will then be made. It is hoped that a terminal can be situated so that this work can be phased in with unproductive time of the circulation desk staff.

University of Surrey:
 conversion cost: £1,850 for 83,000 books = 2.23 new pence per book

University of Essex:
 initial conversion cost: 2.23 new pence × 200,000 = £4,460
 annual conversion cost: 2.23 new pence × 15,000 = £334

COSTING AND ECONOMICS

Depreciating the initial conversion over ten years gives a charge of £446 per annum. The recurrent conversion cost will be taken as increasing at 7 per cent per annum.

	1970/71	1973/74	1976/77
Initial	466	446	446
Recurrent	334	409	501
Total conversion	£780	£855	£947

Estimated volume of loans per year

The student population at Essex is expected to increase from about 2,000 in 1970/71 to 2,500 in 1973/74 and 4,000 in 1976/77.

There seems to be no reliable data or theory for predicting the future volume of loans. The authors think that a doubling of student numbers would involve less than a 100 per cent increase in library borrowing, partly because more books will probably be restricted to use in the Library only and there might be a tendency in some Universities (though strongly discouraged at Essex) for small Departmental collections to spring up, if only on an informal basis.

However, there is no obvious way to quantify these effects and insufficient data to extrapolate from past experience in this or other libraries. Sussex and Lancaster both report a marked increase in the average borrowing per student in the last few years. Perhaps the latter would cancel out the former.

In the absence of quantifiable arguments it is assumed, with reservations, that the volume of loans will be proportional to the undergraduate population. This has no effect on predictions of manual costs but an overestimate here will flatter the predicted computer cost per loan.

	1970/71	1973/74	1976/77
Loans per year	100,000	125,000	200,000

Conversion cost per loan (new pence)

	1970/71	1973/74	1976/77
Automated	0.78	0.68	0.47

Equipment depreciation

It is assumed that the Library will purchase one 25 million character disk drive, one video terminal and the equivalent of an ALS three reader system and the depreciation of those items will be spread over five years.

Purchase prices:	Disc Drive	£7,500
	Badge Readers	£3,000
	Video	£1,500
	Installation	£500
	Total	£12,500
	Annual depreciation	£2,500

It should be noted that the DEC price of the disk drive used at Essex has fallen from £12,000 to about £9,000 in the last three years. DEC is the manufacturer of the PDP-10 computer but not of the disk drives and these can now be purchased direct from Memorex for about £7,500.

One of the factors involved is the introduction by most manufacturers including DEC of a new double density disk. The initial conversion is expensive but thereafter the unit cost of disk drive storage will fall considerably. This is the general trend for all the manufacturers of disk systems. If the Library were to pay for only part of the cost of a disk drive this would reduce the cost of on-line storage to around that of terminal equipment.

Depreciation cost per loan (new pence)

	1970/71	1973/74	1976/77
Automated	2.50	2.00	1.25

Equipment maintenance

It will be assumed that this will remain constant.

Current annual maintenance:	Disk Drive	£550
	Badge Readers	£300
		£850

Maintenance cost per loan (new pence)

	1970/71	1973/73	1976/77
Automated	0.85	0.68	0.43

COSTING AND ECONOMICS

Computer processing

Each transaction is expected to involve up to ten disk accesses. Processer time is not known at present so an arbitrary allowance of 0.05 seconds has been allowed. This is for a PDP-10 (roughly the same power as an ICL 4-70 or 1904A) and is a very high estimate. At a cost of £6 per hour (10 new pence per second) for processing time this would involve 0.5 new pence per transaction and will be taken to include any charge for disk accesses, etc. The computer processing expense will be assumed constant for the period.

Processing cost per loan (new pence)

	1970/71	1973/74	1976/77
Automated	0.5	0.5	0.5

Staff levels under automation

The Circulation Department's circulation work was split into three categories.

1. Unaffected by automation — Shelving — 18.3 per cent — Total 18.3 per cent
2. Affected by automation — Charge — 19.4 per cent
   Discharge — 22.1 per cent
   *Short Loan Collection — 23.9 per cent — Total 65.4 per cent
3. Replaced by automation — Overborrowing — 2.4 per cent
   Recalls — 8.3 per cent
   Reservations — 5.6 per cent — Total 16.3 per cent

* Short Loan Collection means charge, discharge and reservations, etc. for the three hour loans

The effect on the work in category 2 is difficult to assess. Basically, all filing and unfiling will be done by the computer but, although this represents work saved, it does not always mean manpower released for other tasks. This is partly due to the uneven flow of library business. The computer is therefore credited with releasing only a tenth of this time, i.e. 6.5 per cent.

Total time saved: 16.3 + 6.5 = 22.8 per cent of circulation work

Staff cost per loan is therefore taken as 77 per cent of the manual equivalent.

Staff cost per loan (new pence)

	1970/71	1973/74	1976/77
Automated	6.78	8.36	10.30

Savings to library users

At present users average forty-eight seconds per loan completing the loan voucher and twelve seconds being dealt with by the assistant. An automated circulation system will eliminate the former but only slightly improve the latter since books will still be date stamped. Time per issue for an automated procedure will be taken as twelve seconds or 20 per cent of the manual equivalent.

User cost per loan (new pence)

	1970/71	1973/73	1976/77
Automated	0.11	0.13	0.16

University of Essex total automated circulation cost

Automated cost per loan (new pence)

	1970/71	1973/74	1976/77
Conversion	0.78	0.68	0.47
Depreciation	2.50	2.00	1.25
Maintenance	0.85	0.68	0.43
Processing	0.50	0.50	0.50
Staff	6.78	8.36	10.30
User	0.11	0.13	0.16
Total	11.52	12.35	13.11
Manual	9.72	11.90	14.59

Other Universities

Cost per loan in 1970/71 (new pence)

	Manual	Off-Line	On-Line
Southampton	11.4(E)	11.1	—
Southampton, modified by J.D. Ross	12.6(E)	11.6	—
Belfast	3.4(E)	—	3.9(E)
Belfast, modified by J.D. Ross	5.9(E)	—	6.3(E)
Bath	15.8	14.7(E)	18.3(E)
Bristol	13.8	10.3	12.7(E)
Cardiff	15.4	13.8(E)	16.1(E)
Exeter	11.0	10.5(E)	13.0(E)

Cost per loan in 1970/71 (new pence) (continued)

Surrey	12.3*	10.0	—
Essex	9.7	—	11.5(E)

Notes:
* Surrey's manual circulation cost is for 1969/70
Southampton are gradually moving towards an on-line circulation system but were still predominantly off-line in 1970/71.

Conclusions

The cost per loan in academic libraries is in the region of 12 new pence and rising.

Automated circulation control will reduce labour and slow down the increase in costs.

Off-line computer circulation systems are currently as economical as manual ones.

If the difference between on-line and off-line circulation systems is regarded as the cost of a dedicated disk drive, then on-line systems will probably become cheaper than manual ones within the next five years.

Computer equipment prices are falling, especially those for disk storage devices. This trend should bring on-line circulation automation costs down to almost the level of off-line alternatives.

The over-riding factor in costing library circulation is the rate of increase of staff salaries. The size of library, rate of increase of book stock, user time and cost of equipment are likely to be dominated by the effects of inflation.

References

1. KIMBER, R.T. The cost of an on-line circulation system. *Program,* Vol. 2, No. 3, p. 81-94, October, 1968
2. McDOWELL, B.A.J., PHILLIPS, C.M. and WOODS, R.G. Circulation control system. University of Southampton, 1970. (Southampton University Library Automation Project, Report No. 1), and amendment 2, November, 1971.
3. JEFFREYS, A.E. Letter to the editor. *Program,* Vol. 3, No. 1, p. 43-44, April, 1969.
4. FORD, G., HUDSON, R. and APLING, J. Report on circulation prepared for the SWULSCP working party. South-West University Libraries Systems Co-operation Project. 1971
5. SEYMOUR, L.M. Costing of library circulation, University of Surrey Library. Details supplied by the author.

JOEL A. NACHLAS and ANTON R. PIERCE

Determination of Unit Costs for Library Services

As with other public service activities, inflationary trends and public opinion provide a clear mandate for attempts to control the increasing costs of providing library services. Cost control necessarily requires knowledge of the quantities and sources of costs. A methodology, known as microcosting, for identifying the unit costs of providing specific services is presented here. The method is designed to enable library managers to identify at a detailed level the resources consumed in providing a particular service. This information provides a quantitative basis for and a monitor of library management decisions. To illustrate the use of the methodology, it is applied to the determination of the unit costs of tracking overdue materials at a major university library.

THE RAPID INCREASE in the costs of providing library services over the past several years is well known.[1-3] The causes of this increase are difficult to isolate but hold the key to reducing the rate of growth in library costs. While it is a vast undertaking to identify all of the economic, social, and technological factors that have contributed to cost increases, one cause that can be recognized is the lack of impetus for the development and use of effective cost containment methods.

The provision of library services has been viewed by universities as essential for instructional and research programs and by municipalities as required for constituent cultural opportunity. Library services have been viewed in the same light as medical services. A person who needs medical care asks if it can be provided rather than what it will cost. Universities have thus tended to ask if "adequate" libraries and library services can be provided rather than how they can be provided in a truly cost-effective manner. This approach may have been appropriate in the past as the financial resources for providing library services have generally been available.

Recently universities and municipalities have found that their financial resources are more constrained, that there is greater competition for those resources, and that increasing costs for all programs have resulted in a decline in what can be obtained with their resources. As a result, libraries have found that funds are harder to get, must be accounted for more carefully, and still buy less. Thus libraries have recognized the need to manage their resources more carefully and to attempt to allocate those resources more efficiently.

The key to managing library resources is knowing what the costs of providing library services are. A method that can be used to isolate the costs of providing specific services is discussed here. An example of how this method has been applied to the identification of the cost of pursuing overdue materials in a university library is described. Finally, the potential for application of the methodology to other library service activities is discussed.

COST DETERMINATION

Cost determination can be divided into two categories, macrocosting and microcost-

---

Reprinted by permission of the American Library Association and the authors from *College & Research Libraries* 40(3): 240–247 (May 1979); copyright © 1979 by the American Library Association.

COSTING AND ECONOMICS   177

ing. Both types of cost analysis have been used extensively in production environments in industry.[4] During the past few years, they have also been applied to many service organizations, most notably in hospitals.[5]

The purpose of macrocosting is to examine a system such as a library in order to determine its present costs and from these costs to estimate trends and make inferences concerning future system costs. For libraries, this could prove to be a very fruitful endeavor and appears to have been attempted on a limited scale within the context of budget preparation. Nevertheless, there is substantial opportunity to pursue macrocosting studies in libraries especially in the areas of long-range planning and of evaluation of proposed program or service changes.

The purpose of microcosting is to obtain measures by which specific management decisions may be judged. Microcosts can be used to evaluate specific changes within a library system. This is because microcosts focus upon fundamental "unit costs" and can be used to determine the cost of providing a specific service or even a single unit of that service.

The microcosting technique is explained here by example. For illustration, the application of the method to the handling of overdue materials is described step by step. The results of this application are described, and the extension of the method to other library services is discussed.

Microcosting

The underlying framework for microcosting is conceptually simple. The first step is the construction of a flowchart describing the specific tasks and events that constitute the provision of a particular service. Figure 1 shows an example of a flowchart for tracking overdue materials using the Virginia Polytechnic Institute and State University (VPI & SU) automated Circulation and Finding System.[6]

The most important attribute of the flowchart is that it represents all of the events that may occur in the tracking of an overdue item. Thus the flowchart schematically describes the order in which the various tasks associated with tracking an overdue item may be performed. The possibility that certain steps may be repeated is represented by a "feedback" or return loop.

Once the flowchart has been constructed, it is used to design a work sampling study to identify the library resources that are used to track overdue materials. This work sampling study is described in detail below. First, the pertinent costs and the resulting motivation for the work sampling study are discussed.

The total cost of providing a service is composed of four components: direct labor, indirect labor, materials and equipment, and overhead.

Personnel time is a limited resource, the consumption of which carries an associated cost. The personnel time expended in the specific tasks that constitute the provision of a service is called the direct labor commitment to that service. The direct labor component of the cost of providing a service is the cost of the pesonnel time allocated to the provision of that service.

The first step in determining the direct labor cost for a service is to use the flowchart to help enumerate the personnel that participate in the provision of the service. In the case of the tracking of overdue materials, the participating personnel are one librarian, one library assistant, two level B clerks, one level C clerk, one level C clerk typist, and three level B clerk typists. All of these persons devote part of their time to tracking overdue materials.

Identification of the cost of tracking overdue materials requires the determination of what portions of the personnel salaries are appropriately allocated to this service. This determination is made using work sampling.

Indirect labor is classified in two distinct activity categories. The first of these is work that is not related specifically to any procedure or responsibility. Activities that fall into this category are answering telephones and cleanup. The second category is nonproductive time. Nonproductive time includes idle time, standby time, lunch breaks, and personal time for coffee and rest room breaks. The costs of indirect labor time must be apportioned among the various procedures or responsibilities of the personnel. The actual method of apportionment can be determined by existing man-

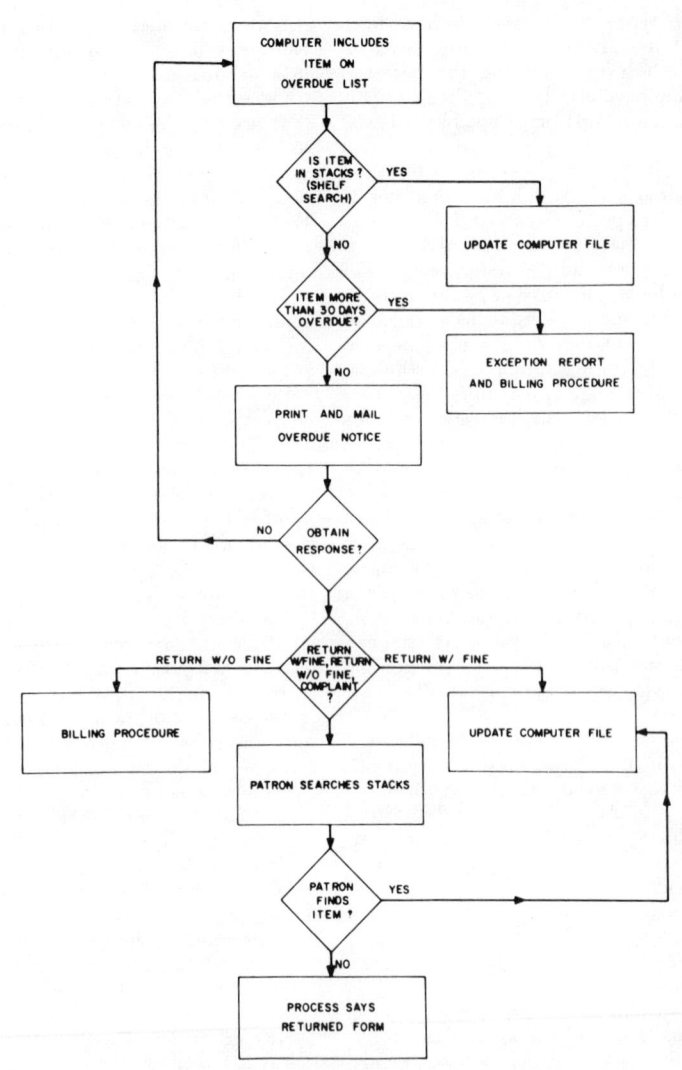

Fig. 1
Flowchart for Overdue Materials Tracking Tasks

agement policy or can be based upon direct labor allocations. In the overdue materials study, indirect labor times were distributed to the task of tracking overdue materials in proportion to the direct labor expended on that activity.

Current materials costs can be obtained from the purchasing agent. In cases where materials costs fluctuate, a moving average can be used to estimate costs of particular items. Equipment depreciation for items used in the performance of a task can be obtained from the accounting department. Care must be taken to allocate the depreciation cost in proportion to its use for the given procedure. In the case of the tracking of overdue materials, the only significant equipment in use is the computer and the computer terminal. Computer-use charges include depreciation. The depreciation cost for the computer terminal is allocated in the proportion equal to the percentage of direct labor committed to tracking overdue materials.

Overhead costs are real costs and must be included in the calculation of the cost of providing a service. Overhead is divided into two parts, departmental and general.

Departmental overhead includes the cost of providing supervision and support personnel. These costs are specific to the department but not to any given departmental responsibility.

General overhead is the cost allocated to the department by the library and includes housekeeping, building depreciation, and utilities.

Both types of overhead are specified by accounting, and both can be distributed over department responsibilities in proportion to the direct labor allocated to departmental procedures. At the VPI & SU library, the circulation department is responsible for the tracking of overdue materials. However, by university policy, departmental and general overhead rates are aggregated and valued at 63 percent of labor costs (direct and indirect).

All four categories of the costs of providing a service have been linked to the direct labor time expended in providing that service. It therefore remains to determine the direct labor commitment to the service. An effective method for doing this is work sampling.[7-9]

Work Sampling

Work sampling is a technique of randomly observing personnel perform their defined tasks and inferring from those observations a profile of the average labor allocations to the various employee responsibilities. By *random observations* is meant that the times at which observations are made are selected by use of a random device (e.g., a table of random numbers) as opposed to their being scheduled at regular intervals. This randomization of observation times guarantees that representative and unbiased data are obtained.

The key to the accuracy of the inferences is to make the observations without disturbing the work environment. Proper introduction of the study and its objectives to the staff prior to execution of the study contributes significantly to minimizing the disturbance of the work environment. An important aspect of this introduction is the emphasis of the focus of the study upon the cost of the service rather than upon individual worker productivity.

To construct the work sampling study, a set of task categories is defined using the procedure flowchart. In addition, general work categories are defined to represent tasks associated with services other than the one under study. Categories corresponding to indirect labor activities are also defined.

Figure 2 shows the task categories used in the overdue materials study. Note that each task category is defined and has been assigned a code. To execute the work sampling study, observation times are selected randomly and recorded on the data sheet shown in figure 3. Then, at each of the selected observation times, a "snap shot" of the department is taken. By "snap shot" is meant that an observer locates each of the departmental personnel and enters on the data sheet the task code corresponding to the activity in which the person is engaged.

Figure 3 shows an example data sheet in which task code entries have been made. In the overdue materials study, 1,013 such individual data entries were accumulated. These data are then analyzed to determine the quantity of direct labor consumed in the provision of the given service.

To analyze the accumulated data, the fractions of available employee time committed to the various tasks are tabulated. Then, the following variables are defined:

T_j = the total available work time for employee j,

t_j = the direct labor time expended by employee j in the provision of the service under study,

s_j = the total indirect labor time for employee j,

r = the aggregate overhead rate (63% in the present study),

d = the computer terminal depreciation rate,

Task Codes

Overdue Materials Tasks

SS — stack search
M — mailing overdue notices
T — computer terminal
RF — returns and fines
E — exception reporting
SR — says returned reporting
C — complaints
RP — running overdue programs
O — other

Non-Overdue-Related Tasks

CHK — checkouts and check-ins
HR — holds and recalls
Res — reserve
Sup — supervision
UP — user problems
O-II — other-II

Additional Designations

P — personal
L — lunch
I — idle

Task Definition for Overdue Materials

Stack Search. Canvassing the shelves to be sure material listed as overdue has not been returned directly to the shelves by the borrower.

Mailing Overdue Notices. Any activity requiring the handling and/or sorting of overdue notices for the purpose of mailing them. This is for the 8-, 15-, and 30-day notices that are automatically generated by the computer.

Computer Terminal. Entering overdue update information obtained from stack search into the computer via the terminal or running the computer programs to generate the overdue materials list.

Returns and Fines. Processing the returns and collecting fines submitted for overdue items.

Exception Reporting. Typing or processing exception reports for overdue materials. This task is specific to items more than 30 days overdue.

Says Returned Reporting. Preparing entries for the "says returned" file.

Complaints. Dealing with patrons who indicate that an overdue item has been returned.

Running Overdue Programs. Running the computer programs to obtain listing for stack search.

Other. Any other task that does not fit into one of the above categories but does relate to overdue materials. Any such entry should be explained on the back of the data form.

Task Definitions for Responsibilities Other Than Overdue Materials

Checkouts and Check-ins. Working at checkout desk.

Holds and Recalls. Processing or working on holds and recalls.

Reserve. Working on reserve book activities.

Supervision. Directing or supervising student employees.

User Problems. Responding to patron requests for assistance that are not related to overdue materials.

Other-II. Any other task that does not fit any of the above definitions. Should be accompanied by a category of task on reverse side of the data form.

Additional Designations

Personal. Individual is involved in a personal activity such as a coffee break or a visit to the rest room.

Lunch. Individual is on a lunch break.

Idle. Individual is at a work station but is idle.

Fig. 2
Task Categories

e = the equipment and materials cost of providing the service under study (computer costs for the present study), and

c_j = the salary rate for employee j.

Then, with the use of these definitions, the total cost of providing the library service is expressed by equation 1, where N is the number of employees that participate in the provision of the service. In this expression that total cost of providing a service is defined in terms of the direct and indirect labor expenditures that are, in turn, obtained from the work sampling study.

Results

Table 1 shows the percentage of available employee time expended in the various direct labor activities associated with tracking

$$C_T = \sum_{j=1}^{N} \left\{ c_j \left[t_j + \frac{t_j}{T_j - s_j} s_j \right] [1+r] + \frac{t_j}{T_j - s_j} d \right\} + e \qquad (1)$$

COSTING AND ECONOMICS 181

ANALYST _____ JOE _____

TIMES / NAMES	7:42	8:12	8:35	8:52	9:16	9:38	9:50	10:11	10:26	10:48
JOHN (Clerk B)	CHK	HR	CHK	HR	HR	HR	HR	P	HR	CHK
MARY (Supervisor)	HR	HR	HR	I	RES	RES	RES	P	RES	RES
BILL (Clerk B)	I	T	SS	SS	SS	SS	P	RES	CHK	I
SUE (Clerk-Typist C)	RF	RF	SUP	I	UP	M	E	E	P	P
ELLEN (Clerk B)	I	T	SS	SS	T	CHK	CHK	P	CHK	CHK
TOM (Library Asst)	RES	HR	RES	RES	C	SUP	HR	RES	CHK	SUP
JILL (Clerk-Typist B)	CHK	CHK	HR	HR	E	E	I	HR	M	M
RICK (Clerk C)	HR	HR	SS	SS	SS	SS	P	CHK	M	M

Fig. 3
Example Data Sheet

overdue materials and the resulting total direct labor fraction commitment to this service at the VPI & SU library. These figures represent the values of the quantities t_j/T_j and are presented as more informative than the actual t_j values. These values are computed using the work sampling data accumulated as are the corresponding fractions of indirect labor times shown in table 2.

The entries in table 2 represent the total indirect labor fraction and the fraction of the available employee time consumed by indirect labor that is allocated to the tracking of overdue materials.

As an example, note that for the supervisor 5.4 percent = [17.7/(100.0 − 23.5)] [23.5]. By adding the allocated personnel times listed in tables 1 and 2, the total fraction of available employee time allocated to the tracking of overdue materials is obtained. These allocations are shown in table 3.

After obtaining computer costs from the computer log, terminal depreciation from accounting, and personnel salary rates from the personnel office, the total cost of tracking overdue materials is computed using the expression defined above, and these costs are distributed to the overdue materials tracked. Using the tabulated data, it is found that the average cost of tracking

TABLE 1
PERCENTAGES OF AVAILABLE EMPLOYEE TIME EXPENDED ON DIRECT
LABOR ACTIVITIES FOR OVERDUE MATERIALS TRACKING

Activity Code	Supervisor	Library Assistant	Clerk Typist B	Clerk Typist C	Clerk B	Clerk C
SS	3.9	1.0	11.1	10.2	18.9	1.0
M	0.0	3.4	0.3	0.0	0.0	0.0
T	0.0	0.5	1.0	0.0	0.0	0.0
RF	0.0	2.9	2.8	0.0	7.8	0.0
E	0.0	0.0	0.0	0.0	0.0	0.0
SR	2.1	0.4	0.0	0.0	1.9	0.9
C	0.0	1.0	0.3	0.0	0.9	1.0
RP	3.9	9.8	0.3	0.0	0.0	0.0
O	7.8	2.4	1.1	0.0	4.1	0.0
Direct Labor Fraction (t_j/T_j)	17.7	21.4	16.9	10.2	33.6	2.9

TABLE 2
PERCENTAGES OF AVAILABLE EMPLOYEE TIME EXPENDED ON INDIRECT LABOR AND ALLOCATED AS INDIRECT LABOR TO TRACKING OVERDUE MATERIALS

Job Class	Indirect Labor Fraction (Percent)	Indirect Labor Allocation (Percent)
Supervisor	23.5	5.4
Library Assistant	25.7	7.4
Clerk Typist B	30.6	7.4
Clerk Typist C	25.9	3.6
Clerk B	20.6	8.7
Clerk C	23.8	.9

overdue materials at VPI & SU is $.22 per overdue item. At VPI & SU this cost amounts to approximately $18,330 per year.

Upon completion of the study, the stack search activity was examined. It was found that fewer than 3 percent of the items listed as overdue had been returned to the shelves without being discharged. As a result of this finding, the stack search activity has been eliminated from the set of overdue materials tasks routinely undertaken. Examining the study results indicates that the stack search activity is time-consuming. In fact, this task requires an average of approximately .61 person-days per day.

Eliminating the stack search frees this time for allocation to other tasks. Including consideration of job category, this time represents $8,000 of the $18,330 annual cost of tracking overdue materials. Now it should be noted that total library operating costs are not necessarily reduced by this amount. Instead, the work avoided by eliminating the stack search creates additional available employee time that is committed to other activities. A follow-up study is planned to determine how much of this additional time is used to provide user services.

TABLE 3
TOTAL FRACTIONS OF AVAILABLE EMPLOYEE TIME ALLOCATED TO TRACKING OVERDUE MATERIALS

Job Class	Total Labor Fraction (Percent)
Supervisor	23.1
Library Assistant	28.8
Clerk Typist B	24.3
Clerk Typist C	13.8
Clerk D	42.3
Clerk C	3.8

CONCLUSIONS

The use of microcosting has permitted the identification of the unit cost of providing a specific type of library service, the tracking of overdue items. Obvious uses for this information are the formulation of overdue return policies and overdue fine schedules. The unit costs can be combined with incentives for efficient materials use to develop operating policies that recover library costs while promoting more responsible utilization of library collections.

It should be noted that the methods by which the indirect and overhead costs are obtained are specific to the particular library being studied. However, it is quite easy to computerize the data manipulation procedure. This permits easy alteration of cost computation formulas and can also be used as a format for refining the method described. The key point is that unit costs of providing user services can be identified using this method.

The method described for microcosting does not require sophisticated equipment or highly trained personnel. In the overdue materials study, library employees with no previous exposure to the technique collected the data. The actual design of the study and the analysis of the data should be entrusted to an industrial engineer. Nearly all university libraries can find an industrial engineer on campus. Urban-based municipal libraries can locate an industrial engineer at a nearby industrial plant or through the state society of professional engineers. Thus the resources required to undertake a microcosting study are likely to be readily available.

A variety of other library services, both routine and special, are well suited to microcosting analysis. Reference services, interlibrary loans, photocopying services, acquisitions and cataloging, and check-in and return services are all reasonable subjects for microcosting studies. In fact, any library service or activity that requires the use of personnel time can be investigated using the microcosting technique. For any given library, the method will have greatest utility in examining services over which some decision-making control is possible.

In summary, a method has been described that will enable library managers to identify the costs of providing specific services. The method was illustrated by application to overdue materials but can be applied to nearly any library activity. In addition, the method can be standardized and loaded on a computer so that it can be applied throughout the library. The value of the method is that it provides a sound approach to determining at a microscopic level how library resources are being consumed.

The information derived can be used to make decisions or formulate library policy.

One approach to taking advantage of the power of the method is to use it both before and after a decision or policy is implemented to determine the effect of the change. For example, the impact of a very stringent overdue fine schedule could be determined by executing the overdue materials study again after the institution of such a schedule. Thus microcosting is a tool that library managers, as they face increasing costs and shrinking budgets, can use to learn about "where the money goes" and how to stretch it further.

REFERENCES

1. William J. Baumol and Matityahu Marcus, *Economics of Academic Libraries* (Washington: American Council on Education, 1973).
2. Richard De Gennaro, "Austerity, Technology, and Resource Sharing: Research Libraries Face the Future," *Library Journal* 100:917–23 (1975).
3. Office of the Executive Director of Universitywide Library Planning, *The University of California Libraries: A Plan for Development, 1978–1988* (Berkeley: Systemwide Administration of the University of California, 1977).
4. Clarence B. Nickerson, *Managerial Cost Accounting and Analysis* (New York: McGraw-Hill, 1962).
5. American Hospital Association, *Hospital Engineering Handbook* (Chicago, The Association, 1974).
6. Systems Development Department, Virginia Polytechnic Institute and State University, *Detailed Documentation of the Library Circulation and Finding System* (Blacksburg, Va.: Virginia Polytechnic, 1978).
7. Association of Research Libraries, *Determining Indirect Cost Rates in Research Libraries*, SPEC Kit No.34 (Washington, D.C.: The Association, 1977).
8. John S. Goodell, *Libraries and Work Sampling* (Littleton, Colo.: Libraries Unlimited, 1975).
9. Lesley Gilder and J. G. Schofield, *Work Measurement and Library Management: Methods of Data Collection*, LMRU Report No.2 (Cambridge, England: University of Cambridge, Library Management Research Unit, 1977).

Unit times in studies of academic library operations

D. H. Revill

Introduction
IN RECENT YEARS various articles have described the results of work study exercises in libraries.[1,2,5,8,9,10] Smith and Schofield see one of the advantages of these studies as offering inter-library comparisons.[1] This article is offered as a further contribution towards this end.

It may be helpful to add one more library's experience in this field as, increasingly, there appears to be developing a consensus, or, at least, a range of unit times which are not so disparate as to preclude their use, if only for purposes of comparison, in other situations.

Unit times are more valuable than unit costs in that the latter may change more rapidly and are, naturally, derived from the former. Various similarities in the data quoted in the surveys occur, *e.g.* book-ordering consumed 11.4 per cent of our Central Services (technical processes) time in 1974 and 13.9 per cent in 1975 compared with Newcastle's 11.7 per cent.[2] The cataloguing process also reveals some similarities. The unit time is roughly (and variously) 28 minutes per item at Liverpool and about 26 minutes at Newcastle.

Liverpool Polytechnic Library Service has conducted several studies since 1972—October 1972 in the Engineering and Science Library, May and June 1974 over the entire system, May and June 1975 on part-time and temporary staff and the work of the Central Services Unit, June and July 1975 again over the entire system. The objectives of the studies were to:

1. Obtain unit times for all functions and tasks performed by library staff.
2. Derive unit costs for all tasks and functions.
3. Identify possible economies of scale.
4. Identify the cheapest method of performing tasks for which various methods exist at present.
5. Define the maximum workload capacity of the library and of its sections at present staffing levels.
6. Identify the variety of tasks performed by library staff.

It must be admitted that we have been more successful on objectives 1, 2 and 5 than on the others.

For ease of comparison we adopted Pritchard's excellent list of codes.[8] It would be extremely helpful if a list such as this could be adopted by libraries. Pritchard's list does seem to strike a nice balance between too great a degree of specificity or generality.

Where Liverpool data is not given this is either because the number of items was too small for confidence or the task is not normally undertaken, *e.g.* having a computerized cataloguing system the only sorting of cards is associated with vertical files and similar items and withdrawals from the former manual catalogues. Where data from other surveys does not conform exactly with the codes used the approximate equivalents are given—for instance some studies give a time for the entire cataloguing or processing system rather than the several stages within these.

The 1972 study used work sheets where the participants recorded a brief description of each task undertaken, the procedures adopted, the time taken and the quantities involved. Quantities are, obviously, essential; however, they can be neglected unless there is close supervision of recording. Greater attention was given to this in the later studies. Many tasks either do not require quantities to be recorded, *e.g.* sick leave, as they are either obtainable from other sources or are irrelevant. However, one has two choices on others. One can either accept the time taken during the duration of the study for a task and gross this up to an annual, or similar, total time, probably making this relative to another indicator (say acquisitions), or one can attempt to count the number of occurrences of the event (amendments, insertions, booksellers reports, etc.) over the longer time period. In the later surveys counts of items processed were made by the staff concerned at the time of recording the activity, thus we were able to relate units of work produced to individual staff members. This was not for the purpose of individual assessment but did indicate the variations likely on identical tasks performed by different individuals. The range of times found in this way gave more confidence in adopting, or calculating, a mean for each activity. Where counts are made once daily rather than at the time undertaken these deviations may be hidden. Extreme deviations may indicate that two different tasks have been coded as a single task, in which case an investigation can be made, or may simply reflect individual staff differences. Standard deviations were not calculated.

The 1974 study used a system of coded tasks for recording. The use of codes for tasks was discontinued in the 1975 study as many staff were unable to memorize them all (including their definitions) and lacked both the time and the patience to look them up in the lists. (Examples and information on the codes are obtainable from the author.) Professional staff checked the verbal descriptions to ensure correctness and lack of ambiguity. In some respects this allowed a cross-comparison within groups of staff. Where one staff member timed and quantified each element of a task or series of tasks these could be aggregated for comparison with another record where a broader more inclusive description had been used (*e.g.* on 'processing'). Actual times of starting and completing tasks were recorded rather than adopting a system whereby the day is divided into equal time intervals. It was felt that the latter introduced too many distortions and could confuse staff. It seemed easier to the staff to simply consult their watches. This had some positive advantage in that interruptions were more easily identified.

The 1974 survey provided an analysis via the computer. This analysis included the proportions of each task which were performed by qualified staff. This is not to say that the proportions are 'good' or 'ideal'. Many reflect the staffing situation at that time and the small site situation where professional staff are obliged to undertake some clerical duties. The program was also intended to provide data on the proportion of each staff members overall time devoted to each task. Unfortunately there was a 'bug' in the program and we failed to obtain this data. It is very helpful to obtain both 'within task' and 'within grade' proportions. The 'within task' proportions of professional time have altered somewhat since 1974. Cataloguing (code 62), other than for difficult items and checking, is now almost entirely a clerical operation. The four surveys covered some 705 man-days.

There are weaknesses in all the studies only too well known to, and acknowledged by the authors. Unit times are not available for all library operations. Professional activities especially are elusive to quantification. The variety of tasks also tends not to be comprehensively listed. Clerical and routine procedures are relatively easily described but items such as 'reading memos', 'writing reports' may be subsumed under general headings. Similarly discovering the number of memos read or reports written, over time, can be difficult. The time taken in discussion, liaison, meetings and merely being seen about the place may not be sufficiently tangible or self-evident. In all the studies, task elements have not been treated at the 'first-generation' level (*e.g.* grasp, reach, etc.) but are more akin to third generation or second generation limited higher orders.

'The use of higher level systems indicates that these times do in practice represent a weighted average and that inaccuracies can reasonably be expected to balance out over a whole task. . . . '[3] A work study engineer would see these methods as a starting point but they would not satisfy a purist.

It is recognized that unit times represent means and that there will be deviations about the mean. Measured at another time with different staff members the results will be different too. However, one would not expect such differences to be vast. Similarly the net error in such figures may be relatively low in that though gross error may be large a great deal of error cancels out. These figures can only be regarded as indicative but better than 'guesstimates'. But they are not 'standard times'.[4] Gilder and Schofield say we should 'accept the resultant measures as indicators rather than precise standards.'[5]

The Department of Employment Tripartite Working Party discussed the problem of the 'average': 'There can be no completely objective or scientifically correct time for a complete task. . . . There are many difficulties and possible errors, both human and technical in arriving at "standard performance".'[6]

So, librarians can be somewhat excused. Nevertheless some form of agreement on definitions and interpretation would seem to be necessary if comparisons between institutions are to be made. The unit times also reflect what is done rather than what ought to be done. For example, greater care and hence time may be necessary on some tasks but pressure of work prevents this. An ideal staffing situation is unlikely (and itself is relative) so one can regard the unit time as variable too. Measured at different times, under different circumstances, it may be different even though the objective description of the task remains unchanged. 'Standard times' assume 'normal conditions'! One objective of work study is to improve the method. Predetermined motion time systems claim to be better able to do this although not all work study people would wholly subscribe to this view.

The surveys discussed here do not always make it clear whether the times refer to 'improved' or 'unimproved' systems. They may simply be statements of what was. Smith and Schofield recommend recording the less regular or unusual activities—their secondary rather than primary tasks. They also advocate the encouragement of self-recording by all grades of staff. It is my hope that an attitude will develop to work which, among other things, sees the recording of the quantity of work done and the time taken as a natural part of any work—a kind of personal feedback on the job.

Masterson points out that the timing of the surveys also affects the results obtained.[7] Ideally one needs to conduct sample surveys throughout the year and repeat them, or parts of them, at regular intervals thereafter both to reconfirm previous data and to cover progressive changes in working methods. The City of London Polytechnic survey (COLP) was carried out in the vacation.[8] There may be considerable differences between the results of term-time and vacation surveys.

Pritchard and others have calculated the **available working time** (AWT) applicable to members of staff.[8] These are usually given as total hours or minutes available in the year. Smith and Schofield, and Newcastle, used the concept of primary task time (PTT)—that time available for the primary or special duties of staff as opposed to the shared and common tasks. Pritchard uses 1,630 hours per annum as AWT. This figure can then become the divisor for staff calculations. The College of Education Libraries Research Project (CELRP) adopted 1,500 hours per annum for professional staff and 1,550 hours for clerical staff.[9]

This idea of 'available working time' is closely involved with and related to the work study engineer's 'relaxation allowances' which would normally be built in to 'standard times' per operation or task. In the library studies these allowances are calculated on an annual hours basis, being deducted before other calculations are made.

Smith and Schofield suggest allowances of from $12\frac{1}{2}$ to 16 per cent for tea and office breaks, fatigue, personal needs and waiting time. The Newcastle study suggested an approximate range of from $12\frac{1}{2}$ per cent to 13 per cent but did include tea breaks in available working time.

At Newcastle some 21.2 per cent of **total time** was lost to sickness, leave, breaks, etc. The percentage at Liverpool was 23.5. The Newcastle study arrived at a figure of 1,687.5 hours of available time per annum (45 × 37.5) but this includes the relaxation element. Agreement should be reached, as advocated by Smith and Schofield, on such figures. It can be seen, in sources, that total annual hours vary from 1,200 to 1,800. Calculations of the number of staff required will obviously vary enormously.

Calculations made at Liverpool suggest that some 9.8 per cent of total time is taken up by leave and a further 13.7 per cent on 'personal needs' (breaks, sickness, etc.). Thus only 76.5 per cent of the working year is available for professional work and some 77.7 per cent for clerical staff. Local circumstances, policy on leave and bank holidays, may affect the figure as far as individual libraries are concerned. However, it appears to me that approximately 1,460 hours for a professional member of staff and 1,480 hours for a non-professional staff member are the maxima one can reasonably expect, allowing for relaxation. The differences in the data may simply reflect differing methods of allowing for absences and relaxation—at the level of gross annual time available, or having calculated 'available working time' then subtracting the 'relaxation' element.

Williams studied the various practises in calculating **relaxation allowances** and has developed tables for use in the Imperial Group.[11] These allowances are grouped under headings:

1. Standard fatigue recovery allowance.
2. Physiological factors.
3. Psychological factors.
4. Environmental factors.

Librarians may be more interested in the third of these which covers discipline, monotony and concentration. A validation test averaged 17.5 per cent relaxation allowance per job studied. The Scott Mulligan Data system, sometimes used for clerical operations, includes a relaxation allowance of 16 per cent in the element times.[12]

In addition to 'relaxation allowances' industry recognizes that 'incidental delays' also occur typically involving from 2½ per cent to 10 per cent of the

Code	Description	Liverpool Professional % of task (1974)	Unit time (mins)	CELRP Libraries (A,D,E,G)*
04	Reading reports, memos, correspondence		8	
07	Timetabling	93		
08	Opening mail		1.2	
09	Gathering management information	73		
10	Stationery, checking, requisitioning, per item	36	1.8	
11	Liaison	79		6.25 hrs per internal committee. 2.5 hrs per external meeting
12	Individual instruction (in use of catalogue, per student, p.a.)		10	39 27 65 23 (mins)
13	Meeting visitors	100		

* A, D, E and G refer to individual libraries studied. See text reference 9.

TABLE 1: *General categories*

COSTING AND ECONOMICS

	Liverpool		COLP	CELRP	CLMRU	Newcastle
Code	Description	Professional % of task	Unit times (mins)	Unit time (mins)	Unit times (mins)	Unit times (mins)	Unit times (mins)
14/15	Current awareness	62	0.66		20 hrs per revision. 30 hrs per new publication		
15A	Displaying new books per book		0.5				
16	External enquiries						
17	Internal enquiries (staff & students) per enquiry		14		75 mins per reader p.a. (includes some of 12)		
17A	Periodical enquiries per enquiry		8			10 mins per issue. Library Q	
18	Issue desk duties per transaction/item, charging, discharging, minor enquiries, renewals, registration		3.3		4.5 mins per issue (includes 25)	4 mins per issue (includes 28). Library R	
20	Issuing and receiving books per transaction	5	0.8 (discharging)		c. 2 mins (includes 24 and 28)	0.66	1.5

23	Conversion to Browne issue system		1	
24	Reservation per item	34	4	A D E 14.4 5.5 9.1 13.5
25	Inter-Library Loans		15	A D E 20.5 16.8 14.7 100 Library Q G 23.7 71 Library R 34
26	Shelving per book	0.75	0.87 (code 110)	2.2 (includes 36)
27	Shelf revision per book	56	0.08	
28	Sending overdues per overdue	8	2	A E G 2–3 0.1 0.1 0.3 5
29	Final letters			
29A	Account queries	20		3

TABLE 2: *Services, counter routines and enquiries*

COSTING AND ECONOMICS 191

Code	Description	Liverpool Professional % of task	Liverpool Unit times (mins)	COLP Unit times (mins)	CELRP Unit times (mins)	CLMRU Unit times (mins)	Newcastle Unit times (mins)
31	Photocopying per page	21			A D E G		0.6
34	Periodicals: acquisition	10	2.1		8.69 2.42 5.75 1.19		2.2
	Display shelving						
	Chasing	16					
	Ordering	37					
35	Binding per volume	62				7 Library Q	4.8
36	Stock editing per book				2.2 (includes code 26)	8 Library R	
37A	Vertical file material: per item		3				
40	SDI Services	11					
41	AV catalogues file maintenance per item		3.3				
44	Indexing periodicals		3.1	3.5			
46	British and International standards			12			
50A	Inserting loose-leaf amendments. Per page		0.9				

TABLE 3: *Periodicals, etc.*

total time. Similarly relaxation allowances between 10 and 20 per cent are often found. 'A basic allowance of 8 per cent can be considered satisfactory... working sitting down. . . . If concentration is important one can add between 2 and 5 per cent. If the operation is of very short duration (*e.g.* 10 seconds) then an allowance of 2-5 per cent is made to provide relaxation from monotony.'[13] A contingency allowance of up to 5 per cent for uncontrollable factors (*e.g.* queries) is also applicable. A relaxation allowance of about 16 per cent does not seem unjustified.

The unit times and other data are given in Tables 1-6. They are largely self-explanatory; however, one or two points could be made. For example Smith and Schofield on inter-library loans in their library 'Q' (Table 2, code 25), state that inter-library loans (ILLs) over a 3-month period were 549, with a unit time of 100 minutes.[14] This suggests a primary task time (PTT) per staff member in the region of 1,220 hours. At Liverpool, in the financial year 1975-6, 11,000 inter-library loans were handled with two, full time equivalent, staff. There may be differences in interpretation here or the possible greater reliance of Liverpool on one primary source in the British Library Lending Division may account for the discrepancy. Similarly 80 per cent of our requests are photocopies. The university situation may well be considerably different.

Kirk gives some useful data derived from studies of university libraries on reshelving.[15] Table 2, code 26, shows 0.75 minutes per item at Liverpool. Reworking Kirks' data gives a rough 1.28 minutes per book for the universities. This difference can, possibly, be explained by the larger collection sizes of the universities and the likelihood of the presence of closed access areas. 'Sending overdues' shows some variation; however, an explanation may be offered. The low figures quoted in the College of Education Survey may be due to 'overdues' being internal mail only.

Within 'ordering' (Table 4) the Liverpool data shows that writing orders is a 61 per cent professional task. This is the consequence of professional staff, partly through convenience but probably mainly through necessity, writing orders during the selection process. This can have advantages in that the degree of urgency and the number of copies required are judged by professionals and included on the 'document request form' (DRF). Code 54/5 checking delivery notes, etc., occupies 1.5 per cent of all technical processes time compared with 9.9 per cent at Newcastle. All delivery notes, orders and invoices are identical at Liverpool. At site libraries, in 1974, unpacking was 43 per cent professional! This probably reflected both a staff shortage and the staff's wish to see and handle the new books! Some familiarization with new stock should take place of course. Currently this tends to be at the classification stage in that, for four site libraries, classification is not centralized being shared by Central Services Unit (CSU) staff and the site professional staff. However, code 105A shows that familiarization with new stock is 85 per cent professional. Code 56 'Accessioning' is primarily undertaken by book suppliers. It is only in the minority of cases that the CSU needs to accession items, *i.e.* where we have not ordered a title via our major suppliers.

Checking against the catalogue and BNB occupied 7 per cent of all CSU time in 1974 compared with 8.3 per cent in 1975; cataloguing reduced slightly from

COSTING AND ECONOMICS

		Liverpool		Hudson and Ford Unit times (mins)	COLP Unit times (mins)	CELRP Unit times (mins)	CLMRU Unit times (mins)	Newcastle Unit times (mins)	% of all processes
Code	Description	Professional % of task	Unit times (mins)						
51	Ordering:			All ordering processes:		(for all acquisition processes):			
	Writing orders	61		6.35 (optimum manual system includes selection)		24 (for most college libraries)		2.9	
	Checking items against catalogue	32				27 (where booka-matic or triggering			
	Checking v 'on order' file Verifying all details	91		4.55 (automated)		22.4 (processed by supplier)			
	Selection	70		9.54 (Bristol) 7.95 (Exeter)		(for all ordering processes)			
	Notification to requester of decision to purchase	18				12 (emergency rate)			
51B	Standing order (per item)		4.4				38 Library Q		
53	Post-ordering (filing, checking, etc.)		2.5				33 Library R		
53A	Chasing orders		3.2						
53B	Filing order forms (DRFs)		1.3						
53C	Withdrawing order forms								
53D	Book order queries	2						1.09	

54/55	Unpacking books, checking delivery notes or invoice (per item). Liverpool includes altering prices and shelving in year order in the CSU						
	At each site level	1.7	All receipt processes: Bristol 7.54 Exeter 6.26	0.56		3	9.9
		1.8	2·65 (optimum manual system for all receipt processes). 1.8 (automated)				
		43					
					A	D E G	
					2.95	3 1.3 3.6	
56	Accessioning Government publications and queries	3.3	2.2	2			1.9 14
							1.7
							3.3 7
57	Packing books for site libraries (per 100 books)	2.7		0.47			
58	Unpacking accessioned books (per 100 books)			0.6			

TABLE 4: *Ordering*

COSTING AND ECONOMICS

		Liverpool		Hudson and Ford Unit times (mins)	COLP Unit times (mins)	CELRP Unit times (mins)	CLMRU Unit times (mins)	Newcastle	
Code	Description	Professional % of task	Unit times (mins)					Unit times (mins)	% of all technical processes
Pre-cataloguing									
61a	Checking v. BNB catalogue	13	8	All cataloguing processes: 29.47 (optimum manual)	6.6 (codes 59–61)				
61b	Allocating expenditures to budget categories. Per item		0.4						
Cataloguing				28.69 Bristol 31.05 Exeter (for whole process to filing cards in catalogue)		A D E G	24 (codes 63 and 68) net 64–69 gross* (codes 63–77 +100)	52.4 of AP2/3 21.8 of AP4/5	
63	Classification (including subject indexing)	62	9.2 (1975) 9.6 (1974)		5.56	5.6 6.4 3.5 5.5		26.3 (codes 63–73) SO2 time	
63a	Queries, revision, reclassification, etc.		6.7				15 net (codes 62 and 63) 55 gross (codes 62–77+100)		

				A	D	E	G	
68	Cataloguing onto input forms	5.9	4.54					
71	Checking cataloguing	2.44		1.9	2.7	0.7	0.6	1.1
					(includes filing)			
72	Checking classification and subject indexing	4.5						
74	Typing catalogue cards	1.1			1.2	0.48	1.8	0.7
78	Proof reading and validation, incl. editing periodical catalogue for input. Per entry.	0.8						
	Proof reading typed catalogue cards. Per card		0.6					
	validation of print-out per entry	0.34						14.9
								12.1 (AV)

* Represents cataloguing for departmental and main or departmental library.

TABLE 5: *Cataloguing*

COSTING AND ECONOMICS

		Liverpool		COLP	CELRP	Newcastle
Code	Description	Professional % of task	Unit times (mins)	Unit times (mins)	Unit times (mins)	Unit times (mins)
100	Labels, jackets, book cards at CSU	2	3.3	2	A 7.6	2.7
	at sites		3			
101	Triggering		1	1		
102	Dymoing spines			1.6		
103	Checking, processing and sorting	14	0.7		0.6 D 1.4 E 17 G 7 0.4 2.3 0.14	
104A	Creating 'quick reference' item		4.2			
104B	Creating 'short loan' item		4.5			
105A	Scrutinizing new books	85				
105–7	Checking v reservation file and informing reader		2.2			
111	Stocktaking losses recording		3			
112	Withdrawing books, removing records		3.7			3.4

TABLE 6: *Processing*

25 per cent in 1974 to about 20 per cent in 1975. This probably reflects the greater involvement of non-professional staff using 'Books in English' (formerly), BNB and CIP information to transcribe data onto the input documents for the computerized catalogue. These are checked by a professional staff member who also does the 'difficult' items. 'Keyword' indexing, classification and subject indexing are a shared responsibility of technical services and site library professional staff. Classification took some 19 per cent of the total CSU time in 1975. Newcastle indicate some 17 per cent of technical services time devoted to 'processing'. In Liverpool, where the greater part of processing is undertaken by book suppliers, the percentage is 6.6 per cent although to this should be added a currently uncertain proportion of site libraries' time. Much of the processing of Liverpool stock is undertaken by suppliers.

The unit times, however accurate or variable, are but one aspect of the problem. A further element in the data is required before one can use the information to free staff for work elsewhere—the time and quantity of work predicted for the year. Using annual report statistics is *post hoc* and hence not entirely reliable for this purpose. Past records of peaks and quantities are a guide only to future expectations. One requires an analysis of work-load and output over time in order to identify any regularities which indicate a consistently light (or perhaps one should say 'less-heavy') load in any section. Projections on an annual basis via time trends and so on may be useful for justifying staff numbers or arguing for others but this is too crude for an adequate response to seasonal or other changes over shorter cycles. What is really needed is a prediction of demands next week and next month even to the extent of morning, afternoon and evening periods. Attempts to do this are being made by sampling output during the year. The principle of relative deprivation may then have to apply—one takes from one section to bolster another that is more heavily committed. This is never easy, not least because one may be limited in one's ability to move staff between sites. Slack may not be experienced by the grade of staff required in the deprived section at that time. There are obvious limits to whom one can transfer to duties elsewhere apart from any job description or union difficulties.

Using the figures to justify additional staff necessitates the adoption of various assumptions which themselves could be challenged being in all likelihood 'improvements' on the present situation. One may have measured the time devoted to, say, shelf revision under the existing system. This may not be the ideal amount of time. One may need shelf revision twice a day as opposed to a possible current situation of once a week. One's superiors may challenge this on the grounds that you did at least survive before. There is a need to predict but one should be wary of Parkinson's law operating. Conversely staff can speed up operations under pressure, through successful staff training, or by better recruitment methods. If all that is required is the appearance of a systematic approach to work levels and staffing needs then the rough 'norms' developed (I believe) at Leicester Polytechnic may suffice. One is all aware that a Churchillian statement on one side of A4 paper may have a greater effect and be better understood than reams of possibly more objective and 'scientific' data. However, it is never easy to justify norms that appear arbitrary. These norms are:

Housekeeping: 1 clerical hour per week per 1,000 stock.
Counter duties: 2 clerical hours per hour open per week.
Mail: 5 clerical hours per week.
Supervision: 2 professional hours per staff per week.
Selection: 5 hours per professional staff per week.
Enquiries: 1 enquiry per 10 *potential* readers per week × 10 minutes.
Tuition and current awareness and liaison: ½ hour per 10 potential readers per week.

Weekly available hours per staff member are assessed to be 35 for this purpose. An example based on one Liverpool Polytechnic site library is shown in Appendix 1.

It can be seen that the present staff of 5½ is nicely inflated to 8.9. Independently we have justified 3 additional staff so in this case the norms appear to work.

Conclusion

There is a need to agree basic parameters with the controlling agency. A personnel department of a local authority may not have norms for such things as 'available working time'. Indeed recent national agreements have been implemented on the understanding that no increase in staff should be demanded consequent on changes in the annual holiday allowances or the length of the working week. Similarly, library staff are assumed never to be ill! On the other hand the personnel department may wish to apply standards to all employees across the entire local authority. If it has not already done so this is a massive undertaking. The result may not be to one's liking. One may be establishing a precedent. There may be other O and M studies showing differing results. It is easier to obtain agreement to the use of such formulae if the institution, of which the library is a part, has the power to allocate staff (as obtains in some polytechnics).

REFERENCES

1 SMITH, G. C. K. *and* SCHOFIELD, J. L. Administrative effectiveness: times and costs of library operations. *Journal of Librarianship* 3 (4), October 1971, p. 247 (referred to in tables as CLMRU).
2 MASTERSON, W. A. J. Work study in a polytechnic library. *Aslib Proceedings* 28 (9), September 1976, p. 288–304. Itself based on: NEWCASTLE UPON TYNE POLYTECHNIC LIBRARY. Planning and research note 3. *Work Study* June–July 1975.
3 DEPARTMENT OF EMPLOYMENT TRIPARTITE WORKING GROUP. *An introduction to predetermined motion time systems.* HMSO, 1976, p. 4.
4 FRENCH, D. *and* SAWARD, H. *Dictionary of management.* Gower Press, 1975. 'Standard time. 1. The time as determined by work measurement, that should be taken to perform a job under specified conditions. It consists of: (a) basic time plus (b) relaxation allowance plus (c) an allowance for additional work (*i.e.* infrequent or irregular tasks that the worker has to perform or time spent consulting a supervisor) plus (d) an allowance for "unoccupied time" caused because a worker has to wait for other members of a team to finish their job or to wait for machinery to be ready.' That is, including tea-breaks, fatigue, personal needs, waiting time and other allowances.
5 GILDER, L. *and* SCHOFIELD, J. L. Work measurement techniques and library management: methods of data collection. University of Cambridge, Library Management Research Unit. April 1976 (LMRU Report No. 2), p. 17.

6 DEPARTMENT OF EMPLOYMENT TRIPARTITE WORKING GROUP *op. cit.*, p. 12.
7 MASTERSON, W. A. J. *op cit.*, p. 290.
8 CITY OF LONDON POLYTECHNIC. Library and learning resources service. A diary survey to establish time and cost data for library processes. COLP, 1973 (referred to in tables as COLP).
9 COLLEGE OF EDUCATION LIBRARIES RESEARCH PROJECT. Final report. Didsbury College of Education, January 1973 (referred to in tables as CELRP).
10 HUDSON, R. F. B. *and* FORD, M. G. South west university libraries system co-operation project: a report for the period July 1969–December 1972. Bristol University, 1973.
11 WILLIAMS, H. Developing a table of relaxation allowances. *Work Study and Management Services* 18 (7), July 1973, p. 478–83.
12 DEPARTMENT OF EMPLOYMENT TRIPARTITE WORKING GROUP *op. cit.*, p. 74.
13 BRECH, E. F. L. (ed.) *The principles and practice of management.* 2nd ed. Longmans, 1963, p. 308–21.
14 SMITH, G. C. K. *and* SCHOFIELD, J. L. *op. cit.*, p. 257.
15 KIRK, R. W. Survey on re-shelving in university and large public libraries. *Research in Librarianship* 4 (22), January 1973, p. 101–16.

APPENDIX I

Construction Library and branch library	'Norm'	Present staff Prof. / Other	Potential readers (total: 1,309) Staff / Students	Present term opening hrs/wk	Stock	Prof. hrs/wk reqd	Clerical hrs/wk reqd
		2 / 3¼	99 / 1,210	46¾ + 37½ = 84¼	32,000		
'Housekeeping'	1 clerical hr:wk:1,000 stock				32 × 1		32
Counter	2 clerical staff:1 hr open:wk			84¼ × 2			168½
Mail	5 clerical hrs:wk						5
Supervision	2 prof. hrs:1 staff:wk	3¼ × 2				7	
Prof. selection	5 prof. hrs:wk	2 × 5				10	
Enquiries	1 enquiry:10 potential readers:week × 10 mins		1 × 130 × 10 mins			21.66	
Tuition and 'current awareness' + liaison staff	5 hrs:10 potential readers:week		130 × 0.5 hrs			65	
Total hours						103.66	206.5
(÷ 35) = Total staff						3	5.9

Programmed budgeting and cost effectiveness

D. Mason

Paper presented at an Aslib one-day Symposium on 'Management in a service context', Manchester, 21st November 1972

Introduction

The importance of being able to demonstrate the effectiveness of information services, in terms of value supplied for money spent, needs no emphasis from me. Industry, in particular, has to show a reasonable return on invested capital, and information services can expect to be supported only as long as they demonstrate their worth.[1] Ideally it would be best to be able to put a quantified value on the information supplied, but there is as yet no acceptable method for measuring, or even estimating this value. This is an area in which research needs to be done, and I hope it will be done in the not-too-distant future. However, the fact remains that at present we cannot, except in a very few cases, estimate this value; and although I have recently been taken to task for refusing to grasp this nettle,[2] I remain unrepentant and continue to insist that for the time being we will have to do our best without it.

It remains my opinion, therefore, that a method for demonstrating cost-effectiveness is the next best thing and that in programmed budgeting we have the necessary techniques.

PPBS

The Planning-Programming-Budgeting System, PPBS for short, was designed as a means of providing policy makers with an analytical evaluation of existing and proposed activities, supported, whenever possible, with quantitative measures of performance. The principal part in the setting up of PPBS is the definition of the overall objectives of the organization to which the system is to be applied; followed by the definition of the objectives of particular activities, and the clarification of assumptions made when planning those activities. The aim of PPBS is to analyse expenditure in relation to purpose, and to relate it with results achieved. The questions which have to be asked, and answered, are:

(a) What are the objectives of the organization?
(b) What activities contribute to these activities?
(c) What resources are devoted to these activities?
(d) What is actually being achieved?

A system like this must obviously lead to a form of budgeting different to the

COSTING AND ECONOMICS

traditional budget, in that expenditure is categorized by the purpose for which it is being spent, rather than by the resource, e.g. staff, materials, maintenance, etc. As it is most likely that normal budgeting systems will continue to operate, a method for linking the two, and for keeping them in step, has also to be operated.

Objectives

No doubt each one of us could draw up a list of objectives for our information service, and this is one of the problems in discussing PPBS, in that no two information services are exactly alike. I make no apology therefore for the following list, but offer it as a 'hard core' around which other, and less important, objectives can be grouped.

The objectives of the industrial information and library service are to assist in the maximizing of the company's projects and in the reduction of operating costs by:

(a) Exploiting the literature and other sources of information in order to provide the company's staff with new and up-to-date information on the company's interests.
(b) Providing an efficient and effective enquiry answering and information retrieval system. (You may wonder why I differentiate here but I am sure you will agree that there is a world of difference between the retrieving of information and its presentation to an enquirer.)
(c) Acting as a centre for the company's information services and materials in order to make generally available important documents that might otherwise not be fully exploited.
(d) Acting as a control point for the filing of the company's own reports and related documents, and organizing them for use in order to aid the exploitation of company know-how, and reduce or eliminate duplication of work. (A good reports centre becomes, over the years, a company's corporate memory.)
(e) Building up a collection of periodicals, books, patents and other publications, and purchasing information services available on a commercial basis, on subjects relevant to the company's needs, in order to support the service activities.
(f) Fulfilling all these objectives in an economic and balanced manner so that only reasonable services are provided, and at as low a cost as possible commensurate with effectiveness.

Activities

Let us turn now to the activities which relate to the objectives. Firstly we have to carry out a number of operational activities. Publications have to be selected and purchased, reports have to be acquired, documents have to be indexed and so on. Then there are the service activities, current awareness, information retrieval, reference and loan services. There are several ways in which this list could be drawn up. I have separated the activities into nine main programmes: four operational and five service. These are:

Operational activities
1.0 Acquisition of materials
2.0 Preparation of indexes
3.0 Stock control and maintenance
4.0 Services and systems (Evaluation and research)

Service activities
5.0 Current awareness
6.0 Information retrieval
7.0 Reference and loan
8.0 Supply and distribution
9.0 Training and advisory

Each of these programmes is made up of a number of elements. The following is an example of an operational programme:

Programme code	Element code	
1.0		Acquisition of materials
	1.1	Books and pamphlets
	1.2	Periodicals
	1.3	Information retrieval publications
	1.4	Information retrieval services
	1.5	Reports
	1.6	Patents

and an example of a service programme is:

Programme code	Element code	
5.0		Current awareness
	5.1	S.D.I.
	5.2	Bulletins
	5.3	Circulation
	5.4	Clippings

Each element has to be clearly distinct from the other elements. In the 'Acquisition programme', for example, information retrieval publications are shown as a distinct element, but it could be argued that they are either in book form or issued as periodicals and do not therefore need to be distinguished. However, there may be many occasions when one would wish to compare the cost-effectiveness of such publications with the cost-effectiveness of in-house indexes in order to decide which to use. There is therefore a case for keeping this type of material as a separate element.

Analysis of procedures

The purpose of and procedures used for each element have to be analysed. What is the objective and how is it carried out? Let us take '1.1 Acquisition of books' as our example:

Element 1.1 — *Acquisition of books and pamphlets.*
OBJECTIVE: To acquire, by purchase or otherwise, and to record the receipt of the books, pamphlets, government publications, trade literature, standards, etc. needed to support or provide the requisite information, reference and loan services.

COSTING AND ECONOMICS

PROCEDURE: Bibliographical details of the required publication are verified; the appropriate bookseller or other agent is selected; an order is typed and despatched. On receipt the publication is checked; receipt is recorded; and the invoice checked and passed for payment.

One could, if one wished, carry out a detailed analysis of the systems, but this, though desirable at times, is not strictly required for PPBS. The main purpose is to show why the activity is being carried out, and what tasks are associated with the activity and the sequence in which they are carried out. This should ensure that nothing is missed when staff and material costs are being ascertained.

Costs

The next step of PPBS required that the costs of each element are worked out. The amount of staff time involved has to be ascertained and then converted into the cash value. It is possible with a lot of hard work to achieve an apparently high level of accuracy in the measurement of staff costs. The accuracy may however be illusory. For the purposes of PPBS it is sufficient to round off each cost to the nearest £100 and this means that it is sufficient to get each member of staff to estimate the percentage of time spent on each activity with which he or she is involved.

An average salary rather than an actual salary should be used. This avoids the need to consider whether a group of people concerned with an activity are at the top of their grades, moving up, or, most probably, a mixture of both. Managerial and supervisory staffs' costs should be included in each activity by percentage of time allocated, if it is possible to estimate this. If not, the costs can be allocated over all activities in proportion to the other staff costs involved, by the simple process of adding the Manager's salary to the total professional salaries, and then dividing by the number of professional staff, excluding the Manager, in order to arrive at an average salary which includes his costs.

Separate costs for professional and clerical (or operational) staff should be obtained, because this enables a check to be made on the proportions of work between the two categories in any particular activity; and also to check that in those activities where the professional involvement should be small, this is in fact the case.

To complete the costing process, it is necessary to obtain the costs of any materials or services, e.g. photocopying involved in the activity. One should also include the appropriate costs for maintenance of buildings, heating, lighting, etc., but as many companies allocate these to a central budget, I have excluded them here.

The costs of materials purchased, books, periodicals, etc. should be obtainable from the normal budget figures, although it may be necessary to analyse expenditure in order to find, for example, the cost of purchasing information retrieval publications. The costs of rented equipment such as photocopiers, punched card machinery can be allocated *en bloc* to the appropriate activities. However, the full costs of purchased equipment will have to be worked out.

Let us take as an example a photocopying machine which cost £1000:

Direct on-cost   £
Depreciation: 1/8th of capital cost = 125.00
Capital: 10% interest charge = 100.00
Maintenance and repairs: estimated at 5% = 50.00
Floor space: 10 square feet at £2 = 20.00

           295.00

Materials
Paper and chemicals for
  c. 5000 copies per annum   150.00

       TOTAL   445.00

To these figures the staff costs must be added, and for full costing one would add the indirect on-costs for supervision, heating, lighting, etc., but I will return to these later when dealing with comparative costs.

One final point on costs. When the current costs have been ascertained, future costs can be estimated for up to, say, three years, by adding the appropriate percentages. With rapidly rising costs there can be no certain figure, but 7% annually for increases in staff costs, and 10% for increases in material costs should give somewhere about the right figure.

Costs for operational activities

I have found that a standard form can be used for the costs of each element. The form has separate parts for direct and associated costs. Operational activities have direct costs, and as they exist only as supports for the service activities, these costs have to be transferred to the appropriate services, where they are entered on the form as associated costs. Here is an example of this:

Programme   Preparation of indexes   *Element code*
  Element   Reports Index   2.2

            1972
            £100
    Direct costs
    Salaries—Information staff   10
    Salaries—Operational staff   2
    Materials   2

       TOTAL   14

Observed use of Reports Index
  Information retrieved from reports (element 6.3) 50%
  Identification of reports required for loan (element 7.4) 50%
         £100
    Transferred costs
    Element 6.3   7
    Element 7.4   7

With the service activities the direct costs are totalled, and then the associated costs which have been transferred from the operational activities. The addition of these two figures gives the full cost of the service. An example is shown in Table 1:

TABLE 1: *Full cost of information service*

Programme Element	Information retrieval Literature	1972 £100	Element code 6.1 1973 £100	1974 £100
	Direct costs			
A	Salaries—Information staff	13	14	15
B	Salaries—Operational staff	8	9	10
	TOTAL	21	23	25
	Associated costs			
1.1	Acquisition—books	4	4	4
1.2	Acquisition—periodicals	4	4	4
1.3	Acquisition—IR publications	16	17	18
2.1	Catalogue	2	2	2
2.3	Suppliers Index	9	10	11
2.4	Trade Name Index	3	3	3
3.1	Selection and disposal	2	2	2
3.3	Binding	4	4	4
4.1	Evaluation	1	1	1
4.2	Research	2	2	2
	TOTAL	47	49	51
	GRAND TOTAL	68	72	76

This example shows a fully worked out cost sheet. The direct costs, as one would expect, are entirely staff costs. The letters A and B shown against these refer to the salaries part of the normal budget and this permits easy reference for the so-called 'crosswalk' technique which can be carried out on a computer if desired. Basically it means that the totals of all A's and B's from the PPBS cost sheets should match the total salaries as shown in the traditional budget. This provides a useful cross-check.

The associated costs have been transferred from the elements as shown, with their codes and headings. The forecast figures have been worked out and show that the cost of providing this service will increase from £6800 in 1972 to £7600 in 1974.

Cost effectiveness

Each activity has now to be examined in order, if possible, to quantify its value. A few of the operational activities will have quantifiable benefits and these should be transferred to the service activities using the same proportions as the transferred costs. All the services should be able to demonstrate benefits, but there may be some for which there is no easy way of measurement and for which the benefits will have to be shown as NQ, i.e. non-quantifiable.

This stage of PPBS is the most difficult part of the system. What is the value of an abstract bulletin, or the results of a search for information? As I said earlier, it is not possible at the moment to put a value on information supplied and we must therefore turn aside from cost-benefits and look instead at cost-effectiveness. If we did not supply a certain service, what would it cost the users of that service to do it for themselves? Most of us know our customers only too well, so I think it is safe to assume that in many cases 50 per cent of them would probably do without the service, which brings us back to the value of the information lost!

However here is an example of cost-effectiveness worked out for information retrieval from the literature (I should emphasize that to carry out this sort of calculation you do need to have reasonably accurate figures for the usage made of the service):

Element 6.1

Approx. 3000 enquiries answered annually, 200 of which require lengthy searches. Minimum savings are estimated at £1 per quick enquiry and £20 for a search.

Additionally 200 quick enquiries are answered from the Suppliers Index and 1000 from the Trade Names Index. Further savings accrue from Information Retrieval Publications (element 1.3).

Costs	£	Savings	£
Direct	2100	Quick enquiries	4000
Associated	4700	Lengthy searches	4000
		I.R. Publications	3500
TOTAL	6800	TOTAL	11,500

As you will see certain assumptions or 'guesstimates' have to be made, but no doubt the system can be refined by more accurate measurement of customer time saved. Perhaps one of you would like to carry out some controlled experiments to this end, that is if you can get your customers to be the guinea pigs!

The system that I have outlined for estimating cost-effectiveness does lean over backwards to be fair. In fact, if anything, it does not put sufficient value on our activities. Nevertheless I have shown, to my own satisfaction at least, that for every £100 spent on information services, there should be a saving of £200 staff time in other departments—and that is not a bad return on capital!

Unit costs

Theoretically it should be possible to calculate unit costs for most library activities in the same sort of way as say the *Builder's Pricebook*. However, practice varies so much from organization to organization that the costs would not be accurate enough to be meaningful. One has only to consider, for example, the costs of indexing. The amount of staff time involved would depend entirely on such factors as depth of indexing, and whether the exercise was entirely intellectual, or partly intellectual and partly mechanized. However, if you do feel the need to have unit costs for your own service, it is not difficult to obtain these from a programmed budget. Taking indexing again as an example, you would know from your budget the total cost of this activity, and from your records you should know the number of documents indexed in the year. Dividing the cost by the number of documents will give you the unit cost for your own service.

Capital expenditure

There are times when we are faced with the problem of deciding which of two items of equipment—for example, photocopiers—we should obtain for use in our unit, and perhaps also whether we should purchase or lease them. Obviously the first factor to be taken into consideration is the quality of the end product. We would not purchase a photocopier that produced prints in which the text was dark grey and the background was light grey! But assuming that we are faced with a choice between two machines, using different processes perhaps, but each producing a copy that is acceptable to our customers, the choice can be guided by calculating the cost per copy, because obviously we are looking for value for money.

First of all then the fixed costs have to be calculated. The machinery will ultimately wear out and photocopying machines tend to have a useful life of about eight years. Then there is interest on capital to consider—that is to say, if the money had not been spent it could have been invested and interest earned. The cost of the floor space occupied, both by the machine and by the person operating it has to be added. One has also to estimate the machine loading. Obviously, although the photocopier is in the library's possession, it can only be used when staff are present, when it is not being repaired or checked for maintenance, and when there is sufficient work for it to be operated. In a library the machine loading will probably be about 50 per cent.

Next the variable costs are calculated, including the cost of maintenance and repairs (covered by a contract, otherwise estimated at 5 per cent), cost of materials, cost of operator's time, and the so-called 'indirect on-costs', which are costs of heating, lighting, supply of electricity, supervision, and costs of staff over and above wages. These are usually estimated at 100 per cent of staff costs.

One final item is the time taken to make a copy; not the machine time, but the total time taken by the operator in picking up the original, placing it in the copier, pressing the button, removing the original, removing the copy. Here is an example:

Direct on-cost	£
Depreciation (8%)	125
Capital (10%)	100
Maintenance (5%)	50
Floor space	25
	300

Estimated machine loading 50% (1000 hrs.)
= 0.5p per minute

Materials

Cost per sheet of paper	3p
Cost of developing fluid per copy	.05p
	3.05p

Labour

Averaged to £800 per annum = 1.8p per minute

Time

Average time to make one copy = 2.5 minutes

TOTAL COST

Labour 2.5 minutes at 1.8p	=	4.50p
Materials	=	3.05p
Direct on-cost 2.5 mins. at 0.5p	=	1.25p
Indirect on-cost (100% labour cost)	=	4.50p
		13.30p

It is almost certain that the sales representative will have told you that the cost per copy would be about 3p, but you and I know better. A similar calculation for the other machine will tell you which one provides the cheaper copy.

Now let us turn to the question of how to pay for what you want. Here, for sake of simplicity, I am going to assume that you have decided to have one particular photocopier but have a choice of rental or purchase. One company offers to sell you the machine for £1000, and your materials' costs will be £500 a year. The other company offers to rent you the machine for £750 per year, the rental includes the materials. Which is the better offer? Obviously the one that costs less. A straightforward calculation, allowing say a five year depreciation at £200 a year plus material costs of £500 per year would suggest that buying averages out £50 per year cheaper than leasing (see Table 2).

TABLE 2

			Year				TOTAL
	0	1	2	3	4	5	
A Purchase price (£)	1000						
Materials (£)		500	500	500	500	500	
	1000	500	500	500	500	500	3500
B Lease (£)	—	750	750	750	750	750	3750

But we have to consider that money paid out in the future hurts less than money paid out to-day (which is why moneylenders flourish). The question is how much less. Table 3 shows the results of Discounting the Cash Flow at two rates, 5 per cent and 10 per cent, as compared with not allowing for DCF at all. If we think, as well we might in these days, that the 10 per cent Discount factor is about right, then Table 3 shows that leasing is cheaper than purchase.

TABLE 3

DISCOUNT FACTOR		YEAR						TOTAL
		0	1	2	3	4	5	
0	Purchase (£)	1000	500	500	500	500	500	3500
	Lease (£)		750	750	750	750	750	3750
5%	Purchase (£)	1000	476	454	432	412	392	3166
	Lease (£)		714	681	648	618	588	3249
10%	Purchase (£)	1000	454	413	386	342	311	2906
	Lease (£)		681	620	579	513	466	2859

Value concept

Finally, and briefly, I want to refer to the concept of value. The principal objective is to reduce the costs of an operation while retaining or enhancing the quality. This requires that staff be trained to look critically, and on a continuous basis, at all the activities in which they are involved, with a view to getting value for money spent.

The techniques I have already described can provide the quantitative basis on which costs and benefits can be assessed, and can help the Information Manager to demonstrate to his boss that the money is being used effectively. This may not prevent demands being made for reduction in costs, but should enable us to insist that quality and performance must be maintained, and what the economic effects will be if they are not.

REFERENCES

1. MASON. D. PPBS: application to an industrial information and library service. *J. Librarianship*, **4**, 2, April 1972, p. 91–105.
2. BLAGDEN, J. Special libraries. *Library Assoc. Record*, **74**, 7, July 1972, p. 122–3.

An Application of Managerial Cost Accounting to a Science Information Center

Michael L. Cochran, A. Gilmore Smith, Jr., and A. Douglas Bender

Introduction

In his recent paper, Helmkamp (1) observed that there have been very few attempts to determine the cost of information centers and their services. The author concludes that sound cost accounting procedures can be applied to the operations of an information center and that relevant cost information may be useful as a measure of the center's operating performance.

We have been concerned for some time with the problem of judging the value of an information service or program in relation to its cost.[1] This has led us to use a cost accounting methodology to determine the cost of efforts in our Science Information (SI) center that would open the operation to an incremental cost-to-value analysis of the service and program offered.

---

[1] This concern of judging the value of information service to its cost is manifested in Phillips' paper entitled "Cost Analysis of a Document Retrieval System," which has been submitted to *American Documentation* (now *JASIS*) for publication. Phillips presents a cost *analysis* technique of assessing the cost-value relationship of an information service, while this brief communication addresses itself to a cost *accounting* technique.

The wide range and sophistication of activities that characterize Science Information at Smith Kline & French (2, 3) and the complexity of user information requests, coupled with the interaction of definable information centers within the SI function, necessitated our calling upon established cost accounting principles and techniques to determine the cost portion of the cost-to-value analysis of SI efforts. We proceeded to determine the costs generated by our SI efforts by using the following steps:

STEP I—ESTABLISH DEFINABLE SCIENCE INFORMATION CENTERS

The first step was to define the types of information service that were being requested by the R&D Division and other operating centers of the Corporation. A total of 22 definable services (effort centers) were identified, e.g., alerting, networking, data processing, etc. Each defined effort center was then costed out by identifying and collecting those expenses that were generated independently by that center, such as salaries, supplies, direct charged depreciation, and allocated overheads. These costs may be defined as variable expenses, in that they respond directly to the degree of activity generated by a demand for that effort's output.

STEP II—DEFINE ADMINISTRATIVE SUPPORT CENTERS

Each effort center that was identified was supported by administrative and supervisory centers. These centers were individually costed out in the same manner as the effort centers. The costs of the administrative support centers were then allocated to their respective effort centers based on the degree of administration and supervision required by each effort center. In some instances, a proportion of the administrative support center's activity was expended directly to the user, thereby bypassing the effort center under its control. By definition, the administrative support cost allocated to the effort centers may be considered as fixed expenses by the effort center. After the administrative support center's costs had been allocated to the effort centers, the total costs for each of the 22 effort centers, which describes SK&F's SI services, were tabulated.

Step III—Determine the Effort Center—User Interface

In step three we assigned effort cost to the user. Within SI, we have a cross allocation of effort direction, e.g., machine records servicing two of the data system effort points, library effort supporting the alerting effort, etc. After the intra-effort cost allocation was made, each defined effort center was then allocated to the operating function within the R&D Division and other operating functions requesting its service. This was accomplished by defining the number of requests by a specific R&D program or function.

The problem of judging the value of an information service or program is not quite as quantitative as costing the efforts of the service or program. However, the fundamental observation has been made that the ability to assess a risk situation is increased if timely information of high quality is brought into the decision-making process. Recently, Dalkey (4) illustrated this observation in his Spectrum of Inputs graph, which describes the increase in the probability of truth that can be applied to a statement as the quality of information moves from speculation through opinion to knowledge. Using this observation, the intrinsic value of a definable SI effort is related to the ability of that effort to define accurately the background of uncertainty against which a risk or investment decision must be formulated. The degree of risk associated with an investment will determine that investment's economic value; the degree of economic value associated with an investment, whether that investment be in future dollars or existing resource utilization, obviously must be related to the magnitude of the cost of that investment.

Conclusion

Certain advantages can accrue by applying established cost accounting techniques to information centers and their services. In our experience, the immediate advantage was to make the effort centers within our SI function visible to management and the users. By costing out the effort centers, both user and management could assess the cost in relation to the value of the information service—an incremental cost-to-value analysis. Expansion or contraction of a specific effort could be more realistically planned via the now available incremental cost-to-value analysis. By defining variable and fixed costs, better budgeting procedures could be adopted. We are now in a position to answer Helmkamp's challenge "for a reliable quantitative measurement with which future manpower requirements can be correlated with the expected service demand (*1*)"; and furthermore, to begin the cost-to-value analysis of information.

References

1. HELMKAMP, J. G., Managerial Cost Accounting for a Technical Information Center, *American Documentation,* 20:111–118 (1969).
2. BENDER, A. D., The Organization and Management of R&D Information Activities at SK&F, *Journal of Chemical Documentation,* 9:196–201 (1969).
3. BENDER, A. D., M. GORDON, and R. L. HAYNE, The Need for Creative Analysis in the Transfer of Useful Information, *Proceedings of the American Society for Information Science,* 5:37–41 (1968).
4. DALKEY, N. C., The Delphi Method: An Experimental Study of Group Opinion, Memorandum RM–5888–PR, Santa Monica, Calif., The Rand Corporation, June 1969, p. 3, Fig. 1.

Teaching costing techniques to librarians and information scientists of the future

R. Sturt

Paper presented at an Aslib Engineering Group Conference on 'Costing library and information services', 25th–27th February 1972

I LITTLE THOUGHT, when our mutual friend, Leslie Patrick, led me last June towards the giving of this paper on costing techniques, that my standpoint would have changed to the extent that it has. As a *teacher* for nine years in the sphere of library management or administration, as it was for so long called, my outlook had been tempered by the Library Association's policy, rigorously maintained, that library education aimed to afford the novice the broadest possible view of librarianship. This meant that the descriptive—no matter how lyrical—was *in*; the evaluative or critical—using techniques or tools—was *out*.

In fairness to the Library Association, as to yourselves, it should be remembered that the major syllabus revision of ten years ago was affected more by the claims of certain groups of librarians to have their practices given an airing than by any latent wish to allow the library student to play around with management concepts or principles. Most of you know the results of that policy if, for example, cost-consciousness is the measure that we apply to library performance today.

Now—as a chief librarian of seven weeks' standing—my outlook has been hammered by harsh economic facts. Whether it is computing the manpower and space budgets for planned growth of stock over the next few years (space, I am warned, at £7 a square foot to rent) or determining the cost basis of photocopying service, the need emerges to have at hand or up one's sleeve a battery of hard costs built up by one's own small garrison from objective data.

But, before this translation occurred, I had attempted to find out to what extent and by what means we in the library schools were teaching costing techniques. To do this I wrote to fifteen schools, including my own, seeking information about teaching programmes and materials on costing. I also asked if cost factors were considered in papers at appropriate points where comparative studies were made, as in cataloguing or processing evaluation, and invited examples of difficulty in securing cost data from libraries. My final two criteria were the response of students to any such teaching and the opportunities given students for projects or exercises in the field.

Twelve of the fifteen replied, some at length with much illustrative material and I am taking the liberty of quoting some of the replies.

Two of the twelve were to the point. One wrote: 'I find that we are not, in fact, doing anything at all about teaching cost techniques but I have thrown everyone into a fine fury of wonder as to whether they should be through asking them!' The other took me to task for pursuing my 'own little pet subject field' at a time when educational courses 'have to be broad in scope and deep in principle.' His next remark introduced the facet which I think merits some further discussion as it recurs in other replies: the longer the course is, the greater the opportunity becomes to study certain topics in depth; if more continual assessment were permitted, topics such as costing techniques may well play a greater part. He was, of course, referring to the quiet, revolutionary process in library education in which the Library Association's two-year syllabus is being replaced by the three- or four-year degree syllabus in most schools. If I may hold to that point for a moment there is a pertinent remark from one other school: 'Student reaction is interesting. L.A. course students tend to the view that this is not relevant to librarianship; persuading them that it is, is on occasion uphill work. Degree students are however much more receptive: they tackle these concepts in fair detail in the final year of the course, and having spent a year in the profession ... the students appreciate the relevance to contemporary library administration.'

The clear-cut nature of this distinction may surprise many, but it is underlined by the experience of two schools which offer evidence of the readiness of postgraduate students to learn and apply costing techniques in projects based upon actual library case studies. There is, however, a different note struck by one school writing about postgraduate and undergraduate finals students: 'I have found that the concepts and methods presented little difficulty; nor do the notions of probability, basic algebra, arithmetic. Further, most students show a satisfying perspicacity in identifying weaknesses in mathematical models presented such as Urquhart/Buckland. However, their criticisms tend, very definitely, to be destructive, and they have little appreciation of how to go about remedying the defects of models. ... The students' mathematical "literacy" is usually poor, and—more's the worry—this does not seem to concern them.'

So much for students' reactions. I think the conclusions one may draw from these statements are that students in the final year of a degree course or on a postgraduate course are learning cost techniques and applying them beneficially, and that the more critical factor appears to be the maturity of the student rather than the length of the course. Maturity, in this sense, does include that acquired during the periods of directed practical work in libraries.

Six other schools planned their teaching to ensure that broad management concepts, rather than particular techniques, were clearly understood by students, with the focus upon budgetary processes when illustration was necessary. No substantial teaching of costing techniques, as such, was undertaken, and the two limiting factors quoted were lack of time and the immaturity of students. It should be understood that a consensus of library school opinion in the matter of teaching management techniques was attained at Cambridge in March 1971, when, at the conclusion of a seminar organized by the Library Management Research Unit, 'it was generally agreed that at levels up to first degree, all that could be given was an appreciation and awareness of management techniques.'

As these schools receive the majority of library students it is fair to note that, within the broad policy framework, the 'awareness' is on occasion taken to interesting stages. To quote one: 'Cost factors are used, whenever necessary, in general teaching. Examples are usually forthcoming from our good friends in neighbouring libraries (although the many variations in accounting practice make it difficult to isolate the components of many so-called unit costs).' Examples on a par with those in *Management techniques with particular reference to local government*, by J. M. Rogers, have proved satisfactory in making the student aware of the technique. Other schools use building costs, to show the comparative cost per square foot, or staffing costs linked with workloads, to arrive at examples of general costings. Cost-consciousness is one thing, but, in the view of one school, the 'ability to *use* the techniques is better taught in special short courses after a few years' more experience—and then only to those who will employ them'. Is that last point, I wonder, significant to us today?

One matter about which I was most curious (and unsatisfied) was the use of costing techniques or costs as a critical factor in the examination of cataloguing processes or retrieval systems. Papers were produced, such as *Information services: measuring the cost*, by J. M. S. Risk, or *An introduction to the study of cost effectiveness in information systems*, by Professor J. N. Wolfe, but it may have been a fault in my letter of enquiry that led to the omission of any precise statement of the part they played in the learning process.

My enquiry about the degree of difficulty in obtaining cost data evoked some blunt comment: 'The problem is not mainly one of what to teach and how to teach it, but one of access to some actual cost figures; the most difficult ones to get hold of are the actual prices of equipment . . . and for consumable materials *in the UK*. What is required are regular tabulations in *Aslib Proceedings* or *LAR* of UK prices as in Hayes and Becker, *Handbook of data processing for libraries*. The second problem area is that of costing policies in various institutions.' Here were stressed the differences in calculating overheads, depreciation and allocation. A third problem in the same area was the unwillingness of institutions supplying data to library schools to permit the publication of cost studies even when the identifying clues had been eliminated. Difficulties were mentioned by one other school in comparing 'bald figures' from two or more libraries without knowledge of the total library systems. The paucity of research studies in this field was stressed by a third school, which thought any present discussion would necessarily be 'tentative' and 'exploratory'.

The final consideration arising from this small survey must rest upon the nature and quality of the projects carried out at schools. One reports that there has been a number of students carrying out systems analysis and design studies as their special study project, with several concerned primarily with costing. Another school supplies three projects and I would like to use the titles to indicate the content and context: The unit cost of circulation in the X library; Determination of the unit cost of the circulation system at X college library; The unit cost of generating one catalogue card set at X college library. They are achievements of which I feel both lecturer and students may be proud, as time limitations were severe.

To conclude on the survey—before turning to teaching itself—it may be said that there is far more attention paid to costing techniques in 1972 than ever seemed possible in 1967, that the transition from two-year to longer or later (i.e. postgraduate) studies is speeding the movement towards a greater understanding of management principles, social context, and values, and that constraints such as insubstantial cost data or undue secrecy on the part of practising librarians probably match the restraints that some library educators impose upon techniques-centred courses. Not least in our discussions should be that small but so important question in a profession which nearly drowned in cataloguing and classification techniques: to whom should we teach costing techniques?

I would like to turn now to a plain account of teaching. As this is the first occasion in this paper that my personal views appear it may help to explain an early process of discolouration, when for eight years I bore the strain of keeping books and not reading them. The raw years of my working youth were spent in devising costing systems for two local authorities and, by maintaining rigid controls over expenditure analysis, it was possible to produce a range of unit costs which must at the time have been as startling to those who took decisions as they were unpredictable to me. One I remember was the cost of replacing panes in windows on Council estates. The results were shattering, too. When you realize that such work was carried out by elderly, semi-skilled men whose propensity for teabreaks was matched by that of the housewives, whose very proper concern to repay such kindness found expression in doing all the odd jobs on gate latches and doors unrecorded, and whose materials were for ever being shipped by a dog-like lorry, the value of the unit cost per pane—no matter how correctly computed—was no more real than the workrate of the workmen. They *did* work hard, and effectively; but, with time units of fifteen minutes, no minor jobs were recorded even if they were legitimate. Standard costs *were* attempted, for example the cost of scarifying a square yard of road surface; but one brave attempt to establish, for comparative and retirement purposes, the cost per mile for each vehicle reached a tricky point when it was discovered that a petrol pump at one depot actually *made* gallons of petrol a month by giving short measure. The effect of such a freak condition upon our figures can be imagined, but that was the major difficulty: ensuring that conditions were stable. We measured *operations*, and it would not, I am certain, have occurred to us to measure or quantify any aspects of *service*. It was, therefore, several years after becoming a librarian that the possibility of arriving at more precise costs occurred to me for those areas of our activity that could be isolated from 'service' connotation. This was in the 1950s, and I wrote to the LA and discovered the names of the other two librarians who shared my notion. We also discovered that two municipal treasurers—living miles apart—had prepared some material on costing library services. It was a brief and fruitless encounter; our best endeavours, as far as we could see, would bring us only to the fringes of any effective cost policy for a library when so much of what was spent—and the manner of its spending—was determined by arbitrary, inconsistent and often extravagant decisions taken in the name of service.

One incident in that period remains in memory. I was determined to use precise general costs where I could, and, as I wanted a wall-hung map unit, I wrote for details of one described in a library journal. I pressed the obliging librarian hard for exact costs for this thing that hung out sheets and sheets of 1" maps. Back it came with a specification, a drawing, labour and materials costs: all admirably tabulated. Neatly written along the bottom was: 'The wall fell down, and had to be re-built.' I have never had a wall-hung map unit.

Today—or last year—as a lecturer, the need to teach costing techniques to young people who, in current parlance, would go into middle management, loomed less large than the need to engage them critically in the study of people in the library (personnel management and reader relations) and of the overall planning of systems. My judgement may have been influenced by my knowledge of the cost of mounting and maintaining effective costing systems; an example of what I mean is given in that rather curious publication, *A report on the use of costing and other financial techniques in technical colleges, 1969*, where, after some fourteen paragraphs explaining and examing a unit cost basis, using the course as the unit and, by division, producing a cost-per-course-student, the Report runs:

> A costing exercise on these lines would be theoretically possible, and, if methods of apportionment of indirect expenses were specified, cost comparisons could be made between colleges. The results obtained would certainly be of interest, but it is doubtful whether the the cost of producing them could be justified.

It goes on:

> Financial control and cost-conciousness could be enhanced both by less ambitious costing exercises within colleges and by the publication of national figures of average costs. The possibility of sophisticated industrial-type costing will therefore not be pursued. . . .

It is difficult, in my view, to arrive at that kind of decision without far greater knowledge and experience of management situations than we are able to project in the classroom or seminar, even with case studies and exercises to help us. A technique is a tool used towards the attainment of an objective. A prerequisite to the use of a tool is understanding of the objective for which the tool is selected. It is that understanding, managerial understanding—insight if you like—which we should be trying to inculcate, to a greater or lesser degree, in the process of library education. There is a danger that competence in the use of techniques, without managerial insights, will lead to a negative or destructive attitude, as has been previously stated by one of the library schools. 'They have little appreciation of how to go about remedying the defects of the model. . .'.

Let me sketch the lecturing programme in order that you may hang your criticism upon it or part of it. I would like to insert a background note. Apart from two major postgraduate institutions the library schools in the main are providing courses in tandem: the Library Association in one seat, a university or CNAA in the other. With some rapidity (and agreement) the two are changing places. The LA is now—as an examining body—taking the back seat, and the library schools are in the steering seat, and choosing, within a local academic structure, the direction the courses will take.

The effects are important in this sense. Studies prepared by individual students are becoming increasingly accepted for assessment as a major element in the examination of that course. Thus, student projects—the study of a topic in depth and at length—are moving into fields where we scarcely put a foot before.

In this changing climate of the past few years there is not only individualized study, on projects, but new variants of traditional courses and also newer ways of learning, such as case studies, simulation and other exercises.

Management is divided into the five elements beloved by Brech, Fayol and Drucker: Planning/organizing/motivating/controlling and innovating. Planning includes financial planning, but in the main the element of controlling brings with it the study of the techniques by which control is established, such as budgeting, costing, work study and so on. The Treasury's *Glossary of management techniques* is used as an authority in the matter of definitions, with minor amendments.

The list of readings is kept small throughout the two-year course, in order to ensure availability and consistency of presentation. Activities such as performance budgeting are studied, with examples from the readings, but there is no attempt to prepare a budget by referring to particular objectives.

Costing, or cost accounting, is explained and considered in the light of various and varying statements from the readings. Direct and indirect costs are considered, and a handout assists the analysis. Unit cost is also looked at in this way, with some crude unit costs calculated, such as the cost of processing a book or of cataloguing a book. Cost–benefit analysis and cost-effectiveness are explained but there is no use of case material, and library examples of any great relevance have not yet been found, to be used.

Later in the course, when two major projects are in train, there is a series of lectures with the problems-approach. 'The problem of money' takes actual examples of money problems or inadequate financial information. The absence of costs as a limiting factor in library development—and the lack of cost-consciousness—are now considered in the light of experiences or observations from fieldwork or other situations. By simple exercises it is shown how, for example, the price of a book is related to the cost of processing it and then to the cost of making it available to the reader, to form a basis for compiling a budget that will bring the resources of manpower, stock and space, among other things, into balance.

Two of the greatest needs in teaching are the materials for case studies and authentic, detailed costings or unit costs. If as a result of this conference's deliberations a more open attitude is adopted towards financial information it will be a matter of joy to my former colleagues and some compensation for the free manner in which they have advanced information about their teaching methods—in many respects their most prized, guarded and secret possession.

5 TOWARDS MANAGERIAL ECONOMICS

5. TOWARDS MANAGERIAL ECONOMICS

The papers reproduced in this section reflect a shift in emphasis from those in the preceding sections; the concern with methods of cost data collection, cost analysis and management accounting give way to a preoccupation with the development of a body of economic theory relevant to libraries, in which cost data plays a significant part. In fact, cost data on library and information service operations is essential if theoretical economic models are to be tested empirically and the results of these models used in operational economic management. A combination of practical studies and theoretical explorations should assist library management to develop a useful corpus of methods, concepts and techniques which could collectively be called managerial economics.

Raffel (1974) explores the relationship between economic and political contexts in managerial decision-making in libraries. His arguments are backed up by the empirical studies which he and his co-worker undertook within the libraries of the Massachusetts Institute of Technology. Cost-benefit emerges as a central tool even if its application is constrained by difficulties in reconciling theory to practice. Raffel's arguments make it clear that cost-based knowledge of library service is essential. The inputs to different library programmes and their output consequences must be known and stated. The importance of the budgetary process is emphasized; it is a complex politico-economic tool.

The need to use concepts such as cost-effectiveness and cost-benefit implies a requirement that the concepts and their context are well understood. Orr's paper (1973) has become a classic exploration of the fundamental elements of this territory. His discussion of the measurement of library activity and service tries to tackle the question of rational analysis within a rather more unstable political context. A general management model has to take account of both costs and benefits; decision-making weighs objective data together with professional judgment. The political theme introduced in Raffel's paper surfaces again in Orr's. Orr's paper is thought-provoking and acknowledges the complexity of libraries as economic sytems, whilst seeking understanding through considering a general purpose model.

Buckland (1982) provides a critical gloss on Orr by considering the idea of "goodness". This paper cautions against the idea that cost data provides a universal panacea for the library manager's problems; cost is only one of a large number of useful measures and concepts which must be used in conjunction.

Cost-benefit and cost-effectiveness in the context of the evaluation of information systems are the themes of Gilchrist's paper. These measures rely on basic cost analysis techniques of the kind discussed elsewhere in this volume (Aslib Research Department, 1970; Smith and Schofield, 1971). Whitehall's paper (1980) continues the theme introduced by Gilchrist and argues first of all for a high level of cost awareness, as an important aspect of the resource allocation decisions of managers and users. The paper goes on to review techniques, relevant to two of the manager's needs: to justify resources consumed, and to choose between different options for providing service.

The contribution by Whitehall, and those which follow by Marchant, Rowe and Bookstein, all suggest ways in which a variety of forms of economic analysis can be used in operational library management, and explore the economic background to a number of library problems. These papers in effect provide a sampler of the content of managerial economics for library management. Marchant (1975) reviews several statistical and econometric studies of academic libraries, in an attempt to identify the variables likely to be the best predictors of total operating expenditures.

Relationships between economic variables are explored by means of regression analysis, in ways which could lead to the prediction of future cost patterns. Rowe (1974) continues to explore the ground for a future theory of library economy. Using a model from the theory of the firm, Rowe argues for the determination of optimum library size in order to minimize long run costs. For microeconomic analyses of this kind, accurate cost data is required. Marchant and Rowe both consider the question of budgetary prediction from models; however, predictive studies of this kind could be used with greater confidence against files of long run real cost data. Rowe poses interesting questions about the relationship between the optimal size of library and the cost-effective library. Bookstein (1981) poses the question "how should libraries be funded?" He then goes on to assess critically the microeconomic models represented by the free market and public goods approaches. The difficulty with libraries is in establishing a measurable output, and Bookstein argues that library circulation is not an adequate measure. Regardless of whether input or output measures and their respective value are considered, however, unit costs are required to test out these models. Bookstein concludes that in economic terms a library is a mixture of public and private components. These four papers provide a variety of views on aspects of the economics of libraries. Although these views are disparate and as yet unintegrated, they all point towards the essential value of developing cost data sources as a primary condition for economic analysis. The testing of library economic models will be severely constrained by the absence of that data.

As an antidote to a succession of theoretical treatments, Line's paper (1979) provides perspective through its refreshing common sense. Pointing out the dangers of a hypereconomic approach, Line's argument is in no way anti-economic. Although libraries should aim for maximization of service and not of profit, they still need to be run economically to achieve this goal; thus, economics must be seen as the servant of the library user. Echoing Sturt's comments in an earlier paper in this volume, Line suggests that library educators need to inculcate an economic and systematic approach. This done, the automatic approach to any problem should be to analyse it, identify possible solutions, and compare the various options for cost and effectiveness. And so much the better if this can be done without losing sight of the cultural and humanistic values which surround libraries. These sentiments form a fitting culmination to the themes explored in this collection of readings.

The final paper by Runyon (1981) argues for the importance of having a conceptual model for library data, of which cost and economic data form an essential part. Library managers have yet to perfect their management information systems; the widespread application of management accounting and costing techniques would certainly stimulate the development of such management information systems. Runyon's proposals may indicate the path for development in the near future, taking a total systems approach based upon standardized terminology, machine-aided data collection, customized computer processing and reporting, as well as systematic training and documentation.

FURTHER READING

HAMBURG, M. et al. *Library planning and decision making systems.* Cambridge (Mass.), M.I.T. Press, 1974.

KANTOR, P. B. Levels of output related to cost of operations of scientific libraries. *Library Research,* 3 (1), 1981, 1–28 and *Library Research,* 3 (2), 1981, 141–154.

KENT, A., COHEN, J. and MONTGOMERY, K. L. The economics of academic libraries. *Library Trends,* 28(1), 1979 (Special issue).
McKENZIE, R. B. The economist's paradigm. *Library Trends,* 28 (1), 1979, 7–24.
MOORE, N. Economics in library management. In *Studies in library management, volume 4.* Gileon Holroyd (ed.). London, Bingley, 1977, 120–137.
OVERTON, C. M. and SEAL, A. *Cataloguing costs in the UK: an analysis of the market for automated cataloguing systems.* Bath, University Library, 1979.
PRICE, D. S. Cost analysis and reporting as a basis for decisions. In *Proceedings of the 1976 clinic on library applications of data processing.* ... Urbana-Champaign, University of Illinois, 1977, 83–106.
RAFFEL, J. A. and SHISHKO, R. *Systematic analysis of university libraries: an application of cost-benefit analysis to the M.I.T. libraries.* Cambridge (Mass.), M.I.T. Press, 1969.
WILKINSON, J. B. Economics of information: criteria for counting the costs and benefits. *Aslib Proceedings,* 32 (1), 1980, 1–9.

Hamburg's monograph is a useful broad discussion of many background issues and problems in librarianship which have managerial economic consequences; Raffel and Shishko provide practical exemplification based on studies of M.I.T. libraries. Moore provides an interesting introduction to the application of economic concepts to libraries and should be read in conjunction with McKenzie. Kantor and Wilkinson cover related themes in the relationship between resource inputs, cost and outputs. The collection of papers edited by Kent and others covers matters of pricing policy (King), sources and uses of funds (Cohen and Leeson), economics of library size (Cooper), costs and benefits of library and information service from the user point of view (Braunstein), and the economics of library innovation (Drake and Olson); these form a good overview of some of the territory of library managerial economics. Overton and Seal's paper is a practical example of cost study applied to a specific decision problem, whilst Price considers matters of relevance to the development of library management information systems.

JEFFREY A. RAFFEL

From Economic to Political Analysis of Library Decision Making*

In general, the more critical the decision, the less useful a cost-benefit analysis is to library decision makers. Political analysis is required, and Easton's conceptual framework is presented to suggest the utility of political analysis. A list of normative issues is derived from raising descriptive questions about the politics of university libraries.

IN 1969 THE M.I.T. PRESS published a new volume, *Systematic Analysis of University Libraries: An Application of Cost–Benefit Analysis to the M.I.T. Libraries,* which might have signaled the entrance of economic analysis into the area of library decision making. As coauthor of the book, I anxiously awaited the reviews I hoped would follow.[1] To date all reviews missed what I regard as the major point of the book: *Although helpful, an economic analysis of a university (or public) library is insufficient because libraries operate as political systems and thus improving libraries requires political analysis.*

The purpose of this paper is not only to argue that political analysis of university and public libraries should be undertaken in conjunction with economic analyses but also to apply a specific theoretical framework and concept to university and public libraries. The improvement of libraries requires an expansion of analysis beyond technical discussions of procedural changes and per item costs to the broader utilization of social science theory and research.

In the past two decades both economists and political scientists have expanded their field of inquiry. Economists have become crucial figures in the analysis of governmental policy, especially in the measurement and analysis of governmental effectiveness through the methodology of cost–benefit analysis.[2] Political scientists have at the same time shifted their focus toward nongovernmental institutions, with some analyzing what were once thought to be nonpolitical governmental institutions (e.g., schools) and others, nongovernments (e.g., private governments). As Mancur Olson has recently observed, the social science disciplines differ by their approaches and theoretical frameworks rather than by their subject matter.[3] Thus libraries, be they primarily publicly or privately operated, are fair game for the frameworks of political scientists and economists.

Each discipline includes an array of theoretical frameworks. The overall ap-

*My frequent co-author, Robert Shishko, has tried to impart the essence of cost–benefit analyses to his audience by telling them about an economist who, when asked if he liked sex, replied immediately, "What are the alternatives?" I thank Bob Shishko for helping me to learn enough about economic analysis to criticize it, and I thank David Schulz and Daniel Rich for their insightful comments on earlier drafts of this paper.

proach of systems analysis stands out within each discipline as a fruitful way to improve libraries, specifically cost-benefit analysis in economics and Eastonian systems analysis in political science.

ECONOMIC ANALYSIS

Brief Description

"Basically, economic analysis is the study of choice: the allocation of scarce resources among alternative uses, and the distribution of outputs among alternative uses—that is, the classic questions of what and how much to produce, and who gets what products."[4] Cost-benefit analysis is a subfield of economic analysis: a specific application of economic analysis to nonmarket activity. We have defined cost-benefit analysis as the analytical examination of the costs and benefits of alternatives designed to meet specified objectives under various contingencies or states of the world.[5] Some differentiate cost-*benefit* analysis from cost-*effectiveness* analysis; the former referring to long-range financial effects (e.g., increased dollar income) and the latter to short-range measured output in nonfinancial terms (e.g., number of books circulated).[6] Although systems analysis has been used to refer to cost–benefit analyses, because its use is much more widespread, having application in areas from computer technology to political analysis, we define systems analysis as the study of systems or complexes or organized and interrelated parts, in terms of inputs, outputs, and internal functioning.[7]

Our definition of cost–benefit analysis has already included most of the elements of the basic analytical framework: costs, benefits, alternatives, and contingencies. What then is cost–benefit analysis? It is a way of looking at the world. Usually one starts from a set of objectives that a decision maker has in mind. The analyst finds measures of the extent to which the objectives may be met. For example, if an objective of a library were to provide reading material to library users, then one measure of meeting this objective would be annual book circulation. One then examines the alternatives for fulfilling each objective.

By constructing models (e.g., formulas, computer simulations), the analyst relates each alternative to its corresponding costs and benefits (i.e., the degree to which objectives are met). The model is used across several contingencies or states of the world. Given the costs and benefits associated with each alternative in each contingency, a criterion or measure of preferredness (e.g., maximizing profits) is selected and the "best" alternative is chosen.

Figure 1 illustrates the cost–benefit procedure. Note that the method is actually circular—objectives are revised in light of feasibility and costs, new alternatives are created, models are refined, and the decision process is continuously in motion.

Brief Critique

The elements of the cost-benefit analysis model serve as the basis for a brief critique of the method. Attempts to define library objectives can lead to clarifications of purpose, yet they often result in futile searches for well-hidden goals obscuring the true clients of the library.[8] While efforts to generate alternatives to perform library services more efficiently and effectively are made, the question of the practicality and feasibility of radically different ideas weights the ultimate analysis against innovative options. Relating costs to alternatives becomes the key task, and numbers generated through cost modeling become the foci of economy drives. Benefit modeling, however, is weakest when the alternatives are most innovative, e.g., public library programs based

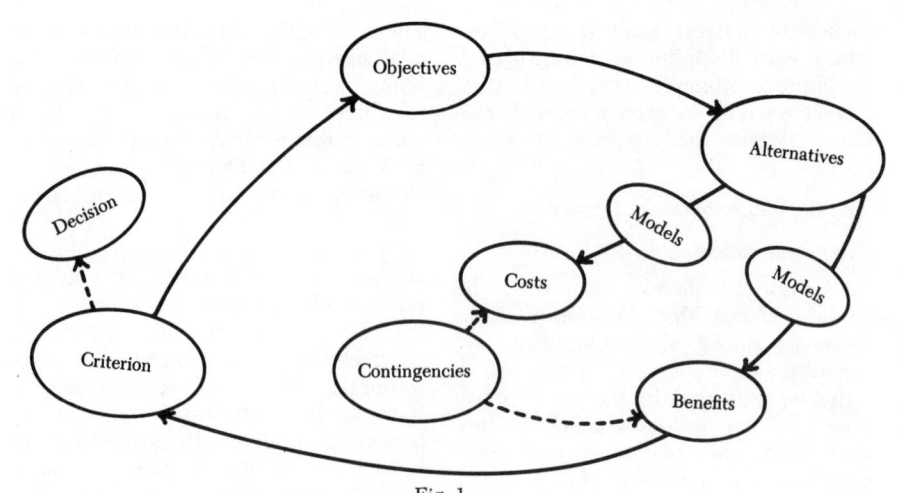

Fig. 1
The Basic Cost–Benefit Framework

on distributing paperback books for disadvantaged patrons, university libraries handing out free copies of required articles to students.[9] Because the contingencies studied most are those thought to affect costs, not benefits, inflation of prices is emphasized over inflation of goals in serving users.

Each of these difficulties is related to the political context in which the economic study is conceived, implemented, and received. The basic political problem with economic analysis transcends operational and day-to-day difficulties and political intrigue. The basic political problem centers on political conflict inherent in all our institutions, including libraries. It is this conflict that is inappropriately dealt with or ignored in economic analysis.

The Political Problem with Economic Analysis: An Example

Near the end of the data collection stage, the economic systems analysis of the Massachusetts Institute of Technology (M.I.T.) libraries yielded a list of twenty library alternatives with associated costs and benefits.[10]

At this stage in the analysis several points were evident:

1. Several alternatives were not worth considering. Alternatives offering fewer benefits at a higher cost than comparable alternatives were discarded. For example, storing books off campus rather than on campus saved no money and resulted in losses of benefits to library users.

2. Many conclusions with major policy implications were already warranted. For example, inexpensive storage appeared to offer little financial savings at a fairly high cost in benefits to a majority of the M.I.T. community.

3. Although alternatives could be described in terms of costs and benefits with respect to the two major library objectives, more information was required to select and recommend a subset of alternatives. For example, should the cost of reproducing copies of library materials be reduced or should many course-required articles be distributed free of charge? Should either

be done with or without a decentralization of library space?[11]

It is at this point that cost-benefit analysis (and economic analysis) comes to a grinding halt. Cost-benefit analysis assumes that the objectives, even if unclear at the beginning of the analysis, can be specified at some point to the satisfaction of the decision maker. Cost-benefit analysts recognize that multiple objectives may exist and suggest that the tradeoffs, the extent to which meeting one objective leads to a failure to meet other objectives, be specified and clearly displayed. But did our analysis indicate objectives that could be agreed upon?

We decided to present the data on alternatives derived from our analysis to the individual members of the university community, thus to allow each to act as if he or she were the ultimate decision maker.[12] Because it would have been too costly to reach all members of the community, we drew a random sample of undergraduate students, graduate students, and faculty and research staff and presented them with twenty alternative changes, with a brief description of costs and relevant benefit considerations, for the M.I.T. libraries. Respondents were given budgets of $0, $100,000, and $200,000 to spend for changes in the libraries.

The analysis of the survey clearly indicates that different subgroups of the M.I.T. community either had different objectives in mind or viewed different means as being best for meeting common objectives:

> The general conclusion is that the three major campus groups differ in the systems they would like the library to adopt. Undergraduates seek to expand and centralize the reserve collection by cutting research services. Graduate students add lower Xerox prices and increased access to this list of desired systems and would prefer to cut seating rather than cataloging. The faculty are the most willing to alter

book storage and cataloging and relatively less desirous of a centralized reserve system. . . .

> The less a respondent reported using the libraries the more likely he was to select saving money on book storage and seating and to spend it on lower Xerox rates, departmental libraries, and an all-Xerox reserve system. Low users thus tend to be outside-use oriented. The high users prefer expanding seating, acquisitions, reference, and access to other collections. The high users thus are research oriented. We have concluded that the library has traditionally served one clientele, the research oriented. There now appears to be, however, a second clientele, who spend few hours in the library and seek not the space but the materials in its collection. We believe, with as yet no proof, that many of those oriented to outside use prefer to work outside the library but are forced, primarily by the reserve system, to work in the library. We hypothesize that these users (and many other potential users) could be served by a library emphasizing distribution as well as in-house facilities and services.[13]

The M.I.T. analysis indicates that the alternatives faced by the M.I.T. library and university administrators involved major choices among various subgroups on campus. Furthermore, the analysis strongly suggests that decisions now favor faculty far more than students.

The political problem with economic analysis is that there is no economic way to resolve differences among alternatives meeting different objectives held by different subgroups; where political conflict exists a political solution must be found.[14] This is not news to most economists. What library decision makers require is help in resolving these political conflicts. Presumably political analysis can help.

POLITICAL ANALYSIS

Political scientists would not agree on the nature of analysis necessary to deal with such political conflict. Some would argue that an analysis should begin with a positivist or descriptive analysis of libraries with a focus on who decides and by what process. Others would argue that an explicitly normative or value based analysis, with a major focus on issues of equity and responsiveness, is required. Because neither of these approaches has been applied to libraries, a first step falling between the normative and positive poles of political systems analysis has been chosen here. Below, David Easton's descriptive framework is used to raise the normative questions which library decision makers should be addressing.[15]

Easton defines politics as the authoritative allocation of values for a society. In the past, many governmental institutions, perhaps education is the best example, have been viewed as being outside of the realm of politics. In 1969, in an introduction to a reader on the politics of education, the editor stated that "The idea that politics and *public education* are intimately related was practically unthinkable as recently as a decade ago. . . . At the very least, any governmental process involving authoritative decisions on matters of public relevance is of a political nature."[16] Thus an entire literature dealing with the politics of education has developed.[17] Certainly it would not be inappropriate to raise issues concerning the politics of public libraries and libraries at public universities.

Studying the politics of university libraries derives from another expansion of political analysis to the area of private government.[18] Public governments have been defined as "those general as well as special-purpose associations and agencies either to which all inhabitants of a given locality are subject or of which all citizens are members"; and *private governments* are "those limited-purpose associations or organizations, usually voluntary in membership, which exist both alongside and subordinate to public governments."[19] Examples of private governments are corporations, trade unions, professional associations, and universities. Indeed, the public versus private distinction has become increasingly blurred, especially as applied to universities, within the past decade.[20] The basic questions one asks about private governments are political: Are (and can) private governments (be) democratic?[21] Related questions include: Who gets what, when, and how?[22]

Although many alternative models of the political process exist, I believe that Easton's framework provides a useful analytical scheme for beginning a political analysis of libraries.[23]

Easton's Framework for Political Analysis

Easton's model (see Figure 2) is simple in its conception but complex in its full description. Dye describes the theoretical framework succinctly:

One way to conceive of public policy is to think of it as a response of a political system to forces brought to bear upon it from the environment. Forces generated in the environment which affect the political system are viewed as inputs. The environment is any condition or circumstance defined as external to the boundaries of the political system. The political system is that group of interrelated structures and processes which functions authoritatively to allocate values for a society. Outputs of the political system are authoritative value allocations of the system, and these allocations constitute public policy.

Systems theory portrays public policy as an output of the political system. The concept of "system" implies an identifiable set of institutions and activities in society that function to transform demands into authoritative decisions requiring the support of society. The concept of "systems" also

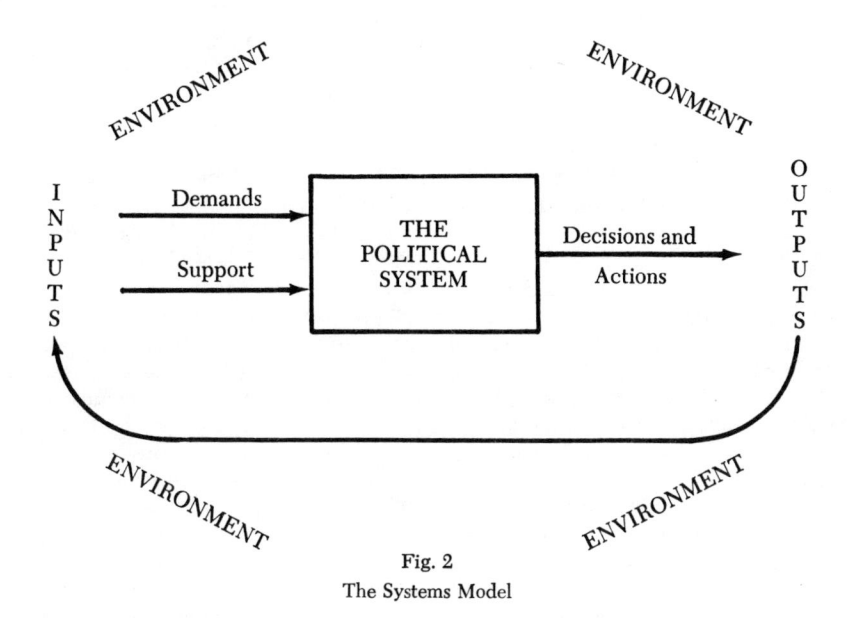

```
                    ENVIRONMENT                    ENVIRONMENT

  I                                                                    O
  N         Demands                                                    U
  P      ─────────────▶    THE        Decisions and                    T
  U                     POLITICAL    ─────────────▶                    P
  T         Support       SYSTEM         Actions                       U
  S      ─────────────▶                                                T
                                                                       S

                    ENVIRONMENT                    ENVIRONMENT
```

Fig. 2
The Systems Model

implies that elements of the system are interrelated, that the system can respond to forces in its environment, and that it will do so in order to preserve itself. Inputs are received into the political system in the form of both demands and support. Demands occur when individuals or groups, in response to real or perceived environmental conditions, act to affect public policy. Support is rendered when individuals or groups accept the outcome of elections, obey the laws, pay their taxes, and generally conform to policy decisions. Any system absorbs a variety of demands, some of which conflict with each other. In order to transform these demands into outputs (public policies), it must arrange settlements and enforce these settlements upon the parties concerned. It is recognized that outputs (public policies) may have a modifying effect on the environment and the demands arising from it, and may also have an effect upon the character of the political system. The system preserves itself by: (1) producing reasonably satisfying outputs, (2) relying upon deeply rooted attachments to the system itself, and (3) using, or threatening to use force.[24]

POLITICAL ANALYSIS AND UNIVERSITY LIBRARIES

System Boundaries and Legitimacy

The first question that arises is whether we can determine the boundaries of a political system. Throughout the M.I.T. library study we felt too constrained by the definition of the system we were studying, "the M.I.T. libraries." The use and evaluation of a university library are not independent of the book stores within (and without) the university. To declare one a legitimate item for analysis and the other as outside of the area of analysis may be to miss the dynamics of the situation. It was surprising to discover that a high-level, library acquisitions department staff member had not only made no effort to buy books from the Harvard Coop but also had never even been to this store, one of the world's largest bookstores. We were surprised to receive veiled threats by a department chairman after we had measured his departmental library's floor-space without his permission. The quality of departmental libraries must surely determine the nature and degree of use of the main libraries. What units should be included in the library decision maker's domain?

Output and Benefits

Unlike Easton, it seems that the most fruitful political analysis must begin with the output stage of the political process. The analysis of output, done within the cost-benefit framework of the M.I.T. study, provides some significant information and raises some important questions.

The best tool available for analyzing policy was (and often is) the library budget. But budgets are usually input based (e.g., cost of books purchased, cost of personnel salaries) rather than output or policy derived (e.g., cost of providing student services for coursework). Perhaps even more interesting, the M.I.T. library budget, divided into parts among discipline-related libraries, was considered confidential. To paraphrase one library administrator, "If the social scientists knew what we were spending on the physical science library, they'd start asking for more funds."

A program budget analysis of the M.I.T. library seems to show quite clearly who benefits from the current decision-making system. Only 23 percent of the total budget is used for providing required reading and facilities for studying, i.e., less than a quarter of the budget is devoted to nonresearch, course-related student services. Of course, this overstates the antistudent bias, for undergraduate and particularly graduate students devote much effort to research both inside and outside of courses.

As noted in the discussion of the cost–benefit analysis of the M.I.T. libraries, the survey analysis challenges the myth of a unitary community.[25] In fact it suggests that the allocation of benefits, if not costs, is weighted in favor of faculty and staff. Why should this be so?

Demand and Democratic Process

The concept of demand is a crucial one in Easton's framework. An analysis of demands made upon library administrators at M.I.T. would probably indicate that a small number of senior faculty are the primary demanders. The library advisory committee contained no students; the administrators themselves spoke almost entirely of faculty complaints.[26] What channels, both formal and informal, are required for those affected by decisions concerning libraries to be adequately heard?

The concept of demands is too limited for the political analysis of quasi-public institutions like university libraries. Few preferences, defined as desired states of affairs, even reach the level of demands. Easton concentrates on the reasons for the weeding of demands and the attrition of preferences in the input stage of the political process. We should ask, as does Easton, what institutions exist to filter and channel demands to library decision makers? How successful are different kinds of people within the university community in making their demands heard? To what extend should access be equalized?

The mobilization of bias should also be considered crucial by library analysts. Several political scientists have criticized their discipline for the substantive conclusion that American institutions are open and responsive to minority groups.[27] They argue that this optimistic substantive conclusion derives in part from a methodological problem, analyzing only decisions made by public bodies. Backrach and Baratz ask, "Can the researcher overlook the chance that some person or association could limit decision-making to relatively noncontroversial matters, by influencing community values and political procedures and rituals?"[28] By limiting political analysis to overt decisions, the role that elites play in mobilizing bias, i.e., in defining the nature and states of the political game, is overlooked.

The mobilization of bias plays a critical role in library policy. One of our early suggestions at M.I.T. was that the price of reproducing pages of library materials within M.I.T.'s libraries should be reduced. Although the price was later decreased, the action was based upon an agreement that decreasing the price would ultimately increase revenue (i.e., elastic demand) and the system would remain self-supporting. *But why should the dissemination of information by copying be self-supporting, and who is disadvantaged by this decision rule?* Whereas many faculty have research grants, departmental resources, and relatively high incomes, students are at a relative disadvantage in the marketplace. Libraries do not break even on providing books. Should they break even on copying materials for dissemination?

One economist has made an argument that could have been based on the mobilization of bias concept:

> Or why do not librarians diminish their stock of hard-cover books and acquire in their stead substantial inventories of paperbacks which they would then give away free? We are inclined to reply, "Why, that would be crazy: our budget would soon be exhausted." And yet that is exactly what librarians are doing now except instead of giving books away free they are giving staff services away free.[29]

Keller calls for implicit (or explicit) pricing of library services.[30]

Easton's framework, indeed all political frameworks, should include a basic economic concept of exit. Hirschman argues that one mechanism of voicing disapproval within the political as well as economic sector is exit, e.g., leaving the organization or not consuming the product.[31] To what extent do potential library users seek other sources of information because of library ineffectiveness? To what extent do some groups lack an effective means of influencing library decision makers by their inability to exit?

The larger question that each of these points concerning demand raises is the appropriateness of democratic norms for library decision making. Should libraries be run more democratically than they now are?

Decision Making and Selecting Decision Makers

The analysis of decisions and decision makers is a crucial aspect of Easton's framework. The analysis of library decision making must reach beyond the traditional organizational bounds of the exercise of rationality. Lakoff has expressed the criticisms of traditional organizational analysis as follows:

> The study of organizational decision-making studiously avoids asking the kind of questions that would render the study of decision-making genuinely political. It does not ask what constituencies are involved, or how the legislative is related to the executive, or how the authority of the decision-maker is made accountable to those he represents. It does not ask whether the system is constitutional or just, legitimate or illegitimate. Instead the study of decision-making in organizations is confined to the question of whether and to what extent the functions of management are exercised rationally. The stress, in other words, is clearly on administration rather than government, on the integrative function of social organization, on improving the efficiency of the decision-maker. There is practically no attention paid to the question of whether people who are members of the organization or who are served by it have or ought to have control over it, whether they have any right (a term which would probably be considered altogether un-

scientific by students of organization) to be consulted in the decision-making process or indeed to decide what form the process will take.[32]

In this conventional sense, the study of organizations, despite its focus on decision making, has been quite apolitical.

Dye's identification of barriers limiting rational decision making, in many ways analogous to criticisms of the use of cost-benefit analysis in libraries, might serve as a starting point for an analysis of library decision making. They are restated below as hypotheses.

1. There are no community values which are usually agreed upon, but only the values of specific groups and individuals, many of which are conflicting.
2. The many conflicting values cannot be compared or weighted: for example, it is impossible to compare or weight the value of individual dignity against the loss of rare books.
3. The environment of library policy makers, particularly the power and influence system, renders it impossible for them to see or accurately weight many community values, particularly those values which have no active or powerful proponents.
4. Library policy makers are not motivated to make decisions on the basis of community goals, but instead try to maximize their own rewards—power, status, money, etc.
5. Library policy makers are not motivated to maximize net goal achievement, but merely to satisfy demands for progress; they do not search until they find "the one best way" but halt their search when they find an alternative which "will work."
6. Large investments in existing programs and policies (e.g., cataloging systems, library buildings, and other "sunk costs") prevent policy makers from reconsidering alternatives foreclosed by previous decisions.
7. There are innumerable barriers to collecting all of the information required to know all possible policy alternatives and the consequences of each alternative, including the cost of information gathering, the availability of the information, and the time involved in its collection.
8. Neither the predictive capacities of the social and behavioral sciences nor the predictive capacities of the physical and biological sciences are sufficiently advanced to enable policy makers to understand the full range of consequences of each library policy alternative.
9. Library policy makers, even with the most advanced computerized analytical techniques, do not have sufficient intelligence to calculate accurately cost–benefit ratios when a large number of diverse political, social, economic, and cultural values are at stake.
10. Library policy makers have personal needs, inhibitions, and inadequacies which prevent them from performing in a highly rational manner.
11. Uncertainty about the consequences of various policy alternatives compels policy makers to stick as closely as possible to previous policies to reduce the likelihood of disturbing, unanticipated consequences.
12. The segmentalized nature of policy making in large library bureaucracies makes it difficult to coordinate decision making so that the input of all of the various specialists is brought to bear at the point of decision.[33]

Testing these hypotheses requires an analysis of the values and personal goals of library decision makers, the power of competing interests in universities, the incentive structures surrounding library administrators, and the nature of information available to decision makers. Significant normative questions follow. Should library decision makers be more representative of those who use the libraries? Should the incentive structure for advancement in library administration be altered to better reflect user and potential user demand?

Lessons for Librarians

Unfortunately, whereas economists can advocate that library decision makers try to maximize benefits at a given budget level, political scientists can offer no clear-cut decision rule as an alternative. This paper ends with questions that library decision makers should ask, but no simple answers of what actions to take if answers are found can be offered at this point.[34] Future research is needed, although this obviously will not solve all the political problems of librarians.

Following the more complete Easton model, library decision makers should ask themselves:

1. What is the relevant library system? Have I excluded a key component that determines user behavior but has traditionally fallen outside my purview? Can I coordinate decisions between my area and the additional area?
2. What are the *environmental* constraints that appear to limit my discretion? Can they be altered?
3. What groups (and individuals) make *demands*? Are they representative of the potential users of the library? What preferences do not become demands? Are new or revised mechanisms needed to encourage more demands?
4. What is the general climate of opinion with respect to the library, e.g., *support* for library? Has the climate provided me with so much latitude that demands remain unmet? What assumptions (of users or administrators) limit the consideration of alternative policies? Who benefits from these assumptions? Who does not benefit? Can the asumptions be changed?
5. *Who plays a role in decisions* about library allocations? To what extent are users or potential users involved? To what extent are those affected by decisions helping to make them?
6. Who *benefits* from (and pays for) the library? Does the budget show this? What services serve what groups? How well are they served?
7. What *feedback* is available to the decision maker to evaluate current allocations? What mechanisms for feedback exist? Are they successful in bringing evaluations of users to decision makers? Do nonusers have access and do they use feedback systems?

In brief, political systems analysis is analogous to economic systems analysis: it is a way of thinking.

Woodrow Wilson, asked whether he had much difficulty in accustoming himself to practical politics, stated that after his experience in university politics at Princeton everything else seemed simple. It is time that we all recognized the politics of libraries and acted accordingly.

References

1. Jeffrey A. Raffel and Robert Shishko, *Systematic Analysis of University Libraries: An Application of Cost-Benefit Analysis to the M.I.T. Libraries* (Cambridge, Mass.:

M.I.T. Press, 1969). Our M.I.T. editor said goodbye to us with the comment, "I hope you get some reviews." When we replied, "You mean some *good* reviews," she responded, "No, just some reviews."

2. General references in the area of cost–benefit analysis include Charles J. Hitch and Roland N. McKean, *The Economics of Defense in the Nuclear Age* (Cambridge, Mass.: Harvard Univ. Pr., 1960); and David Novick, ed., *Program Budgeting: Program Analysis and the Federal Budget* (Cambridge, Mass.: Harvard Univ. Pr., 1965). References on the "economics of information" can be found in Harold Anker Olsen, *The Economics of Information: Bibliography and Commentary on the Literature* (Washington, D.C.: ERIC Clearinghouse on Library and Information Sciences, 1971). (ED 044 545).

3. Mancur Olson, "Economics, Sociology, and the Best of All Possible Worlds," *The Public Interest*, no. 12 (Summer 1968), p.96–118.

4. Olsen, *Economics of Information*, p.1.

5. Jeffrey A. Raffel and Robert Shishko, "Cost–Benefit Analysis for Library Administrators," paper presented to Massachusetts Chapter of the Special Libraries Association on March 11, 1969, in Boston, Massachusetts.

6. Melvin R. Levin and Alan Shank refer to cost–benefit analysis "as a measurement technique in which the total costs of a given project or program are compared with the probable total benefit. . . . The result is a numerical ratio. . . ." Cost–effectiveness is viewed as a variation of cost–benefit analysis where the output is expressed in "raw form without conversion to dollars." See Levin and Shank, eds., *Educational Investment in an Urban Society: Costs, Benefits, and Public Policy* (New York: Teachers College Press, 1970), p.1–2.

Using this distinction, I refer primarily to cost–effectiveness analysis in its application to libraries and cost–benefit analysis as the general approach.

7. Raffel and Shishko, "Cost–Benefit Analysis," p.2.

8. Late in the M.I.T. analysis it became evident that an advertising objective of the library was also significant; that is, librarians wanted to encourage those in the university community to increase their use of the library. Thus attempts were made to entice book use by lavishly furnishing lounges in the libraries. This goal was rarely acknowledged.

9. In the M.I.T. study we tried to resolve this problem by asking potential users to judge benefits themselves.

10. Raffel and Shishko, *Systematic Analysis of University Libraries*, p.50–55.

11. Ibid., p.46–67.

12. Terry N. Clark, in an unpublished paper titled "Please Cut the Budget Pie" (research paper #37 of the Comparative Study of Community Decision-Making, Summer [1972]), develops a further rationale and somewhat different methodology to measure citizen preferences for various public policies.

13. Raffel and Shishko, *Systematic Analysis of University Libraries*, p.65.

14. There is a literature in economics (welfare economics and public choice economics) on this subject. The proposed solutions include: (1) maximizing total utility across individuals—but this requires the interpersonal comparison of utility and the measure of utility, both problematic procedures; (2) transforming costs and benefits into dollars and maximizing the net figure—but the full transformation is usually impossible and questions like those raised in the first method still arise; and (3) only taking those actions that make no one worse off and at least one person better off—but this case arises infrequently in the era of declining or steady budgets.

I am indebted to the critiques of cost–benefit analysis by Aaron Wildavsky. See his "The Political Economy of Efficiency: Cost–Benefit Analysis, Systems Analysis and Program Budgeting," *Public Administration Review* 26:292–310 (Dec. 1966); and "Rescuing Policy Analysis from PPBS," in *Public Administration Review: PPBS Reexamined* 29:189–202 (March/April 1969).

15. David Easton, *A Systems Analysis of Political Life* (New York: Wiley, 1965).

16. Alan Rosenthal, ed., *Governing Education: A Reader on Politics, Power, and Public School Policy* (Garden City, N.Y.: Anchor Books, 1969), p.viii–ix.

17. See Frederick Wirt and Michael Kirst, *The Political Web of American Schools* (Boston: Little, 1972), for one volume applying Easton's framework to the politics of education.

18. See Sanford A. Lakoff and Daniel Rich, eds., *Private Government: Introductory Readings* (Glenview, Ill.: Scott, Foresman, 1973), for an excellent discussion of the rationale for studying the politics of private government and case studies, including the politics of university governance.

19. Ibid., p.3.

20. See Sanford Lakoff, "Private Government

COSTING AND ECONOMICS

in the Managed Society," in Lakoff and Rich, eds., *Private Government*, p.218–42.
21. Lakoff and Rich, *Private Government*, preface.
22. Harold Lasswell, *Politics: Who Gets What, When, and How* (Glencoe, Ill.: Free Press, 1958).
23. Thomas Dye recently described several models used in analyzing public policy: (a) elite-mass model, (b) group model, (c) incremental model, (d) institutional model, (e) systems model, and (f) rational model. See Thomas R. Dye, *Understanding Public Policy* (Englewood Cliffs, N.J.: Prentice-Hall, 1972).
24. Dye, *Understanding Public Policy*, p.18–19. Dye's conceptualization is based upon David Easton, "An Approach to the Analysis of Political Systems," *World Politics* 9:383–400 (1957); and Easton, *A Framework for Political Analysis* (Englewood Cliffs, N.J.: Prentice-Hall, 1965).
25. In the preference survey at the $0 budget level, although differences were small, faculty were somewhat more satisfied as measured by the percentage desiring changes from current allocations.
26. The reader should note that this paper is not an indictment of M.I.T. in particular, although there is evidence that the libraries are governed in the same way as are other elements of the university (e.g., health services, graduate school).
27. These arguments relate to a larger battle among elitists, pluralists, neoelitists, and so on. See Dye, *Understanding Public Policy*.
28. Peter Bachrach and Morton S. Baratz, *Power and Poverty: Theory and Practice* (New York: Oxford Univ. Pr., 1970), p.9.
29. John E. Keller, "Program Budgeting and Cost Benefit Analysis in Libraries," *College & Research Libraries* 30:160 (March 1969).
30. It should be noted that many university libraries charge fees for use, for reproduction and for organizational users. My own opinion is that fees for the former are far too high and the latter far too low. In any event, both require further political analysis.
31. Albert Hirschman, *Exit, Voice, and Loyalty* (Cambridge, Mass.: Harvard Univ. Pr., 1970).
32. Lakoff, "Private Government in the Managed Society," p.229.
33. Dye, *Understanding Public Policy*.
34. Note that analogous questions arise about public libraries. Political scientist Edward Banfield is one of a few people to raise explicit political questions about public libraries. Banfield begins his discussion of urban libraries with the question of their purpose. "It [the urban library] is trying to do some things that it probably cannot do, and it is doing others that it should not do."

In Easton's terms the question expands: (a) What is the relevant *system*? Educational institutions? Information institutions? (b) What are the *outputs* of the library? What groups does it serve? How well does it serve them? (c) Why does the library try to serve these groups? What *demands* does it try to meet? What preferences never become demands? What tasks might it accomplish that are not now viewed as appropriate?

Banfield argues that libraries should serve "serious," not "light," readers; the latter group could be served by rental and paperback libraries. But most serious readers can pay for the services they receive. Should the general public then pay for a subgroup to receive the services?

Perhaps what Banfield is trying to communicate is that although the *cost* of library services may serve as the focal point for library decision making and public concern (e.g., closing and reduction in services of public libraries), the basic problem of public libraries is not an economic problem. Rather, we have not examined library priorities and reallocated library resources to meet changing political circumstances. Only a political analysis will indicate why this is so and what changes should be made.

See Edward C. Banfield, "Some Alternatives for the Public Library," in Ralph W. Conant, ed., *The Public Library and the City* (Cambridge, Mass.: M.I.T. Press, 1965), p.102–13.

MEASURING THE GOODNESS OF LIBRARY SERVICES:
A GENERAL FRAMEWORK FOR CONSIDERING
QUANTITATIVE MEASURES

R. H. ORR

INTRODUCTION

THE LITERATURE OF the last few decades reflects a steadily increasing concern with quantitative assessment of libraries and their services. This concern is both the result of, and a reaction to, growing pressures from within and without the library profession to adopt the tools of the management sciences. The pressures are generated by many factors including the success of these tools in other fields and their adoption by the organizations supporting libraries, the increasingly explicit character of competition for funds at all levels, and the complexity and critical nature of decisions on the host of new options being created by technology and by formalization of library networks.

The literature also reflects the profession's conflicting attitudes toward this development. At the risk of oversimplification, these attitudes may be grouped into two opposing schools, whose respective positions can be summarized as follows: One school feels that some of the major benefits derived from libraries are intangible (i.e., not measurable); that attempts to quantify services lead to the aggregation of units that are qualitatively different; that each library is unique and should be assessed in the context of its own particular history, constraints, users, and environment; and that the subjective judgement of professionals should be respected. Members of this school commonly complain that 'administrators' insist on 'performance figures', which can be misleading and do not adequately represent what the library really does, and view quantitative measures as being, at best, a 'necessary evil'.

In contrast, the other school believes that it will eventually be possible to measure objectively the goodness of most, if not all, library services; that imperfect measures can be useful if their limitations are appreciated; that libraries are no more varied than other organizations where the tools of management science have been applied profitably; that subjective judgement should be checked against objective measures whenever possible; and that quantitative measures offer great promise as aids in obtaining proper support for libraries and in achieving better services at an acceptable cost.

The positions of both schools are tenable in their less extreme forms. Analogous schisms have developed in other professions at crucial phases in their evolution from an art or craft to an applied science; and the optimistic view is that we are witnessing such a phase in the evolution of librarianship. The resulting dialogue can be healthy in so far as it stimulates careful reappraisal of traditional approaches to library management and also helps to ensure that innovations are subjected to the test of active, informed criticism before being adopted. My purpose here is not to moderate this critical test of quantitative measures, but rather to sharpen it.

This paper presents a general framework for considering the relative advantages and disadvantages of different quantitative measures, citing selected reports to illustrate points or to indicate where a fuller discussion can be found. Although measures can be valuable tools for research aimed simply at increasing our understanding of libraries as complex organizations, and for professional bodies and government agencies concerned with whole populations of libraries, the present focus is on their use as practical aids in the management of individual libraries.

TASKS COMMON TO MANAGEMENT AT ALL LEVELS

In thinking about such use, it is helpful to have a relatively concrete model of the decision-making processes the measures are intended to aid; and for this purpose, the construct of a highly simplified library will be introduced from time to time. This hypothetical library is part of a larger organization, and the Librarian reports directly to the Administrator of the parent organization. The library's services are grouped into broad categories, each of which is managed by a Section Head, who reports to the Librarian. At all three management levels, the manager has the following tasks: (1) to obtain, from the next higher level of management, the resources (funds, personnel, space, etc.) necessary to meet his responsibilities, which are defined in terms of specific goals; (2) to allocate the resources thus obtained among activities at the next lower level in such a way that the resultant effects make the greatest possible contribution toward these goals; and (3) to ensure that the resources allocated to any particular activity are employed to maximal advantage.

Each of these tasks, which will be called justification, allocation, and maximation, respectively, entails making decisions based on the predicted effects of alternative actions (planning) and on the results of past decisions (control). This statement of tasks merely formalizes what managers have always done, whether their style was 'traditional' or 'scientific'. Central to all decisions required for planning and control is the exercise of weighing the goodness of results (expected or realized) against the resources required. Again, this is true regardless of the manager's style—the exercise has always been carried out; all that varied has been whether it was performed more, or less, consciously and systematically.

A whole family of closely related management science techniques—cost-effectiveness analysis, cost-benefit analysis, systems analysis, and the so called planning-programming-budgeting system (PPBS)—has been developed to make this exercise more systematic and objective, and to ensure that it is carried out explicitly in planning and control. However, all these techniques require that not only the resources needed, but also the goodness of results, be expressed quantitatively. Now, library managers generally have long been reconciled to the necessity for quantifying, at least crudely, the resource factors considered in the weighing exercise, which are commonly thought of collectively as costs; but few are accustomed to treating the goodness of results similarly. Although the philosophical and practical problems of achieving proper measures of library costs are far from trivial, these problems are less formidable than those of measuring the goodness of results; and the former problems will not be discussed in this article.

ULTIMATE CRITERIA FOR QUALITY AND VALUE

Intuitively, the concept of 'goodness', as applied to a particular library service, seems to have two basic aspects, which are reflected in the simple questions—'How good is the service?' and 'How much good does it *do*?' For want of better labels, the first aspect may be called quality, and the second, value. For present purposes, I prefer these labels to their apparent equivalents in the jargon of information science—effectiveness and benefit. As terms, quality and value quite obviously have the fuzziness of meaning one expects of non-technical words—in contrast to words that have secondarily acquired a technical meaning and are therefore assumed, sometimes wrongly, to be precise and reliable tokens for communication within a given realm of discourse. Apparently, effectiveness and benefit were used in several, somewhat different senses in other disciplines and fields before these terms were borrowed for information science; and although most of the formal definitions that have appeared in recent library literature are reasonably consistent (e.g., *see* Martyn,[1] Lancaster,[2] and Gilchrist[3]), the terms are often used in confusing ways, some of which may be traced to their common meanings or to senses carried over from economics and administration. Also, because effectiveness is commonly defined in very general terms (e.g., 'the extent to which a system or service achieves its objectives'), it has little intuitive meaning; and it can, and does, lend itself to paradoxical applications and to confusion with benefit.*

With minimal refinements, the primitive notions of quality and value reflected in the two simple questions can serve as ultimate criteria. About the only desirable refinement is agreement that the ultimate criterion for assessing the quality of a service is its capability for meeting the user needs it is intended to serve, and that the value of a service must ultimately be judged in terms of the beneficial effects accruing from its use as viewed by those who sustain the costs. As will be seen later, these formulations are still quite fuzzy, particularly that for value. But further refinement involves risking the loss of their utility as intuitively meaningful and simple statement of ideal standards to which one can refer when considering various substitute, or proximate, criteria that may be easier to implement—and this is the prime function of ultimate criteria.

DIRECT AND INDIRECT MEASURES OF QUALITY AND VALUE

Measures of quality and value may be characterized as direct when they are based on these ultimate criteria, and indirect when some presumably related criterion is substituted as the basis for judgement. In examining how the various criteria employed for this purpose are related, one can start with the following basic propositions, which are almost truisms because they are so strongly qualified: (1) that, *other things being equal*, the capability of a service will tend to increase as the resources devoted to it increase, *but not necessarily proportionately*; (2) that, *other things being equal*, the total uses made of a service (utilization) will tend to increase as its capability increases, *but not*

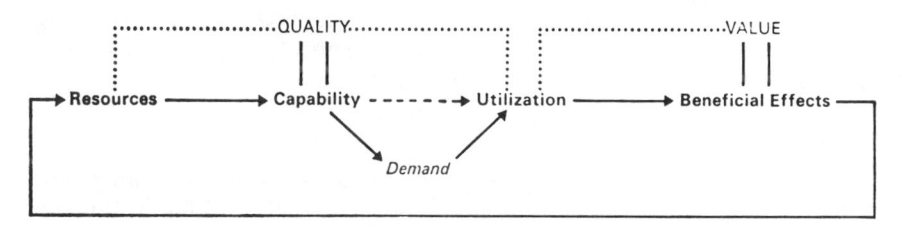

FIG. 1. *Relations among criterion variables*

necessarily proportionately; (3) that, *other things being equal*, the beneficial effects realized from a service will increase as its utilization increases, *but not necessarily proportionately*; and (4) that, *other things being equal*, the resources devoted to a service will increase as its beneficial effects increase, *but not necessarily proportionately*. The postulated relations among these four variables is depicted in Fig. 1 as a cause-and-effect sequence looped on itself.

* For example, it is proper, but confusing, to speak of the effectiveness of a management information system whose objective is to increase efficiency (or cost-effectiveness), and of a service designed to increase the value (or benefit) realized from the scientific literature.

Since, in the real world, 'other things' are never equal, this sequence should not be assumed to be more than loosely coupled, even when time lags between cause and effect are taken into account.*

Although this diagram is grossly simplistic and does not attempt to show many important interactions, such as the effect of utilization (service loads) in degrading capability, it can be useful for examining the logical support for indirect measures of quality and value. Of the four variables in the loop, resources lend themselves most readily to quantification in that they seem, at least superficially, to have 'natural' units, which should be countable. Hence, the library 'statistics' usually compiled are very largely measures of resources, most of which can be derived more or less directly from records maintained for other purposes. Utilization is somewhat more difficult to quantify. First, except in libraries where service is almost completely staff-mediated, it requires substantial effort and expense to maintain records of utilization that are at all complete. Second, units of output for a number of important services must be defined relatively grossly for practical purposes, since the output is heterogeneous. Nevertheless, it is becoming increasingly common, in reports intended to justify support, for service output to be expressed in terms of rather crude units (e.g., reference questions handled, bibliographies prepared, students instructed, etc.) as well as in terms of what are superficially more refined units (such as items circulated and pages photocopied).

In contrast, the other two variables in the loop—capability and beneficial effects—have proved much more difficult to measure directly; and in the absence of satisfactory direct measures of quality and value, indirect measures have been substituted. Thus, measures of resources are very commonly interpreted as indicators of quality, as suggested by the dotted line from quality to resources in Fig. 1. The rarely explicated assumption underpinning this interpretation is actually the first of the propositions on which the diagram is based—with the vital difference that the proposition's two critical qualifications are either ignored or dismissed as of little practical consequence. In effect, the size of a library, in terms of resources, is equated with its quality. Many have pointed out the inadequacies of library standards' expressed in terms of resources alone; and standards that specify resource per unit of some measure of potential demand, e.g., volumes per student, represent an attempt to make somewhat more tenable the assumption of 'other things being equal'. However, the central question of how well the resources are managed is still begged.

Another kind of indirect measure of quality that has been used in the absence of a satisfactory direct measure is symbolized in the figure by the dotted line from quality to utilization—for example, measures such as the number of items circulated per member of the potential user population.

* However, an optimist would favour a fifth proposition: that ... the closeness of coupling will tend to increase as library management improves...

Here the underlying assumptions concern the qualifying phrases of the second proposition, but there is an additional complication in that the relation between capability and utilization is mediated through demand, which is itself a highly complex variable. Since demand is so important in considering measures of both capability and utilization, its nature will be analyzed later.

The most commonly employed indicators of value are measures of utilization, such as those previously mentioned as being used in annual reports for justification purposes. These indirect measures of value rest on analogous assumptions about the qualifiers in the third proposition. Finally, there is yet another kind of indirect measure of value that could have been symbolized by a dotted line from value to resources. If one remembers that the ultimate judges of value are those who sustain the costs, then accepting some measure of support, such as the size of a library's budget, as an indicator of the value accruing from its use perhaps involves no more outrageous assumptions than do some of the other indirect measures of value and quality that have been discussed. Although librarians are generally unwilling to make such assumptions, economists and others may not have similar qualms. For example, Hamburg and his co-workers,[4] estimated the total value of services provided by the Free Library of Philadelphia in 1970 by computing the total costs for that year (including depreciation of the collection, buildings, and equipment) and assuming that this investment of government funds resulted in social benefits exceeding costs by the 'expected' margin (10 per cent).

The purpose of this critical examination of the logical basis for indirect measures of quality and value currently employed was not to suggest that they are worthless. These measures do meet real needs and will continue to be used until library managers become convinced that better measures are available. In recent years, considerable effort has been devoted to developing new kinds of measures, each of which entails its own set of assumptions. Only by explicating the assumptions underlying the measures now used and exploring their vulnerability to violations of the critical conditions upon which their validity depends, and doing the same for any new measures that may be considered as replacements, can one make a rational assessment of relative acceptability on the score of validity.

SPECIFIC NEEDS FOR MEASURES OF GOODNESS

Let us return to our hypothetical library and develop the construct in more detail so that it may be used to illustrate specific needs for different kinds of measures. In this library, the budget-making cycle is initiated by requests from the service level; and a manager's responsibilities are usually defined by the next higher level only in rather general terms. He is expected to suggest and defend specific performance goals for his own level in the process of budget negotiation. The strategy when negotiating with a higher-level manager is to present arguments for the proposed performance goals, and the estimated costs, in terms that are convincing and valid within the superior's frame of reference, and to demonstrate one's managerial competence by showing that goals for the previous budget period were met or, better, exceeded within budgetary limitations. The presentation is buttressed with summary data in a form that is meaningful to the superior and that he can use at the next higher level of budget negotiation.

The Librarian believes it will be impossible to implement this strategy at his level unless performance goals for the entire library can be expressed in terms of service outputs that the Administrator will recognize as being functionally related to the parent organization's programs, and that collectively represent the library's total effort, thereby making it possible to account for all expenditures in terms of these outputs. To this end, the Librarian has adopted a classification of services based on what the user receives (ultimate service outputs), which accommodates both services that are staff-mediated and self-mediated.

One classification that might meet the Librarian's requirements has six broad categories of services to individuals: (1) document services, (2) citation services, (3) answer services, (4) instruction services, (5) facilities services, and (6) adjunct services. Details of this classification, which has been developed in considerable depth, with operational definitions of specific services, are given elsewhere;[5] and for present purposes, a brief summary will suffice. Document services include all the means a library may employ to provide a user with the specific document he wants, given that he already has an adequate bibliographic description for this document.* Citation services include all the ways of providing a user with bibliographic descriptions of some or all documents relating to a particular subject (subject searches) and of providing him with a correct citation for a specific document when he has only an incomplete or inaccurate bibliographic description of it (citation verification). Answer services provide the specific information required to answer a user's question—as contrasted with referring him to a document that may contain the answer. Facility services include provision of space equipped for the user to work in the library. Here, work is defined very broadly to cover any user activity that the given library is intended to support. Instruction services cover various ways that library staff, individually and collectively, plays the role of teacher or advisor. The category of adjunct services includes certain less common services, such as editing, translating, providing non-print media, etc. In this scheme, technical services, such as acquisitions, cataloguing, etc., are viewed as enabling activities that contribute to user-service outputs; therefore, it lends itself to planning and budgeting in terms

* Here, and throughout this article, the term 'document' is used in the broadest sense and means any discrete unit of recorded information, regardless of its type or form.

of service outputs or programmes (e.g., PPBS). However, since it only covers services to individuals, a similar categorization of services to other libraries (e.g., I-L lending, central processing, etc.) is required to encompass the full service output of libraries that devote a significant part of their efforts to such services. The archival and museum-type functions served by some libraries in preserving documents and artifacts, which are not so much services to individual users or other libraries as to posterity, should also be included in total service output when appropriate.

Our hypothetical library has many distinguishably different kinds of service output; but to simplify his management tasks, the Librarian ignores minor differences when counting units of output. He has organized the staff associated with closely related outputs into Services, and grouped the Services into three Sections. Analyzing the needs of the Librarian, and one of the Section Heads, for measures of goodness will suggest the corresponding needs at higher and lower levels of management. It is instructive to look first at the kinds of ideal measures each of these managers might wish to have before turning to what he has at present.

The Librarian's ideal tool for the justification task would be a global measure of the total value of the library's services, representing the sum of values attributable to all uses of Services A, B, C, D, E, etc., and expressed in two ways: (1) as a summary figure-of-merit in whatever units of value the Administrator employs in justifying his own budget, and (2) as an index relating the total value *actually* realized to an estimate of the total value that *could* be realized if the library had 'optimal' support. This estimate would be based on empirically-derived mathematical models for each service showing how value increases as support increases. The Librarian could use this measure both to defend his budget request and to demonstrate how the over-all performance goal for the previous period was met.

If the Administrator is sophisticated, the Librarian would want also to review how the allocation and maximation tasks had been handled at his level.* In the former task, the Librarian would have used the information incorporated into the measure already described, but before aggregation, i.e., figures representing the realized and the potential values for Services A, B, C, D, E, etc. On the basis of this information, supplemented by his knowledge of factors not included in the mathematical models, he would have decided how to allocate the total resources available to the library among Services A, B, C, D, E, etc.

To insure that the resources that have been allocated to each service are employed to maximal advantage, the Librarian needs additional information. In the sequence depicted in Fig. 1, the link between capability and utilization is particularly vulnerable to factors outside the library's control;

* To facilitate presentation, justification, allocation, and maximation are treated as if they were separate tasks, rather than closely related activities. Also, any interactions among services have been ignored.

and in addition, there is often a considerable time lag between changes in capability and changes in utilization because, as will be discussed later, this link must be mediated through changes in users' perception of capability and consequent changes in their habits. Now, even if the Librarian had a mathematical model of the relation between resources devoted to a given service and its realized value *over the long term*, as we have postulated, the relation could change materially if changes are made in the processing activities contributing to the output of this service. Yet, only by changes in these operations can the Section Head responsible for this service hope to realize a greater return from given resources. Therefore, to follow the Section Head's progress in this effort, the Librarian would like a direct measure of the capability of this service, since it will react to changes in the processing sequence more rapidly than measures of value, and more sensitively, in that it will not be subject to as many extraneous factors. When employed with a mathematical model of the capability of the service, this measure would serve to check the predicted effects of altering the processes contributing to the service, and the differences between observed and predicted capability would provide an empirical basis for improving the model. Actually, the most desirable model would be one that related resources to capability, to utilization, and finally to value, thereby providing a much more versatile aid for planning and control than simply having some arcane formula or curve for estimating realized value from the resources devoted to the service. For checking and adjusting the latter model, a measure of utilization of the service would also be necessary.

To summarize, the principal yardsticks needed by the Librarian, aside from measures of costs, would ideally be direct measures of capability, utilization, and value for each of his library's services. The measures of capability and utilization would be suitable for checking the predictions of mathematical models relating capability, utilization, and value; and the units of the measure of value would be suitable for aggregation into a global measure of the total value realized from all services.

The Section Head's needs for aids in carrying out the management tasks at his level can be treated more briefly since, for justification and allocation, he would employ the measures postulated for the Librarian, except that, since the Section Head is concerned only with particular services, he would have no use for the global measure of value. However, for his maximation task, he would like somewhat more detailed models of individual services than have been specified earlier; and in addition to measures of capability, utilization, and value for these services, measures of goodness for individual operations in the contributing processing activities would be needed to guide decisions on how these activities should be changed to realize a greater return for given resources.

This hypothetical library has few, if any, close counterparts in the real world today; and the ideal measures and refined mathematical models postulated are only approximated by the management aids that have been developed to date. Nevertheless, the construct serves to suggest some goals for work toward better measures, as well as to illustrate the different management applications of measures of goodness and indicate the different kinds of measures needed.

PROBLEMS OF DIRECT MEASURES OF GOODNESS

Much has been made of the importance of drawing a sharp distinction between the criterion, or concept, upon which a measure is based and the operational procedures required to carry out the measurement.[6,7] While this distinction has some logical appeal, and it is certainly much easier to suggest criteria than to develop workable procedures to implement them, the distinction quickly blurs in practice. There is a continuous spectrum ranging from a simple notion, through progressively more precisely defined statements of the notion and of the acts to be carried out, to very detailed and explicit instructions that have been extensively tested for clarity and precision At what point along this spectrum does an idea become a measure? If one used the criterion for adequacy of methodologic description that is standard in most sciences—namely, that the method be described in enough detail to insure independent replication of results—few methods for assessing library services would qualify to be called measures. Thus far in this article, the term, measure, has been used loosely to refer not only to the operational means for describing something quantitatively, whether the means have been carefully spelled out or merely implied, but also to the numerical results obtained by these means. As long as one is discussing measures on an abstract level, such imprecision seems unavoidable and should cause little confusion. In the following sections, where emphasis shifts to the 'how' of measurement and discussion of particular measures that have been proposed or developed, the context should make the intended sense of the term clear.

We have seen how indirect measures of quality and value have been, and are being, employed as substitutes for measures that are based directly on the ultimate criteria for quality and value. Now it is appropriate to look at some of the general problems that help to explain why direct measures have not yet replaced these substitutes. For direct measures of quality, or capability, the main problems seem to be those of defining operationally, the universe of needs a service is intended to meet—i.e., needs for specific documents, for specific items of information, or for whatever the service is intended to provide—and, second, those of determining which of the needs so identified has been (or could be) met by the service. Fig. 2 suggests the complexity of the concept of needs and of its relation to demand and ultimately to utilization. This diagram focuses on the capability-demand-utilization triangle in the earlier figure. One concept of needs allows of the possibility that some may be unrecognized by the user, at least until such time as they are brought to his attention by accident, by colleagues, or by an 'active' type of library service designed to convert unrecognized (or very poorly defined?) needs into 'wants'. With this concept, the problems of defining the total universe of needs, and identifying specific examples of these needs, are difficult indeed since the necessary operations would seem to entail extensive trials with representative users. Another concept has a strong

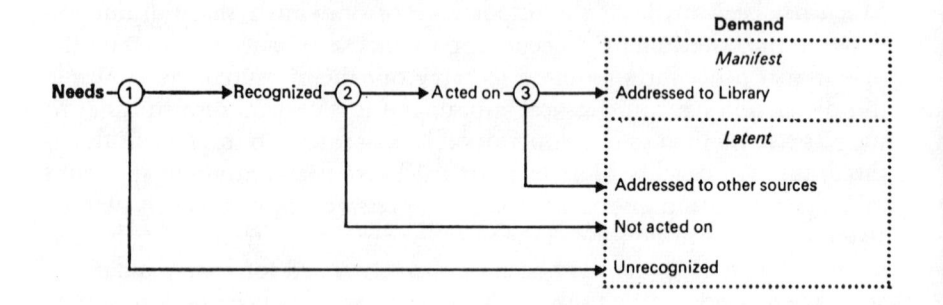

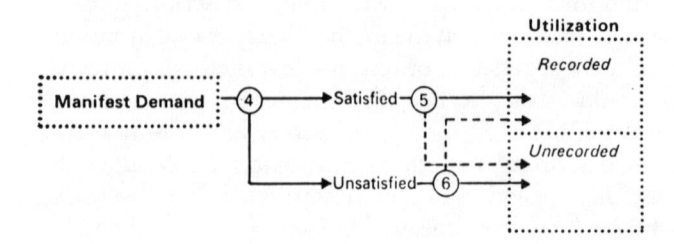

FIG. 2. *The nature of demand and its relation to utilization*

normative element in that it assumes that appropriate 'authorities' or 'experts' can determine what a user needs. Whether this view is defensible depends on the particular application. It has the merit that a definite set of needs can be identified much more easily, e.g., by combining required, or recommended, reading lists.

Once needs have been recognized, or have been both recognized and 'acted on', it is at least theoretically possible to identify an unbiased set of such needs by asking users to record them, as has been attempted in numerous 'diary' studies.* The easiest and most commonly used approach is to limit consideration, either explicitly or implicitly, to only those needs that have both been acted on and 'addressed to' the library, which the diagram shows as comprising 'manifest demand'. However, except in libraries where the service of interest is completely mediated by staff,

* Line has recently reported, with refreshing candor, the problems he encountered in such a study.[8] His report also discusses the disadvantages of measures based on only a subset of potential demand.

identifying even this limited set of needs operationally may prove difficult. Where self-service is possible, users can address needs to the library, i.e., can try the library, without necessarily making these needs known to staff.

However needs are defined, there remain the problems of determining what proportion of these needs are met or 'satisfied'. Again, for libraries where self-service is the common mode, this problem can be formidable. As the diagram suggests, the usual ways of recording utilization include neither all the satisfied, nor all the unsatisfied needs. In addition, such records may not differentiate between satisfied and unsatisfied needs. For example, a loan record may represent a book borrowed only because the title really wanted was not available—if the substitute proved to be a poor one, should this record be counted as a satisfied need? Some different solutions to the problem of determining the proportion of satisfied document needs are exemplified by the Shelf Failure Survey,[9] in which this ratio is established by questioning a sample of users about their activities during a library visit, and the Document Delivery Test,[10] in which someone simulates users and records the availability status of items the users are postulated to need. Certain methods of assessing answer services [11,12,13] also employ someone who is not actually a user to record the data required to determine the satisfaction ratio.

A further complication in determining the ratio of satisfied to total needs stems from the complex effects of capability. The numbered junctions in the diagram indicate some of the ways in which capability can interact with demand and utilization. A library's capability, *as perceived by its users*, can obviously influence decisions at points 2 and 3 with the result that, as perceived capability increases, so does the ratio of manifest demand to potential demand (manifest plus latent demand). Thus, one can postulate that perceived capability is an important factor in determining a library's service loads, which are usually more accurately represented by manifest demand than by recorded utilization. The influence of perceived capability at junction 6 may not be as obvious; but it seems reasonable to believe that, when users have a high regard for the library's capability, they are more likely to make their unmet needs known to staff.* By definition, a library's actual capability influences the outcome at junction 4; and depending on one's concept of needs, it may be appropriate to postulate an effect at junction 1 produced by active modes of service, as discussed earlier. The net effect of all these interactions is that, unless one is very careful about how the ratio of satisfied to total needs is established, the results may show a paradoxical relation to efforts to improve capability—similar to the experience of librarians who have been discouraged and puzzled, at first, when their efforts at improvement seemed to result in more unsatisfied users.

* The outcome at junction 6 is also, in part, determined by the nature of the service and policies on recording use; and these factors control junction 5 almost completely.

Difficulties of a different order of magnitude are met in trying to devise a direct measure based on the ultimate criterion of value; and it is easy to become trapped in a philosophical quagmire in the attempt. The first problem is—Who are 'those who sustain the costs'?—and to avoid any unnecessary trouble, let us define costs to exclude such things as users' time and effort, which can be handled in other ways. Except in the rare instances where a library that enjoys no tax preference is entirely supported by charges or fees paid from its users' own pocket, the question can have several possible answers if one considers ultimate as well as proximate courses of support. However, this phrase in the statement of the ultimate criterion was purposely left somewhat vague so as not to exclude those who control the library's support. Therefore, for most libraries, there are two possible answers; and the appropriate choice depends on the purpose for which the measure is intended. If it is intended for a theoretical analysis of library economics, the choice may be those who are the ultimate source of support. But for the pragmatic purposes of library management, the choice is those who approve requests for funds, space, etc. at the next higher level of management; and this commonly reduces to one person although he may be advised by a group.

Given that the question of the ultimate judges' identity has been settled in favour of the pragmatic choice, one approach is to start by postulating that the 'value system' of these judges should logically be determined only by the objectives of the parent organization and then proceed by trying to assess the beneficial effects attributable to a particular service of the library (or to all of its services collectively) in terms of how much the service contributes toward achieving these organizational objectives. This contribution need not be reckoned in monetary units; indeed, it can be expressed in several different, and incommensurable, units.* In theory, given sufficiently precise organizational objectives, the beneficial effects attributable to a service could be measured very directly by controlled experiments designed to determine how the value realized from the service varies as its quality or level of support varies. But, with the exception of businesses, where the objective is to increase profit, few of the organizations that support libraries have defined their objectives sufficiently precisely to make this approach even theoretically feasible. However, even if such experiments were feasible and the postulate of a *logically* determined value system is tenable, it would hardly provide a practical means of measuring value. In one variant of this approach, the problem posed by lack of precisely defined organizational objectives is by-passed by the assumption that any saving of users' time (or organizational funds) attributable to the service will contribute to

* Among recent publications treating the assessment of benefits in non-monetary terms, one of the more pertinent and interesting is Zvezhinskii's brief discussion of appropriate measures for assessing the contribution of information services in an engineering design unit operating within a socialist economy.[14]

organizational objectives by making these resources available for other, presumably productive, activities. This basic idea has been implemented in many ways and with varying rigour—for example, by asking users to estimate time savings, by employing mathematical models to estimate savings of users' time, etc. Although this general tactic may be useful and justifiable for certain management purposes, it has obvious inherent limitations.

A second, and basically different, approach emphasizes the essentially subjective nature of value judgements and proceeds to assess the beneficial effects of a service by determining the value people attribute to these effects. The resulting methods vary widely with regard to what assumptions are made (e.g., assumptions that allow users or librarians to act as the judges) and how values are made explicit; but they can all be considered to be relatively direct measures as long as the central question is not begged entirely by equating value with what is expended (i.e., the resources devoted to a particular service or to the library itself). Although the methods may be quite different in procedural details, they all fall in one of two classes— either the judges are asked to indicate their values (elicited values), or values are inferred from their actions (inputed values). For example, in SCOUT,[15] and the Standardized Inventory of User Services'[16,17] the elicited values of librarians are used to weight the contributions of different services to a global measure of overall service; whereas, Hawgood started with the actions (decisions) represented by a library budget and from these actions derived a set of inputed values by computer.[18] Although the feasibility of employing values elicited from users has been explored, the notion of deriving values from users' actions seems to have had more appeal. One of the first to see the possibilities of this notion was Meier, who in 1961 suggested that the amount of personal time users allocated to a service might provide a basis for a measure of value.[19] Others have explored the problems of developing measures of this type at the theoretical level (e.g., Hawgood[20] and Elton[21]); but thus far, only some rather crude measures have been tested operationally.[22]

DESIDERATA FOR MEASURES

To complete the general framework for considering measures of goodness, it is necessary to give some attention to factors that cannot be covered here in any detail. Table 1 is a checklist intended to suggest the whole array of factors to be considered in deciding whether a particular measure is suitable for a particular application and preferable to alternative measures. In the explanatory comments and suggestions, the viewpoint of a decision-maker who is considering a candidate measure for use in his own library has been adopted; and it is assumed that he has a specific application in mind. These comments will serve the dual purpose of recapitulating certain of the points made earlier and of indicating some of the questions that should be asked about factors that have not been mentioned thus far.

TABLE 1. *Desiderata for measures*
1. Appropriateness
2. Informativeness
3. Validity
4. Reproducibility
5. Comparability
6. Practicality

Regarding appropriateness, some of the questions to be asked are: Is the measure of the proper type? For example, the allocation task hinges upon the relative value of different services; and measures of value, rather than quality, are indicated for this task. Are the units and scale suitable? If the results of different measures are to be aggregated, they must be in the same units, or convertible to common units. The scales of most measures of quality impose certain limitations on the arithmetical operations that are permissible for relating quality and costs. An index-type scale is natural for setting performance goals. Are the operations required to implement the measure compatible with the library's procedures, physical layout, etc.? Is the viewpoint and/or service philosophy implied by the measure appropriate? Some measures are predicated on a philosophy of 'active' as opposed to 'passive' service; and some are based on the premise that the library should be viewed as part of a larger system, rather than as a self-sufficient entity.

For lack of a better word, 'informativeness' refers to the help in suggesting sources of operational problems and possible solutions that is provided as an additional benefit by some methods but not others. For example, suppose one measured the capability of a service by asking users how many times they had tried the service and how often their needs had been met. Although an index of capability could be based on the ratio of successes to total tries, carrying out the procedure would provide little help in pinpointing what was affecting the success rate. Best of all would be a method that supplies the key data needed for employing a mathematical model to determine the relative importance of existing operational problems and to predict the likely effects of alternative actions.

Only in the special cases where a universally accepted 'standard' measure exists against which a newer measure can be formally 'validated', and in those cases where there are reasonable grounds to believe that the results obtained by a measure will be systematically and materially biased in an uncorrectable way, can the validity of a measure be assessed at all objectively. Measures falling in the latter category include those whose implementation is likely to change the very thing that is being measured, as contrasted to 'unobtrusive' measures, which are free of any such risk. In most cases, assessment of validity is essentially subjective and depends, ultimately, on the judgement of those who are expected to accept the results. In judging 'face' or prima facie validity, one may ask: Are the assumptions underlying the measure acceptable, including those made in arriving at a criterion as well as those made to simplify data collection? But most operationally-defined measures depend upon several assumptions that are demonstrably 'untrue' in some sense. An alternative approach is to ask: Will the results be unacceptably distorted if the assumptions are violated? Measures that have face validity for users and non-librarian administrators, as well as for librarians, are certainly preferable for many applications. Indeed, it can be argued that much of the difficulty experienced in getting adequate support for libraries is attributable to the use of measures of quality and value that have little validity for non-librarians.

Reproducibility, or reliability, is considerably easier to assess. Here the main question is: Are the procedures for implementing the measure carried out in such a way that standard statistical techniques can be employed to estimate the size of errors to be expected—i.e., Is the reliability statistically determinate? All measures are subject to errors, which are tolerable only if one can be reasonably confident (and prove to others) that the errors are not large enough to affect decisions seriously.

Comparability considerations are relatively simple when the aim is to obtain data useful for monitoring changes in whatever is being measured, and one is concerned only with a single library (as opposed to groups of libraries).* The key question is: To what extent will results be affected by factors one would wish to control? For example, for monitoring progress in improving the capability of a service, it may be undesirable for the results to be affected by transient service over-loads or cyclic variations in service loads.

Practicality is of prime importance in considering measures intended for routine use as management aids, in contrast to one-time or infrequent 'studies'. Among the many questions to be asked are: To what degree will library operations be impeded? Can the reliability needed for management decisions be achieved at acceptable costs in terms of staff time and operating expenses? What is required in terms of users' time, effort, and patience? Can the procedures be carried out by library staff with little or no outside help?

At the outset, I stated that my purpose was not to moderate criticism of innovations in library management, but rather to sharpen it. I hope the conceptual framework presented here will serve this purpose and prove of some value as a general aid in assessing developmental efforts in an area where the *caveat emptor* principle still prevails.

* However, since it is often useful to compare results obtained in one's own library with results in similar libraries, inter-library comparability should always be given some weight.

REFERENCES

1. MARTYN, J. Evaluation of information-handling systems. *Aslib proceedings*, vol. 21, 1969, p. 317-24.
2. LANCASTER, F. W. The cost-effectiveness analysis of information retrieval and dissemination systems. *J. ASIS*, vol. 22, 1971, pp. 12-27.
3. GILCHRIST, A. Cost-effectiveness. *Aslib proceedings*, vol. 23, 1971, pp. 455-64.
4. HAMBURG, M. *et al*. Library objectives and performance measures and their use in decision making. *Library quarterly*, vol. 42, 1972, pp. 107-28.
5. ORR, R. H. *et al*. Development of methodologic tools for planning and managing library services: III. Standardized inventories of library services. *Bulletin of the Medical Library Association*, vol. 56, 1968, pp. 380-403.
6. SNYDER, M. B. *et al*. Methodology for test and evaluation of document retrieval systems: A critical review and recommendations. Washington, DC, National Science Foundation 1966, NSF C-418.
7. EVANS, E. *et al*. Review of criteria used to measure library effectiveness. *Bulletin of the Medical Library Association*, vol. 60, 1972, pp. 102-14.
8. LINE, M. B. The ability of a university library to provide books wanted by researchers. *Journal of librarianship*, vol. 5, 1973, pp. 37-51.
9. URQUHART, J. A. *and* SCHOFIELD, J. L. Measuring readers' failure at the shelf in three university libraries. *Journal of documentation*, vol. 28, 1972, pp. 233-41.
10. ORR, R. H. *and* SCHLESS, A. P. Document delivery capabilities of major biomedical libraries in 1968: Results of a national survey employing standardized tests. *Bulletin of the Medical Library Association*, vol. 60, 1972, pp. 382-422.
11. BUNGE, C. A. Professional education and reference efficiency. (Research series, no. 11). Springfield, Illinois State Library, 1967.
12. UNIVERSITY OF THE STATE OF NEW YORK. Emerging library systems: The 1963-1966 evaluation of the New York State public library system, Library Extension Division, Albany, 1967.
13. CHILDERS, T. Managing the quality of reference information service. *Library quarterly*, vol. 42, 1972, pp. 212-17.
14. ZVEZHINSKII, S. N. Criterion and indicators of technico-economic effectiveness of information utilized in planning-design work. *Nauchno Tekhnickeskaya Informatsiya*, series 1, no. 6, 1967, pp. 3-6. (Translation issued by US National Technical Information Service as AD 680978.)
15. WESSEL, C. J. *et al*. Criteria for evaluating the effectiveness of library operations and services: Phase III. Recommended criteria and methods for their utilization. Washington, DC, John I. Thompson and Co., 1969, AD 682 758.
16. ORR, R. H. *et al*. User services offered by medical school libraries in 1968: Results of a national survey employing new methodology. *Bulletin of the Medical Library Association*, vol. 58, 1970, pp. 455-92.
17. OLSON, E. E. Survey of user service policies in Indiana libraries and information centers. Bloomington, Ind., Indiana University, 1970, ED 044 139.
18. HAWGOOD, J. *and* MORLEY, R. Project for evaluating the benefits from university libraries. University of Durham, 1969, OSTI 5056.
19. MEIER, R. L. Efficiency criteria for the operation of large libraries. *Library quarterly*, vol. 31, 1961, pp. 215-34.
20. HAWGOOD, J. The scope for automatic data processing in the British Library. Supporting paper I. 2: The British Library in its relationship to national library provision: An approach to library resource allocation. 1971, NAB 800-I. 2.
21. INSTITUTE FOR OPERATIONAL RESEARCH. Scope for operational research in the library and information services field. London, 1972, OSTI 5136.

22. ORR, R. H. The scientist as an information processor: A conceptual model illustrated with data on variables related to library utilization. *In:* Nelson, C. E. and Pollock, D. K. Communication among scientists and technologists. Lexington, Mass., D. C. Heath and Co., 1970, pp. 143-89.

Concepts of library goodness

Michael K. Buckland

The study of "library goodness" is an underdeveloped area. There has been some speculation that there might be some general universal measure of library goodness. The idea is appealing. Imagine a Monday morning in the office as a university president, mayor or corporation chief executive officer arrives and the secretary says: "Good morning! The financial crisis is looking even worse but you'll be pleased to know that the librarian reports that the library's performance went up half a point on the library goodness scale last week." It is a nice thought but not very probable.

Single measures of library goodness[1] can be concocted but their credibility is undermined by the number of arbitrary assumptions that have to be made to piece the parts together. Nor should this be surprising. When choosing an automobile, a variety of different factors: safety, appearance, economy, speed, comfort and so on, are considered. The problem is to relate this battery of factors to resources, intentions and personal set of values.

Although the quest for the Grail of Library Goodness has not (yet) been successful, there has been no lack of measures of performance proposed nor lack of people proposing them. The principal guide is Lancaster's *Measurement and Evaluation of Library Services.*[2] There have been plenty of suggestions: What is lacking is coherence, a sense of the whole. It is not that there has not been progress. Lancaster's work is rather complete through about 1973, with some later work. A comparable volume written in 1963 would have been a lot thinner. Yet there is a long way to go, and it is noticeable that the numerous empirical efforts need to be counterbalanced by a greater attention to theory and to context.

Three paradoxes

There are plenty of gaps and intellectual problems in librarianship and it can be stimulating to attempt to resolve apparent contradictions. In approaching library goodness, consider three paradoxes.

The evaluation of catalogues. Books are catalogued and, therefore, retrieved by their attributes. Usually these attributes reduce to what they are "about," who their authors were, what their titles are and where and when they were published. A narrow definition of evaluation would be concerned with whether or not the catalogue (or any retrieval system) does in practice yield the items with the desired attributes.

On the other hand, it has been argued that the proper criterion for evaluation of the items retrieved should be their utility to the user, rather than their "aboutness"

Reprinted from *Canadian Library Journal,* 39(2), 1982, by permission.

COSTING AND ECONOMICS

or other attribute used for retrieval. This sounds plausible but the utility depends on the user's state of ignorance and motivation at that particular time. So, in a sense, the catalogue would be evaluated not on its own characteristics but in terms of matters (ignorance, personal values) that are extraneous to it. This seems a little unfair, albeit desirable.

Optimal library size. In many areas of manufacturing, commerce and engineering, matters of size and scale are of central interest. The same could reasonably be expected to be true in librarianship. After all, every increment in size costs money. Yet that is not the case. The literature of librarianship is almost silent on the topic and what little there is does not get one very far and, I suspect, is little read. In brief, the literature is very limited on what might be a central concern.[3]

Lenin's view of public libraries in the U.S. The third paradox is quite different again. Many people connected with U.S. public libraries do not realize that a great admirer of the American public library scene was Lenin. Lenin was quite knowledgeable about libraries: His wife, Krupskaia, was a librarian.[4]

In the U.S. public libraries are viewed as a bastion of western liberal democracy and are seen as playing a significant role in free access to information, in establishing a well-informed electorate and so on. Since these are not goals generally attributed to the Soviet Union (or to Lenin), it seems paradoxical that he should have been so enthusiastic.

Orr's schema

A discussion that can be helpful in trying to grapple with concepts of library goodness was published by Orr in the "Progress in Documentation" series of the *Journal of Documentation* in 1973.[5]

Orr points out that there is a fundamental ambiguity in discussions of library goodness because there are two quite different sorts of goodness:

- How good is it? — a measure of *quality*.
- What good does it do? — a measure of *value*.

Suppose that a collection of Persian prayer books was amassed and that, through assiduous purchasing and photocopying, this collection came to be the most complete collection of its kind in the world. Unquestionably this would be a good collection. If good cataloguing and knowledgeable staff were added, then we would have a good library. It would be good in the sense of quality. We can, in fact, say more than this. Quality in this sense implies capability. Such a library collection is of good quality because it is highly capable of meeting the needs of persons seeking to learn about Persian prayer books.

On the other hand, it does not necessarily follow that even the highest quality library would have beneficial effects. Let us imagine that this collection of Persian prayer books were to be in Bella Bella, B.C., or some other relatively inaccessible and sparsely populated area. What good would it do? In the absence of civilization it is difficult to imagine any beneficial effects.

Measurement

Unfortunately both quality (capability) and value (beneficial effects) are difficult to measure, especially the latter. In practice we tend to fall back on surrogate measures. See Fig. 1. In particular income or resources are assumed to indicate capability: "With a book budget that low they can't do much!" or "That should be a good library, just look at the resources they have!". There is an implied causal connection. So there should be in the sense that a skilled librarian ought to be able to improve the quality of a library given improved resources. However, the improvement is not automatic any more than buying expensive ingredients guarantees a good meal if the chef cannot cook. Similarly, it is assumed if utiliza-

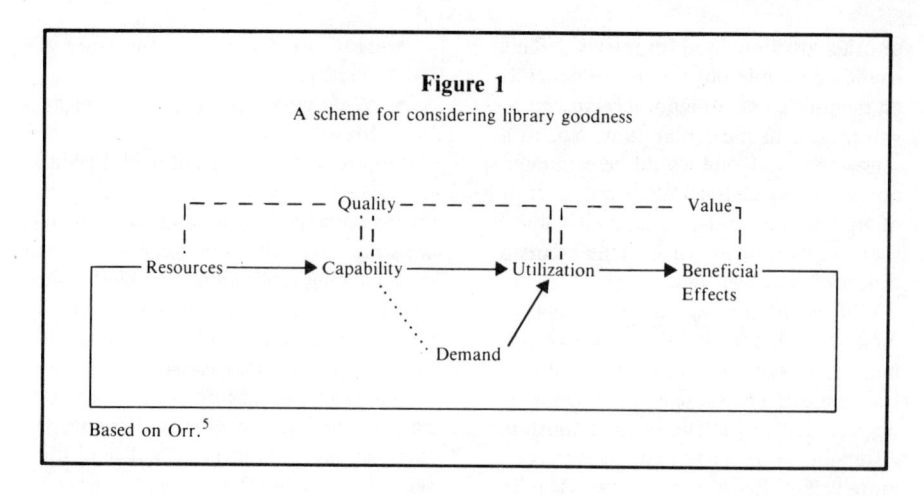

Figure 1
A scheme for considering library goodness

Resources → Capability → Utilization → Beneficial Effects

Quality ----- Value
Demand

Based on Orr.[5]

tion is increasing, then beneficial effects are increasing. "The children's library is packed, it must be doing a good job."

These assumed connections, which are depicted by dotted lines in Fig. 1, are not unreasonable so long as it is remembered that the tightness of the connection can vary. Several things can go wrong. In particular the capability being offered may be more or less appropriate for the pattern of demand in the context where the library service is provided. We can imagine library collections more appropriate to probable demand in Bella Bella than Persian prayer books. Similarly relocating the latter in Vancouver or, better yet, Teheran would increase utilization and hence, beneficial effects.

Appropriateness

Library services are paternalistic in the sense that they are ordinarily provided by some for others. The appropriateness of the provision for the context in which it is provided deserves recurring consideration. In this regard there is more theoretical work to be done on the demand for library services. What are the crucial attributes of demand such that the detailed profile of services provided is appropriate?

Let us imagine a situation in which the dominant form of demand is for identified documents and in which promptness of service is desirable but not critical. What profile of library service, what capability would be most appropriate? Since the emphasis is on obtaining specific, known documents, a premium should be placed on author and title catalogues. Tools of subject access play a minor, auxiliary role. Reliable document delivery is important because requests are for specific documents and, by implication, substitution of alternative titles is likely to be inappropriate. A high level of immediate availability on open-access shelves would seem desirable for convenience but, in fact, open access does not seem essential. Lengthy loan periods are tolerable if a particular item can be recalled from loan on request. Good service would be possible from closed stacks (even with shelving by size and accession number in compact storage) if documents are to be kept secure and in good order. Urgency permitting, interlibrary loan could serve this demand better than any other kind of demand. This sort of demand calls for investment in union catalogues and finding lists. The need for expert reference staff would appear to be at a minimum. ("I know what I want, please get it!")

Let us now imagine what an appropriate profile of library provision might be like if we were dealing with a demand pattern characterized by specific subject inquiries and urgency. In this situation there would appear to be a premium on subject access, including both a subject arrangement of documents and subject indexes that provide additional points of access to them. The indexes might be purchased bibliographical tools or locally produced. A special emphasis on computer-based reference services and on local indexes, because of the additional power each can bring, might be expected. Indepth indexing of parts of documents would seem, in general, to be desirable, though not necessarily affordable. Experienced subject specialist reference staff or information officers can play a substantial role. To the extent that one document may be substitutable for another, low levels of immediate availability and lengthy loan periods become tolerable. Large but not necessarily exhaustive local collections within the subject area concerned are desirable to provide for browsing. Access to large holdings is also likely to be needed because the result of a subject search might become a search for one or more particular documents. In that case interlibrary loan would suffice for providing access to documents unless urgency is a major concern. The collection, even if large, ought to be on open access and arranged by subject in order to facilitate browsing even though one can also browse in subject indexes.

The two profiles of library provision that just imagined represent quite different patterns of library provision: the former resembles a traditional university library and the latter a typical special library. Other scenarios are possible. The recognizable difference between the two profiles illustrates the extent to which a library's "capability" may need to be made appropriate to the pattern of the demand to be served.[6]

Paradoxes revisited

Let us reconsider the three paradoxes in relation to library goodness and preceding discussion.

The paraxodical situation with respect to the evaluation of catalogues can be resolved by reference to Orr's schema in Fig. 1. Retrieval evaluation in the narrow sense is a matter of quality and capability. A retrieval system that consistently and reliably retrieves just those items that have the specified attributes is, unquestionably, a good retrieval system, whether it is used or not.

The extended definition of catalogue effectiveness is concerned with the utility of what is retrieved. This approach differs from the narrow definition in two ways: Firstly, it is an evaluation of the combination of a retrieval system and its users; secondly, it corresponds to Orr's second type of goodness — what good does it do? It is concerned with value and beneficial effects. It is, therefore, different in kind from the narrow definition.[7]

The question of optimal library size has an explanation of a different sort. There may be circumstances in which library books ought to be relegated to less accessible storage, and there may be circumstances in which staffing ought to be increased relative to acquisitions. A change in size is a change in kind and some restructuring of the pattern of provision, such as decentralization or automation, becomes desirable. However, after all appropriate restructuring, the acquisition of one more book would seem to continue to be advantageous, even though, with diminishing returns, the advantage might become small. In other words, the marginal benefit of increased size appears to remain positive, however slight. Bigger, from this perspective, remains better.

The restraint lies outside of the library. At some point the marginal increase in the benefit to be derived from the next dollar to be spent on books is less than the benefit to the city of the next dollar to be spent on road repairs, or the benefit to the university of increasing the number of teaching assistants or whatever. We should expect the literature of librarianship to be rich in dealing with the problems of handling increases in size. However, we cannot expect it to be other than impotent in relation to optimal library size because the problem is in large measure external to librarianship and can only be resolved in relation to the context of library services.

The paradox of Lenin and American public libraries becomes less paradoxical if we review it in terms of Orr's schema and also ask about social values to define what constitute beneficial effects. It is perfectly reasonable for Lenin or anybody else to respect and admire public libraries for the capability they have to inform, educate and amuse.

The precise tuning of the capability through, for example, book selection and censorship will depend on the social values defining what beneficial effects are being sought. It is these social values that constitute the difference. Lenin was not seeking to achieve a western liberal democracy. This paradox is only a paradox so long as we fail to distinguish between the two sorts of goodness with respect to public libraries.

Conclusion

The concept of library goodness is ambiguous: "How good is it?" and "What good does it do?" are valid but quite different questions. Orr suggests another goodness, the goodness of library management, that would be reflected in tighter connections between the elements in his schema: more capability for any given increase in resources, more utilization for every increase in capability and so on.

Such improvement in the effectiveness of library management and in our ability to grapple with concepts of library goodness call for a greater emphasis on the theory and context of library service.

Footnotes

1. Hamburg, M. and others. *Library Planning and Decision-Making Systems*. MIT Press, Cambridge, Mass., 1974.
2. Lancaster, F.W. *Measurement and Evaluation of Library Services*. Information Resources Press, Washington, D.C., 1977.
3. A noteworthy exception to this neglect is Gore, D. ed. *Farewell to Alexandria: Solutions to Space, Growth, and Performance Problems of Libraries*. Greenwood Press, Westport, Conn., 1976.
4. Raymond, B. *Krupskaia and Soviet Russian Librarianship, 1917-1939*. The Scarecrow Press, Metuchen, N.J., 1979.
5. Orr. R.M. "Measuring the Goodness of Library Services: A General Framework for Considering Quantitative Measures," *Journal of Documentation*. 29, 3, Sept., 1973. p. 315-332.
6. For a fuller discussion of the appropriateness of provision in relation to the sorts of inquiries served see Buckland, M.K., "Types of Search and the Allocation of Library Resources," *Journal of the American Society for Information Science*. 30, 3, May, 1979. p. 143-147.
7. For further discussion of uses of the term 'relevance' see Wilson, P. *Two Kinds of Power: An Essay on Bibliographical Control*. University of California Press, 1968, especially chapters II "Describing and Exploring" and III, "Relevance." Wilson is concerned primarily with the extended definition of relevance and utility: "textual means to an end," (p.50). In Wilson's terms the narrow definition of relevance should not be called relevance but "fitting a description," (p. 46); "To say of something that it fits a certain description is not to employ the concept of relevance," (p.47).

COST-EFFECTIVENESS

ALAN GILCHRIST

An analogy

THIS CONFERENCE is an information system—you are the users and I am one of the documents that has been retrieved by the system operators. Each of you will 'read' up to six documents and will, I hope, discuss them with each other. The cost to each one of you is the £14 conference fee plus incidentals. Few of you will have met this cost yourselves, having persuaded your employers to foot the bill as well as giving you a day off to attend the conference, making a total cost of the order of £25 per organization. The conference organizers have controlled the finances and, like you, have chosen to expend energy on this exercise rather than some other activity. Three groups of people, the conference organizers, your organizations and yourselves, all have individual expectations and when the conference is over will assess to what extent these expectations have been met. The conference organizers will heave a sigh of relief before becoming involved in planning next year's conference, when they will take into account those of your views of this year's conference that they come to hear about. Your views, I suggest, will depend to a considerable extent on chance: the conversation you happened to have with the person sitting next to you at dinner; a train of thought stimulated by a discussion of one of the papers and, in the even longer term, the unforeseen connection between something a speaker said and a problem encountered a month later. As for the people who actually paid the money—some organizations require delegates to present formal reports when they return to work, and must rely on this method of assessing whether their money was well spent. As conferences continue to be organized for the exchange of information we must assume that they are worthwhile. I personally think they are, and though I hate to say so at this particular moment, there is clearly a lot of truth in the often heard general assessment: 'It's not the papers you listen to, it's the people you meet.' Incidentally, if this assessment is accurate, it is worth considering to what extent conferences are organized to meet this primary objective.

This analogy underlines I think some of the problems of cost-effectiveness:

(a) The different standpoints from which we may judge success.
(b) The different ways in which success can be judged from these standpoints.
(c) The existence of long term effects.
(d) The difficulty of relating a cost to a complex purchase.

Cost-benefit analysis

The idea of relating resources expended in producing an output to the effects of that output are, of course, not new. I was, though, surprised to read in a survey of cost-benefit analysis (CBA)[1] that a classic paper on the utility of public works appeared in the economics literature as long ago as 1844. CBA is defined by the Treasury[2] as being 'a systematic comparison between the cost of carrying out a service or activity and the value of that service or activity, quantified as far as possible; all costs and benefits (direct and indirect, financial and social) being taken into account'. This definition is accompanied by the explanation that 'CBA involves the listing and consideration of as many effects as can be identified—beneficial and adverse, short-term and long-term, tangible and intangible—on all persons and groups likely to be affected (however remotely) by a proposed project or service. The value of this appraisal depends on how completely all effects can be traced and the extent to which they can be evaluated in comparable (normally monetary) terms.'

CBA has been used extensively in many areas such as health, education and transport. You will all have heard mention of its application, for example, when the M1 motorway and the Victoria Line were being planned. The M1 analysis was a complex exercise which classified net annual savings under four heads:

1. those relating to diverted traffic;
2. those relating to generated traffic;
3. savings in non-business time;
4. the effects on the growth of the GNP;

but still it was criticized for omitting:

1. allowances for police and administrative costs;
2. benefits accruing to pedestrians and cyclists;
3. advantages of more reliable goods deliveries.

It was also criticized for introducing inconsistencies between long-term and short-term views and for an inadequate appraisal of the savings due to accident reduction. Since the M1 study we have seen the Buchanan Report—a study of no less a topic than the long-term problems of traffic in urban areas. This report included the notion of 'environment' in calculations for urban road improvements which makes the estimation process extremely complex, if it is feasible at all. More recently still, there has been a small furore over the application of CBA to the siting of London's third airport. An article written by Peter Self, Professor of Public Administration at the University of London, engagingly titled 'Nonsense on stilts: the futility of Roskill',[3] attacks the basic methodology adopted by the Commission. He says, for example: 'CBA gets its plausibility from the use of a common monetary standard, but the common value of the £ derives from exchange situations. Outside such situations common values cannot be presumed, and symbol and reality become easily confused...' Later on he says: 'It is just possible that cost-benefit exercises have some utility as supporting evidence for certain kinds of decision. But when this art is elevated to the level of a comprehensive framework for decision-making, the costs of cost-benefit become severe indeed, amounting almost to actual vitiation of proper professional and political procedures.' More recently, Buchanan, who was a member of the Roskill Commission, was reported as saying that 'he "quite literally" failed to understand the details of the massive cost-benefit analysis—the biggest of its kind ever undertaken in this country—which had dominated his colleagues' decision to go for Cublington rather than Foulness'. The report went on to say that 'as the mathematics involved were extremely complex it would have been surprising if any non-specialist had followed the analysis, but more important—he doubted the relevance of economics to the issue. His decision was made finally "on a hunch"—a deep down feeling telling him where to go!'[4] It can be seen how difficult it is to identify all effects, beneficial and adverse, long-term and short-term, tangible and intangible. Furthermore, the effects of a system may be far reaching, as the wake of a river boat is far more pronounced than the ripples which erode the banks. The system is part of a larger system and is related to many others but where does one draw the line? Finally, CBA requires very careful interpretation but still the hunch may be more important.

Cost-effectiveness analysis

Cost-effectiveness analysis (CEA) is a less romantic and more down-to-earth variant of CBA, and again I turn to the Treasury glossary[2] which gives definitions of two aspects:

'a method of finding either
  (a) the cheapest means of accomplishing a defined objective or
  (b) the maximum value from a given expenditure.'

and as examples of these

(a) 'would be the analysis of the cost of cleaning office buildings to see whether contract or directly employed labour provides the cheaper method of cleaning to a reasonable standard;
(b) 'may often be the more difficult exercise to carry out: it may be necessary for example to try to measure the combined effectiveness of a mixed military force. This form of analysis has been used particularly in the defence sector where the benefit in terms of military capability or military effectiveness cannot necessarily be expressed in financial terms.'

Evaluation of information systems

I shall now discuss briefly three recent research projects which have been based on cost-benefit and cost-effectiveness analysis.

I hope you will forgive me for taking you yet again into the well-charted Wessel territory,[5, 6] but his project was so thorough and well-informed that it would be less sensible to avoid mentioning it. Wessel started with a survey of the literature and state-of-the-art from which he concluded that, for his needs, CEA was one of only three techniques of central importance. He also recognized four general aspects of library performance:

1. Philosophical—relating to the statement of the reasons for the library's existence.
2. Management—relating to the influence on the efficiency and effectiveness of the library of management practices.

3. Services and products—relating to the library outputs and measures of service or product effectiveness.
4. Operations—potentially useful as a basis for performance evaluation of the staff's professional actions.

In one use of CEA, Wessel identified each significant service, activity and operation and constructed a procedural model based on these components. The model included alternative routes because, of course, each chain has one or more entry points. Each event block in the flow chart, e.g. 'User contacts library or librarian to satisfy informational need', was then assigned a figure representing the probability that that event would occur. This figure was based upon past experience, subjective analysis or statistical sampling. Now, each activity is represented by the connecting line between events, and those activities which accrued significant costs were assigned standard cost data, these data also being derived from past experience, or generated by techniques such as work measurement. It was then possible to derive measures of effectiveness from the probabilities that events would occur when a number of needs were processed. The first use of this analysis was to identify and investigate 'effectiveness causal factors'. For example, events with low probabilities of occurring were investigated, as were the effects of activities on the probability of occurrence of a subsequent event. The second use of this analysis was to arrive at a figure of effectiveness for any chain of events and activities expressed as the product of effectiveness probabilities. For example, one objective of reference service or search service may be simply to identify some candidate documents for an informational need. The effectiveness of this service in meeting this objective can be measured by the probabilities of communication of needs, of the librarian beginning a search and of the librarian identifying some candidate documents. This technique is based on the correct formulation of goals and objectives, a point which Wessel emphasizes particularly strongly, and this in turn is based on the proper determination of the services needed by the user.

A project undertaken at Durham University[7] started with the intention of assessing the benefits accruing from a university library by gathering subjective evaluation from the academic staff. This approach was later changed to a methodology which assumed that the library manager, by intelligent and constant interaction with the users, was highly likely to optimize his system. The Durham team constructed a model into which they fed:

(a) the total resources—in terms of labour time, money, seats, and shelf space available during, say, the coming year;
(b) the unit cost of each activity in these terms;
(c) the present volume of each activity—items acquired, loans per year etc.

A computer was then used to manipulate these figures and to show that, for the library being examined, adding one item to stock appeared to be rated as equal in user benefit to:

–providing 4.5 inter-library loans;
–catering for 1,270 user-hours of reading on premises;

COSTING AND ECONOMICS

—providing 90 items on long loan;
—or 203 items on short loan;
—using 3.4 hours of senior librarian's time on advisory work;
—or 9 hours of junior librarian's time.

By manipulating the model in the opposite direction (a technique known as inverse linear programming) the librarian may determine the best way of allocating resources in the changed circumstances. In addition, the model allows the librarian to make subjective alterations to ratings and for certain constraints to be built in.

The third study I want to refer to was undertaken by consultants[8] on behalf of the Department of the Environment as part of the latter's programme of investigation into the problem of data co-ordination in the Construction Industry. The consultants were asked to investigate the feasibility of setting up a central file containing information about commodities used by the construction industry. During the second phase an attempt was made to estimate the cost benefit of about fourteen alternative systems. The study which will be published later this year identified twelve characteristics which could provide potential benefits:

Response time—savings in time to answer enquiries.
Increase in complexity of enquiries leading to further time savings.
Reliability or system.
Reliability or accuracy of data.
Up-to-dateness.
Comprehensiveness of coverage—increased choice.
Depth of data for products—including ease of comparison.
Presentation—including ability to provide hard copy.
Browsability.
User convenience.
Feedback to users.
Feedback to manufacturers.

Of these they concluded that 'Response time' was the one item that related directly to the number of enquiries put to the file. The value of the 'annual user time saved' by a particular alternative was compared with the cost of that system and the result expressed as a net benefit if positive or a net cost if negative. The 'annual user time saved' was based on survey, past experience and estimation. The report concluded that the evidence from the various approaches suggested that a computer system would show a total benefit of the order of £10 million per annum as against £5 million per annum for a microform system, the others being non-starters.

At this stage, like Buchanan, you might feel inclined to give up the detailed argument and rely on your hunches. You might also, with some justification, question the validity of such analyses, and certainly they should be approached with a healthy degree of watchful scepticism. At least five points emerge from these projects:

1. Such studies are detailed and complex. Think particularly of Wessel's

procedural analysis. At broader levels the figures become very large and difficult to assess. The commodity file study was based on estimates of 18,500 organizations, posing 125,000 enquiries per day, concerning some 360,000 products and marketed by some 12,000 manufacturers.
2. They rely on detailed and reasonably accurate costing.
3. They rely very often on some pretty broad assumptions. For example, Durham based their whole methodology on the assumption that a librarian was likely to optimize his system, but one may question whether the benefits as assessed by the librarian are adequately related to the needs of the community served by the library. The availability of services, and the user's expectation of success will have marked effects on demand.
4. They are based on evaluation of criteria which are difficult to assess objectively. It is significant that the Department of the Environment's study used the single criterion of saving the time of the user.
5. Though the methodology may be widely applicable, the collected data is not, in general, universally true. For example, the figures of equivalent benefits obtained in the Durham project related only to a particular library at a particular time.

I should like now to restate the problems, how I think they should be viewed and what we can all do about it.

Aiding decisions
One of the clearest writers on this subject (in the information science literature) is Lancaster and I can strongly recommend a recent article of his in the *Journal of the American Society for Information Science* with the title 'The cost-effectiveness analysis of information retrieval and dissemination systems'.[9] Lancaster says that an information system can be evaluated from any one of the following viewpoints:

1. How well the system is satisfying its objectives, which will usually mean how well it is satisfying the demands placed upon it. Here we are evaluating the effectiveness of the system.
2. How efficiently (in terms of costs) it is satisfying its objectives. This is cost-effectiveness evaluation.
3. Whether the system justifies its existence (i.e. the system worth). In evaluating system worth, we are concerned with cost-benefit relationships.

These three viewpoints incorporate three vital measures. Costs can be classified as the prime expenses of documents and direct material, labour and expenses, and as the production overheads attributed to indirect material, labour and expenses. But in cost-effectiveness analysis we must also be aware of variable costs. For example, if we increase the number of retrospective searches conducted from 1,000 per year to 1,500 per year, the cost per search may be reduced by £x. We are still very short of comparative cost figures which we can use with any degree of confidence. The second measure is effectiveness and this is a measure which can be calculated only if we have defined our objectives and the criteria by which we can assess to what extent those objectives have been met. The feasibility study of a central commodity file listed some user criteria. These are possibly based on the user criteria for a document retrieval system listed in an earlier article by Lancaster[10] as Coverage, Usability, Recall, Precision, Response time, Presentation and User effort, of which the most important appear to be Coverage, Response time, User effort and our old friends Recall and Precision. Lancaster also pointed out that these user criteria were not the only ones and that it was necessary to consider two groups of management criteria:

(a) the criteria of system operators and of the immediate administrators of the system;
(b) the criteria of 'top management'.

The third measure is benefits and these are more difficult to quantify. Lancaster lists four broad benefits:

1. Cost savings in using the system as compared with the costs of finding needed information elsewhere.
2. Avoidance of loss of productivity.
3. Improved decision making or reduction in the level of personnel required to make decisions.
4. Stimulation of invention—a serendipity factor.

At lower levels the relationship between cost and effectiveness may be somewhat difficult to distinguish from the relationship between cost and benefits. An example is given by Lancaster:[9] 'Suppose we reduce the average number of terms assigned in indexing, and thereby reduce the average indexing time per item. We could say that an immediate benefit of this action is to reduce input costs. On the other hand, such an action is likely to have a very definite influence on the effectiveness of the system (the average precision of the system may increase—and this in itself may be regarded as a form of benefit—while the average recall will almost certainly decrease). In other words, this action has had immediate observable benefits (in terms of cost saving at input), it will have a long-range influence on the effectiveness of the system and it may have an even longer range influence on the benefits of the system's products to the end user.' This is not playing with words, but is a good illustration of the balancing of costs, performances and benefits in relation to time. And it is balance which one is seeking in system design and performance, which is why one should be conscious of such factors as 'trade-off'—the comparison of the benefits which would arise from alternative uses of given limited resources (for example, almost invariably economies in input procedures will result in an increased burden on output processes and thus output costs) and 'diminishing returns'—graphically summarized by Bourne[11] in the statement: 'We can design a system capable of satisfying, efficiently and economically, 90 per cent of the user requirements, but to satisfy the remaining 10 per cent would require a disproportionate increase in costs and in effort.'

So, the examination of costs, performance and benefits and their correlation using such concepts as trade-off and diminishing returns is an analytical aid to decision making and not a magical trick which is going to solve all our problems tomorrow. In a much quoted statement, Quade[12] has said: 'It is important to remember that all analysis of choice falls short of scientific research. No matter how we strive to maintain standards of scientific inquiry or how closely we attempt to follow scientific methods, we cannot turn cost-effectiveness analysis into science. Its objective, in contrast to that of science, is primarily to recommend—or at least to suggest—policy rather than merely to understand and predict.' Aiding decisions by the use of cost-benefit and cost-effective analysis is important to the librarian for two inter-related reasons—justification and resource allocation.

The problems of dwindling resources and the growth of knowledge are real and serious and libraries are in competition with other services for funds. Some convincing arguments must be produced. It will not be enough to rely on horror stories of wasted money and wasted endeavours caused by poor information systems: Carlson[13] has in any case shown that these are generally apocryphal—in particular the old chestnut that 'it is probably cheaper to do a research job under $100,000 than to search to see if the work has already been done'. Carlson found that what was actually said was: 'if it were not for the creation of such centralized documentation services as ASTIA it might be supposed that some day in the future a research manager could find it more economical to do the research than to search the literature—if the research cost less than some figure, such as $100,000'.

What librarians and information officers, particularly in industry, must do is to establish a stronger relationship with management. I know this has been said before, but I am not aware that very much has been achieved in this direction. Firstly, what we need collectively is an objective argument based on the economics of information, its handling and its value. A classic paper by Carter and Williams[14] appeared twelve years ago. The authors observed a direct relationship between technical progressiveness and financial success, which was demonstrated by such characteristics as:

Good information sources.
Readiness to seek information and knowledge of practice from external sources.
Willingness to share knowledge—technical, managerial and commercial.

I wonder whether it has affected management thinking or whether its findings have been used or extended by information scientists?

Secondly, I think that information scientists must be prepared to extend their horizons, so that instead of being content to provide a service, they are in a position to work out with management what objectives they should pursue in order to be more closely integrated with the information needs of decision makers. I know that information officers are a community particularly hard worked in maintaining their services, so I hope you will not think it impertinent of me to suggest that it is possible we are not making the best use of our intellectual resources in a rapidly changing environment. Shoffner[15], writing in the US, reports that there has been virtually no increase in productivity in library operations over the past twenty years, and Schon[16] in last year's Reith lectures gave a fascinating account of radical changes in organization and objective-setting in systems as disparate as NASA, the 3M Company and the underground student movement. We too may have to make some radical changes in the design and organization of our information systems.

Having justified our existence we must allocate our resources in the best possible way and it is guides to resource allocation that come out of the work of Wessel, the Universities of Durham and Lancaster and others working in the general area of management science. These are complex and time-consuming exercises probably beyond the resources of most information officers to set up for themselves. Some of these projects will undoubtedly produce usable data or mathematical models from which data may be derived, but what can the average information officer do for himself? I think he can do two things:

(a) learn something about management techniques so that he can use what he finds useful, particularly for control; and talk to his managers in their own language;
(b) collaborate in schemes for the pooling of basic data.

I should like to end by outlining two research projects which should help in both these approaches.

The Library Management Research Unit of the University of Cambridge is designing a Management Information System for library administration, the methodology involving techniques of data collection, analysis and presentation. It is the Unit's intention to design a simple-to-use system, which initially will be applicable to university libraries. The collection of data on times is based on a simple diary technique and we at Aslib are investigating with the Unit the possibility of devising a standard form of cost analysis based on diaries which could be extended for use in other types of library. Activity times can be arrived at analytically by diary techniques, activity sampling and direct observation. One can either break off at a procedural level, or one can go further to the task level to produce synthetics which can be reconstructed. Aslib is also investigating this approach and eventually will attempt to relate the two approaches. In the current part of our project, data of the following form has been collected: time taken to perform an operation on a particular item (e.g. abstracting, cataloguing, classifying), together with some information about the item or the process (e.g. language, how many cross-references or analytical entries were required—these being the variables we think will have a major effect on the time). The problem has been to analyse the quantitative effect of each variable. It proved useless to examine each variable separately, ignoring all the others, as each effect was distorted or swamped by all the others. It has therefore been necessary to develop a method (a form of multiple regression) which will take account of all variables simultaneously. We are now getting results which make reasonable sense (e.g. in the system studied the major effect on the cataloguing time was whether and how many analytical entries were required). One very encouraging result is that in the one case where we had two people doing the same job, we analysed the results, considering the person doing the job as a further variable, and found this to be the least significant of all the variables. At the most superficial level, we intend to identify just which variables affect processing time and rank these. This will be of some value in itself to designers. More importantly, we hope to produce standard costs which will be defined in terms of variables and context and so may be used with greater confidence. This is a huge undertaking which we do not ourselves have the resources to complete, so we shall be inviting the Aslib membership to take part. As soon as we have established the methodology (which we want to keep as simple as possible) we shall conduct a pilot run in which information officers will collect data in their own libraries, reporting to us in a standard format. If this is successful we shall extend the project to include anybody who would like to use the technique. The more that take part, the wider will be the range of information available and the more accurate the data.

This talk was entitled simply 'cost-effectiveness', a term which the Treasury glossary includes as being synonymous with 'cost-consciousness'. This is a condition we can hardly avoid in the present economic climate.

REFERENCES

1 PREST, A. R. *and* TURVEY, R. Cost-benefit analysis: a survey. *Economic Journal*, 75, 300, Dec. 1965, p. 683–735.
2 H.M. TREASURY. *Glossary of management techniques.* London: HMSO, 1967.
3 SELF, PETER. Nonsense on stilts: the futility of Roskill. *New Society*, 2nd July 1970, p. 8–11.
4 DIMBLEBY, JONATHAN. Profile: Colin Buchanan. *New Statesman*, 30th April 1971, p. 586.
5 WESSEL, C. J. *and* COHRSSEN, B. A. *Criteria for evaluating the effectiveness of library operations and services. Phase I, Literature search and state-of-the-art.* ATLIS Report no, 10. Feb. 1967.
   WESSEL, C. J., MOORE, K. L. *and* COHRSSEN, B. A. Ibid. *Phase II, Data gathering and evaluation.* ATLIS Report no. 19, Aug. 1968.
   WESSEL, C. J. *and* MOORE, K. L. *Recommended criteria and methods for their utilization.* ATLIS Report no. 21, Jan. 1969.
6 WESSEL, C. J. Criteria for evaluating the technical library effectiveness. *Aslib Proc.*, 20, 11, Nov. 1968, p. 455–81.
7 DURHAM UNIVERSITY. *Project for evaluating the benefits from university libraries; final report.* Durham: University Computer Unit, 1969.
8 DEPARTMENT OF THE ENVIRONMENT. *Commodity information in the construction industry* (to be published).
9 LANCASTER, F. W. The cost-effectiveness analysis of information retrieval and dissemination systems. *JASIS*, 22, 1, Jan./Feb. 1971, p. 12–27.
10 LANCASTER, F. W. *and* CLIMENSON, W. D. Evaluating the economic efficiency of a document retrieval system. *J. Doc.*, 24, 1, March 1968, p. 16–40.
11 BOURNE, C. P. Some user requirements stated quantitatively in terms of the 90% library. *In*: *Electronic information handling*, edited by A. Kent and O. E. Taulbee. Washington, DC: Spartan Books, 1965, p. 95–110.
12 QUADE, E. S. Introduction and overview. *In*: *Cost-effectiveness analysis: new approaches in decision making*, edited by T. A. Goldman. New York: Praeger, 1967, p. 1–16.
13 CARLSON, W. M. The economics of information transfer. *Trans. N.Y. Acad. Sci.*, 31, 7, Nov. 1969, p. 803–13.
14 CARTER, C. F. *and* WILLIAMS, B. R. The characteristics of technically progressive firms. *J. Ind. Econ.*, 7, 2, March 1959, p. 87–104.
15 SHOFFNER, RALPH M. Economics of national automation of libraries. *Lib. Trends*, April 1970, p. 448–63.
16 SCHON, D. The loss of the stable state. Reith Lectures 1970. Published in *The Listener*, 19th November 1970, *et seq*. Now published in book form under the title *Beyond the stable state*. London: Temple Smith, 1971.

User valuations and resource management for information services

T. Whitehall

Paper presented at the fifty-third Aslib Annual Conference, University of Sussex, 18-21 September 1979

Being able to show a benefit for information services to balance against their cost, and knowing what criteria to use for choice among the options for their provision—these are needs which loom large for information people. This paper reviews what techniques have been found useful, and tries to show how valuations from the clients of information services can be brought into the equation.

THREE SORTS OF people are involved in managing the resources of a library/information service—the funder, the clients, and the manager of the service.

The funder hopes to see some return for an investment in the service, and really ought to set out a policy for the service as well.

The client has some idea of the types of services he can use, and some expectations about their quality. The client may need documents themselves, or a list or a summary of documents, or the answers to questions, and may need to be kept informed on new developments affecting his/her work. The client will expect the service to save at least the time otherwise spent on looking for things personally, will expect the service to be easy to use, and will expect it to be reasonably successful.

The manager of the service needs at various times some or all of the following:

—some indication on what to do for the clients;
—pointers on how to allocate what funds are available among the different needs involved;
—to be able to justify the resources consumed at present, or those required in the future, to the funder; (This need arises when the manager is obliged to formulate a policy for the service, in the absence of one from the funder.)
—help in choosing among various modes of provision of some services;
—to ensure that labour and materials are being consumed efficiently;
—to maintain the quality of services.

This paper reviews techniques appropriate to two of the manager's needs: justification of resources and choice among options.

Reprinted from *Aslib Proceedings*, 32(2), 1980, by permission.

User valuations and resource management

Oldman[1] describes two different orientations in the literature of library and information systems, one focussing on the user, the other on the system. The user orientation says, in effect, 'Let us listen to our clients and plan the service around their needs.' The system orientation is about resource allocation. It says, 'We have these resources, which must be managed in a responsible manner.' Oldman argues for an amalgam of these two orientations. She reminds us that many systems studies are made with scant regard for the user, incorporating dubious assumptions about user behaviour.

There is a long history of asking library users about their needs and how they feel about a service which has already been set up for them. The responses are generally unhelpful. Their information needs are usually expressed in terms of a document or a type of document. Also one is left with the impression that there is a great deal of unspoken information need, either because clients do not recognize needs, or because they do not see a library as the place to satisfy them. Responses from users about how the services provided suit them are just as unhelpful. People are grateful for information services, and their gratitude seems to get in the way of making a useful assessment. People are conservative to the extent that the service they are receiving at the moment is quite often preferred to one that might force a change in their habits. What I am saying is that it is difficult to combine a user orientation with the system orientation, because we cannot rely on the answers we get from the users.

Nevertheless it is vital to have some input from the clients to illuminate decisions about design and allocation. A serious problem in any sort of service organization is through lack of user input to end up doing the wrong things very efficiently.[2] Arnold points out that heavy reliance on cost-benefit analysis in library planning could mean that one or two services that looked well on net benefit would be provided, to the neglect of other essential but apparently unprofitable contributions to the work of the clients.[3]   In this review I have taken up Oldman's challenge, and tried to show how the user orientation can be combined with techniques for resource management. I think we may have been asking the user the wrong questions.

Justification of resources consumed

'Why is there a credibility gap between management, which thinks that information services cost far too much, and represent a luxury, and librarians and information managers who believe that such services are indispensable?' asks Wilson.[4] The librarian or information officer is like a general practitioner—using knowledge and special skills to give a service which is appreciated when it succeeds, but at the same time given only grudging financial support. This could merely betray society's lack of faith in the continued support of its physicians, and management's of its information providers. Fortunately it is not as simple as this. Why *does* management regard information services as a luxury? There are several contributing factors.

A lot depends on the sort of management we are talking about. The manager who holds the purse strings may have a scientific approach to problem-solving, or may like to play things largely by ear. The first type of manager can see some advantage in the systematic collection of information about the task in hand, and its dissemination to staff. A person of the second type is more likely to see a library as educational in function, and be less able to see the need for an organized information service.

In many organizations, library and information services are part of the general overhead, their cost being spread over all departments in the organization. At times of financial stress there will inevitably be pressure on top management from department heads to reduce the burden of overhead charges, so that they may see a larger part of the organization's revenue available for running their departments. At these times the canteen, the gardens and the library can suffer. The need to reduce the size of overheads shown on a cost analysis submitted in support of a merger or takeover bid can have a fatal effect on libraries and other service departments.

A concept that has done more harm than any other to library funding, in industry at least, is that of the profit centre. It became fashionable a few years ago to regard each department of a company as having a financial input and output, and to encourage at least a balance if not a net profit from departmental operations. Applied to marketing, sales or production departments the profit centre concept can give a departmental manager a convenient yardstick for measuring efficiency. However, as in the case of 'management by objectives' a few years earlier, the profit centre idea is not applicable to all departments with equal success. Yet in the profit centre era a department without a cash output, or one capable of easy conversion to cash, becomes a 'non-profit centre'. Guess what happens to non-profit centres when we need to show a convincing cost analysis. This is another reason why 'information is considered less indispensable at times of economic recession' as Oldman puts it.

Librarians' recipes for dealing with what Armstrong[5] describes as 'a keen smell of corporate surgery in the air' are mostly reactions to the impositions laid on them by accountants which have been described above. If library services are charged to the departments which receive them, the library is no longer part of the general overhead. If a value in terms of cash can be ascribed to the effects of library activities on its clients or on the organization, then the library has a cash output to balance against the money consumed in its running, and can assume the more respectable status of a profit centre.

These and other approaches to justification will be discussed under five headings:

The use of performance measures;
Attempts to show a benefit in terms of cash;
Measuring the total client time 'spent' on the services;
Charging for services;
Demonstrating that the funds provided have been used to supply specific information inputs to the work of the clients.

Performance measures as a means of justification

We can think of an information service as having inputs of labour, materials and uncommitted cash,[6] and outputs of two types, as in Figure I. The intermediate outputs are the services which arise from the library/information system (loans, photocopies, SDI notifications, etc.). The final outputs relate to the impact of these services on the clients or on the organization to which the clients belong (advantage gained, time saved, etc.). Performance measures are intermediate output measures, and a list of some of these is given in Table 1.

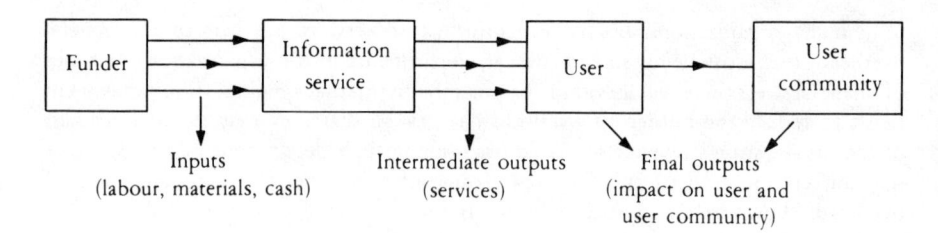

FIG. 1. *Information service inputs and outputs*

Inputs (labour, materials, cash)
Intermediate outputs (services)
Final outputs (impact on user and user community)

TABLE 1. *Intermediate output measures for library and information service*

Performance measure	Reference
Number of library users	Rzasa & Baker[7]
Acts of use of the library	—
Photocopies requested/supplied	—
Enquiries made/answered	—
Loans to clients	—
Amount of study space used	Rzasa & Baker[7]
Satisfied demands	Buckland et al[8]
Time taken to get requested document to user	Orr et al[9]
Number of document exposures	Hamburg et al[10]
Item-use days	Meier[11]
Time user is exposed to documents	Hamburg et al[10]

Use of intermediate output measures for justification has been heavily criticized on two counts. Firstly the number of things produced by a service is proof only that the service has an output. It could be doing the wrong thing very efficiently. Secondly acts of use are suspect as measures of value because it cannot be assumed that a client will obtain something of value just because he has borrowed a book or sat at a table or asked for a photocopy. However Klintoe[12] found that the presentation of an analysis of costs and intermediate outputs to his funder was a useful justification technique. He used this method successfully at the Danish Technical Information Service. His regular statement to his funders has two columns (Figure 2). In the first column is a breakdown of costs into salaries and materials for each of several services provided. The second column shows opposite each service a list of accomplishments for that service during the same period. Klintoe describes the main advantages of his presentation as follows: 'discussions with the Board of Directors can be conducted on the level of policy issues, not on detailed expenditure' and 'the public auditor ... can see exactly how the money is spent and the use to which it is put'.

Costs		Accomplishments
b) Requests for procurement of information (DK/S tasks)		
Salaries, engineers (2594 h)	Dkr. 118.333	213 tasks from 116 diff. inquirers, i.e.
Salaries, office staff (914¾ h)	− 15.994	3 organisations
Consultants	− 5.117	8 centres of spec. knl.
Information materials	− 5.127	104 mfg. companies
Transportation and car-fare	− 4.875	1 public service
Hotel and board allowances	− 1.295	213 tasks have been:
	Dkr.150.741	199—procurement of information
		14—planning and management of courses and conferences
Cost per request: Dkr. 708		Turnover per order: Dkr. 606
c) Requests by telephone	Dkr. 31,602	Approx. 2000 requests.
Salaries, engineers (660 h)		
Salaries, office staff (86¾ h)	− 1,524	
	Dkr. 33,126	
Cost per request: approx. Dkr. 17		Free of charge.
d) Requests from foreign centres or from own organization (DK/U and DK/AD tasks)		
Salaries, engineers (339½ h)	Dkr. 15.826	74 tasks, i.e.
Salaries, office staff (101¾ h)	− 1.834	58 foreign
Information materials	− 1,386	16 internal
Transportation and car-fare	− 353	
Hotel and board allowances	− 100	
	Dkr. 19,499	
Cost per task: approx. Dkr. 264		Free of charge.

FIG. 2. *Extract from a statement of costs and intermediate outputs presented to the funding agent for justification purposes, after Klintoe.*[12]

Showing a cash benefit as a means of justification

The several approaches to justification by showing a monetary advantage as a result of information services are summarized in Table 2.

(a) That information has been supplied which can be shown to have given an advantage to a client or to the organization is a powerful source of justification for an information service. One tends to think here of massive sums saved in investment funds or research time. Martyn[22] and Strable[23] give examples of this. Moisse[14] describes losses due to lack of information. Hanson and Slater's excellent

TABLE 2. *Justification techniques which show a monetary advantage from services*

Monetary advantage	Reference
(a) Tracing a money-saving event back to information supplied by the service.	Hanson & Slater[13]; Moisse[14]; Arnone & Jackson[15]; Hess[16]; Martyn[22]; Strabel[23]
(b) Showing the cost of supplying information as a small fraction of the possible advantage gained from using it.	Wills & Christopher[17]
(c) Showing time saved for the client.	Nightingale[18]; Fearn & Kovalik[19]; Wolfe[20]; Mason[21]
(d) Asking what it is worth to continue to supply the service.	Univ. of Durham[6]; Wolfe[20]

summary[13] gives examples of both. Obviously one or two corporate triumphs traced to information supplied by the service will help. However, in creative work of any kind, there is a quiet series of useful inputs of lesser magnitude going on all the time. The problem is to identify what part information from the service played in the success of a venture.[15] Hess suggests that when people bring items back to the library, they should be asked what use has been made of each item and for what purpose.[16] I suggest that something more than discreet enquiries at the library desk is needed, and that the need for justification is another good reason for working close to the clients. Some of the benefits of a good information service may be more subtle than the advantage gained from a speedy end to a project. Hall[44] tried to show how possession of an information service can make its clients more used to looking for information and putting it to use in their work. It seems difficult to get clients to admit that the information service, however good, has had an effect on their habits, in my experience.

(b) Another justification is to relate the cost of getting information to ensure success for a project to the profits expected, or loss to be avoided. The cost can usually be shown be a very small fraction of the expected loss or profit. Wills and Christopher[17] give an example in which the project is the launch in another country of a product currently sold in the UK. How much should the company be prepared to spend on information to help with the decision? The payoff at various percent shares of the new market is calculated. Prior to collecting any information, there will be an estimate of the probability of achieving various shares of the new market. The lowest likely profit (or highest loss) to the company represents the maximum sum it would be worth paying to avoid an unfavourable outcome.

(c) Perhaps the most commonly reported approach to justification is to balance the cost of a service against the time saved the client by not having to do things personally which the service does.

A very direct approach is that of Nightingale.[18] To justify the expenditure on a current awareness bulletin, he found how many journals the clients would have to

TABLE 3. *Scanning time saved by one SDI service*[19]

Number of clients	Hours per week saved
1	¼
3	½
12	1
29	2
7	3
8	4
5	5
1	6
1	7
1	

scan themselves if no bulletin were available. The total annual cost of all this scanning he found to be £29,600. The bulletin costs £2,500 per year, so there is a saving of £27,000.

Fearn and Kovalik[19] asked the clients of their computer SDI service to state how many hours of their time per week were saved by elimination of the need to scan abstracts, current contents pages, etc. (Table 3).

They were able to calculate that a total of 8,000 man hours per year was saved by the sixty-eight recipients of their service. The average hourly salary of a client multiplied by 8,000 minus the cost of the SDI service gave a figure for net benefit from the service. They found a benefit of three dollars from every dollar spent.

Mason[21] calculates the difference between the cost of an enquiry service given by the information unit, and the cost of the clients' doing it for themselves. The advantages of centralized documentation and the expertise of the information workers shows through in the results of such a calculation and makes it useful for justification purposes. He also justifies the activities which contribute to an information service by showing how much more they would cost if done in another department of the organization.

An oft-repeated criticism of time saved the user as a measure of benefit of information service is that 'a saving of time is not necessarily an increase in productivity unless the time saved is used for something productive' (Bowerman[24]). Wolfe[20] points out that one cannot assume that one hour saved on information seeking is necessarily equivalent to one hour spent on one's work. In an investigation of the value of abstracting and indexing services to clients, he asked researchers how many extra hours they would need to work to maintain their research output if they had no secondary services to supply information.

(d) The value of an information service to its clients could be indicated by the amount they were prepared to pay to keep it going. This is the thinking behind the attempt by Morley and Hopkins[6] to justify a current awareness bulletin. They found that staff in receipt of a bulletin would give an average of £6 per head of their own money to keep it going. (On the other hand they would vote £32 of university money for this purpose!) If questions about payment to sustain information services are asked in an attempt to justify them, it is as well to pretend that the questions are not hypothetical. The Durham University survey included the sentence, 'Please note that you may well be asked to pay the amount to which you commit yourself.' In the event, twenty-two of the recipients of the bulletin were prepared to vote sufficient funds to pay for the labour cost of producing a bulletin for thirty people.

Clients' time 'spent' on the service as a means of justification

In a market situation, goods are manufactured at a certain cost to the provider and sold at a certain price to the customer. Their value is thus apparent to both parties. In the case of library and information services, their cost is clearly apparent, but as their customers do not have to put their hands into their pockets on each occasion of use there is no awareness of value. The user of library and information services does pay for them however, *with the amount of time personally spent on the service.*

This briefly is the argument for justification of free services by measurement of the time their clients are prepared to spend in using them. It can be developed as follows: in a bad library clients may spend a great deal of time in getting what they want, but they will not do this very often. They will eventually go elsewhere for the documents or information which are so hard to obtain through the library. In a good library, clients may well spend less time per visit, because their requirements are easily met. However they will come again and again, because it costs less of their time to use the library service than other competing sources of the same information. One could define a good library and information service as one that can supply useful information at the lowest possible cost to the client in terms of client time that must be put into the transaction.

Orr[26] discusses the pros and cons of collecting information on the time spent by library clients on using library services by the diary method and by random time sampling using an alarm carried on the person. He comes down on the side of the second method, and gives examples of its use.

Kochen's measure of the effectiveness of an information service is the number of clients who, having used the service once, come back to it a second time.[25]

Justification of services by charging for them

The transfer of cash from the clients of an information service to the suppliers provides the information department with a monetary output to balance against the funds it consumes. It has another advantage in that one of the problems with a free information service is that, if it is a good one, everyone wants its products. Charging for services helps to reduce the 'me too' usage by people who want the service but do not necessarily need it.

There are three approaches to charging for information services:
(a) to make a token charge in order to show that the services are valued;
(b) to charge so as to cover the cost of the services;
(c) to sell the services in an attempt to make a profit.

(a) Any charge which the clients will bear can be used to demonstrate the value of a service, but Zais[27] reports that the appropriate price is the cost of producing the single items provided. This price is open to detailed interpretation, but the idea is to ignore the fixed costs of the whole operation. For instance the price of a manual search might be the cost of the searcher's time, ignoring the cost of the stock or data base he searched. A bulletin might be supplied at the cost of paper, printing and distribution for a single copy, ignoring the scanning cost and the cost of material scanned. Provided that a simple formula for calculating charges could be worked out, this system of pricing could be used to give the funder an idea of the value of the services to the clients. However one thinks of Arnold's comment that unless large amounts are to be transferred it 'may be absurd' to set up an accounting system to deal with them.[3]

(b) Charging to recover all costs of the library/information service on the face of it seems a sensible procedure, but it is probably the most difficult of the three approaches to get started. A costing exercise on the library and information system has to be done, and some way found to allocate the costs of materials, machinery, the manager, the doorman and the teaboy to the services consumed by the clients.

The usual approach to costing services is firstly to identify the *activities* that go on in the unit day by day, and decide in what proportion they contribute to the *services* consumed by the clients. Then the activities are costed in terms of labour and materials and machine costs. Finally the costs of activities are distributed among the services (Mason,[28] Raffel & Shishko,[29] Price[34]). The cost of items which cannot be traced through to particular services are allocated to all services at the same rate (Marron[32]) or in proportion to the labour cost of services (Price[33]). Armstrong[5] has something useful to say about overhead costs and their allocation during costing. Vickery[30] reviews methods of measuring how labour costs are distributed across library services. A common technique is for library and information staff to keep a diary of how they spend their time on their main tasks, or alternatively a record of time spent on tasks other than the main task (Smith & Schofield[31]).

Some system of charging has to be agreed with the clients of the service, and arrangements made for a charge to be made across departments.

When users of the library and information services have to pay for them on the basis of the amount of use they make, instead of a standard overhead charge which is levied whether they use the services or not, they begin to weigh up the value of their transactions with the library and their use of it may decline. Hence one of the problems of operating a cost recovery system for information services is that more flexibility than usual has to be available in the staffing of the service. A fair proportion of part-time staff on limited contracts can give this flexibility, together with the use of outside consultants. Another problem is that the charges made on departments, because they have to be loaded with overheads of the library and costs of materials acquired but not necessarily used for a particular service, may have an inhibiting effect. One answer is to make a charge which covers the labour cost of services, and to agree with departments an annual sum based on their use which will go towards the cost of materials and library overheads (Cook[35]).

(c) Perhaps the happiest way to justify the funds invested in an information service is to make a profit, by selling services to customers other than one's own captive audience. Examples of situations where this is possible are the information services of research associations and professional bodies, when there is no restriction on their commercial activities. Both sorts of organization have a ready-made clientele, which can be extended. An area of the country which has a high degree of technical or commercial activity, but no good information service besides one's own provides a similar opportunity. One has to consider how unique is the service that can be offered, and what potential use there is for it. Norton[36] gives a checklist of questions for those information units thinking of going commercial'.

The pricing of information services sold on the open market does not have to conform to one's management accountant's way of seeing things, so one has a freer hand. A common starting point is to see what it costs people to obtain the product one has for sale by other means, either by their own efforts or from a commercial source. The less work the customer has to put into making use of what one provides, the higher can be the charge. People will pay more for evaluated information than for a list of references (Koch[37]). A loose-leaf updated handbook or compilation is much easier for them to use than a hardbound book with innumerable supplements, and will attract a higher price. For a service which is unique, one can charge what people are prepared to pay.

The above sketch of commercial practice in this area should be supplemented by Lutz[38], White[39] and Zais[27] on the theory of pricing, and the interesting discussions of charging written at the time when information centres in the USA were being encouraged to pay their way (Veazie[40], Schwuchow[41], Wilson[42]).

In whatever manner charges are made for information services, there will be resistance from clients who previously received documents or information for nothing. Veazie[43] says that charges affect use in the majority of cases. In his experience 8–15 per cent of clients will drop the services altogether, and 16–28 per cent will reduce the use they make of them. Terry[45] describes the introduction of voluntary charges at the regional Primate Information Centre in Washington, where imposition of fixed charges would have been unfair to researchers and students. A fee for each service was suggested, and the client given the opportunity of paying all or some or none of it. Terry found that long-time clients did eventually adjust to the need to buy information, previously obtained free of charge. She makes the point that voluntary payments for services could be used as a guide to the value placed on them by clients.

Justification by demonstration that the funds provided have been used to provide specific information inputs

One problem of justification is that information is not seen as a resource, by either the funder or the client. (Universities are built from concrete and bricks and mortar and trees and water, but without information these things might never emerge as a useful campus.) To be able to show a list of *information inputs* essential to the work of one's clients could be a powerful argument in obtaining the funds to supply these inputs.

The approach is illustrated in Figure 3 by a *task analysis* of basic research. Each task requires some information for its successful completion, and some of these information inputs are shown.

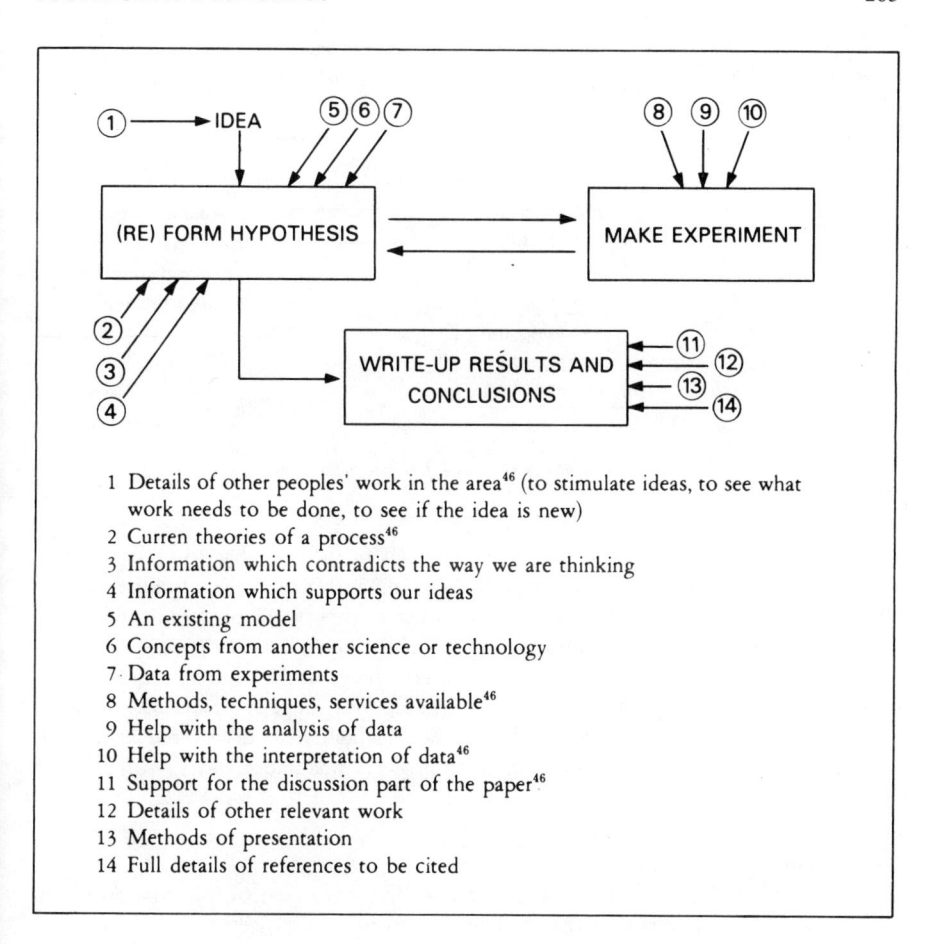

```
                        ┌─ IDEA   ⑤⑥⑦         ⑧ ⑨ ⑩
                   ①         ↓  ↙↙↙           ↘↓↙
                   ┌──────────────────┐      ┌──────────────┐
                   │ (RE) FORM         │ ───→ │ MAKE         │
                   │ HYPOTHESIS        │ ←─── │ EXPERIMENT   │
                   └──────────────────┘      └──────────────┘
                   ②  ↗↗↗         ↓       ┌───────────── ⑪ ⑫
                   ③             ┌────────────────────┐ ← ⑬
                   ④             │ WRITE-UP RESULTS   │ ← ⑭
                                 │ AND CONCLUSIONS    │
                                 └────────────────────┘
```

1 Details of other peoples' work in the area[46] (to stimulate ideas, to see what work needs to be done, to see if the idea is new)
2 Curren theories of a process[46]
3 Information which contradicts the way we are thinking
4 Information which supports our ideas
5 An existing model
6 Concepts from another science or technology
7 Data from experiments
8 Methods, techniques, services available[46]
9 Help with the analysis of data
10 Help with the interpretation of data[46]
11 Support for the discussion part of the paper[46]
12 Details of other relevant work
13 Methods of presentation
14 Full details of references to be cited

FIG. 3. *Task analysis of basic research, with information inputs to the tasks*

Figure 4 illustrates a task analysis of product development, and Table 4 shows some of the information inputs which contribute to each task. Despite the generality of approach it will be seen that the information inputs give a clear idea of the sort of information which could be collected and disseminated by an information unit serving product development work. Commercial as well as technical information is involved.

The literature contains several papers which describe different types of work in terms of tasks, and describe the sort of information which is put to use in those tasks (the papers by Chaddock[47] and Wolek[48] on the information requirements of engineering design for instance). Radley[49] gives a task analysis of company operations as a whole and lists the information inputs, but not in enough detail to provide a convincing demonstration for justification purposes. Some indication of information inputs for investment decisions, forward planning and marketing are given by Aguilar,[50] Schoner,[51] and Jones[52] respectively.

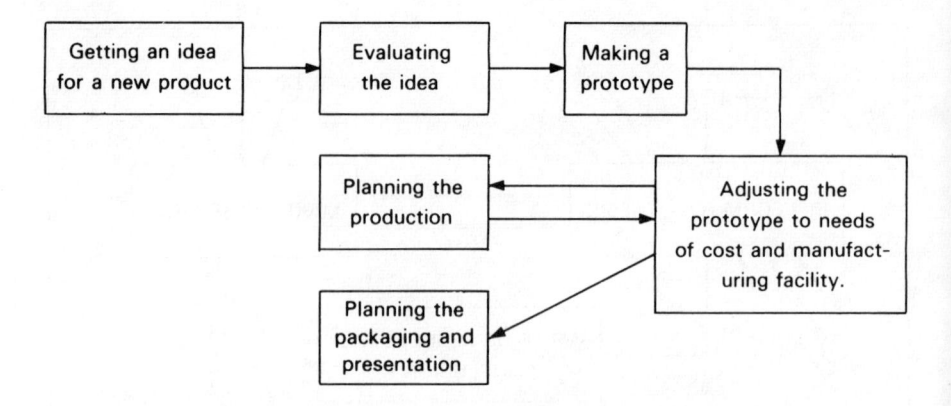

```
┌─────────────────┐     ┌─────────────┐     ┌─────────────┐
│ Getting an idea │ ──▶ │ Evaluating  │ ──▶ │  Making a   │
│ for a new product│    │  the idea   │     │  prototype  │
└─────────────────┘     └─────────────┘     └─────────────┘
                                                    │
                        ┌─────────────┐     ┌──────────────────┐
                        │ Planning the│ ◀── │  Adjusting the   │
                        │ production  │ ──▶ │ prototype to needs│
                        └─────────────┘     │ of cost and manufact-│
                                            │  uring facility. │
                        ┌─────────────┐     └──────────────────┘
                        │ Planning the│            ▲
                        │ packaging and│ ◀─────────┘
                        │ presentation│
                        └─────────────┘
```

FIG. 4. *Task analysis of new product development*

The value of this technique for justification lies in the fact that to construct the analysis the information manager needs the help and agreement of the funder and the clients, so that the true nature of the contribution to their work becomes obvious to them. Information managers can take the lead in the construction of a task analysis, where their overall view of the work of their clients is helpful. As regards the information inputs, many of those shown in the figures were got by discussions with clients using the critical incident technique, and others were discovered at a time when a programme of evaluation of research projects was under way.

Choice among options

The literature of choice tends to be dominated by comparison of information given with the aid of computerized abstracting and indexing services versus services relying on the resources of a library. I think this is unfortunate, because such studies tend to obscure the real problems of choice, which were here before computers came into the picture. The studies are often occupied with attempts to justify the installation of a terminal for on-line work, in which case they attempt to show how cheaply on-line searches may be run in comparison with the cost of labour, materials and travel associated with manual searches of the same sort. They may be studies which use the measures of recall and precision to compare on-line and manual searching, in imitation of earlier work in which these measures were used to compare the effectiveness of alternative indexing techniques in a controlled experiment. My contention is that neither type of study gets to the heart of the matter of choice among various techniques for giving an information service.

The problems are twofold:

First there is a variety of choice due to information services' being produced by sources which are in competition with information officers. Furthermore these services can often be used directly by technical and commercial people without the intervention of their librarian or information officer. (I mean services like reproduced contents pages of journals, printed or computerized abstracting and indexing services, subsets

TABLE 4. *Product development—task analysis and information inputs*

Tasks	Information inputs to tasks
Idea for a new product	Areas in which product development is needed Consumer need Competitor's product Patent applied for or granted Results of basic research New techniques for production Raw materials used already Production processes used already News of alternative materials for formulation Company markets
Evaluating the idea	Cost of developing the idea into a saleable product Cost of alternative routes to the product Consumer acceptance Relevant legislation Activities of competitors in the area Price at which product would sell Size of market for product
Making a prototype	Has anyone solved the problem in another way? Results of basic research Available materials and recipes Available methodology Design information
Adjusting the prototype to needs of cost and production facility	Alternative materials and recipes Alternative methodology Costs of raw materials Costs of production
Planning the production	Available equipment Design data for equipment Alternative processes and their cost Facilities available within the company Information on where production plant might be situated
Planning the packaging and presentation	Packaging materials Effect of air, water, time, etc. on the product Packaging methodology and equipment Consumer expectations of the product

of these and alerting services from them, bulletins produced and sold by other organizations, updated compilations of facts and figures on paper or machine.) *They are produced with a market, not individuals, in mind.*

Second, different types of client value different characteristics of an information service, and the value systems of the clients differ from those of the information service manager. Hall[53] reports that an information manager would tend to choose a service for clients on the basis of its reliability and its compatibility with the existing pattern of service from the information unit. Secondly the manager might look at the cost and timeliness of the service. Not until services have been ruled out on these considerations does the information manager consider things like ease of use and availability of the original—factors which the client sees as highly related to the value of the service to him.

Choice among options for information service clearly has to be done by techniques which allow combination of the manager's orientation towards cost and efficiency with the client's value system. Such a technique is cost-effectiveness analysis.[54] The key to the analysis is that a list of characteristics of a service is drawn up *which relate to its benefits*. Then a mode of giving the service under consideration is rated for each of these features, and an index of effectiveness is obtained for that mode by combining them. If this is done for all possible modes of giving the service under consideration, they can then be compared for effectiveness and cost.

Features of information services which have been used for purposes of comparison are listed below:

Coverage of scanning or of data base
—by subject area
—by type of publication

Timeliness
—relating to use of primary material
—relating to speed of processing of service

Precision
—the proportion of items notified which are relevant

Recall
—the proportion of relevant items in the literature which are notified

Novelty ratio
—the proportion of items notified which client has not seen before

Ease of use
—amount of information supplied by notification
—availability of original document

Blick[55] shows how a cost-effectiveness analysis can be used to advise on the choice among various approaches to giving a current awareness service (Table 5). The options, along the top of the table, are scored for various features which relate to the value of the service. Blick gives reasons for his scores. For instance a bulletin with titles only scores higher for 'timeliness' than one with abstracts, because of its much shorter production time. Blick has included cost as a feature, instead of calculating a cost-over-effectiveness ratio for each alternative, as described by Flowerdew and White-

TABLE 5. *Five alternative approaches to current awareness notification from Blick*[55]

Feature	Titles-only Bulletin	Abstracts Bulletin	SDI Titles-only	SDI Abstracts	SDI On-line Titles-only
Timeliness	8	4	4	4	6
Relevance	7	7	4	4	6
Cost	6	3	8	7	6
Customer convenience	4	10	3	8	3
Suitability for large No. of customers	7	7	3	3	3
Total	32	31	22	26	24

head.[54] Also his analyses include features related to benefits to the information service as well as benefits to the clients. (See his 'suitability for large numbers of customers' in Table 5, and factors for 'skilled labour commitment' and 'controllability' in the other analyses in his paper.)

Both Blick and Flowerdew and Whitehead indicate that if the effectiveness analysis is to be a reliable aid to choice, the scores should be weighted in some way, since the different features of a service are unlikely to be of equal concern to any set of clients. (Clients might consider timeliness to be of paramount importance, much more so than precision, for instance.) Flowerdew and Whitehead say this can be done by the service manager alone, or from a survey of clients' attitudes and use.

Clients of manual SDI services were asked to say how six features of the service they were enjoying were related to its value to them.[56] They could score the degree of relevance to value for each feature on a six point scale. Figures 5–7 show that there was substantial agreement about the relevance to value of features like size of a batch of notifications (not related at all to value), and coverage of the service and recall (highly related to the value of the service). Timeliness (Figure 8) was seen as important, but many clients did not see it as so highly related to the value of SDI as recall and coverage. About the relevance of novelty and precision ratios to value (Figures 9 and 10) there was a range of attitudes all the way from not relevant to value to highly relevant to value.

It certainly does no harm to make one's clients think about things of this sort. If they could be educated to give responses which reflected their priorities with accuracy, a valuable input from the user to the manager's analysis would be obtained.

REFERENCES

1 OLDMAN, C. *The value of information.* Bradford: Management Consultants (Bradford) Ltd, 1976.
2 MCCONKEY, D.D. *MBO for non-profit making organisations.* American Management Association, 1975.

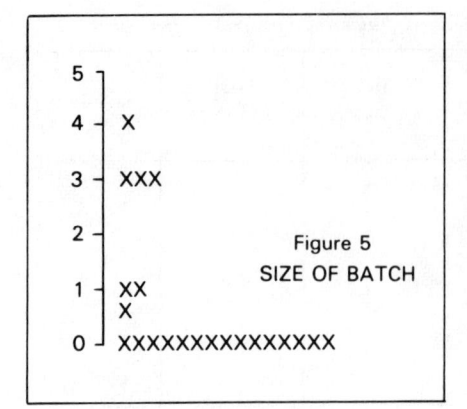

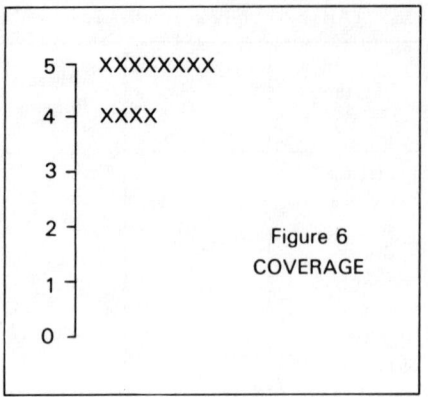

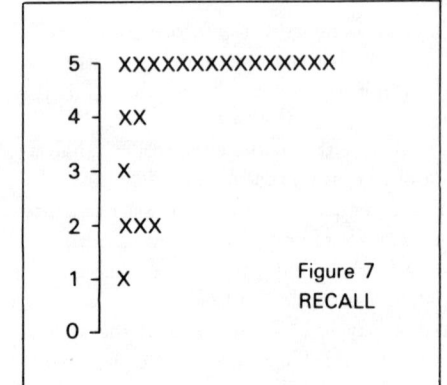

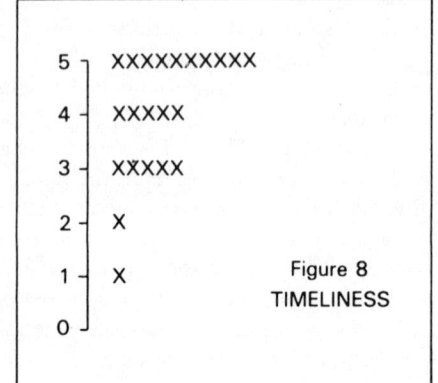

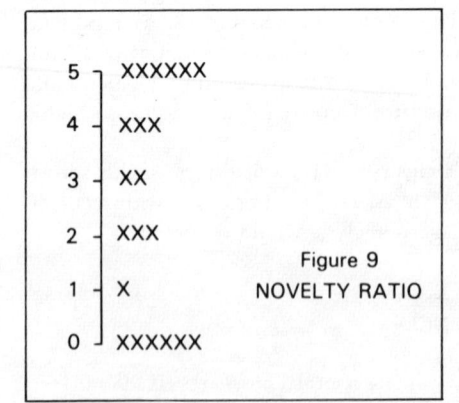

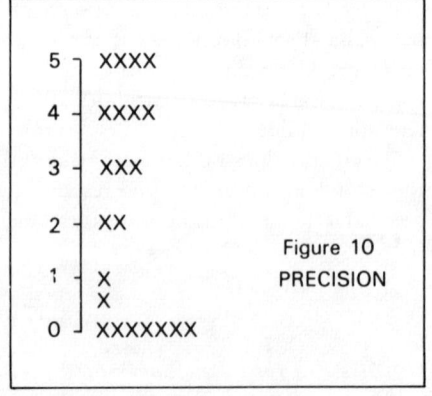

```
Figure 5                Figure 6
SIZE OF BATCH           COVERAGE

5 |                     5 | XXXXXXXX
4 | X                   4 | XXXX
3 | XXX                 3 |
2 |                     2 |
1 | XX                  1 |
  | X
0 | XXXXXXXXXXXXXXXX    0 |


Figure 7                Figure 8
RECALL                  TIMELINESS

5 | XXXXXXXXXXXXXXXX    5 | XXXXXXXXXX
4 | XX                  4 | XXXXX
3 | X                   3 | XXXXX
2 | XXX                 2 | X
1 | X                   1 | X
0 |                     0 |


Figure 9                Figure 10
NOVELTY RATIO           PRECISION

5 | XXXXXX              5 | XXXX
4 | XXX                 4 | XXXX
3 | XX                  3 | XXX
2 | XXX                 2 | XX
1 | X                   1 | X
                          | X
0 | XXXXXX              0 | XXXXXXX
```

FIGS. 5-10. *The degree of relevance of some features of an SDI service to its value to clients of the service—how the clients voted (0 = not relevant to value; 5 = highly relevant to value)*

3 ARNOLD, D. V. *The management of the information department.* London: Andre Deutsche, 1976. pp. 101-2.
4 WILSON, JNR. J. H. Improving costing technique and cost-effective operations for technical libraries and information centres.
 In: REES, A. ed. *Contemporary problems in technical library and information centre management: a state of the art.* American Society for Information Science, 1974. pp. 177-99.
5 ARMSTRONG, A. Analysing industrial information service costs: a simple check-list. *Aslib Proceedings,* November 1972, (24) 11, 635-40.
6 *Project for evaluating the benefits from university libraries: final report.* University of Durham, October 1969. (OSTI Report 5056.) Chapters 2 & 7.
7 RZASA, P. & BAKER, N. R. Measures of effectiveness for a university library. *Journal of the American Society for Information Science,* 1972, 23(4), 248-53.
8 BUCKLAND, M. K. et al. *Systems analysis of a university library.* Lancaster University, 1970. p. 48.
9 ORR, R. H. et al. Development of methodological tools for planning and managing library services. *Bulletin of the Medical Libraries Association,* 1968, 54, 380-403.
10 HAMBURG, M. H. et al. *Library planning and decision making systems.* London: MIT Press, 1974. pp. 18-24.
11 MEIER, R. L. Efficiency criteria for the operation of large libraries. *Library Quarterly,* 1961, 31, 215-34.
12 KLINTOE, K. Cost analysis of a technical information unit. *Aslib Proceedings,* July 1971, 23(7), 362-71.
13 HANSON, C. W. & SLATER, M. *Does your firm need its own information service?* OECD, 1963. Publication 15101. pp. 35-44.
14 MOISSE, E. Costing information in an independent research association. *Information Scientist,* June 1976, 57-68.
15 ARNONE, G. A. & JACKSON, M. E. An information system as a cost-reduction tool in the transfer of knowledge. *Proceedings of ASIS,* 1973, 10, 3-4.
16 HESS, E. J. Towards the measurement of benefits from the use of information services. *Proceedings of ASIS,* 1973, 10, 91.
17 WILLS, G. & CHRISTOPHER, M. Cost-benefit analysis of company information needs. *Unesco Bulletin for Libraries,* January/February 1970, 9-22.
18 NIGHTINGALE, R. A. A cost-benefit study of a manually-produced information bulletin. *Aslib Proceedings,* April 1973, 25(4), 153-7.
19 FEARN, R. A. C. & KOVALIK, G. Cost/benefit analysis of a computer-based agricultural information system. *Proceedings of ASIS,* 1973, 10, 62-3.
20 WOLFE, J. N. et al. *The economics of technical information systems.* New York: Praeger, 1974. p 14.
21 MASON, D. Programmed budgeting and cost-effectiveness. *Aslib Proceedings,* March 1973, 25(3), 100-10.
22 MARTYN, J. Unintentional duplication of research. *New Scientist,* 6 February 1964, 21, 338.
23 STRABLE, G. *Special libraries; a guide for management.* Special Libraries Association, 1975. p 8.
24 BOWERMAN, C. M. The development, cost and impact of a current awareness service in an industrial organisation. *Journal of Chemical Documentation,* 1971, 11(2), 72-5.
25 KOCHEN, M. What makes a citizen information system used and useful.
 In: KOCHEN, M. ed. *Information for the community.* American Library Association, 1976. p. 151.
26 ORR, R. H. The scientist as an information processor.
 In: NELSON, C.E. & POLLOCK, D. K. *eds. Communication among scientists and engineers.* Heath Lexington, 1970. pp.143-89.
27 ZAIS, H. W. Economic modelling: an aid to the pricing of information services. *Journal of the American Society for Information Science,* March 1977, 89-95.

28 MASON, D. PPBS: application to an industrial information and library service. *Journal of Librarianship*, April 1972, 95–101.
29 RAFFEL, J. A. & SHISHKO, R. *Systematic analysis of university libraries: an application of cost-benefit analysis to the MIT libraries*. London: MIT Press, 1969. Chapter 1.
30 VICKERY, B. C. Research by Aslib into costing of information services. *Aslib Proceedings*, June 1972, 337–41.
31 SMITH, G. C. K. & SCHOFIELD, J. L. Administrative effectiveness: times and costs of library operations. *Journal of Librarianship*, September 1971, 245–66.
32 MARRON, H. On costing information services. *Proceedings of ASIS*, 1969, 6, 515–20.
33 PRICE, D. S. *Collecting and reporting real costs of information systems*. ASIS, November 1971. (ED 055 592.)
34 PRICE, D. S. The cost of information: a prerequisite for other analyses.
   In: TAYLOR, R. S. ed. *Economics of information dissemination*. Syracuse University, New York: 1973. pp. 21–48.
35 COOK, J. Financing a library/information service by operating a cost recovery system. *Aslib Proceedings*, June 1972, 24 (6), 342–9.
36 NORTON, J. Information analysis centres and the private sector.
   In: SMITH, W. A. ed. *The management of information analysis centres*. COSATI, 1972. (ED 059 412.) pp. 187–92.
37 KOCH, H. W. Marketing the products and services of information analysis centres.
   In: SMITH, W. A. ed. *The management of information analysis centres*. COSATI, 1972. (ED 059 412.) pp. 20–34.
38 LUTZ, R. P. Costing information services. *Bulletin of the Medical Libraries Association*, April 1971, 254–61.
39 WHITE, R. *Consumer product development*. London: Penguin, 1973. pp 107–15.
40 VEAZIE, W. H. The marketing of information analysis centre products and services. ASIS, 1971. (ED 050 772.)
41 SCHWUCHOW, W. Fundamental aspects of the financing of information centres. *Information Storage and Retrieval*, 1973, 9, 569–75.
42 WILSON, J. H. & BARTH, J. W. Cost analysis for community information services.
   In: KOCHEN, M. ed. *Information for the community*. American Library Association, 1976. pp.171–82.
43 VEAZIE, JNR. W. H. DOD policy on cost recovery as viewed from an information analysis centre.
   In: SMITH, W.A. ed. COSATI, 1972. (ED 059 412.) pp. 160–69.
44 HALL, A. et al. The effect of the use of an SDI service on the information-gathering habits of scientists and technologists. Institution of Electrical Engineers (Report No R/72/11.) pp.4, 8–13.
45 TERRY, M. W. Voluntary charges: experience on the middle road. *Proceedings 4th ASIS half-yearly meeting*, 1975, 171–5.
46 SLATER, M. & FISHER, P. *Use made of technical libraries*. London: Aslib, 1969. pp. 72–81.
47 CHADDOCK, D. H. Information used in design. *Engineering Materials and Design*, April 1970, 471–2.
48 WOLEK, F. W. The engineer: his work and needs for information. *Proceedings of ASIS*, 1969, 6, 471–6.
49 RADLEY, G. W. *Management information systems*. London: Intertext, 1973. pp. 14–31.
50 AGUILAR, F. J. *Scanning the business environment*. London: Macmillan, 1967. Exhibit III–1.
51 SCHONER, B. & UHL, K. *Marketing research: information systems and decision making*. London: Wiley, 1975. pp. 130, 173–8, 194–8.
52 JONES, H. *Preparing company plans: a workbook for effective corporate planning*. Farnborough: Gower Press, 1974. pp. 56–97, 121–150.
53 HALL, H. J. Which service to buy, and why? *Proceedings of ASIS* 1976, 13. Abstract p.47, and microfiche.

54 FLOWERDEW, A. D. J. & WHITEHEAD, C. M. E. Cost-effectiveness and cost/benefit analysis in information science. London: OSTI, 1974. (Report 5206.) pp. 28–35.
55 BLICK, A.R. Evaluating an in-house or bought-in service. *Aslib Proceedings,* September 1977, **29** (9), 310–19.
56 WHITEHALL, T. Personal current awareness service: a handbook of techniques for manual SDI. London: The British Library, 1979. (BLRD Report 5502.) pp.101,114.

MAURICE P. MARCHANT

University Libraries as Economic Systems

The possibility of developing an economic theory of libraries is explored. The concepts of economic theory, economic system, and economic model are discussed as potentially applicable to libraries. Two types of such models are developed from data drawn from university libraries. One predicts professional staff size from two variables: collection size and collection decentralization. The other identifies a set of library inputs composed of professional staff size, subprofessional staff size, and annual acquisitions rate as a consistently good predictor of library expenditures and a stable measure of library input.

THE FEASIBILITY OF AN ECONOMIC THEORY of the library has recently been suggested.[1] Were such a theory to be developed sufficiently to provide mathematical models, it is suggested that library planning and budgeting might be measurably improved.

Economic theory attempts to define and generalize the relationship existing among variables having to do with the production and distribution of wealth. Its method is largely deductive: on the basis of a set of known or assumed facts, a hypothesis is established and a model is set up. While the model may be simple or complex, it is a simplification of the real world to the extent that it does not include all the variables that could possibly be included. It is likely to emphasize those that are important to the needs of the study and those that are readily measurable. The effect of those not included cumulates as error variance in the model. An example of an economic theory is that price tends to move to the level at which demand is equal to supply. Another is that a rise in price tends, sooner or later, to decrease demand and to increase supply.

Such theories require checking against data obtained from the real world. If empirical data support the relationship proposed by the theory, we may accept the theory as a useful assumption until additional evidence appears which conflicts with the theory, requiring its modification or abandonment. Because of the difficulties associated with environmental control in economic studies, economic theories indicate tendencies rather than universal laws.

Two different concepts are covered by the term "economic system." Both are concerned with the interrelationship of a set of economic variables. One is concerned with the ways in which a given society organizes its means of production and distribution of material wealth

Reprinted from *College and Research Libraries*, 36(6), 1975, by permission.

and services and might be referred to as, for example, the American or British economic system. The other concept adheres to general systems theory and is concerned with identifying interrelationships between variables within a system: the processing of inputs into outputs, the effect of change in one variable on others, and so forth. This paper is concerned with the second concept, but is limited largely to the study of inputs.

The kinds of variables incorporated into economic models are those associated with production. They might be measures of wealth or productivity or those thought to affect or to be affected by them. Obviously, personnel, materiel, and money are important economic variables. For example, the model presented later in this paper in which physical decentralization serves as a predictor of staff size is an economic model because the emphasis is on personnel as a representation of funding. In another context, physical decentralization might be fitted into a political, rather than an economic, model in which the object is to study faculty influence.

In model building, theoretical assumptions of cause and effect relationships are made and tested. In doing so, within the concept of general systems theory, variables become categorized as input, intervening, and output variables. Speaking generally, they might be described as follows. Inputs are those things that enter the system from outside, such as books and personnel in a library. Outputs are products which are created in the system with the use of inputs and exported back into the environment, such as library service. Intervening variables are affected by inputs and, in turn, affect outputs. But the label given a variable under one set of circumstances may not apply in another. Thus an input variable in one system might be an intervening or output variable in another system.

Variables are also categorized as independent and dependent. An independent variable has the capacity to predict the value of a dependent variable, and there is often a presumption of causal relations between them. These terms are more general than, but not unrelated to, the concepts of input, intervening, and output. Within a systems study, one would expect inputs to be independent variables, outputs to be dependent variables, and intervening variables to be both.

Two relevant research projects regarding libraries have emerged recently. One computed the annual growth rates of several variables in academic libraries and developed prediction equations for estimating various staff, collection, and cost values.[2] The other, noting that the distribution of many library statistics is skewed, approached the study of those statistics with improved success through their logarithmic values.[3]

These studies provide a sense of confidence to the assumption that generalized influences are at work which affect all or large groups of academic libraries. If so, their identification and measurement may help in the construction of an economic theory of the library which librarians might find useful in decision making.

The thrust of this paper is to provide recently identified evidence supportive of that position. However, these studies have been confined to academic libraries of limited size range, above 500,000 volumes. They were undertaken to explore a set of readily available data for evidence that might support the concept that libraries are economic systems and to identify points of departure for further research. Two groupings of predictive models will be discussed, one dealing with the size of the professional staff and the other with measures of input.

PROFESSIONAL STAFF SIZE

It was found in a study of twenty-two libraries of Association of Research

Libraries (ARL) member institutions that the ratio of professional staff members (mostly librarians) to 1,000 students was 4.4 (with a standard deviation of 3.5).[4] Comparisons with other variables in the study demonstrated that the ratio had a high relationship with several funding measurements. It took its place among them as a measure of library wealth, indicating that it reflects financial input in relation to the number of students who have a potential call on the library. This relationship was confirmed by factor analysis as well as by the magnitude of the Pearson product-moment correlation coefficients, which was as high as .99.[5] It was apparent that funding is a fairly good predictor of professional staff size. The high standard deviation relative to the mean of the librarian-to-student ratio results from both high variance in wealth among libraries and a skewing toward high wealth caused by a few especially wealthy libraries.

The number of professional staff members was also found to be highly related to several other organizational variables. Moreover, when their interrelationships were graphically depicted, number of librarians occupied a central position among them much like the axle of a wheel.[6] These variables, along with their correlations with professional staff size, were: (1) collection size, .72; (2) currently received serial titles, .54; (3) number of volumes acquired during the school year, .56; (4) physical decentralization of the collection, .71; and (5) number of doctoral degrees (excluding law, medical, and dental doctorates) granted that year by the university to which the library belongs, .62.

It is not difficult to imagine staff size being affected by these variables. The size and growth rate of the collection generate work to process and service it. A large graduate program, which is the primary justification of a large collection, would be expected to generate service demands. Overfragmentation of the collection could cut down on the efficient use of personnel.

However, considering these variables' lack of independence from each other and the small number of libraries in the study, it would be surprising if they could all fit significantly into a formula predicting professional staff size. The easiest procedure for constructing an optimum predictive equation is through linear multiple regression analysis, in which combinations of independent variables are tested for significance and compared for predictive capacity. The best combination, as it turned out, included two variables: collection size and decentralization. Together, they explain almost 80 percent of the variance in professional staff size. If these relationships are causal and accurate, they offer help in predicting staff needs under changing conditions of collection size and decentralization. The predictive equation is

$$Y = 22.9 + 0.235X_1 + 67.8X_2$$

in which Y is number of professional staff members, X_1 is collection size in 10,000s of volumes, and X_2 is the decentralization index. The decentralization index is computed from the formula

$$D = B^2/C_t$$

in which D is the decentralization index and is equal in this case to X_2, B is the number of branches, and C_t is the total number of volumes (in 1,000s) in the university library system and is ten times the value of X_1 in this case. The derivation of the formula for decentralization is explained in the dissertation.[7] While the correlation between the independent variables was insignificant (.28), the involvement of collection size in both made the formula nonlinear.

The prediction equation has certain limitations. First, it was derived from libraries varying in size from 500,000 to 2,100,000 volumes and with a mean size of 1,160,000 volumes. The mean of the decentralization indexes was 0.084, and the indexes ranged from 0.000 to 0.586. The equation functions best with libraries having values close to the mean, and the extent of error can be expected to increase as the values deviate from it.

There is also a certain potential for error in the prediction due to the 20 percent of the variance which was unaccounted for. The expected error is as much as 17 about once in twenty cases.

Sets of Library Inputs

The usefulness of professional staff size as a measure of input requires testing. But it is part of a more general question which asks what measurements constitute interrelated sets of inputs. It would be helpful if a set of mutually complementary inputs could be identified which are stable over time.

Inputs in this case consist of resources entering the library from the environment. Funding can be thought of as an input. So can the resources the budget provides, such as personnel and library collection components.

The dollar has been used as a measure of input by most libraries; but it has both advantages and disadvantages. As a means of exchange, it can stand for many different inputs, including personnel playing different roles and drawing differing salaries, books and serials, and various other materials and services libraries need. Consequently, the dollar can be used as a unit of input by which, in one sense, various inputs can be compared. For example, a librarian costing $10,000 a year can be equated to 1,000 books averaging $10 each.

But the potentially available freedom to choose what inputs to exchange the library's budget for may be delusionary. If a given set of goals is desired, its actualization may predetermine the optimum mix of inputs required. If so, and we understand the optimum system that will achieve it, the choice of inputs and their quantities have already been determined, and the inputs are not independent of each other.

Another weakness in using money as a measure of input is its instability during periods of inflation or recession. Consequently, it would be helpful if other, more stable, inputs could be identified.

Research Methodology

To study input stability, two sets of data were subjected to regression analysis. The first had been collected for the dissertation. It included three measurements of funding (total operating expenditures, staff expenditures, and library materials expenditures) and five measurements of the basic groups of resources funded by libraries (the total number of staff members, professional staff size, subprofessional staff size, the number of volumes acquired, and the number of current serials received). However, it was also limited to one year's data from only twenty-two libraries. The second set was the data based on punched cards regarding the libraries of fifty-eight ARL member institutions compiled by the Purdue University Library and Audio Visual Center.[8] While it lacked measurements for number of current serials received, the sample size was much larger and the data covered twenty-one years. Consequently, the smaller data base was used for a series of preliminary analyses to determine whether the lack of that one measurement might be a serious loss. The second set was then analyzed, first, to see to what extent it confirmed the preliminary analyses and, second, to determine the extent to which the relationships might have varied over time.

Preliminary Analysis Series

Total operating expenditures were best predicted, using the first set of data, by the size of the professional staff and number of acquisitions. Once they had entered the regression analysis, none of the other measurements had a significant further predictive capability. The two, as a set, accounted for 83 percent of the variance in total operating expenditures.

Expenditures for library materials were best predicted by annual number of acquisitions and the professional staff size, which accounted for 76 percent of the variance in library materials expenditures.

Staff expenditures (including salaries and wages) were best predicted by the size of the professional staff alone, which accounted for 77 percent of the variance in these expenditures. None of the other potential dependent variables, including the number of subprofessional staff members, contributed significantly to the prediction.

The relationships between the three expenditures were also probed. Adding the staff and library materials expenditures together accounted for nearly 90 percent of the total operating expenses in the average of the libraries studied and would be expected, therefore, to provide an excellent prediction. Staff expenditures alone explained 91 percent of the variance in total expenditures, and library materials expenditures added 8 percent more to the explanation, for a total control of 99 percent.

Anticipating that the relationships identified in these preliminary analyses would be generally consistent with those in the larger study, several insights were possible.

First, the number of current serial titles offered little supplementary predictive potential to any of the expenditure variables. This is not to say that the cost of serials is unimportant. Rather, it suggests that (1) the number of serial titles is not a good indication of serial cost, and (2) the number of serial titles varies with such other variables as number of professional librarians to such an extent that its predictive potential, such as it is, is largely duplicative.

Second, the strongest predictors of total operating expenditures are professional staff size and number of volumes acquired. Of these, professional staff size appears to be the stronger. Number of volumes acquired affects expenditures largely through library materials expenditures, as would be expected; but professional staff size is an important predictor for both library materials and staff expenditures.

Third, with an increase in the number of libraries in the study, number of subprofessional staff members might emerge as a significant predictor of total operating and staff expenditures.

Fourth, total staff size did not provide a useful index for this study. The components of it, professional and subprofessional staff size, are more useful.

ANALYSIS OF SERIES OVER TIME

The preliminary analyses provided a sense of confidence that the lack of data regarding serials from the larger data base would not result in the lack of an important variable for the purpose of this study. As the regression analyses were completed, using the data for each year for making a set of regression analyses like those in the preliminary series, the patterns that had been expected emerged. Since there was some overlap between the libraries represented in the two data bases, this should not come as a surprise. But neither was it certain beforehand. Of the twenty-two libraries in the preliminary series, four were not among the fifty-eight libraries of the larger series. No library over 2,100,000 volumes in size in 1968 was among the twenty-two in the preliminary series, whereas twelve of the fifty-eight in the larger data base were above that size in 1968. That the pattern was similar between the two samples and from year to year in the second sample suggests that the pattern can be relied upon, within limits, from year to year and across a fairly wide size range. Moreover, predictions of individual library expenditures and their confidence intervals were made possible.

It is that measure of consistency, supplemented by the Baumol and Marcus and Pratt observations, which provides encouragement to persist in the search for a theory of library economy.

One purpose of this study was to try to determine whether the staff size and acquisitions measurements might have greater stability over time than the expenditures measurements. One way to test stability is to see how constant the cumulative proportionate variance, as a measure of predictive capacity, remains from year to year as compared with the regression coefficients which are generated in sets of yearly regression analyses in which the staff size and acquisitions variables serve to predict the expenditures levels. Another evidence is the extent to which variance in the cumulative proportionate variance and regression coefficients is a function of time.

If the ability of a set of independent variables to predict the value of a dependent variable remains constant, the cumulative proportionate variance would not change. But the effect of inflation on the cost of the independent variables over the years would cause changes in the regression coefficients. The magnitude of variance from year to year is measured by the standard deviation. The extent to which the variance is constant over time would be expressed by a simple correlation between value of the variable and the year.

Summaries of the sets of analyses are given in Tables 1 through 4. They provide the data required to evaluate (1) the ability of specific sets of independent variables to predict library expenditures, (2) variance over time in that predictive capacity, (3) the mean value of regression coefficients associated with each independent variable in the set, (4) variance in the regression coefficients, and (5) the extent to which variance was a function of time. In addition, in order that a rough comparison can be made of the difference in variance between the regression coefficients and cumulative proportionate variance, the standard deviations were normalized by showing them as a ratio of their mean values. This normalized value is known as a coefficient of variation.

Table 1 summarizes data regarding the relationships of total operating expenditures with staff and library materials expenditures during the twenty-one-year period. These data are presented largely to provide a basis for comparison with the other three tables. This set of independent variables is shown to be an excellent predictor of total operating expenditures (predicting, in an average year, with 98.47 percent accuracy) with little deviation in predictive capacity from year to year (1.94 percent standard deviation). Staff expenditures is the more stable predictor. (Comparing the coefficients of variation determines their relative variability.) Neither the regression coefficients nor the cumulative proportionate variance changed in

TABLE 1

SUMMARY OF ANALYSES RELATING TOTAL OPERATING EXPENDITURES TO STAFF AND LIBRARY MATERIALS EXPENDITURES OVER TWENTY-ONE YEARS

	Mean	Standard Deviation	S.D./Mean	Correlation with Year
Regression coefficients				
Staff expenditures	1.1553	0.1281	0.1114	–0.1390
Library materials expenditures	1.1085	0.2383	0.2150	–0.1951
Cumulative proportionate variance	0.9847	0.0194	0.0197	–0.1089

TABLE 2

SUMMARY OF ANALYSES RELATING TOTAL OPERATING EXPENDITURES TO PROFESSIONAL AND SUBPROFESSIONAL STAFF SIZE AND NUMBER OF VOLUMES ACQUIRED OVER TWENTY-ONE YEARS

	Mean	Standard Deviation	S.D./Mean	Correlation with Year
Regression coefficients				
Professional staff size	12418.	6028.	0.4854	0.9179
Subprofessional staff size	3915.	1601.	0.4088	0.4658
Acquisitions	4.0917	2.1690	0.5301	0.2736
Cumulative proportionate variance	0.9309	0.0309	0.0385	−0.2194

a pattern associated with time. (The correlations with year were low and not significant at the .05 level, which was the lowest significance level tested throughout the study.) Since all three variables were affected by inflation, these nonsignificant correlations were expected.

Regression coefficients associated with more constant inputs as predictors of expenditures, being immune to inflation, should be more highly correlated with time because the resources acquired will increase at a slower rate than the funding expended to acquire them. Tables 2, 3, and 4 provide the data generated to test the constancy of three such input variables and their predictive capacity. In each case, the input variables listed are those which contributed significantly, at the .05 level or better, to the prediction and which, as a set, provided the best prediction available.

All three input variables were able to enter the analyses, in Table 2, predicting total operating expenditures. Note that the larger sample size and breadth of years covered allowed for the inclusion here of subprofessional staff size, which did not emerge in the preliminary study. In seventeen of the twenty-one yearly analyses, it emerged as a better primary supplement to professional staff size than did number of volumes acquired.

Together they explained an average of 93.09 percent of the variance with a standard deviation of 3.09 percent, a substantial improvement over the preliminary analysis results of 83 percent. The inclusion of the larger number of libraries appears to have improved the statistical measurements of the relationships.

While the prediction is lower than was attributed to the two expenditures variables in Table 1, it is remarkably high and stable. In only one year did it drop below 90 percent.

The coefficients of variation (S.D./Mean) of the regression coefficients were much higher than those in Table 1 and indicate a fairly high variation in regression coefficients over the years. Much of the variation was not random but, rather, was the result of increases

TABLE 3

SUMMARY OF ANALYSES RELATING LIBRARY MATERIALS EXPENDITURES TO PROFESSIONAL STAFF SIZE AND NUMBER OF VOLUMES ACQUIRED OVER TWENTY-ONE YEARS

	Mean	Standard Deviation	S.D./Mean	Correlation with Year
Regression coefficients				
Professional staff size	3491.	1691.	0.4844	0.8186
Acquisitions	2.7042	1.1832	0.4375	0.5000
Cumulative proportionate variance	0.7508	0.1441	0.1919	−0.5109

TABLE 4
SUMMARY OF ANALYSES RELATING STAFF EXPENDITURES TO PROFESSIONAL AND SUBPROFESSIONAL STAFF SIZE OVER TWENTY-ONE YEARS

	Mean	Standard Deviation	S.D./Mean	Correlation with Year
Regression coefficients				
Professional staff size	8845.	4549.	0.5143	0.9198
Subprofessional staff size	3119.	955.	0.3062	0.6896
Cumulative proportionate variance	0.9371	0.0495	0.0528	−0.3576

over the years that are the result of inflation. That was particularly true of the regression coefficients associated with professional staff size and, to a more moderate extent, with subprofessional staff size.

Tables 3 and 4 summarize the data from the sets of analyses predicting library materials expenditures and staff expenditures, respectively. As expected from the preliminary analysis, professional staff size entered both sets. In addition, subprofessional staff size entered the staff expenditures set, and acquisitions entered the library materials set.

In each set, the correlations between year and regression coefficients for both input variables were positive and significant, indicating that the regression coefficients grow larger over the years. The staff size variables explained 93.71 percent of the variance in staff expenditures, which is comparable with the predictive power of the three input variables in Table 2. But control over variance in library materials expenditures, of 75.08 percent, was less strong and was associated with a standard deviation more than four times as large as was found in total operating expenditures.

The correlations of year with the cumulative proportionate variance associated with staff and library materials expenditures indicate a tendency for a decline in predictive power in recent years. The decline is more pronounced regarding library materials expenditures, with which the correlation is significant at the .05 level, than regarding staff expenditures.

Overall, the data support the hypothesis that the staff size and acquisitions input variables have retained their powers to predict library expenditures. But their control has been better over total operating and staff expenditures than over library materials expenditures. Apparently, stability of prediction is greater for more general funding measures than for more specific ones.

CONCLUSIONS

A pattern of relationship between major personnel and materials inputs with library expenditures has persisted in American university libraries for two decades. The major inputs are professional and subprofessional staff size and number of volumes acquired. Together, they constitute a set of inputs that are stable over time and can be used in systems studies comparing conditions in one year with those in another in place of the expenditures variables which are not stable.

While a budget officer may not be willing to predict next year's funding needs in a specific library without greater specificity than these three gross measurements provide, that officer could probably estimate this year's expenditures within a margin of error as small as 6 percent with 95 percent confidence and as small as 7.5 percent with 99 percent confidence. With some experience, he or she could likely improve substantially.

Such accuracy is possible because many other expenditures are reflected in these three. Materials, such as paper, pencils, and card stock, are a function of the number of personnel and books acquired. While an administrator might control the costs involved in such items somewhat by bulk purchases and watching for bargains, control through these types of activities is only marginal. Moreover, attempts to economize unduly in these areas can readily result in operational bottlenecks that inhibit effective service. When a library acquires a new reference assistant, the resource commitment that will result, after the library has adjusted to the stress imposed by that increase, will be a great deal more than that staff member's salary and fringe benefits. It is more likely to be nearer $20,000 than a $10,000 annual salary.

The demonstration, in the first part of this paper, that professional staff size is a function of decentralization and collection size is a minor contribution to a developing economic theory of libraries. It suggests that organizational patterns might be a fruitful area for future study into that development. Another area would be to identify the interrelationships between the three staff and acquisitions input variables and other resources, perhaps as part of the type of systems analysis studies and model building carried out with the use of techniques and concepts used in econometrics.

Radical changes in the pattern of library organizational behavior might affect the basic economic patterns identified in this study. But the pattern has remained fairly constant over a twenty-year span characterized by constant change. At least for the near future, those relationships are likely to persist and to provide a basis from which future costs can be predicted.

References

1. Michael K. Buckland, "Toward an Economic Theory of the Library," in Robert S. Taylor, ed., *Economics of Information Dissemination: A Symposium* (Frontiers of Librarianship 16 [Syracuse, N.Y.: School of Library Science, Syracuse University, 1974]), p.68–80.
2. William J. Baumol and Matityahu Marcus, *Economics of Academic Libraries* (Washington: American Council on Education, 1973).
3. Allan D. Pratt, "A Theory of Lognormal Size Distribution of Academic Libraries in the United States" (Ph.D. dissertation, Univ. of Pittsburgh, 1974).
4. Maurice P. Marchant, "The Effects of the Decision Making Process and Related Organizational Factors on Alternative Measures of Performance in University Libraries" (Ph.D. dissertation, Univ. of Michigan, 1970), p.108–11.
5. Ibid., p.120–21.
6. Ibid., p.123.
7. Ibid., p.96–97.
8. Oliver C. Dunn and others, *The Past and Likely Future of 58 Research Libraries, 1951–1980: A Statistical Study of Growth and Change* (8th issue; Lafayette, Ind.: University Libraries and Audio Visual Center, Purdue University, 1972), p.5.

APPLICATION OF THE THEORY OF THE FIRM TO LIBRARY COSTING

D. Rowe

This article suggests limitations in Douglas' model for the optimum size of a library of monographs. It proposes a micro-economic model for determining optimum library size and minimum unit costs.

I A. DOGULAS' PROVOCATIVE ARTICLE on the optimum size of a library of monographs (*Aust.Lib.J*, November 1973) provides a useful starting point for analysis of library costing. The determination of the optimum size of a collection is surely one of the central problems of librarianship today. Libraries are becoming big business as library capital and budgets continue to grow ever larger. Resources are limited, nonetheless. Misallocation of scarce resources deprives the public of additional benefits. Most librarians are aware of the short run need to obtain a maximum return from money, labour and other resources. Fewer librarians however seem to have considered the need to determine optimum library size in order to minimize long run costs. That may result from the interdisciplinary gap that seems to persist in Australia at least between librarianship on the one hand, and mathematics, economics and operations research on the other.

The title of Douglas' article indicates his model is designed to determine the optimum size of a collection of monographs, but implicitly excludes serials and other materials. Those omissions may detract from the usefulness of Douglas' model as in many libraries non monograph materials may be so numerous as to constitute a high proportion of total holdings. In addition, Douglas seems to assume all monographs in libraries are available for loan and inter-library loan. He ignores reference books and rare books. His model may be of little use to a large reference library that ordinarily does not lend to the public.

I question Douglas' assumption in equations (5) and (8) that the cost of holding a book in the library, C_s, can be related directly to the cost of arranging an inter-library loan, C_i, and to the cost of handling an inter-library loan, C_h. The cost of having a book in the library, C_s, varies over time, but inter-library loan unit costs, C_i and C_h, (corrected for inflation) are constants over time. In Douglas' equations (5) and (8) it seems that if the period for determining the cost of holding a book, C_s, is varied, the value of C_s varies, and thus n, the 'optimum' size of the collection varies. That is to say, the size of Douglas' 'optimum' collection depends in part on the arbitrary time period used.

A further criticism is that Douglas has failed to indicate whether unit holding costs are total costs including rent on library capital, or whether they represent only explicit budget costs. When opportunity costs of library capital and buildings are considered, and their magnitude realised, it is necessary to define closely the composition of unit holding cost. In the absence of a precise definition of the cost of holding a volume, variable cost data in Douglas' model could yield a variety of 'optimum' monograph collections in a given library.

MICROECONOMIC MODEL

Douglas' pioneering work has stimulated my independent development of a micro-economic model[1] for determining optimum size and minimum costs of a library that includes monographs, bound serials, audio visual materials, archives, and other materials. Each piece is counted as one book unit, costs being averaged for each unit.

The microeconomic model relies on the availability of accurate assessments of the

Reprinted from *Australian Library Journal*, 23(3), 1974, by permission.

library's real costs. Real costs comprise budget costs plus implicit costs.[2] Implicit costs include returns that would be received on capital invested in the library if the library were owned by a commercial firm operating for profit. Library users do not pay directly for their use of libraries. Consequently it is impossible to obtain data for intersecting supply and demand curves as indicators of libraries' economic efficiency. In the absence of a demand schedule the most practical way to assess efficiency is to examine the supply side and determine minimum average cost.

The theory of the firm determines optimum or least expensive output per period. Similarly, the library model developed below shows the optimum or least expensive bookstock available during a given period. Minimum average cost of a library bookstock may be defined as the library's total cost for a given period divided by the library's optimum size bookstock for that period. Assuming that library personel and internal services are efficient, the major step towards minimizing average (i.e. per volume or unit) cost is to relate it to optimum or most efficient bookstock, as in the following diagram.

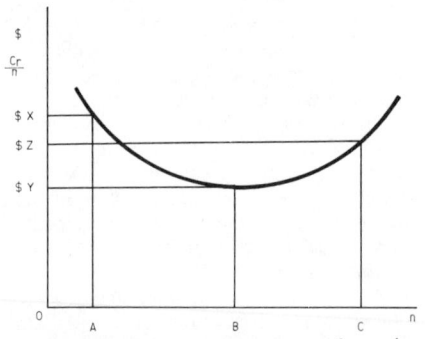

Figure 1: Long run average cost curve for various sizes of library bookstock per period. Cr/n = long run average cost; n = size of library bookstock per period.

Average cost is shown in the diagram in the long run.[3] By the long run is meant a period of time long enough to vary all library resources, including buildings, equipment, bookstocks, management, and expertise. Long run average cost is comprised of a package of unit (per volume) component costs for library functions and services that include, for the given period, storage, acquisitions, lending and reference services, inter-library loan activities, management, rent on capital, and other heads of real expenditure.

In the above diagram it will be seen that while bookstock is relatively small, OA, unit (per volume) real cost will be $X. As bookstocks and related library services grow there occur overall economies of scale[4] in the library's unit costs. When the bookstock reaches a size of OB, average (per volume) cost will be minimised at $Y. With a bookstock larger than OB there occur diseconomies of scale,[5] and average cost begins to increase. With a bookstock of increased sizes OC, average cost rises to $Z. When average cost is least, at $Y per volume per period, the optimum bookstock OB has been achieved, determined by the criterion of economic efficiency.[6]

It should be noted unit costs of component library services and functions may not individually minimize with an optimum bookstock. That fact however is irrelevant to the principal task of securing minimum total costs per volume per period.

If different bundles of services are provided in various kinds of libraries the underlying component cost structures differ and optimum size of collections and minimum average cost of bookstock may vary as the proportions of component costs vary. For those reasons different kinds of libraries are not directly comparable as to average costs. Similarly, underlying component costs of identical goods and services used by libraries may vary in different regions and cities. It is quite possible that the long run average cost curve and associated optimum library size may be unique to the individual library, because of its unique cost structure.

It may be deduced from Figure 1 that if long run average cost of a library, with a constant package of services, persistently slopes downwards or upwards (after being corrected for general inflation) as the size of bookstocks changes, the library is not operating with an optimum bookstock. The slope of the average cost curve over the initial period tested will provide a rough indication of target optimum size and target minimum unit cost. The library's target position will become clearer as subsequent data is plotted on the average cost curve. If for a variety of reasons [7] however the empirical curve is irregular or if the base of the curve is found to extend horizontally for some distance the library's optimum size will be determined within a certain range rather than at a particular point of growth.

The long run average cost curve, provided it is reasonably smooth, provides a ready and simple means for calculating the warranted library budget per period.[8] If the library holds OA volumes the warranted (real) budget for that period is $X.OA. If bookstocks expand from OA towards the optimum size OB the warranted (real) budget per period will become $Y.OB. With optimum size bookstock OB the warranted budget $Y.OB will provide for minimum average cost per period.

ECONOMIC SURVIVAL

To this point we have seen that the theory of the firm applied to the library determines optimum library size, minimum unit costs, and warranted budget per period. Warranted budget so determined may be used as a basis to compare library transaction cost with the transaction cost of using an alternative information service. At this time the nearest practical alternative to using material in the library is the obtaining of original and copy material by inter-library loan. With future technology the nearest alternative to using materials in the library may be widespread use of computer information services, provided commercially or by governments. If library services are to survive economically in a future of expected rapid technological change, it is argued the cost of using the library must remain lower than or equal to that of a substitute non library service, other things being equal. Having established a model for lowering unit (per volume) costs in libraries, this article would be incomplete if it failed to establish a simple framework for comparing the real cost of using the library with the cost of using a non-library information service.

For a given library the number of lending and reference transactions per period may be counted or estimated fairly exactly by statistical methods. The average cost of a lending or reference transaction per period is calculated by dividing the library's warranted (or other) real budget for that period by the total number of transactions. The relationship that emerges between average transaction cost and warranted library budget is illustrated in the following diagram.

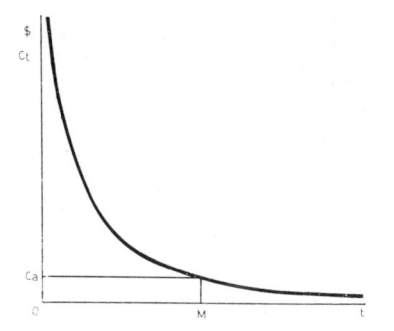

Figure 2: Total of lending and reference transactions per period, t, plotted against average transaction cost, C_t, with warranted level of budget for that period.

This diagram shows how the average cost of using the library, C_t, diminishes the more frequently the library is used. The transaction cost of using a non library information service is shown as C_a, on the vertical (cost) axis. The diagram shows that if the number of library transactions per period fails to reach a level of OM, the average real cost of a library transaction exceeds that of a non library competitor. However when library transactions per period exceed a level of OM library transaction costs are less on average than those of the non library competitor. It is argued that if the library's average transaction costs exceed those of a non library competitor the continued existence of the library cannot be justified by economic criteria, assuming the non library service is a satisfactory substitute. It is unlikely computer services will become satisfactory substitutes for libraries in the foreseeable future. Nevertheless, librarians who dismiss altogether that eventual possibility may be like Lot's wife: looking back and not forward.

SUMMARY AND CONCLUSION

The practical application of the model developed in this article relies on the availability of long run real cost data to determine minimum unit (per volume) cost of a library and corresponding optimum library size. Consequently it appears the model may be of most relevance to established libraries able to provide real cost data over a long period. In addition to determining minimum unit cost and optimum size the model determines warranted library budget. The budget determined by the model may be used as a basis to compare the transaction cost of using the library with the transaction cost of a non library information service.

As an indicator of costs, the long run average cost curve could be a useful policy tool for restricting the growth of libraries to an optimum size. As a cost indicator it could be used to initiate development of low cost/decentralized/co-operative storage schemes for little used materials.

It remains now for individual libraries wishing to determine their optimum size to plot empirical long run average cost for various sizes of bookstock, as in figure 1. Before being plotted, average cost data should be corrected carefully for inflationary changes using a price index with a suitable base year. The long run period used initially should be such as to provide a reasonable opportunity for plotting significant change in unit (per volume) holding cost and size of bookstock. After plotting data the curve that emerges should be part of the U-shaped curve shown in figure 1. The curve may be completed subsequently by plotting additional data. The application of empirical average cost data to the theoretical model developed in this article promises to be an interesting and rewarding, if painstaking, task.

[1] The microeconomic model is an adaptation of that more fully described in Leftwich, R. H. *The Price system and resource allocation* (Dryden, 1970) : chapter 8.

[2] Ibid : 144-5.

[3] Ibid : 146-8. In the long run microeconomic model while the average cost of holding a book varies over time, that does not alter optimum library size corresponding to minimum average cost. The lowest point on the long run average cost curve in figure 1 may move vertically but not horizontally if the long run period is varied.

[4] Ibid : 162-4.

[5] Ibid : 164-5.

[6] Ibid : Note qualifications.

[7] Ibid

[8] As we are dealing with the long run period, the warranted budget may extend over several years. The long run budget is converted to an annual budget by dividing it by the number of years included in the long run.

AN ECONOMIC MODEL OF LIBRARY SERVICE

Abraham Bookstein

In times of economic distress, the roles and activities of institutions are scrutinized with particular fervor. The library is no exception. Yet, though library activity is increasingly being discussed in economic terms, no economic model exists that expresses what it is that a library does. At the core of the difficulty is the abstract character of library output. To circumvent this difficulty, various measures of library performance, for example, circulations of library material, have been recommended as criteria for funding libraries. In this paper I suggest a microeconomic model of library activity. This model treats library output as an abstract quantity and shows how it relates to other components of library performance. In terms of this model, the likely consequences of basing funding on such measurable outputs as circulation are analyzed. In both the "centralized authority" and "free market" versions of the model, we conclude that basing funding on circulation will result in a diminution in service level, as defined in the paper. Because of the abstract nature of library service, it is not possible to derive the optimal amount of money to be allocated to libraries. However, models such as this one do allow us to assess how libraries are likely to respond to changing economic conditions, and provide conceptual guidelines for rational decision making in the allocation of library funds.

Introduction

Economic theory attempts to answer two fundamental questions: In a complex society, what determines how scarce resources are distributed? How should these resources be distributed to maximize the benefits they provide to society? These are questions that have always fascinated social thinkers. Never do they do so as intensely as when these resources are perceived as being especially limited and the competition for them acute. For the library, as an institution whose access to resources is highly dependent on the political process, how these questions are resolved will be critical in shaping its character and, perhaps, even deciding its existence.

Economists have developed very sophisticated and powerful concepts and modes of analysis in response to the questions posed above. The debate regarding library support is increasingly argued in these terms. Yet, when asked to justify the maintenance or expansion of library service, the library community has been reluctant to present its case in economic terms. Instead, when asked to explain the library's allocation of resources, the library community tends to respond in terms of moral values, referring to the library as something intrinsically good, and producing intangible, but socially valuable outputs. While it is correct that much of the library's output is intangible, this unfortunately is not true of the resources it consumes, and the ultimate question is whether we can justify a dollar being used to subsidize library service rather than, say, opera or art museums or public parks, or to be left with the public to purchase beef or beer. If libraries are to defend effectively their share of society's resources, it is imperative that librarians become conversant with the terms in which these issues are discussed, and that microeconomic models that accurately capture what it is that libraries provide be developed. My impression is that such models do not currently exist.

Efforts have been made to adapt models created to analyze the activity of profit-making firms to libraries. Although these models provide important insights into library operation and have caused us to look at libraries from a fresh perspective, they often fail to capture some of the library's most essential features. The purpose of this paper is to indicate some limitations of these earlier models and to present a simple microeconomic model of library activity that captures some characteristics that seem particularly salient to me. This model is intended to clarify the essential differences between libraries and those firms that traditionally have been the focus of economic modeling.

Many earlier writers have studied how resources should be allocated rationally to and within libraries. Philip Morse [1] and Ferdinand Leimkuhler [2] have pioneered the application of operations-research models to understanding library operations, and today a substantial literature taking this approach is available [3]. Among the notable early contributions by economists interested in library activity are Baumol and Marcus's examination of cost trends in libraries [4], and the papers in *Libraries at Large* [5]. Black [6] and Goddard [7] explicitly apply mathematical economic models to the library setting. Also interesting is the commentary by Machlup [8] regarding the lack of data needed for a proper economic analysis of library operations.

The recent deterioration of economic conditions has been paralleled by an increase in economically oriented publications about libraries. Among the more substantive are books by Machlup, Getz, and White [9–11]. A survey of classic economic theory and its application to libraries, as well as a more complete bibliography, can be found in DeWath [12].

Classic Economic Model

Traditional microeconomic theory was developed to study, and most successfully describes, the production and distribution of tangible goods. One component of the theory is the producer, who combines various inputs to produce a quantity of an item, which is then brought to market for sale. At a given level of technology and a given price structure for the various inputs and products, microeconomic theory indicates how much of each input should be used to create a given quantity of output most efficiently, and how much of that output to produce. By bringing together the output of many producers, the market provides the consumer with a variety of goods from which to choose. Classical economic theory assumes that each consumer will buy goods so as to get the greatest benefit, given the constraint that he not exceed his income in purchases. In this manner, consumers and producers interact at the marketplace, one trying to optimize personal satisfaction, the other profit, also a form of satisfaction. Collectively, they determine the price of goods and how much is produced.

The theory of the free market has much appeal. Probably of most significance is that we can show that, given certain simplifying assumptions, the forces acting at the market produce a price structure that allows an optimal allocation of society's resources. Further, all of this occurs automatically, without any outside agency having to estimate on behalf of others what market baskets of goods are best for them, or how much of each input should be available to a firm: this is settled by the market itself by means of prices. Of course, the free market is a theoretical ideal. However, the theory developed for the free market can be extended to analyze various breakdowns of the free market, and its effect on public welfare.

The goods analyzed by the traditional theory are tangible. That is, a specific, measurable quantity of them are produced, and they sit around bringing attention to themselves until someone buys them. Once sold, such a good becomes the property of an identifiable person who had to pay to gain access to the benefits provided by the good, and who is then able to enjoy exclusive rights to it.

Some kinds of goods cannot be described in this way, and how to treat such goods often eludes a free market solution. Of particular interest are the so-called public goods: these are goods, usually nontangible, such as defense and clean air, which, once created, are shared without diminution by any number of people (are "nonconsumable") and for which it is difficult to collect a price for consumption (are "nonexcludable"). It is for such goods that societal intervention is generally regarded as necessary. Although traditional theory is frequently used to describe the private service sector, this represents an extension of the theory. Because of the nontangible character of these goods, the extension may not always be satisfactory, and variations of the models developed below may well be better suited to describe some components of the private service sector as well as libraries.

The Library

A question of prime concern for us is, What is the library's output, and is it best conceived as a marketable good, or as a public good? If the former is the case, then the level of library funding should be determined in a free market by means of a system of fees for service. If a library produces public goods, then a case can be made for continued subsidy. I believe that neither model completely captures what it is that a library produces. It is certainly not a public good, in that access to it can easily, if not happily, be controlled; and, to a degree, use by some does interfere with use by others. On the other hand, neither does the free-market model of the trade of tangible goods apply.

It has been suggested that the library does in fact have a measurable output for which it can charge—that is, its book circulation [11]. Certainly book circulation is an important aspect of library activity, and it is easy to see why one would wish to treat it as a conventional economic good—the library's product. Reasons for doing so include: (1) Circulation is a measurable output of the library, so charges can easily be levied on a basis resembling the charges for traditional goods in a free market. Circulation may not be a perfect measure of library output, but it is workable and at least approximately correct. (2) It may be the single most important output of the library, and much of other library service is in fact ancillary to getting a book to a patron. (3) Even if the library does provide other services (for example, in-house use of materials), these, at least approximately, tend to be proportional to circulation, and thus even if circulation does not measure everything a library does, it could serve as an index of these. (4) Even when circulation does not adequately measure overall library service, it is nonetheless an important component. If so, we can model the library as a multiproduct firm, with circulation as one of its products, and apply classical theory at least to this component, perhaps treating other components differently.

But treating book circulation in libraries as analogous to bushels of wheat in farming is not without its problems, both practical and conceptual: *(a)* Simple circulation is a very crude measure of a library's benefit to society. At minimum, we should distinguish categories of items, and perhaps users, before assessing how much benefit society receives from a given level of circulation and thus the income a library should receive. A community may very well not wish to equate the circulation of a popular mystery with that of an economic history of the country. *(b)* Libraries provide services quite unrelated to circulation; for example, preservation of local history. If too much attention is focused on tangible output, these activities may suffer. More specifically, *(c)* by rewarding a library solely for circulating books, society will encourage libraries to reduce other socially desired functions to increase circulation, just as rewarding libraries on the basis of how many people enter the library encourages the substitution of library "happenings" for book-related service.

But more serious from a theoretical point of view is that circulation, or any other chargeable service provided by the library, such as reference, is not a library's product in the same way that wheat is a farmer's product. Unlike the case of the traditional firm for which economic theory was developed, the input of books, staff, etc. does not result in an inventory of circulations that must then be cleared at the marketplace. Thus, the theory by which the prices of goods are determined through free-market interactions would have to be modified before it can be applied to library circulation. Similarly, even though the inputs and technology are held fixed, circulation can vary, depending on demand. Thus, rather than serving as the output of a library, book circulation is in fact as much a measure of community interest, or demand, as it is a measure of library productivity. Thus, circulation does not represent either the supply curve of the library, nor the demand curve of its market, but rather reflects the interaction of the two. For this reason, to analyze a library by economic modeling, it is necessary, at least in principle, to determine how to conceptualize a library's output and to relate this to consumer demand. In such a theory, circulation would be a derived quantity, rather than a direct output of the production process.

Model of Library Activity

Traditionally, the analysis of the supply side of a market begins by constructing the production function of a firm, a relation between the firm's inputs and the quantity of its product. Given the prices of the various inputs, this permits the construction of a cost function that relates the quantity of goods produced to the amount of money it would cost a firm to produce this quantity of goods. These goods are tangible outputs, are measurable, and directly involved in the producer-consumer interaction.

Libraries do not have a tangible output that they produce and then sell. As we noted above, measures that have been used, such as circulation or number of people entering the building, represent demand for, as much as they do supply of, library output, a quality shared with many other producers of services. On the other hand, regardless of interest in library service, no circulation would be possible without the existence and maintenance of libraries, so something does result from library expenditure: the output of a library is the capability to provide benefits. This capability may or may not itself be susceptible of measurement. It is an abstract quantity. Nonetheless, to establish it requires resources, and once established it results in measurable consequences. Defining the library's output as an abstract state variable makes the formulation of library policy very difficult, as we shall explore below. But this characteristic is not unique to libraries; it is shared with other public goods and services, such as the readiness of the fire department, as well as some segments of the private service sector. Libraries differ from at least some public goods in that this state variable, the capacity to provide service, yields tangible benefits upon demand by users. These interactions resemble the trade of tangible goods; however, we must create the intermediary variable, service capability, if we are to distinguish conceptually what is supplied from what is demanded, and to create a logically coherent model of library activity that will allow us to explore the consequences of various funding approaches.

Thus, central to our model is an abstract state variable, S, which conceptually quantifies a library's potential for providing service. More generally, it is possible to consider the library as a multiproduct firm, with several distinct dimensions of service potential, $S_1, S_2, \ldots S_n$. For example, S_1 might represent access to printed material and S_2, reference capability. The theory presented below can, and should, be generalized to include this complexity. The most important aspects of this model, however, can be presented most clearly if we defer consideration of these complexities in library service and concentrate on the simple single-output model, which I shall refer to as circulation to be concrete.

The size of the output variable is influenced by the amount and type of inputs a library receives. We represent this schematically by a type of production function:

$$S = f_S(x_1, \ldots x_n). \tag{1}$$

Here S represents a library's service potential, and the x's represent the amounts of various inputs, for example, books, equipment, and personnel of various types. Thus, parallel to the tangible goods produced by the traditional firm is the intangible "state" of the library. Although S is not directly measurable, several measures of library effectiveness suggested in the literature are, in fact, indexes of S. Examples include: the percentage of a checklist of items owned by a library, the average time to get a desired item, and the probability of a desired book being on the shelf. In practice, having an actual measure of library quality is highly desirable for purposes of accountability. In this regard the abstract character of library service acts as a serious impediment to rationalizing budget allocation for libraries—an impediment shared with many other components of government service. In such situations, an index or other approximation of output must be used. But such an explicit measure is not required for our development. We will, instead, assume that such a variable does exist, detail its role in our model, and examine the consequences of having such a quantity at the core of our analysis. As we saw above, the quality of service provided by a library interacts with the demand for library service to produce such transactions as book circulation. Part of our concern below is to analyze the consequences of basing financing, using one mechanism or another, on such an indirect measure as circulation. But before we can do this, we must complete the supply side of our model of library service.

The second component of our model is the library's budget. If given B dollars, the library's inputs must obey:

$$C_0 + \Sigma C_i x_i = B, \qquad (2)$$

where C_0 is a fixed cost and the C_i the unit costs of inputs, for example, various categories of labor or supplies. (Book expenditures are likely to be included here, though they in fact have characteristics of capital investments as well as of inputs in the usual sense. It is important to recognize, however, that acquiring books is not considered an output of library activity or directly a measure of library service.) Once the optimal mix of inputs is known, this equation can be combined with equation (1) to yield:

$$S = f_S(B), \qquad (1')$$

a function relating B to the potential for service that it is possible to attain with B,[2] given the state of the library's technology. It is reasonable to assume f_S increases with B, though, most likely, a given increase in B will have less impact on S as B gets large.

---

2. Technically, this is a different function than that appearing in eq. (1), as it has different arguments. I shall here and below use the same notation for related functions when confusion is not likely to result. This will enormously simplify the notation.

Three Models of Library Finance

In the above discussion we examined the character of a library's output and indicated how this is related to a library's budget. We still must describe the demand side of library service and show how this is related to the level of library support. Below I shall describe three models of library financing.

Public Finance Model
In this model, the library's budget is provided by some agency that is intended to represent the interests of the user population. This may be a taxing body in the case of a public library, or a superordinate institution, as for a special or university library. Presumably, the supporting agency is willing to divert a certain amount of money from other uses because of the benefits provided by the library, and the agency expects at least a certain amount of service for its money. Thus, in this model, the agency replaces the direct user population as the source of demand for library service. The multiple demand function of the free market is replaced by the single demand function of the funding agency. The relation between a given amount of money, B, dedicated to library service and the minimum service level, S, acceptable for that level of expenditure is given by a "demand function:"[3]

$$S = f_D(B). \qquad (3)$$

The function f_D is, in principle, determined in a variety of ways. In an industrial library, S itself may be viewed as an input into production and ultimately to profit. The level of S purchased would in this case be determined in much the same way as would any other input of the production process. Although the output of universities is less tangible, the level S here would, in principle, be determined similarly.

The demand curve for public libraries is more complex, since it is so intimately tied to the political process. Some consider the decision regarding library budgets to be made arbitrarily, almost haphazardly, by the funding agency. Others see the budget as resulting from the balance of power of various special interests. Without denying the reality of either of these models of public financing, it is nonetheless of interest to ask whether there is any rational basis, at least in principle, for determining the level of library financing. I shall suggest a model of library financing that is very similar to models used to analyze public goods [13].

---

3. The function, f_D, is a demand function in that it relates a level of service to the amount of money a community will pay for that level of service. It is not the same as the marginal utility function that economists usually mean by demand function.

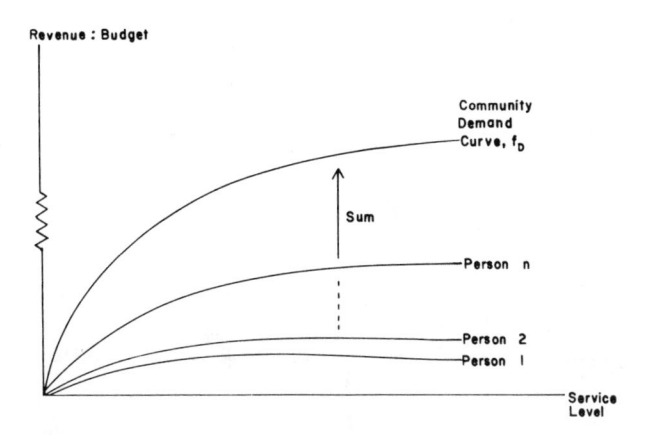

FIG. 1.—Definition of a community's demand function, relating the level of service (S) provided by a library to the amount of money (B) a community would provide for that level of service.

Because of the abstract character of library service, it is not possible to use this model to determine explicitly the optimal level of library funding. The model does, however, establish some principles, or ideals, for funding such agencies as public libraries, and ideals, if accepted, do influence behavior.

I shall define the public's demand for library service as the aggregation of the demands, or "pseudodemands," of the individuals making up the public. That is, for each person in the community, we can imagine asking how much he would (or should) be willing to pay, for whatever reason, selfish or altruistic, to establish a given level of library service, given the current distribution of income, and given the prices of other goods. The community demand curve can then be conceptualized as the sum of these individual demand curves (fig. 1). It indicates how much money would be available to a library operating at a given service level, if it were possible to evaluate and collect from each person the value to him of that level of service. Many have observed that library service provides "externalities," that is, they provide benefits to others than those who use the library directly. This observation is quite consistent with this model; we simply incorporate the external benefits to a person into that person's pseudodemand function.

The proper level of support, under this model, is given by the intersection of curves f_S (see eq. [1']) and f_D (see eq. [3]), as shown in figure 2. If curve f_D represents a community's willingness to pay for library service, then a is a point at which library service would stabilize. To justify the expenditure of B_0 dollars, the community demands at least a level of service equal to S_0, and the library is able to provide that level of service

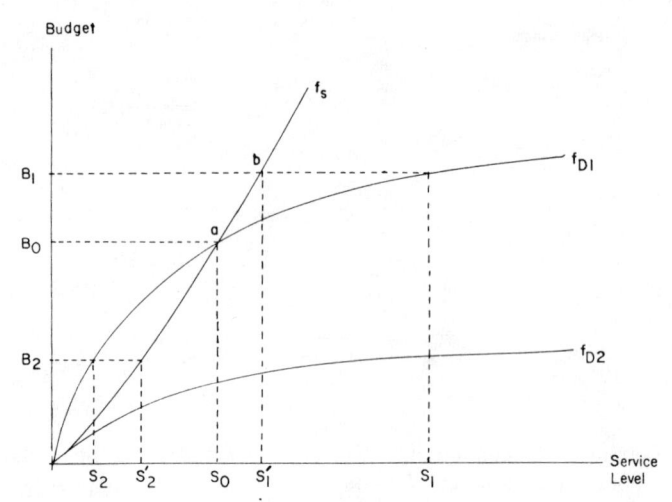

FIG. 2.—Determination of level of public library support in the public finance model

given that level of funding. On the other hand, if the library were funded at level B_1, the community would expect a level of service S_1, but the library could only provide a level of service S'_1, and not be able to promise improvement to the degree required to justify expanding its operation by increasing funding. The pressure is thus to reduce funding until B_0 is reached. Notice that if a community providing funds at level B_1 experiences a change of priorities, thereby lowering its demand for library service, the effect would be the same as moving from a to b on the current graph.

If, on the other hand, the library were funded at level B_2, it would be providing service at a level exceeding the minimum demanded by its community. However, the community would be willing to pay extra for extra service, and the annual budget is likely to increase until a is reached. Thus, a represents the long-term operating point of a stable community. Note that if the community's demand curve were f_{D2}, no library service would be provided. (If we analyze service as multidimensional, this could correspond to the elimination of one segment of service—perhaps other segments would be funded.)

As the final component of this analysis, we must represent actual community use of library service, since library service was presented not as actual use but rather as a potential for such use. Library use is complex and multidimensional. We shall, for conceptual simplicity, continue to represent this use in terms of a single variable, C, visualized as the circulation of library material, and referred to it as such below. The importance of C for our development is that it is measurable and can be associated with specific individuals. We will examine the consequences of this below. If we wished to consider library use as multifaceted, then C, like S, could be modeled as having a number of components.

The amount of circulation, C, is schematically given by:

$$C = f_C(S, p), \qquad (4)$$

where p represents the price, if any, charged for each circulation. In the current model $p = 0$, but the price is included to increase generality. We are leaving f_C as a general function, although we demand that it have the following properties: we expect C to increase as S increases, and to decrease with increases in p. To increase generality further, we could modify equation (1') to include the effect of increased circulation on service level: $S = f_S(B, C)$, since increasing C will tend to reduce the level of service S, for example, because of queuing effects and increased costs associated with library use. We will omit these considerations in this paper for purposes of simplicity.

In the model we are proposing, circulation is explicitly a consequence of both the library's output (S) and the price of a transaction (p), the relation between the two being given by a function representing the community's response to these factors. It is easy to see, however, how some could perceive circulation as a direct library output. For, if we substitute equation (1') into equation (4), we find (ignoring p):

$$C = f_C(S) = f_C[f_S(B)] = f_C(B). \qquad (4')$$

That is, because of circulation's direct dependence on service capability, there is a functional relation between the library's inputs as represented by the budget level, B, and the consequent circulation level. Because of this relation, we can influence the circulation level directly by changing the library's inputs, or, indirectly, by modifying the budget. This permits us to act as if circulation is a library output and to create something resembling a production function for book circulation. However, this is accomplished at the loss of conceptual clarity and obscures the actual interaction of causal factors. For example, it obscures how a change of community interest could result in changing levels of circulation, even if B is constant.

Our model includes two functions representing the public's attitude toward the library: the desire for a high level of service, and the actual use of this service through circulation. In fact, although an individual's demand functions, representing his desire for service capability and his actual use, will be closely related, they will not by any means be identical. There are many reasons why a person will be willing to support a public library even though he makes little or no use of it. Some people simply feel a library system is an intrinsically good thing and want to have one in their community, at least if the cost is not too high. Others may believe a strong library system will attract to their community an educated middle-class population, and thereby contribute to maintaining property values and enlightened civic leadership. Or, a person may wish to support a quality library system, in anticipation of future occasions when it will prove to be of value. People have different reasons for supporting a public library, not all of which are directly, or to the same degree, tied to the immediate use of its facilities.

But equating circulation with library output is not merely conceptually problematical. Basing library support on circulation statistics alone may possibly cause an actual decline in library quality as evaluated by the funding agency. For suppose circulation is in fact influenced not only by S, a "true" measure of library quality, but also by another service variable, S', under the library's control, but valued less than S by the funding agency. For example, S' may measure the library's ability to provide, upon demand, a popular novel. Then, if we assume a dollar spent on S' increases circulation more strongly than does a dollar spent on S, a library can increase the size of its budget by transferring funds from improving S to improving S'. Such a transfer would be interpreted by the funding agency, the purchaser of library service in this model, as a diminution in the quality of library service. Nonetheless, since institutions tend to prefer more money to less, there will be a tendency to make this shift.

The impact of shifting funds from S to S' can be described more precisely in terms of the library's demand and supply functions. Suppose that a library has the discretion of directing a part of its budget, say α, to S' and another part, $1 - \alpha$, to S. If so, the circulation level is given by: $C = f_C(S, S')$. Since $S' = f_{S'}(B_{S'}) = f_{S'}(\alpha B)$ and $S = f_S(B_S) = f_S[(1 - \alpha)B]$, the circulation level can be reexpressed as a function of α and B: $C = f_C(\alpha, B)$, with C increasing with α for B fixed.[4] But we are assuming B is itself determined by the value C takes, so we must satisfy:

$$B = f_D(C) = f_D[f_C(\alpha, B)]. \qquad (5)$$

The relationship between α and B is illustrated in figure 3, which shows the demand function $f_D(B)$ and the circulation function f_C evaluated at $\alpha = 1$ and $\alpha = 0$. These graphs define B, and thus C, as a function of α. We are assuming that B is maximized by setting α equal to 1, achieving a budget of B_1.

Suppose that a library operating under these conditions nonetheless desires to maximize S, or equivalently, B_S. To do this analytically, we must solve equation (5) to find the relationship between B and α. If we

---

4. Once again, I am simplifying the model. Most likely both S and S' depend on both B_S and $B_{S'}$: $S' = f_{S'}(B_{S'}, B_S)$; $S = f_S(B_{S'}, B_S)$.

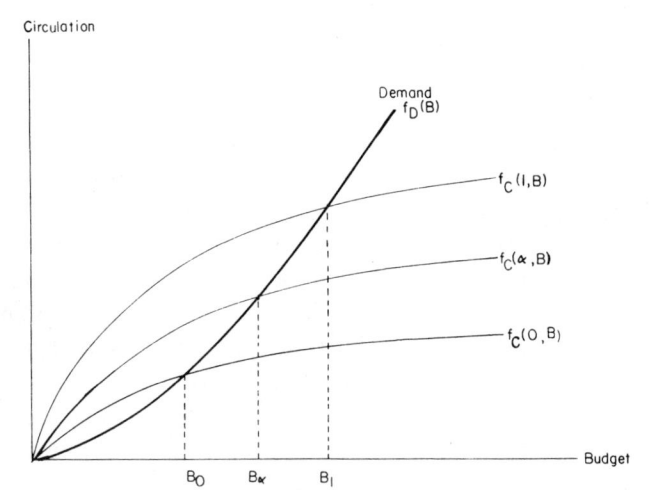

FIG. 3.—The influence of budget distribution on the level of library funding

denote by g the function relating B to α, that is, $B = g(\alpha)$, then we must find α which maximizes $B_S = (1 - \alpha) B = (1 - \alpha) g(\alpha)$. This will occur when

$$\frac{d\,g(\alpha)}{d\alpha} = \frac{g(\alpha)}{1 - \alpha},$$

if such a value exists,[5] or else at $\alpha = 0$.

5. The condition on g can be described in terms of the functions f_D and f_C. The equation $B = f_D\,[f_C\,(\alpha, B]$ implicitly defines B as a function, g, of α. Using the implicit function theorem, we can assert that

$$\frac{dg}{d\alpha} = \frac{df_D}{dC}\left(\frac{\partial f_C}{\partial \alpha} + \frac{\partial f_C}{\partial B}\frac{dg}{d\alpha}\right).$$

Solving for $\frac{dg}{d\alpha}$ we found

$$\frac{dg}{d\alpha} = \frac{df_D}{dC}\frac{\partial f_C}{\partial \alpha} \bigg/ \left(1 - \frac{df_D}{dC}\frac{\partial f_C}{\partial B}\right).$$

One interesting result follows immediately. We are assuming $(dg/d\alpha)$, (df_D/dC), $(\partial f_C/\partial \alpha)$, and $(\partial f_C/\partial B)$ are all positive. For this to be true, we must have $(df_D/dC)(\partial f_C/\partial B) < 1$. Since $(df_D/dC) = 1/(df_D/dB)$, treating f_D as a function showing B as depending on C, and taking notational liberties, we conclude $(\partial f_C/\partial B) < (df_D/dB)$. In other words, for our equations to be consistent, the slopes of the circulation and demand curves must be as shown in fig. 3. If this condition holds, the above equation would allow us to determine the optimal value of α if we are given specific functions for f_D and f_C. It is also possible to give some conditions for a solution to exist for $\alpha \neq 0$. Since $g(\alpha)$ is positive, if $dg(\alpha)/d\alpha$ is never infinite, and is greater than $g(0)$ at $\alpha = 0$, a solution will certainly exist in the interval (0,1). If the derivative is less than g at $\alpha = 0$, then a solution will exist if the derivative can catch up with the right-hand side. This will be the case unless $dg(\alpha)/d\alpha <$

Thus, even if it is accepted that S is the most appropriate measure of library service, and that a given budget is most effectively used if dedicated to increasing S, in the above circulation-oriented system, a librarian who is both rational and altruistic may very well have to divert funds to less desirable programs in order to serve the community as well as possible. Both S and C are indexes of library effectiveness; however, in some cases, the maximizing of one may be inconsistent with maximizing the other. Thus, if we wish to use a political mechanism to determine in a rational manner the level of library financing, we face a dilemma. The crux of the matter is that the quantity we wish to base our budget on is not measurable. If we simply make funds available and rely on the librarian's judgment to make the best use of these, we lose the semblance of objectivity. However, if we create a readily available measure of performance, such as circulation, we find that we may, in our attempt to create an objective criterion for allocating funds, in fact be encouraging an inefficient use of these funds. In the next section we shall see that this contradiction also holds true in a for-fee library system.

Free-Market Model

The previous model treated the case in which library service was considered a public good and supported by public monies. In that model, it was the level of service that we intended to support publicly, and we saw how actual use was a consequence of both service potential and public demand. At the opposite extreme, we may consider the model of the pure for-fee service: all revenues available to the library are the result of fees collected for items circulated. Once again we assume equations (1) and (1'). Our circulation demand function now resembles the downward-sloping curve of traditional economic analysis: $C = f_C(S, p)$ is the number of circulations generated collectively by individuals of the society; it is again the sum of individual demand curves, but with the sum taken horizontally rather than vertically. Thus, the operating level of the library must satisfy $S = f_S(B)$ and $C = f_C(S, p)$. But now, without subsidization, B is determined by the magnitude of C and the price of a circulation:

$$B = p f_C(S, p) \qquad (6)$$

and, thus, substituting equation (6) for B in equation (1'),

$$S = f_S [p f_C(S, p)]. \qquad (7)$$

$g(\alpha)/(1-\alpha)$ for all the values in the α-interval (0,1). If so, $(1/g)(dg/d\alpha) = (d/d\alpha) \ln g$ must be less than $1/(1 - \alpha)$ for all α in the unit interval, so $\ln g(\alpha)/g(0) < \ln 1/(1-\alpha)$ in this interval, or $g(\alpha) < g(0)/(1 - \alpha)$. Funds will be diverted from S to S' unless such diversion causes too little improvement in S; this analysis makes this statement precise.

COSTING AND ECONOMICS 319

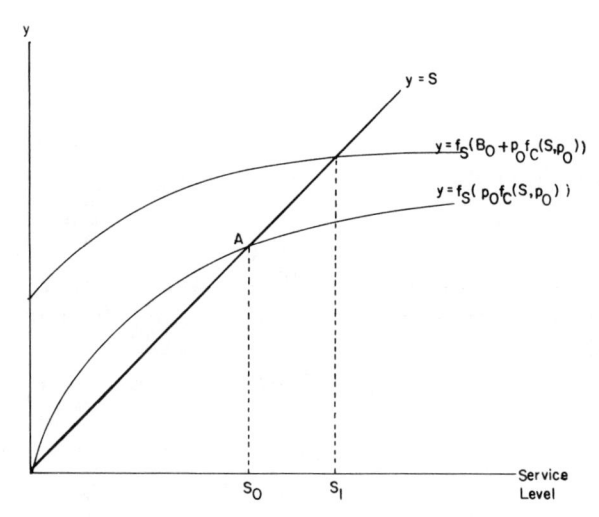

FIG. 4.—Graphic solution of equations (7) and (7'). The intersection of the two curves with the line $y = S$ defines the service level, S, as a function of the price charged for checking out a book for the cases where no subsidy ($B = 0$) is provided, and where the subsidy has a nonzero value ($B = B_0$). Alpha is defined in the text.

If we can solve this equation for S, we can relate S to p in that community. Note that $S = 0$ is the only solution at $p = 0$, assuming reasonable behavior of the functions; $S = 0$ remains a solution for p greater than zero, but a positive value of S becomes a possibility. For $p = p_0 \neq 0$, we can graph both the left- and right-hand sides of equation (7) as in figure 4, using y as a dummy variable. Ultimately, we expect $f_C(S, p)$ to level off as S increases—use will ultimately be saturated. Thus, if $f_S[p_0 f_C(S, p_0)]$ rises fast enough, that is, if $[df_S(0)/dB] \times p_0 [\partial f_C(0, p_0)/\partial s] > 1$, then at some point the two curves will meet, denoted by A in figure 4. At that value of S, denoted S_0 in the diagram, equation (7) is satisfied. Thus, when $p = p_0$, $S = S_0$ solves equation (7). In any case, $S = 0$ is a solution (assuming $f_s[0] = 0$ and $f_C[0, p] = 0$). In this manner, we can define S as a function of p: $S = f_S(p)$. As p increases from $p = 0$, we expect that $pf_C(S, p)$ will initially increase, so $f_S(p)$ will initially increase. At some point, p_m, the decline in $f_C(S, p)$ due to increasing price will no longer be compensated for by the increase in price, and B, and thus S, will decline. Thus p_m is the price at which library capability takes its maximum value; this is the price the library should charge if it is to maximize service level. Note that since this is the point at which the library's revenue is maximized, we must satisfy:

$$\frac{d}{dp} p f_C(p) = f_C(p) + p \frac{df_C/(p)}{dp} = 0,$$

or

$$\frac{df_C}{dp} = -\frac{f_C/(p)}{p}.$$

Note, however, that the condition for circulation to be maximized is given by $(df_C/dp) = 0$. Since $f_C(0) = 0$ (at zero price the library has zero funds), if the library is to function at all, (df_C/dp) must initially be positive. Eventually, $f_C(p)$ is maximized, $(df_C/dp) = 0$, and at higher p, decreases in size: $(df_C/dp) < 0$. It is in this region of negative (df_C/dp), at a price greater than that which maximizes circulation, that S is maximized. That is, on a pure for-fee basis, maximizing circulation and maximizing service level are inconsistent. Service level is maximized in this model when income is maximized. But to maximize income, it is necessary to raise the fee for service beyond the point where it begins to discourage actual use. The decline in use is, initially, compensated for by the higher price for each use.

Mixed-Economy Model

As our final model, we consider the possibility of partial subsidy. Suppose the community provides a subsidy of B for library service and the library charges a fee of p dollars per circulation. Then equation (7) becomes

$$S = f_S [B + p f_C (S, p)], \qquad (7')$$

which is represented graphically in figure 4.

We see that now a solution always exists: $S = f_S(p)$, for all p, and the solution occurs at an increased level of service, S. If we maximize $f_S(p)$, we find the price, p, that is required to maximize service capability, S, and the level of service provided at that level of subsidy:

$$p = f_p(B), \qquad (8')$$

$$S = f_S(B). \qquad (8'')$$

Finally, we can answer the question, how much subsidy is the community to provide? This is given by plotting the service demanded by the community for a given level of subsidization and the enhanced service curve (8")—we would allot the amount of public monies for library provision given by the intersection of the two curves, as in figure 2. We will then charge a price p per use corresponding to that level of subsidization, as given by equation (8'). It is interesting to note that if the introduction of fees for service does not change the demand function, then the movement to the right of the supply function will cause both service and dollar support to increase. (This does not imply that the introduction of fees is in fact associated with increased subsidization, since fees are introduced, typically, in response to a falling demand curve. Rather, the practical effect of fees, in such circumstances, is to prevent the level of subsidization from falling yet further.)

Conclusions

This is not an empirical study, and I have not attempted to develop measuring instruments or to collect data. Rather, I have tried to develop a conceptual model of library activity that may be an alternative to models adapted from the for-profit sector of our economy. In creating this model, I have intentionally eliminated complexities that are features of a library setting in order to accentuate those aspects of library behavior that I believe best characterize this institution and distinguish it from other institutions.

The salient features of the model are: (1) The output of the model is a potential for service, that is, a state variable, rather than tangible goods. It is this that society pays for when it supports its library system. In this, libraries are like many other providers of personal services and resemble public goods. Indeed, for many reasons [12], libraries are publicly funded, which creates a further resemblance to public goods. (2) On the other hand, unlike many public goods, potential for service is translated into actual service by means of palpable voluntary interactions between the library and its public. These interactions are measurable, can be controlled, and can be charged for. In this, libraries resemble traditional firms, and some have considered these interactions as the library's output.

It is this mixture of private and public components that makes the library unusual, though not unique. The purpose of this paper was to make this distinction precise, and to create a model that indicates how these characteristics interact to create the library component of our economic system.

The public-good component of libraries also explains the tenacity with which libraries have resisted satisfactory economic analysis. This point can best be made by comparing the treatment of public and private goods in our economic system. In both cases, analysis typically begins by assuming the existence of abstract and difficult to measure quantities, the utilities of goods for individuals. In both cases, the assumption that these utilities exist allows us to establish conditions, in terms of these utilities, that must be satisfied for a given distribution of resources to be optimal. But here the treatment of the two categories of goods diverges in a crucial manner. In the case of private goods, it can be shown that, given a free market, the conditions for optimality are automatically satisfied. Thus, in a free market, we simply need to assume the existence of utilities, not measure them. Nor does some agent have to intervene to see to it that the conditions deduced for optimal social welfare are met—this occurs automatically by means of the price mechanism.

The situation vis-à-vis public goods is very different. Here, no free market for the exchange of goods exists. Though the concept of utility remains central to the theory and the conditions for optimization are established, there is no precise way to measure this utility and no mechanism to see to it that the conditions for optimization are in fact met. Instead, the decision regarding resource allocation is made by political means. But, at best, the agents responsible for these decisions are imperfect assessors of social welfare, and there is no self-actuating mechanism to prevent some from substituting their own utility for that of society when determining how resources are to be distributed. Taking this to its extreme, this situation does resemble a market, but one in which it is power and favors that are exchanged rather than goods, and the utility functions that are maximized are those of a relatively small part of the population at the expense of the rest. Further, we have seen that attempts at rationalizing this process by establishing objective criteria, for example, circulation levels that the library must satisfy to justify a level of public support, are only partially successful, and may encourage an inefficient use of resources. The essence of the problem is the nonmeasurability of library output.

We have become very sensitive to the dangers to our physical and social environment of uncontrolled big business. More recently, we have been recognizing with alarm the nonbenign impact of a large centralized government created to correct these defects. Probably the most critical issue facing our society today is how to use political mechanisms to correct breakdowns of the free market, or provide services for which the free market is inadequate, while correcting the very serious distortions that take place when political power replaces free exchange. One attractive possibility, at least for some cases, is to try to create mechanisms by which public support is provided in such a way that some of the efficiencies of the free market are retained. One example of this is the usually unrecognized, but very real, subsidization of part of the publishing industry by means of public funding of libraries. This in fact diverts public monies to publishers, a situation that may be justified by the externalities involved in book creation, while maintaining a healthy competition among publishers. This consequence of libraries is overlooked by those who see the library as reducing the demand for books by providing free access. Because of libraries, book production has become a free market activity with some of the nonexcludable characteristics of public goods.

In a sense, my third model does accomplish some of the same. It permits public support of libraries, but at the same time creates a market for library service. Pseudodemand functions cannot be measured, but to the extent that individuals valuing libraries are more likely to use them often, they are approximated by actual use. Similarly, those valuing the service most pay the most for it. On the other hand, the model does recognize the existence of benefits not directly tied to immediate use by means of the subsidy provided.

REFERENCES

1. Morse, Philip M. *Library Effectiveness: A Systems Approach.* Cambridge, Mass.: MIT Press, 1968.
2. Leimkuhler, Ferdinand F. "Library Operations Research: A Process of Discovery and Justification." In *Operations Research: Implications for Libraries,* edited by Don R. Swanson and Abraham Bookstein. Thirty-fifth Annual Conference of the Graduate Library School. Chicago: University of Chicago Press, 1972.
3. Bookstein, Abraham, and Kocher, Karl. "Operations Research in Libraries." *Advances in Librarianship* 9 (1979): 143–84.
4. Baumol, William J., and Marcus, Matityahu. *Economics of Academic Libraries.* Washington, D.C.: American Council on Education, 1973.
5. Knight, Douglas M., and Nourse, E. S., eds. *Libraries at Large: Tradition, Innovation, and the National Interest.* New York: R. R. Bowker Co., 1969.
6. Black, Stanley W. "Library Economics," Appendix F-2. In *Libraries at Large: Tradition, Innovation, and the National Interest,* edited by Douglas M. Knight and E. S. Nourse. New York: R. R. Bowker Co., 1969.
7. Goddard, Haynes C. "Analysis of Social Production Functions: The Public Library." *Public Finance Quarterly* 1 (April 1973): 191–205.
8. Machlup, Fritz. "Our Libraries: Can We Measure Their Holdings and Acquisitions?" *AAUP Bulletin* 62 (Autumn 1976): 303.
9. Machlup, Fritz, et al. *Information through the Printed Word: The Dissemination of Scholarly, Scientific, and Intellectual Knowledge.* New York: Praeger Publishers, 1978.
10. Getz, Malcolm. *Public Libraries: An Economic View.* Baltimore: Johns Hopkins University Press, 1980.
11. White, Lawrence J. Public Library in the 1980's: The Problems of Choice. Unpublished manuscript, New York University.
12. DeWath, Nancy Van House. "Demand for Public Library Services: A Time Allocation and Public Finance Approach to User Fees." Ph.D. dissertation, University of California, Berkeley, 1979.
13. Musgrave, Richard A., and Musgrave, Peggy B. *Public Finance in Theory and Practice.* New York: McGraw-Hill Book Co., 1976.

The Psychopathology of Uneconomics

MAURICE B. LINE

THIS PAPER MAKES NO PRETENSE to be a scholarly review of the literature on uneconomic things done in, by and for libraries, and the attitudes responsible for and resulting from them. I am not an economist nor a psychologist (let alone a psychopathologist), but a librarian who spent all his working career in university libraries until a few years ago; this paper is a set of personal observations.

The subject of this paper could hardly have been chosen twenty years ago, and if it had been chosen it would hardly have been understood. The idea that libraries should pay much attention to economics is a relatively recent one. Librarians have, of course, always complained of insufficient money to buy all the books they wanted to buy, and to this complaint was frequently added demands for more staff. A big library was, almost by definition, a beautiful library — the bigger the more beautiful. What is relatively recent is the concept that libraries are systems or organizations consuming and deploying capital and recurrent resources that can be optimized — as is the discovery that not only was optimization attained, if at all, only by accident, but that some libraries actually approached "pessimization" by using their resources in almost the least effective way possible. Little in the structure of the university has given the librarian any incentive to think in economic terms. Indeed, there are some inducements not to economize. For example, if he does not spend all his budget in one fiscal year — even if in the process he knowingly wastes money — his budget for the following year may be reduced. There is no profit motive to inspire the librarian, and there is no paying market for his services. Moreover, many of the most costly elements of the library operations, such as storage, heating and lighting, do not have to be funded from the library budget.

The changes have come about for several reasons. Most obvious is the combination of the increasing growth of published material, with its implications for acquisition and storage costs, and increasing restrictions on funds. This is only an aggravation of a problem that has always existed, but when the problem is aggravated beyond a certain point it almost begins to constitute a new problem. At least as powerful a factor has been an unparalleled increase in demands from users, as their numbers have grown at an enormous rate and as traditional disciplines have given birth to new subdisciplines and broken their boundaries to constitute numerous interdisciplines. Increase in user demand has also been greatly stimulated by improvements in bibliographic control, both in comprehensiveness of coverage and in speed of notification.

These changes in libraries are paralleled by, and are in part the consequence of, changes in their parent institutions. Academic institutions have developed from cottage industries to large and complex organizations absorbing ever-increasing portions of the national (or state) budget. Inevitably, a more careful watch has been kept on the money they spend and how they spend it; and attempts have been made to measure the contribution they make to the economy. Universities have therefore been forced to think in economic terms, to justify their estimates in detail, to allocate their resources with great care, and to measure their outputs. Not only have they had to consider how best to use new resources, but in many cases how to allocate *reductions* in resources. Various techniques and approaches have burgeoned, such as PPBS and, most recently, zero-based budgeting, which demand that every expenditure be justified from scratch, as if it were entirely new.

These developments have affected the library, as they have every other part of the university. For librarians to say in such circumstances merely that they need more money to buy more books, more staff to serve more readers, and more capital to build new buildings to house more books and readers, is clearly not enough. The apparently fundamental truth that libraries must expand to buy the books available has been challenged by hard reality. Some librarians have still not accepted this fact, maintaining that the hard reality is temporary, while the need for growth is eternal. Other librarians, perhaps making a virtue of necessity or perhaps by a happy coincidence, have challenged the very concept of "big is beautiful," arguing that the criterion by which libraries must be judged is not their size but their service. By this reasoning, the library is no longer a thing-in-itself but an integral element in the university, in scholarly communication, in education and in society itself; it can be understood only in relation to its context, and the main commodity in which it deals is not books but information. There has been a gradual but profound shift from the book-oriented library to the user- and information-oriented library, from the more or less self-sufficient collection to the switching center, from the storehouse of knowledge and cultural heritage to the information broker. The conventional objectives of the library have thus been challenged. It is not, of course, axiomatic that the information center is always cheaper than the conventional library; it is quite possible to save money on books and waste it in other ways.

The question of the library's objectives is vital to economic considerations, because economies cannot sensibly be discussed except with reference to objectives. To run the library as economically as possible is not a meaningful objective unless the "library" is defined, any more than economy in itself can be a principal aim; otherwise, the most economic library would be one that was closed down and its contents dispersed. Economic success or failure depends on what one is trying to achieve.

Almost all librarians have been forced by economic pressures to reexamine not only their functions, but also the methods by which they try to achieve them. Here, too, recent years have seen some fundamental questioning, striking at the roots of traditional theory and practice. In this case, librarians have not generally had to conduct their reexamination in public in order to justify their estimates; rather, they have been obliged to try to economize in order to keep within their reduced budgets, and the debate has been an internal and private one. The question "How can we reduce the costs of the present catalog on its present lines?" must have been asked by many librarians for many years. "Do you need a catalog at all, and if so, what sort?" is a much more fundamental question, which librarians have been most reluctant to answer, let alone ask. Skipping the first part of the question, they have tended to answer, "One with the fullest details, of course." This answer is not necessarily true, even if the need for a catalog is assumed and the time and convenience of use taken into account; the fullest catalog is not necessarily the one that serves readers best. However, again assuming that a catalog is needed, it is reasonable to ask: "What is the best catalog that can be provided at the least cost?" In the attempt to answer this question, a better catalog — one that serves more readers more adequately — may be designed than if no costs are taken into account. Similar questions may be, and have been, asked about classification and subject indexing, issue systems, acquisition systems, and other routine practices and operations.

Among the various economies that might be made in a library with more or less conventional objectives are the following:

1. Cataloging is a very labor-intensive operation. Costs can be cut, perhaps by half, by the use of records from an external data base, use of lower-level staff, and shorter records.
2. Classification in most libraries is at least as costly as cataloging, and often more so. The more detailed it is, the more costly it is to use, and still greater costs are incurred when changes are introduced into the scheme. For browsing purposes, extreme detail may be more confusing than helpful, while for information retrieval, few classifications are sufficiently detailed or convenient to use.
3. Subject indexing along traditional lines is also very costly. It can be reduced by the use of keywords in titles, enhanced where absolutely necessary. The cost can be eliminated entirely if bibliographies are used to guide readers to books on specific topics, just as abstracting and indexing services are used for subject access to journal articles.
4. Book selection can absorb a great deal of staff time and effort, although it appears that many books are still selected that are never used at all. Crude selection might be just as effective and a lot cheaper.
5. Acquisition budgets, especially for journals but also for books, can in many cases be greatly reduced with only a minimal reduction in service. Since in any large library the vast majority of demand falls on a small proportion of the collection, trimming the fringes does no harm and can produce great savings in staff, processing and binding costs as well as in purchase costs.
6. Permanent retention of stock that need never have been acquired in the first place, or that served its entire purpose long ago, is expensive because of the space it occupies. Even if discarding costs are not negligible, they should be easily outweighed by space savings over a period of ten or twenty years at the longest.

Most of the above examples concern methods of providing access to books that have been acquired, but the last two represent an attack on acquisitions and disposal — a more fundamental attack, because the stock, according to the traditional concept, is the heart of the library, without which it would not be a library at all. To suggest that cataloging and classification can be simplified is bad enough; to suggest that fewer books might be bought and more discarded is much worse. The ultimate blasphemy is to suggest that the library need not even ask for as much money as it does, either for staff, books or buildings. The largest savings can usually be made in the area of staff, since several tasks could be eliminated or simplified, or carried out by lower-level staff than at present.

The application of economics need not, of course, concern only a reduction of existing costs. The increased utilization of capital resources of stock, and of the skill and expertise of staff, is an economic good, and this can be encouraged by improved circulation practices and policies, and by opening the doors of the library more readily to outsiders. It may even be possible to earn money for the library by selling services to industrial organizations.

Money saved in one or more of the above ways can be used in various ways — if indeed the reason for saving in the first place is not a reduced budget. For example, more can be spent on services and less on processing; a wider variety of current books may be bought, cheaply processed and drastically weeded after four or five years; and so on. The question must always be what kinds of services users really need, and how best to provide them.

When the attackers are from "outside" the library — from the university or its funding bodies — they can be dismissed as ignorant barbarians, appeased as angry gods, or submitted to as irresistible conquerors. However, much of the assault in recent years has come from within the library community itself, and this has been more difficult to deal with. Wherever the attacks and pressures have come from, librarians have generally been singularly unprepared for them. In few cases have they even known what the true costs of their existing operations are. This ignorance has had some strange results. For example, gifts of books, however useless, have been welcomed as "free," although the costs of processing books are high (indeed, considerably higher than the purchase price of most deliberately acquired books). Journals are all bound and stored permanently, when it may be far cheaper to discard some of them unbound after two or three years and rely on interlibrary loans for the occasional requirement. Numerous other examples could be given of uneconomic things done in unwitting or willful ignorance.

The reactions and responses of librarians to economic pressures may take a variety of forms, not necessarily mutually exclusive. Some of these are described below.

The simplest response is the *traditional*. This response takes the form not of an argument, but of an assertion that the library is by definition a collection of books, as large as possible, cataloged, classified and indexed according to traditional standards. "We must be very careful before we change established practices" is a common expression of this attitude.

Allied to the traditional response is the *perfectionist* response: "Only the best is good enough; we must maintain our standards." "Best" and "standards" are undefined, but are usually assumed to mean "most detailed and elaborate." One manifestation of the perfectionist attitude is the urge toward constant improvement, whatever its cost. It is cause for some amazement that new and "improved" cataloging rules and revised classification schemes can be, and frequently are, devised and adopted without full prior consideration of the costs of implementing them.

Also related is the *cultural* response: "The library is a storehouse of culture, and to damage or erode it in any way is to damage or erode the cultural heritage." This is indeed true of national archival collections and portions of many other libraries, but not of the generality of libraries, which are funded by institutions in order to serve them here and now. Some librarians appear all too ready to sacrifice the needs of the present, which can be known and largely met, to the dead needs of the past and the unknown needs of the future.

Allied with any of the above may be *passive resistance:* "Don't do anything and it may go away; it's only a fad that will go the way of other fads." This response may be deliberate (and sometimes quite effective), or it may represent the paralysis of the rabbit confronted by the snake. It may be expressed openly as the *mañana* approach: "Make my library economic, o University, but not yet."

The above attitudes do not enable libraries to avoid the hard facts of economics, but they can easily result in their sub-optimizing — doing the same thing, only a little less expensively: buying fewer rare books, spending a little less on rebinding, and so on. More commonly, these attitudes are combined with some of those below, or those below are used as "fronts" for those above.

The *political* response appeals to prestige and status: "To reduce our acquisitions would gradually make our library smaller than X or Y, and we might even fall behind Z." The fact that the most prestigious universities tend to have the biggest libraries is adduced in support of this argument, although the most obvious reason for this fact is that the most prestigious universities usually have the most money to spend on libraries, as on other things. (They also tend to have the oldest buildings, to enhance their university status.)

The *psychological* or *pseudo-altruistic* response is also quite popular: "Users won't stand for it/won't adjust to it/shouldn't be expected to accept it"; "You can't recruit staff to work in a library with reduced acquisitions/a withdrawal policy/simplified processing"; "Libraries must be thought of in terms of individual users whose needs are all different — optimization is concerned only with groups and averages." The obvious answer to this is that a library that tries to satisfy everyone is in danger of satisfying no one; and that a library whose basic procedures are geared to the greatest good of the greatest number can still aim to serve individual needs as exceptions.

Another group of responses apparently concedes something to the economic approach, and can carry some superficial and temporary conviction. The first is the *mini-economic* response: "But I *am* economizing — I saved $1000 last year by using a different printer for bookplates." The implication is that the librarian has looked at all details of his operations to see where economies might be made.

More impressive is the *pseudo-economic,* expressed in "cooperation" and "resource-sharing." On investigation, most exercises in resource-sharing appear to save little or no money, but cost quite a lot to operate. Very often, *more* money is spent on making more extensive resources available to a group of libraries, though the use of these resources, and the costs of satisfying the occasional needs through other channels, are rarely compared with the cost of this additional provision. (In the United Kingdom, the argument that resource-sharing saves money has now been virtually abandoned, and it is admitted that more money is needed for it, though little or no evidence is offered that the need for it is there in the first place.)

The *marginal-economic* approach argues that while some aspects of libraries can and should be costed, these are only minor, and the most important things cannot be measured, let alone costed. "What is the value of information?" is a popular question with this school, as are assertions about the value of browsing, which is usually confused with serendipity. (Incidentally, serendipity would be best served by the random arrangement of books on the shelves, which would avoid classification and thus save a great deal of money.) It can easily be shown that some things cannot be measured, and the implication is that the economic approach should therefore be used only in marginal ways, and then very carefully.

The *false economy* riposte is also common: "It costs too much to change procedures; discarding costs more money than new buildings; interlibrary borrowing costs more than acquisition," and so on. If these statements are not made as mere assertions, they are supported by one-sided and shortsighted costings. One can make procedural change, discarding or interlibrary borrowing cost whatever one likes, within limits, just as other costs, such as those for storage (including the cost of half-empty buildings), can be ignored or minimized. This is not to say, of course, that change should not be costed before it is decided upon, that discarding is cost-free or that it should be applied to any but very little-used stock, or that it is not more economical to buy books of which more than minimal use can be expected. The full economic facts are needed in all cases.

The *overkill* response is less often encountered, but not unknown: "There is no point in altering the present system because the whole pattern of primary communication will change in the foreseeable future"; or "We have a very big automation program ahead which will change all our procedures anyway" — whether for the better or worse, or at what cost, is rarely stated. This is in fact a subtle variant, albeit starting from different premises, of the *mañana* approach. It can carry some conviction because the librarian appears to be forward-looking; indeed, his eyes are looking so far forward that he is in danger of falling into an economic pit a few yards in front of him.

Most of these responses have something to be said for them, and a reasonable, or at least plausible, case can often be made in their support. However, they can also be rationalizations for attitudes based on deep and often primitive emotions. Of these, insecurity is probably the main one, leading to fear of change, acquisitiveness, reluctance to shed possessions, and clinging to the past. Also, many librarians are not ready to accept that their past training — in history, literature or philosophy — is an irrelevant anachronism. To recognize oneself as a dodo on the way to extinction cannot be a happy experience.

Emotions such as these are so universal that it may seem hard to refer to them as pathological. They are pathological only if their existence and strength are not recognized and if they intrude into decisions that should be made on rational grounds. The personal emotions of librarians have no place in running an efficient library service. However, the personal emotions, and likely reactions, of users certainly must be taken into account. Moreover, a wise library director would not attempt to ride roughshod over the primitive emotions of his own staff: they too have to be persuaded. A rational librarian has, as part of the process of reaching a rational decision and implementing it, to consider the psychopathology of others as one essential fact, as real as library procedures and costs. In other words, he should be an amateur psychologist as well as an amateur economist.

So far I have considered the responses of those who oppose or resist change, arguing that many of them have a psychopathological basis. However, it is equally true that there is a psychopathology of excessive change. The conservative traditionalist is, or was, a more common type in libraries than the restless "change-for-change's-sake" librarian, but the latter has gained much ground in recent years. Automation programs in the 1960s provided many striking examples of bandwagon jumping. Some experiments undoubtedly had to be conducted in order to find out how best to use the power of the computer, and in the process some mistakes were bound to be made. Deliberate experimentation is, however, something different from the exceedingly incautious programs embarked upon in some libraries — programs on which much money was wasted. There must be numerous other, less spectacular, examples of forward plans that were never properly costed but were entered into as facts of faith. There is some danger that massive withdrawal programs will fall into this category, though the obstacles to such programs are so great, and withdrawal decisions involve so many people besides the librarian, that overly hasty action is less likely than with automation.

A different pathological type is the *hypereconomist*. This is the librarian who tries to reduce everything to numbers and costs, who considers that what cannot be measured either does not exist, or should not exist, or is not worth bothering about if it does exist. The term "cost effectiveness" is ever on his lips, and value judgments are alien to his conceptual world. He may appear at first to be at an opposite extreme to the overcautious traditionalist concerned with the perfectibility of cataloging, but in fact he is a mutation of the same species. Like the professionalist cataloger, he is an obsessional, insecure individual who seeks security, not in catalog entries but in numbers. The one catalogs and classifies experience; the other counts and costs it. Both feel safer because they have reduced the infinite range and variety of knowledge and life to something visible, filable or measurable. The hypereconomist is merely a perfectionist who has learned a bit of economics, or perhaps a second-rate economist who has strayed into libraries and seen easy pickings there. There may in fact be a place for these people, for a time at least. If it had not been for obsessional counters like Sir Francis Galton, the science of statistics would have developed more slowly (though it may still be doubted whether Galton's efforts to measure the protuberance of Hottentot women's bottoms or the efficacy of prayer constituted great advances in knowledge). Likewise, a few obsessional hypereconomists may be a useful counterbalance to the uneconomists of the past.

Discussion to this point has made the uneconomic or hypereconomic librarian the object of scrutiny. However, libraries do not exist without users (in spite of the efforts of some librarians), and the total ecology and economy of libraries must take users into account.

The attitudes of faculty toward an economic approach to libraries are likely to be ambivalent. On the one hand, the library is competing with departments for limited institutional funds, and it is in the faculty's interest to resist increases, or even to seek reductions, in the library's budget. On the other hand, one of the main resources of research — in the humanities and many of the social sciences, *the* main resource — is the book collection, and every department wants as good a collection as possible. The department may react to this clash of interests with confusion, or by arguing different ways on different occasions, or by pressing for more library funds for books in their subjects and for fewer in other subjects. Attitudes may be partly determined by the nature of the discipline. A historian is less likely to take, or accept as valid, the economic approach than an economist, a technologist or even a physicist; his values will be different, and he will be less likely to view resource allocation in a systematic or scientific way.

However, faculty reactions are not generally predictable. What can usually be predicted is that if the librarian cuts resources or services in particular subjects or areas, there will be an angry response, even if the cuts are the direct result of budgetary reductions approved by the faculty itself. Similarly, if the librarian reallocates resources from stock to service — sacrificing, say, some acquisitions in order to pay for better information services in the form of access to computer data bases — there may well be an outcry. Even if it can be shown that the service aids faculty in its research and teaching more than stock, faculty still tend to prefer stock; and if they have the choice of sacrificing primary literature or secondary services such as indexing and abstracting journals, they will sacrifice the latter. If a suggestion is made that some stock could be disposed of or relegated to low-use storage, there are protests from faculty, even when it can be shown that none of the present faculty has used any of the stock in question, or that much of it has never been used by anyone.

The desire to maintain the stock in a department's own subject is understandable enough; the unwillingness to accept services instead of stock, or to accept relocation of unused material is not rational, and comes at least partly within the realm of psychopathology. The possessive instinct familiar to nearly everyone is one obvious explanation. No one likes to throw away household goods acquired years ago or inherited, even though they have never been used; after all, "it may become useful some time."

Apart from possessiveness about stock, faculty do not exhibit much psychopathology. They may want or expect the library to do uneconomic things, but this rarely becomes a major issue. Also, faculty can use libraries in uneconomic ways unwittingly. For example, they may ask for some documents on interlibrary loan that they would not request if they were aware of the true cost of borrowing. Indeed, faculty use of libraries takes place in almost total ignorance of the actual and relative costs of different activities, so that uneconomic behavior is inevitable. Education in the economic facts of libraries rather than psychological treatment is indicated for faculty; and this is the responsibility of the librarian.

The attitude of students is less easy to identify or categorize because it varies so much, both within and between generations (student generations are very short), and because students are generally not much concerned with the economic operation of the university. The only time they want the library to economize is when they take up some particular cause, such as free contraception for themselves or Stetsons for poor Peruvian Indians, which they consider to be a more important use of funds.

More often, students want more books on their subjects, more copies of books, more space in which to work and, in general, more of everything. There may be some conflict with faculty, since with a limited budget it may not be possible to provide enough textbooks for all students as well as serve faculty research needs adequately.

One quite common student attitude is a reaction against hypereconomics, not on traditional and conservative grounds but on antiscientific grounds. The spirit, emotions and senses are everything; reason, particularly as exemplified in science, economics and statistics, is nothing. Indeed, the whole library may be seen as a storehouse of the knowledge and reason they detest, and acts of arson and other forms of destruction have not been unknown. These are truly pathological.

The university administrator must not be ignored. It is from or through him that pressures to economize come, and he is much more likely to be concerned with economy than effectiveness, let alone cultural values. He may, however, be open to conviction that the library is a valuable cultural asset to the university, and hence worth defending. He may within himself contain the conflict between various warring elements in the university at large — the admirer of size and prestige versus the cost-conscious administrator, the preserver of culture versus the servant of modern science and technology.

With all these existing conflicting attitudes and values, the ensuing debate is bound to bring forth some prime examples of psychopathology. The net result may be the worst of all possible economic worlds, but is more likely to be a sad compromise between hard economic facts, entrenched attitudes, the needs of the majority, and the wishes of the powerful. There is all the more need for a librarian to have appropriate knowledge and apply it carefully and rationally. The forces of unreason have much more chance of victory when a rational case is not argued fully or carefully presented.

Library directors may presently be pulled in two different directions: toward the humanistic and cultural approach, in which many of them were bred and which can seem antipathetic to an economic approach; and toward a half-baked economic approach which can be destructive as well as superficial. The solution surely lies in better education and a more comprehensive vision. Library education must not merely teach a few economic techniques, but inculcate as deeply as possible an economic and systematic approach. This is all the more vital because libraries, as nonprofit organizations, offer very little economic motivation — no extra money is to be earned by economizing. Library administrators, at whatever level, spend most of their time in problem-solving — small day-to-day problems as they arise, and much larger, long-term problems (which really must be solved first if wise day-to-day decisions are to be made). The automatic approach to any problem should be to analyze it, identify possible solutions, and compare the various options for costs and effectiveness. Librarians do not all need to be economists or systems analysts, but the economic and systematic attitude toward the library should be second nature.

This alone is not enough, and a comprehensive vision is needed that embraces cultural and humanistic values as well as economics and systems analysis. Far from being in fundamental conflict, the two should be seen as complementary. The library needs to be run economically and effectively *in order* to provide the best possible service with the resources available. If it is not run economically and effectively, a few may receive a good service at the expense of the many. Nor is designing the basic system to satisfy the most common needs speedily and efficiently in conflict with serving special and individual needs; these can in fact be served better, if the main system runs smoothly and there is spare capacity to provide individual service where it is needed. In place of the commercial objective of the maximization of profit, the librarian's objective should be the maximization of service.

Economics must be seen as the servant of the library user, and of the objectives of the university, including cultural and even traditional objectives. To question radically the means by which values are served is not necessarily to question the values themselves. The implication of this is that some economics certainly must be taught to librarians but only in a much wider context. And librarians need to be constantly reminded that they are supposed to be serving users, not books, shelves, catalogs or buildings. Finally, none of these skills is of much practical use unless the library director develops political skills: he can learn from Machiavelli as well as Panizzi.

ROBERT S. RUNYON

Towards the Development of a Library Management Information System

This paper outlines an approach, with both widespread implications and specific practical steps, for assembling some of the data that library administrators now require in order to make libraries operate more effectively. These data have not been assembled in the past because the costs in staff time alone have been and continue to be prohibitive for most institutions.

One major impediment to effective library administration is the lack of a comprehensive management information system (MIS). Some investigators in this area seem to have become fascinated with the potential value of various elusive and fugitive library statistical measures, but they have given little attention to the operational systems that would be required to assemble these data. The proposal outlined here stresses the need for a total systems approach, based upon standardized terminology, machine-aided data collection, and customized computer processing and reporting as well as systematic training and documentation.

After the proposed MIS is developed, it can be offered to subscriber libraries by a bibliographic utility or network system at variable rates determined by input data volume, processing times, and output report requirements.

INTRODUCTION

One of the persistent problems in academic library planning and decision making is obtaining an accurate picture of exactly what is going on within the library. We are used to keeping counts of our operations, but we are seldom comfortable with the accuracy, timeliness, or completeness of this data once assembled. All libraries have some kind of statistical data system, but I would venture to say that in few libraries is the system considered adequate. Some reasons for this unfortunate situation are presented in this paper along with a general outline of an improved system and the steps that may be necessary for its realization.

THE NEED

Investigators have repeatedly decried the lack of needed data to conduct research in library operations.[1,2] Doubtless the problem exists in many areas, but there are signs that we now have the knowledge and the tools required, and that it may be an appropriate time for the initiation of specific projects within certain organizations to address the overall need. That need was concisely summarized by Urquhart in a paper that was suitably addressed primarily to service considerations:

> Nowadays we must recognize the need to quantify the problems of librarianship so that management can plan their policies on a rational basis. There is a particular need to develop measurement techniques which can be used to describe library processes, and provide management with up-to-date information. Such techniques must operate within three restraints:
> they must be inexpensive to operate;
> they must not interfere with existing services;
> they must provide reproducible results.[3]

One hopeful sign is the growing professional interest and publication in the area of library measurement and evaluation. Fifteen years ago this kind of work was being done on the outside, and confined typically to university operations research departments. Now it is beginning to form a widening stream in our professional literature, and as indicated by the 1980 ALA Preconference on Library Effectiveness, much of the quantitative work is now being done within the profession by library practitioners and library school faculty members.[4]

Whereas a few years ago, the requirements and processes for generating library statistical data were largely external to the library, the situation has begun to shift. Now there is both a high degree of need and matching technical capability for developing sophisticated statistical records within each academic library. This is not to say that individual librarians will now become operations research experts, but that through the marriage of newer conceptual developments in library measurement and computer processing we can now accomplish that which could not be done before. This will become clearer as we examine long-standing obstacles to statistical record keeping. But first we need to outline a conceptual model for library data to support administrative decision making.

A CONCEPTUAL MODEL

In most statistics committee discussions and in the published literature, we continue to speak of library measurement in terms of isolated tallies of individual items and events occurring within a library. Our thinking has remained fixed on the relatively narrow issue of how to define and report several limited categories of measurement. In addition, those categories of data, collected for purposes of local operational control and national reporting, tend to have very little relationship to those which are called for or utilized in empirical research studies. The reason for this lies in the absence of a broad conceptual model of library data that can be used in the development of a detailed statistical data system applicable to a wide range of operational planning, reporting, and research purposes.

The models which need to be constructed include both verbal and graphic descriptive and explanatory models as well as mathematical and statistical models. It would be as serious a mistake to rush into the premature construction of the more precise quantitative models as it would be to avoid quantification when it becomes possible. In any complex organization where there are many variables which must be considered in the resolution to any problem, it is necessary to become specific and quantitative about the factors which must be changed.[5]

In order to develop such models we must turn our attention to the key decision-making issues about and within the library. Our question must be, "What data is needed in order to derive more timely, reliable, and far-reaching decisions?" Doubtless there are also other decision-making criteria that should be considered, and those might be best addressed within a special task force of library administrators representing a sampling of major library organizational types. Numerous writers have pointed out the necessity for administrators to be involved at the outset in the establishment of goals and objectives for the development of an MIS.[6] Unfortunately, this critical and most difficult first step is frequently overlooked or delayed beyond the point at which the system design has become frozen in its basic data structure and organization.

The conceptual model that seems to be required here is a set of integrated, decision-related data categories appropriate to the overall administration of a library. An abbreviated example of such a data set for an academic library is outlined in appendix A. This illustrative example is suggested as a monthly planning report to senior-level administrators. Other more or less detailed reports might be useful at other intervals for different purposes.

For an MIS to be detailed in coverage and broad in application, it is imperative that the data categories be precise and well defined. Fortunately, the process of developing many of the fundamental terms, definitions, and relationships has been effectively begun in the work done so far on the National Center for Educational Statistics (NCES) *Handbook of Standard Terminology for Recording and Reporting Information about Libraries*. The long and complicated history of this important document is summarized in the 1980 *Bowker Annual*.[7] The introduction to the *Handbook* points to the required expansion

COSTING AND ECONOMICS

of our vision from microscopic counting activities to overall management and decision-making concerns:

This *Handbook* describes basic management information useful in academic, public, school, and special libraries. An underlying premise of the *Handbook* is that all types of libraries have a common set of functions, purposes, and resources which outweigh the differences in setting, size, or organizational goals. The data base is built upon a common set of terms related to those common functions, purposes, and resources, while accommodating and providing for those terms unique to each type of library.[8]

As indicated above, it should now be possible to proceed towards the development of a generalized MIS that addresses the needs of academic, public, special, school, and other types of libraries. The examples and allusions in this paper are drawn largely from the academic library scene, but that simply represents this writer's experience and bias. Other related and compatible examples (in terms of an integrated, multitype library MIS) could be offered to illustrate the application to other types of libraries.

One benefit of an overall conceptual model is to allow a detailed specification of the data to be collected at the level of individual library operations, which can later be grouped and regrouped into regional and national summaries and profiles. As of yet, we don't have this kind of data-handling capability in libraries, and we are not likely to achieve it until we have thought our decision-making needs through in terms of a comprehensive MIS, over and above the need for consistent rules in the counting of minute items and events.

CHARACTERISTICS OF THE MODEL

A number of library investigators have described statistical measures and related interpretations useful in evaluating library performance and effectiveness.[9] During the past several years, there has also been extensive study and effort directed towards the standardization of library statistical terminology. These efforts will be discussed later. What is now needed is the combination of broad management reporting concepts with the detailed technical description of library measurement parameters. Again the NCES *Handbook* appears to be the most ambitious effort in this direction to date. One of the early NCHEMS reports that led to the development of the *Handbook* summarized its seven major data categories as follows:

... the data contained in the management information system describes the environment, the overall resources, and the programmatic activities of the library. The environmental data of the library includes information which describes the external setting of the library, the internal organization of the library and the target group served by the library. The overall resources of the library include four major types of data: collection resource data, human resource data, financial data and facility resource data. Finally the data concerning programmatic activities organizes the library into major activity or functional areas. For each of these, a series of measure categories are used to describe and evaluate the activity of the library. These measures describe revenues/expenditures, personnel, facilities, activities, users, and outcomes/performance of each of the activity areas.[10]

Two useful features of the *Handbook* in its current form are a data classification and hierarchical coding scheme. These, in combination with a glossary of all terms employed, will enable the administrator to specify precisely the type and level of data to collect and report in order to compile a comprehensive, quantitative description of an individual library.

When the re-edited version of the NCES *Handbook* is ready for field review, librarians should be thinking in the broadest possible terms about uses, permutations, and combinations of the data. Other categories that we have tended to overlook in the past, but which should increasingly occupy our attention, are indexes and output or performance measures. We are familiar with some useful applications of index numbers in reporting publishers' price changes and national economic trends, but it seems possible to conceive of "the construction and use of index numbers"[11] also in some areas of library resources and operations. One of these may be the profiling and shorthand description of library collections and user response rates. We already have indexes for retrieval efficiency[12] and the technical services cost ratio,[13] but we haven't been able to include these research-oriented measures in a library MIS. Now that we have examples and case histories of the application of MIS in business and university environments,[14,15] it seems feasible with network resources to apply such systems in libraries. In the ALA Preconference on Library Effectiveness, there was an outline of a quite advanced design for an MIS in a public library.[16] Drawbacks with such localized system developments are that they are costly, and in addition, it is unlikely that they will be compatible for transfer to other library settings.

Cost is a consideration, and the MIS must have a reasonable cost compared to its worth. The economics of information systems requires constant balance between the value of the information carried in the system, and the cost of designing and operating it.[17]

Of course if the development of a generalized MIS is long delayed, it is quite likely and even feasible for a library to develop its own, using some of the NCES *Handbook* data categories and definitions. Certain flexible and user-oriented software packages, such as MARK IV, SCRIPT, and FOCUS, are now available and can facilitate the writing of the requisite computer programs. Another option is the use of an "electronic worksheet" program such as VISICALC which is now available on many microcomputers.

TERMINOLOGY

The problem with terminology has impeded the development of a generalized library MIS in the past. It seems now that there is well-grounded hope for progress in this area. Librarians will doubtless settle their terminological confusions and disputes if there are short-term, positive benefits in doing so. One such benefit will be the ready availability of the kind of statistical tabulations and output reports proposed here. Another major incentive to agreement will be the adoption of the new standards for library statistical terminology being considered in 1980–81 by the American National Standards Institute (ANSI Committee Z39.7).

The committee is working on a draft standard that contains 482 categories of library data. This compares to only 31 items in the Association of Research Libraries annual statistics, and 70 items in the LIBGIS survey form. The ANSI standard is now being developed in coordination with the NCES *Handbook* revision process. Concerted effort is being applied to assure that measurement terms and their definitions cover a broad range of conventional and potentially innovative measures. Terms must be given precise delineations so there is little question about what item counts are to be included with a category. As an example, the definitions used for government documents and microforms in most current statistical surveys are insufficiently precise. Built into the design of the terminology must be the possibility of combining atomic and molecular terms (and tabulations), either on input or in processing. This is necessary in order to customize data collection forms and output reports to meet the requirements of different types of libraries. For example, it is possible to specify media and microform types in great detail, but for certain users or certain reports, aggregate or generic tabulations may be more useful.

ORGANIZATIONAL CONSIDERATIONS

For years, there have been manifold ALA committees humming with projects directed towards the rationalization of library statistical terminology and concepts. Beyond this, there have been numerous committee efforts to support the definition, collection, analysis, and reporting of specific new measurement categories. One example has been the innovative work of the ALA Committee on Statistics for Reference Services, which produced, under the direction of Katherine Emerson, several new publications, conference programs, and training activities related to the measurement of reference transactions.[18] Despite the effort of many hard-working people, it took this committee several years of intense work to arrive at acceptable definitions of directional and reference transactions. Additional effort and time was expended in trying to insert these new "standardized" terms into nationally distributed data collection forms. It was a major victory to get the categories incorporated as cells in the LIBGIS reporting forms for academic libraries. After this was done, and the filled-out forms started coming back from the field, it became apparent that librarians were still unclear about the purpose, definition, and relationship of the reporting categories.

The point of all this is not simply to belabor the obvious fact that national committee activities grind exceedingly slow, even when favored with superior leadership and expert participation. Rather, it is to suggest that far-reaching change in library statistical reporting may have to follow a different path and implementation strategy than in the past.

Once the concepts, terminology, and categories have been developed by professional committees and project research groups, they are usually reviewed in the field, and finally revised for publication. There is probably not much that can be done to shorten these time-consuming editorial and review processes until computer conferencing is more widely available.

It has also been customary to rely upon the federal government to implement library statistical standards through the collection and summarization of data supplied by individual libraries. This process has resulted in protracted delays in the publishing of results and in the modification of categories and terminology as described above. Further, the existing process of national reporting has been a separate, add-on function for most libraries, not yielding timely operational data that can be used for internal planning and control. That is, the data collected and ultimately reported in national summaries has not been skimmed efficiently off the top of a constantly updated database of detailed library measurements. Rather, it has been generated ad hoc, under pressure of external deadlines and constraints. The process has been additionally exacerbated by frequent organizational and personnel changes within the Office of Education (now Department of Education).

On the other hand, the bibliographic utilities are not subject to these forces, and the task of library data handling is central to their overall mission. Likewise, they have daily and direct operational involvement in individual libraries, which provides them with the information and motivation required to design and maintain an effective MIS. It is hoped that after the above handbook and standards have been published, the definitions and specifications for library statistics will be sufficiently explicit for the bibliographic utilities to begin to address the problem of implementation within a new subsystem of their current network-based catalog systems.

Implementation

The essential thesis of this paper is that what is now required to translate the studies and projects cited above into practical results is a complete, off-the-shelf MIS that a library administrator could purchase and install in any library. Like most generalized, commercial software and utility programs, such a system should be designed in a standardized and modular form, so that libraries of different types and sizes could select only those elements that suit their particular needs. If this is done on the basis of the conceptual model proposed earlier, it will be feasible for libraries to disregard data of certain types and at certain levels, and yet remain compatible within a system of broad regional and national coverage. Also, since the model has been thought through on the basis of the items and tasks shared by many individual libraries, the use of the MIS should assure enhanced planning, accountability, and operational control within each library.

When one thinks about the development of the OCLC system, beginning as it did with the early premise that each library should be able to select or maintain its own catalog card print format, the parallels with the needed MIS are recognized. If the statistical report formats are highly flexible, then each library can still devise reports that reflect its own particular needs. Since tables and graphs can be computer printed, there would be a saving in specialist skills and staff time at the individual library level. Like the catalog system on which it is modeled, the statistical data system would soon become so necessary and cost-effective that libraries would be unable to avoid the terminological standardization and uniform reporting that it will exact. By the same token, the provision of frequent, comprehensive, and up-to-date statistical reports will vastly enhance the decision-making and budget analysis capabilities of administrators at all levels.

What is proposed here is that the MIS be designed and installed as a subsystem of one of the existing network-based computer systems, such as OCLC, RLIN, or WLN. In terms of developmental difficulty, the system should present much less complexity than the cataloging subsystems already developed.

Two of the persistent problems in setting up and maintaining an MIS are (1) deciding who counts what and (2) assuring that the daily counts are fed on a scheduled basis to a central collection point. Counting goes on in most library departments, but in order to assure consistency and total coverage and to eliminate overlap, it is necessary to assign responsibility for specific data to appropriate departments and sections within the library. As an example, recently acquired microforms might be counted either in the acquisitions department (where they are received), the cataloging department (where they are processed), or the media department (where they are stored and serviced), but it is redundant and wasteful to have them counted in several departments as many libraries now do.

Input processing should be simplified on standardized, machine-readable reporting forms (mark-sense, optical scanning, etc.) that can be easily filled out at service desks and other points of activity. Forms can be collected and sent periodically for batch machine processing. Alternatively, data might be periodically keyed into a central computer through a general communications terminal.

Output reports should be highly flexible, allowing individual departmental as well as total library summaries on both a month-to-month and annual basis. It should be possible in the institutional profile or system specification to delete or combine various counts, cross-tabulations, percentages, rankings, and other computations. Modular and flexible report formats and statistical computations are necessary in order to adapt to changing local and national reporting needs. Often, the prime reason that required statistical reports are not forthcoming is that there is insufficient staff to process or recombine the raw data already available but dispersed or inaccessible in various office files.

Each user would contract with the vendor for the level and amount of detailed processing and reporting required within the individual library. The specifications for processing of the data would be drawn up in a manner comparable with the OCLC profile now used to determine card format and other characteristics for each member library. Some available data cells could be left unspecified (distinctly not a possibility with the current LIBGIS forms) so that each library might assign some new measurement parameters that may be experimental, customized, or otherwise unique to its own particular operations, holdings, and services.

As with any computer system for the processing of library operational data, there will be a need for extensive documentation and training. Adapting the system to a given library's needs would be roughly analogous to the procedure now involved in writing an OCLC user profile. There will be a need for a comprehensive user manual explaining the system, terminology, and all procedures, with detailed examples. It will also be desirable to include practical guidance in the application of different sampling techniques to library data in the training sessions to be offered in subscriber libraries. While it is not feasible to collect certain types of activity and performance data on an ongoing basis, experience indicates that this is not required, since most library statistical activity measures tend to be very stable over time. Since fairly large samples are generally available, random or sampling errors are usually easy to avoid.[19]

FUTURE RESEARCH

An expanded range and depth of library statistical data could be used for research purposes. We need data that can assist in constructing simulation models of individual libraries and distribution models of regional and national resources. Such data are required to plan a truly effective national library network. Generally, if librarians and researchers have been able to assemble the kinds of comprehensive data proposed here, it has been only episodically with significant summaries and interpretations limited to annual and usually less frequent reports.

For an example of the benefits that effective data and analysis can provide, one need only look to Baumol's fundamental work on library economics.[20] This important study was based upon the Office of Education's *Library Statistics of Colleges and Universities: Fall 1968*,[21] and the annual statistical summaries of the Association of Research Libraries. The study is one of the most fundamental, empirically based analyses of library growth and cost trends available anywhere in the literature. Unfortunately, the data on which it was based was five years old at the time of publication, and there has been no comparable long-range interpretation of longitudinal data for libraries since 1968.

As regards the further elaboration of library data analysis based upon the use of the NCES *Handbook*, there are several topics on which future research is needed:

The basic areas which need additional work are: implementation of the suggested system in a wide variety of libraries; monitored testing of school and special library components; development of methods to measure the results of reserve sharing and networking; development of methods to record data on the agency roles of state and national libraries; and the development of adequate performance and outcome measures for all kinds of library services.[22]

A distinction about the availability and use of input versus output data seems appropriate here. Almost all historical data that has been assembled on academic libraries has been of the input nature, i.e., number of books held, dollars spent, staff available, etc. Increasingly, our funding authorities and accrediting agencies are asking for data on the educational outcomes of these costly resource investments. As enrollments drop and resources diminish, it becomes more important for administrators to provide evidence of the impact and results of expenditures. The MIS proposed here could, because of its flexibility and operational simplicity, make it feasible for many libraries to collect operational and performance data on an ongoing basis. By the same token, it is unlikely that this kind of data will ever be generated on a very wide scale if the procedures for processing the primary input data remain as they are now: rudimentary and inefficient.

We now have the operational capability of constructing comprehensive statistical summaries for libraries of all types. Once such a database has been assembled, it is interesting to speculate on the types of theoretical and policy studies that could then be pursued. One that fascinates this writer would be a study of branch units in academic libraries. Various configurations of academic libraries could be examined, while testing cost/benefit factors in highly centralized versus other more decentralized organizations. Given that this is one of the most resource intensive and poorly documented areas in academic library organization and management, the results could be quite interesting.[23]

REFERENCES

1. Philip M. Morse, *Library Effectiveness: A Systems Approach* (Cambridge, Mass.: M.I.T. Pr., 1968), p.5.
2. Edwin E. Olson, "Research in the Policy Process," in Irene Hoadley and Alice S. Clark, eds., *Quantitative Methods in Librarianship: Standards Research, Management* (Westport, Conn.: Greenwood Pr., 1972), p.102.
3. John A. Urquhart, and J. L. Schofield, "Measuring Readers' Failure at the Shelf," *Journal of Documentation* 7:273–86. (1971); in M. G., Beeler, and others, *Measuring the Quality of Library Service: A Handbook*, (Metuchen, N.J.: Scarecrow Pr., 1974), p.85–86.
4. American Library Association, *Library Effectiveness: A State of the Art*. An ALA Preconference sponsored by LAMA, LRRT, and RASD, Cochairmen: Neal K. Kaske and William Jones. (Chicago: The Association, 1980), 413 p.
5. Olson, "Research in the Policy Process," p.102.
6. Ralph Van Dusseldorp, "Some Principles for the Development of Management Information Systems," in Charles B. Johnson and William G. Katzenmeyer, eds., *Management Information Systems in Higher Education: The State of the Art* (Durham, N.C.: Duke Univ. Pr., 1969), p.33.
7. Eugene T. Neely, "Recent Developments in Library Statistical Activities," Filomena Simora, ed., in *The Bowker Annual of Library and Book Trade Information* (New York: Bowker, 1980), p.368.
8. National Center for Educational Statistics, *Handbook of Standard Terminology for Recording and Reporting Information about Libraries*, in Mary Jo Lynch, ed., *Library Data Collection Handbook: A Report Prepared for The National Center for Education Statistics* (Chicago: American Library Assn., 1981), p.3.
9. F. W. Lancaster, *The Measurement and Evaluation of Library Services* (Washington, D.C.: Information Resources Pr., 1977).
10. Dennis Jones and others, *Commentary to Library Statistical Data Base* (Boulder, Colo.: National Center for Higher Education Management Systems, 1977), p.iii.
11. Robert S. Richard, *The Numbers Game: Use and Abuse of Managerial Statistics* (New York: McGraw-Hill, 1972), p.99–121.
12. Cyril W. Cleverdon, "Cranfield Tests on Index Language Devices," *Aslib Proceedings* 19:173–94 (June 1967).
13. Helen Tuttle, "TSCOR: The Technical Services Cost Ratio," *Southeastern Librarian* 19:15–25 (Spring 1969).
14. Michael S. Morton, *Management Decision*

Systems: Computer-Based Support for Decision Making. (Boston: Harvard Univ. Graduate School of Business Administration, 1971).
15. J. Victor Baldridge and Michael L. Tierney, New Approaches to Management: Creating Practical Systems of Management Information and Management by Objectives (San Francisco: Jossey-Bass, 1979).
16. Kenneth E. Dowlin, "A Public Library Management System," in American Library Association, Library Effectiveness: A State of the Art (Chicago: American Library Assn., 1980), p.85-110.
17. James J. O'Brien, Management Information Systems: Concepts, Techniques and Applications (New York: Van Nostrand, 1970), p.11.
18. Katherine Emerson, "National Reporting on Reference Transactions, 1976-1978," RQ 16:199-207 (Spring 1977).
19. Morris Hamburg, "Statistical Methods for Library Management," in Ching-Chih Chen, ed., Quantitative Measurement and Dynamic Library Service (Phoenix: Oryx Pr., 1978), p.38.
20. William J. Baumol and Marcus Matityahu, Economics of Academic Libraries (Washington, D.C.: American Council on Education, 1973).
21. Joel Williams, Library Statistics of Colleges and Universities (Data for Individual Institutions, Fall 1968) (Washington, D.C.: National Center for Educational Statistics, U.S. Office of Education, 1969).
22. National Center for Educational Statistics, Handbook of Standard Terminology, p.8.
23. Robert S. Runyon, "Power and Conflict in Academic Libraries," Journal of Academic Librarianship 3: p.202 (Sept. 1977).

APPENDIX A
DECISION SUPPORT SYSTEM SUMMARY REPORT*

	This month this year	This month last year	Y-T-D this year	Y-T-D last year	% Change monthly	% Change Y−T−D

(month)

SERVICES

Users

Turnstyle count
Patrons registered (Faculty, students, staff, etc.)
Total target population (Faculty, students, staff, etc.)
% of target population registered
Active users (% of population with charges by user group)

Circulation

Charges (Faculty, students, community users, etc.)
Reserves
Discharges
Holds
Recalls
Overdues (1st notice, 2d notice, etc.)
Fines collected ($)
Interlibrary loan (Loans, requests, etc.)
Items in circulation
Average charges per user to: (Faculty, students, staff, etc.)
Average loan duration
Average charge per patron fined

*The author is indebted to others for several ideas incorporated in this outline: Kenneth E. Dowlin, "A Public Library Management System," in American Library Association, Library Effectiveness: A State of the Art (Chicago: American Library Assn., 1980), p.85-110.; Robert D. Woodley, "A Performance Based Statistical Information System for the Library Services Division of the Merrill Library" (Utah State University, 1976).

COSTING AND ECONOMICS

	This month this year	This month last year	Y-T-D this year	Y-T-D last year	% Change monthly	% Change Y–T–D

SERVICES

Information and Instructional Services

Questions answered (Directional, reference, research, etc.)
Tours and attendance
Classes offered and attendance
Bibliographies prepared
SDI notifications
Outside contacts
Database searches

Special Collections

User count
Reference and research questions
Materials paged

FACILITIES

Space Utilization

Shelving (linear feet)
  -Expansion space available
  -Additions:
    Reference collection
    General collection
    Serials Collection
  — % utilization
Seating
  — Total available
  — Sample use counts
  — % utilization
Faculty studies
  — Reservations
  — Sample use counts
  — % utilization

COLLECTIONS

Collections Growth
Print Materials Added

Books — Volumes
Serials issues
U.S. documents
State and local documents
United Nations documents

Nonprint Materials Added

Microfilm rolls
Microfiche
Microcards
Cassettes
  Audio
  Video
Phono discs
Kits

Materials Withdrawn

Total Items Added to Collections

	Budgeted	Expended to date	Expended this month	Current balance	% utilized

BUDGET

Personal Services ($)

Faculty
Library assistants
Part-time employees
Total savings

Departmental Allocations for Hourly Employees ($)

Administration
Circulation
Collections development
Reference
Technical services

Acquisitions Expenditures ($)

Books
   Direct order (Faculty, library, etc.)
   Approval plan
   Standing order
Serials
Departmental allocations
   (Anthropology, biology, . . . etc.)
Cost per item purchased
   Dept. personal expenditures/items purchased

CONCLUSION

Every selection of readings carries its inherent limitations, stemming both from the viewpoint of the editor and from the pool of literature from which it has been drawn. For those who need to acquire the full range of costing and accounting skills there is no other way than to tackle the literature of those two subjects and extract what is relevant to library and information service management. But the intelligent application of those basic skills has to be performed against a professional background, which shows an understanding of the needs and problems of library management. It is to the requirements of this latter end that these readings have been chosen, and if they are followed through some pattern should emerge. The early sections attempt to show something of the purpose and nature of cost study and they are followed by papers which show the progressive development of techniques and applications. The ultimate goal must be to set cost analysis within the framework of management information and decision making. This would be fulfilled by the kind of managerial economic approaches suggested by the later papers.

Many library problems have to be seen as economic problems of choice and allocation amongst limited resources and much less constrained aims and goals. Cost data can play an important part in assessing solutions, and if this is grasped and understood, then the motivation to collect cost data will grow. Those managers and practitioners who reach this point will no doubt be motivated towards any further reading which is needed; they will draw widely and from several disciplines, and perhaps make their own contribution to the literature of this field. If these readings stimulate action in that direction, then the modest purpose of this reader will have been fulfilled.

AUTHOR INDEX

Page numbers in bold type refer to papers reprinted in this volume. All others refer to papers cited by the editor in his commentary sections.

ARMSTRONG, A. **107**
ASLIB RESEARCH DEPARTMENT **55**
ASSOCIATION OF RESEARCH LIBRARIES 154

BECKER, J. 7
BENDER, A. D. **212**
BIRMINGHAM LIBRARIES CO-OPERATIVE MECHANIZATION PROJECT 154
BOOKSTEIN, A. **305**
BROOKS, J. **165**
BRYANT, P. 154
BUCKLAND, M. K. **258**
BURNS, R. W. **46**

CHAPMAN, E. A. 36
CLEMENTS, D. W. G. **93**
COCHRAN, M. L. **212**
COHEN, J. 227
COOPER, A. 2
COOPER, M. D. **134**

DIVILBISS, J. L. **77**
DOUGHERTY, R. M. 2
DRAKE, M. A. 154
DRUSCHEL, J. 154

FLOWERDEW, A. D. J. 6

GILCHRIST, A. **263**
GILDER, L. 36

HAMBURG, M. 226
HAYES, R. M. 7, 154
HEWGILL, J. C. R. **87**
HINDLE, A. 2
HUMPHREYS, K. W. 85

KANTOR, P. B. 226
KENT, A. 227

LANCASTER, F. W. 154
LEIMKUHLER, F. F. **134**
LEONARD, L. E. 2, 154
LINE, M. B. **324**
LUBANS, J. 36

McKENZIE, R. B. 227
MAGSON, M. S. 154
MAHAPATRA, M. 37
MAIER, J. M. **155**
MARCHANT, M. P. **292**
MARSTERSON, W. A. J. 36
MASON, D. **202**
MICK, C. K. 2
MITCHELL, B. J. 85
MONTGOMERY, K. L. 227
MOORE, N. 227

NACHLAS, J. A. **176**
NEEDHAM, A. 154

ORR, R. H. **240**
OVERTON, C. M. 227

PIERCE, A. R. **176**
PRICE, D. S. 227

RAFFEL, J. A. 227, **228**
RAPER, D. 2
REVILL, D. H. **184**
REYNOLDS, R. 71
ROBERTSON, S. E. 71
ROSS, J. **165**
ROWE, D. **301**
RUNYON, R. S. 337

ST. PIERRE, P. L. 36
SCHOFIELD, J. L. 36, **112**
SCHWUCHOW, W. **26**
SEAL, A. 227
SELF, P. C. 77
SHISHKO, R. 227
SIZER, J. 6
SMITH, A. G. **212**
SMITH, G. C. K. **112**
STURT, R. **216**

TUCKER, C. J. 154
TUTTLE, H. W. 154

WHITEHALL, T. **273**
WHITEHEAD, C. M. E. 6
WILKIN, A. P. 71
WILKINSON, J. B. 227
WILSON, J. H. 2